RESEARCH GUIDES
TO ANCIENT CIVILIZATIONS
VOL. 4

ANCIENT
CARIBBEAN

GARLAND REFERENCE LIBRARY
OF THE HUMANITIES
VOL. 1705

RESEARCH GUIDES TO ANCIENT CIVILIZATIONS

JOHN M. WEEKS
Series Editor

MAYA CIVILIZATION
by John M. Weeks

GREAT ZIMBABWE
The Iron Age in South Central Africa
by Joseph C. Vogel

ANCIENT CARIBBEAN
by John M. Weeks
and Peter J. Ferbel

ANCIENT CARIBBEAN

John M. Weeks
Peter J. Ferbel

GARLAND PUBLISHING, Inc.
New York & London / 1994

Library of Congress Cataloging-in-Publication Data

Weeks, John M.
    Ancient Caribbean / John M. Weeks, Peter J. Ferbel.
        p.   cm. — (Research guides to ancient
        civilizations ; v. 4) (Garland reference library of
        the humanities ; v. 1705)
        ISBN 0–8153–1303–9
        1. Indians of the West Indies—Bibliography.
    2. Indians of the West Indies—Antiquities—Bibliography.
    3. West Indies—Antiquities—Bibliography.   4. Caribbean
    Area—Antiquities—Bibliography.   I. Ferbel, Peter J.
    II. Title.
    Z1209.2.W47A53   1994
    [F1619]
    972.9'01—dc20   93–51063
                                                        CIP

Printed on acid-free, 250-year-life paper
Manufactured in the United States of America

CONTENTS

ILLUSTRATIONS

TABLES

SERIES EDITOR'S PREFACE

In recent years there has been a significant increase of academic and popular interest in the study of past civilizations. This is due in part to the dramatic coverage of the archaeological profession in popular film and television and extensive journalistic reporting of spectacular new finds from all parts of the world. Yet, because archaeologists and other scholars have tended to approach their study of ancient peoples and places exclusively from their own disciplinary perspectives, there has long been a lack of general bibliographic and other research resources available for the nonspecialist. This series is intended to fill that need.

Volumes in the Research Guides to Ancient Civilizations series are principally designed to introduce the general reader, student, and non-specialist to the study of particular ancient civilizations. Each volume is devoted to a specific archaeological culture (for example, the ancient Maya of southern Mexico) or cultural region (for example, ancient Anatolia and Mesopotamia) and seeks to achieve, by use of careful selectivity and a critical assessment of the literature, an expression of a particular civilization and an appreciation of its achievements.

Each volume is written by an authority in the field and will provide a selective, annotated guide to the readily available literature (books, journal articles, essays in edited volumes, dissertations, etc.) in relevant languages. Each volume will also include an introductory essay that reviews appropriate literature for the field, suggests areas for future research, and describes the scope and organziation of the work. In addition, each volume will contain indexing for personal names, subjects, and other areas as appropriate.

The keynote of the Research Guides to Ancient Civilizations series is to provide, in a uniform format, an interpretation of each civilization that will express its culture and place in the world and qualities and background that make it unique.

Ancient Caribbean, the third volume in the series, is concerned with the archaeology and prehistory of the insular Caribbean, including the Greater and Lesser Antilles, and the Bahamas. Forthcoming works will include Paul Zimansky's volume on the Urartu kingdom in eastern modern Turkey and the Indus Valley civilization of South Asia by Rita Wright. Other projected volumes will cover the Hohokam culture of the American Southwest, the Phoenicians of the eastern Mediterranean, Mycenaean culture of southern and central Greece in the late Bronze Age, and the Nile Valley civilizations among others. Still others are in the planning stage.

Ancient Caribbean considers the indigenous remains of the territory into which Columbus sailed when seeking a sea route to Asia. The prehistory of the Caribbean remains one of the least known in the Americas. The speed of European-sponsored genocide left few cultural groups who maintained traditional culture beyond the sixteenth century. Consequently little ethnographic information is available.

The known prehistory of the Caribbean is the prehistory of migration. The earliest archaeological remains are found in the Greater Antilles, possibly associated with the sunken Caribbean shelf that connected Central America with these islands at 4000 B.C. A second group appeared at 2000 B.C. from the South American mainland and eventually extended its influence to the Mona Passage between Puerto Rico and eastern Hispaniola. A third population movement originated in the Orinoco River Valley of northeastern South America and appeared in the Lesser Antilles at 200 B.C. and eventually penetrated as far as eastern Hispaniola. The fourth, developed locally in the Caribbean at A.D. 600, eventually moved into the Bahamas and western Cuba. Within these larger divisions there are further subdivisions and local developments defined by stylistic differences.

After sailing around the Bahamas and the north coast of Cuba, Columbus' ship the *Santa Maria* ran aground on the north coast of modern Haiti. Soon thereafter the Spaniards began a plan of environmental exploitation and colonization. Fortresses, churches, and towns were built throughout the region and a new political order was imposed on the Caribbean landscape. Disease, warfare, and enslavement all contributed to the destruction of the indigenous people. While the period of contact between Spaniards and indigenous populations was very brief, it left an indelible mark on the character of the Caribbean region. *Ancient Caribbean* explores the scholarly examination of the people who confronted Columbus.

INTRODUCTION

This volume is designed for students in search of published material on the archaeology and prehistory of the ancient Caribbean. The bibliography is intended to introduce the reader to the regional and subject literature that may be used to begin further research or for comparing with other cultural traditions. Although the bibliographic entries emphasize literature written in English, important works in Spanish, French, and Dutch are also given. While this guide focuses on archaeological and historical approaches to the Caribbean past, we have also included references to numerous linguistic, ethnographic, and demographic studies.

The following introductory essay provides an overview of the ancient Caribbean and critiques of its sources, methods, and study. Numerals used throughout the text refer to entries in the bibliographic sections.

Peoples and Places of the Contemporary Caribbean

The Caribbean is a region of tropical islands and water passages lying between the continents of North and South America and to the east of Central America. There are three principal island chains in the Caribbean: the Lesser Antilles, the Greater Antilles, and the Bahamas. The Lesser Antilles consist of the 'stepping stone' Windward and Leeward Islands, which extend in a gentle arc from Trinidad on the northern coast of South America to the north and northwest, ending with the Virgin Islands. The Greater Antilles, lying in the center of the region, contain the four largest islands of the area: Cuba, Hispaniola (divided by Haiti and the Dominican Republic), Jamaica, and Puerto Rico. The Bahamas are a large cluster of coral islands located east of Cuba and Florida. The Caribbean Sea extends approximately 1,500 km from Cuba southward to Colombia, and 3,300 km from Martinique westward to Belize, and it covers a total of some 1,250,000 sq. km.

There are smaller island chains off the northern coast of Colombia and Venezuela, and near the eastern coast of Central America. The adjacent continental coast can also be considered as part of the larger Caribbean area; nevertheless, for our purposes we have restricted the scope of the Caribbean region only to its islands and water passages. While we do not specifically consider the Río Orinoco region of South America, we include several important sources on cultural migration from this area into the Caribbean.

The contemporary Caribbean is a dynamic mixture of independent nations, as well as colonies, states, and territories under the jurisdiction of Great Britain, the Netherlands, France, and the United States. Languages spoken include Spanish, English, French, Dutch, and various creoles and dialects. Ethnicity varies from island to island, as well as within islands, and includes various African, European, Asian, and American Indian ancestries and cultural heritages.

The islands of the Caribbean are also geographically diverse. Most of the Lesser Antilles were formed volcanically. Trinidad, Barbados, and the islands off the northern coast of South America are of sedimentary origin, linked geologically to the mainland. The islands in the Greater Antilles are considerably larger than the other islands of the Caribbean

Figure 1.
Map of modern political boundaries within the Caribbean region.

and support significant river drainage systems, deserts, and lakes. The Bahamas are low coral reef sea islands.

We have arranged the bibliographic section in this volume by emphasizing island groups and individual islands. While it seems logical to consider islands as bounded culture areas, and indeed, they set most political boundaries for the contemporary Caribbean (Haiti and the Dominican Republic, and St. Martin/St. Maarten are exceptions), this was not always the case in prehistory. While our modern sense of geographical boundaries is water oriented, the seafaring peoples of the ancient Caribbean were more constrained by land, and established boundaries around water passages. However, since the literature has traditionally been oriented by islands we have retained this perspective in our bibliographic organization.

Peoples and Places of the Ancient Caribbean

Each Caribbean island chain has a different history of cultural migration and occupation. While some parts of the Caribbean have been inhabited for 5,000, and possibly as many as 9,000 years (256), others, notably the northern Bahamas, have been settled for only a little more than 800 years. Although we have considerable information about the indigenous cultures at the time of European contact, we can only speculate on the total number of different cultures, languages, and lifeways that may have existed before 1492.

Many archaeological studies from the Caribbean employ material culture typologies that group cultures by variables of time and space on single typological charts. The core of the problem is that while a cultural group may be stylistically definable during a particular period of time on one island, the same group may have different periods of occupation on adjacent islands. There is the additional problem of whether new material styles or assemblages are indicative of in-migration or of local cultural change. Basically the archaeologist may be able to identify stylistic differences in material culture but it may not be able to determine whether those differences are reflective of different cultural groups and/ or different time periods. Finally, it is also cautioned that even the most stable of ceramic styles may, in fact, represent a multitude of distinctive cultural groups.

In this volume we refer to the time period before Spanish contact in 1492 as 'prehistoric' and the period after 1492 as 'protohistoric.' We refer to the peoples of the prehistoric period as 'indigenous,' and those of the protohistoric period as 'Indians.' While the terms 'Native American,' 'First nation,' and 'First People,' may be preferred by some contemporary indigenous groups, the term 'Indian' best describes the individuals who experienced contact in the Caribbean with Europeans. They were misidentified as 'Indians,' murdered and enslaved in their own land as 'Indians,' dehumanized by European chroniclers as 'cannibal savage Indians,' and to this day, continue to be mystified or romanticized into social invisibility in many parts of the Americas. The point to be made here is that 'Indians' have been, and continue to be, defined by other people. This is a result of the European colonization of the Americas and reflected by the fact that we do not even know the true names of the inhabitants of the Caribbean at the time of European contact. It is for our lack of knowledge that we refer to them as 'Indians.'

The commonly used terms for Caribbean cultures at the time of European contact, including Taíno, Arawak, and Carib, are also problematic. The term 'Taíno' derives from the Arawak word 'nitaíno' meaning noble. The Spaniards were told by the Indians of the Greater Antilles that they were different from the 'Carib' or 'Caribal,' referring to their enemies in the Lesser Antilles. It is unknown whether the concept of a 'Taíno' ethnic community that transcended local political and geographic boundaries existed or whether this was a European creation. It is probable that the prehistoric groups of the Caribbean identified themselves with a specific geographic area rather than sharing the European perspective of cultural boundedness by more abstract categories such as religion or social class. In fact, several names for regional groups are mentioned in the documentary sources, such as Lucayos in the Bahamas and Ciguayos in northeastern Hispaniola.

The term 'Island Arawak' may be a more accurate designator for the indigenous groups of the Caribbean because most languages in the region originated from the Arawakan (Arahuacan) language family. The Guanahatabey, possibly derived from Chibchan-speaking groups in lower Central America, would be an exception. It should be noted that there are still indigenous peoples known as 'Arawak' who live in South America today, whose culture and language developed differently from the Island Arawak-speaking peoples.

In the archaeological literature, names based on ceramic and lithic assemblages such as Casimiroid, Ortoiroid, Saladoid, and Ostionoid are often imparted onto the peoples who made particular styles and forms of material culture. This is simply another naming strategy employed due to the lack of knowledge of these cultures.

Why Is So Little Known about the Ancient Caribbean?

There are several reasons why the prehistoric and protohistoric cultures of the Caribbean remain among the least known in the Americas.

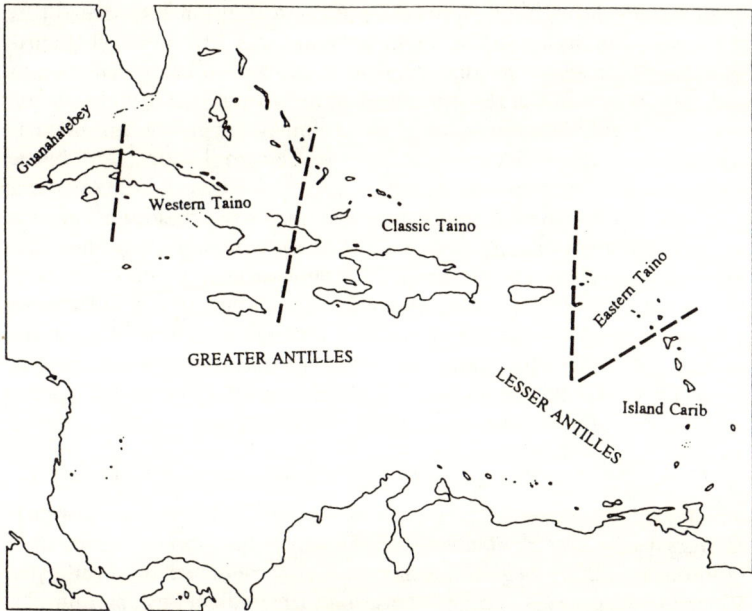

Figure 2. Map of the distribution of prehistoric indigenous groups within the Caribbean region.

Source: I. Rouse, *The Taínos: Rise and Decline of the People Who Greeted Columbus.* New Haven: Yale University Press, 1992. Figure 2.

The indigenous peoples of the Caribbean rapidly fell victim to a European-sponsored genocide and did not leave any form of written record of their ancestral origins or early history. The speed at which the indigenous populations of the Caribbean were decimated, displaced, or creolized left relatively few cultural groups who maintained distinctly traditional lifeways beyond the middle of the sixteenth century; consequently little early ethnographic information is available. The activities of the United States, Spain, France, England, the Netherlands, and other European countries with interests in the region prescribed the role of their Caribbean colonies merely as economic ventures, ultimately attaching the record keeping, scholarly research, and cultural artifacts to museums, archives, and universities of the mother country, thus scattering information throughout the world. The history studied and taught for some four hundred years in the Caribbean tended to focus on the past of the mother country rather than the prehistory of the specific island; indigenous culture was thus unimportant for national identity. In the past century, even with most Caribbean colonies becoming independent nations, an economic dependence on Western Europe and North America has given most Caribbean countries 'third world' or dependent state status. These new nations have been unable to consider history and archaeology high priority endeavors and consequently many sites have been destroyed to accommodate economic development schemes or looted for a foreign antiquities markets. Also, because few contemporary peoples of the Caribbean are identified as indigenous there is little interest in their study. Finally, most professional archaeologists have simply neglected the Caribbean as an area of research for the larger archaeological sites of Mesoamerica and South America.

Are There American Indians Still Living in the Caribbean?

Today there are still people living in the Caribbean who consider themselves 'Indians.' There is a Carib Indian reservation on the island of Dominica (1239–1242) and other Indian settlements on nearby St. Vincent (1394–1398). There are also remnant indigenous communities found in Cuba (570, 572, 576) and Puerto Rico (1069). And along the Caribbean coast of Central and South America the Garifuna (Black Carib) have insular Indian ancestries (1398, 1399, 1401). In other parts of the Caribbean, notably in the Dominican Republic and Puerto Rico, while few people claim to be 'Indians,' there is a growing national consciousness of the indigenous contributions to their cultural and biological heritage (714, 739, 741, 742). While some claims to indigenous ancestry can be seen to be politically motivated (for example, in Puerto Rico the anti-statehood/pro-nationalist movement emphasizes the nation's indigenous past), this should not be considered a reason to discount contemporary claims to an indigenous past.

There is a considerable body of literature in the disciplines of anthropology and sociology that addresses the concept of ethnicity as a dynamic and evolving cultural construct. The definition of a group's ethnicity is not a simple and static measure of blood quanta or a catalog of cultural traits, but rather involves the interrelations of collective thoughts, emotions, and shared experiences, which are constantly changing through time and space. The question of the authenticity of an ethnic group can become politically charged if issues such as autonomy and land tenure are under consideration. Governments often discourage marginal ethnic groups from strengthening their corporate identities so that they do not become political threats. In other words, ethnic authenticity has less to do with the ways people feel bounded together as a group, but how larger political bodies view them.

Caribbean Indian ethnicity is similar to that of many American Indian groups presently unrecognized by the United States federal government that have mixes of Indian, African, and European culture and bloodlines. It is often difficult to administratively define the 'Indian'-ness of these Afro-mestizo groups because most of the tangible emblems that have been historically associated with their tribe, including the traditional anthropological markers of language, religion, and costume, have been 'lost' or creolized. Caribbean Indian identity is often based on kin ties to ancestors, oral traditions passed on through time, a legal or emotional bond with a fixed geographic homeland, and the collection of artifacts and social practices that symbolize their shared history. While many facets of contemporary Caribbean Indian culture are also tied to an identification with their nation's particular history and with African and European culture, many salient themes from their shared Indian past can be said to constitute a distinctive Caribbean Indian identity.

Are there any Indians living in the Caribbean today? We would argue there are, contrary to the many references to the extinction of Caribbean Indians found in scholarly and popular books. Perhaps equally important is a recognition that indigenous culture survives in the modern Caribbean in a variety of dynamic forms, including foodways, folklore, art forms, and technology.

Summary of Caribbean Prehistory

While syntheses of the archaeology and prehistory of the Caribbean region have been rare (11–18, 235, 385), several excellent regional summaries have recently appeared (409, 422, 445, 470). Irving Rouse's *The Taínos: Rise and Decline of the People Who Greeted Columbus* (422) summarizes much of his work over the past fifty years and can be considered the best available overview in English on the archaeology and prehistory of the Caribbean.

Caribbean archaeology can be characterized to a certain degree by its reliance on ceramic and lithic typologies to define prehistoric and protohistoric culture groups and population movements. Other material remains from archaeological sites including bone, botanical remains, pollen, and phytoliths are more difficult to retrieve, and have only recently been studied by archaeologists.

Throughout his professional career Irving Rouse (346, 422, 971) has contributed greatly to the issue of archaeological classification and the delineation of population movements, and has had a great influence on the development of Caribbean prehistoric archaeology (293). Jalil Sued Badillo (149) has recently argued that archaeology, as a discipline, is overly concerned with culture-historical studies while ethnohistory and ethnic studies have made greater contributions to the understanding of the Caribbean past.

Archaeologists create cultural divisions between preceramic lithic and ceramic populations; that is, people who made and used pottery and those who lacked either the knowledge or ability to do so. It is assumed that the technological innovation of pottery production reflects a significant corresponding cultural development as well. The origins of the first groups to settle in the Caribbean is a topic of some controversy. The earliest archaeological materials are found in the Greater Antilles, perhaps associated with the sunken Caribbean shelf that connected Central America with these islands at about 4000 B.c. (256). These initial Preceramic peoples are referred to as 'Paleo-Indians,' and their lithic assemblages are termed 'Casimiroid' after a type-related site in the Greater Antilles. A second group of Preceramic peoples appeared at about 2000 B.c. from the South American mainland, and eventually moved to the Casimiroid frontier at the Mona Passage between Puerto Rico and eastern Hispaniola. These Archaic peoples have been termed 'Ortoiroid,' after a type-related site as well.

There were two principal migratory movements of Ceramic populations through the Caribbean. The first was by a culture referred to as 'Saladoid,' more specifically Cedrosan Saladoid, which originated in the Río Orinoco valley of northeastern South America. They appear in the Lesser Antilles at about 200 B.c. and eventually penetrated as far as the Casimiroid frontier in eastern Hispaniola. The second migration has been termed 'Ostionoid,' developed locally in the Caribbean at about A.D. 600, and eventually moved into the Bahamas and to the frontier of remnant aceramic groups in western Cuba.

Within these larger migratory categories, there are further subdivisions and *in situ* (local) developments defined by stylistic differences in the material culture. The question of whether stylistic changes reflect an *in situ* development or is the product of trade, warfare, migration, or some other form of cultural contact, is a difficulty often addressed by archaeologists in the Caribbean area. For the purposes of this volume, only the major cultural divisions will be addressed, and have been summarized as follows:

Major Cultural Divisions	Time	Location	Origin
Ceramic			
Ostionoid	A.D. 600– A.D. 1500	Lesser Antilles Greater Antilles (except western Cuba)	Caribbean
Saladoid	200 B.C.– A.D. 600	Lesser Antilles Puerto Rico eastern Hispaniola	South America
Preceramic			
Ortoiroid	400 B.C.– 2000 B.C.	Lesser Antilles Puerto Rico	South America
Casimiroid	400 B.C.– 4000 B.C.	Hispaniola Cuba	Central America

Preceramic Cultures

While the origins of the earliest Preceramic cultures of the Caribbean are still somewhat speculative, Casimiroid stone tools from Cuba and Hispaniola exhibit strong similarities to material culture from Honduras and Belize in Central America. Casimiroid lithics are characterized by a chipped stone technology which later developed into the Courian subseries in Hispaniola and the Redondan subseries in Cuba at about 2000 B.C., sometimes referred to as the Archaic period, when groundstone implements first appear.

Very little is known about the Casimiroid peoples despite their lengthy early occupation in the Greater Antilles. The fact that Casimiroid material culture is found only on the large islands of Cuba and Hispaniola suggests that these people were land-oriented. However, axes and gouges, possibly used for the construction of boats, have also been found. Lithic assemblages include knives and projectile points, and may have been used for exploiting available terrestrial resources, including ground sloths. The existence of beads and pendants broadly suggests an elaborate ceremonial component to Casimiroid culture.

The Ortoiroid culture derived from South American origins at about 2000 B.C. and, while similar to the Casimiroid in its lack of ceramic technology, was different in its orientation towards the sea and coastal resources. Ortoiroid culture has been divided into a number of subseries, including Boutbois, Jolly Beach, and Corosan, which occur on specific islands. Certain forms of material culture, such as stone-grinding platforms, bone barbs, and projectile points, are irregularly distributed, possibly indicating a shift from terrestrial resources in Trinidad to maritime resources in the more northern islands of the Lesser Antilles. Ortoiroid artifacts lack the artistic decoration found in the Casimiroid tradition. It has been suggested by Keegan (488) and Watters (376) that the Ortoiroid were transient peoples, moving often to exploit new insular environments.

From the period 1000–400 B.C. the Ortoiroid and Casimiroid were evidently in contact with each other, just across the Mona Passage between western Puerto Rico and eastern Hispaniola. Due to a lack of excavated sites and reliable information, questions concerning culture contact, commerce, warfare, and diffusion have only recently been addressed by archaeologists.

One last subject to be considered is the question of the Guanahatabey culture, previously identified as Ciboney. In western Cuba it appears that the Preceramic period extended to the end of the fifteenth century when the first Europeans arrived. Historical evidence suggests that archaic groups were living in caves, subsisting primarily on fishing, and did not make or use pottery. While Keegan (401) has suggested that the existence of such people is based on Spanish misinformation and perhaps on the mistaken understanding of Taíno mythology, Rouse (422) points out that no archaeological sites in extensively investigated western Cuba have yielded pottery. Rouse further postulates that the existence of an archaic culture in western Cuba may explain the lack of cultural contact by providing a buffer zone between the Taíno chiefdoms of the Caribbean and state-level societies of Mesoamerica and northern Central America.

Ceramic Cultures

There were two principal migrations of pottery-using populations in the Caribbean: the Saladoid and the Ostionoid. The Saladoid originated in the Río Orinoco valley of northeastern South America and migrated north through the Lesser Antilles, Puerto Rico, and the eastern coast of Hispaniola. It is believed however that the Ostionoid developed from cultural interactions already in place in the Caribbean, and then migrated west to the point of the Guanahatabey frontier in Cuba, south into Jamaica, and north into the Bahamas.

The Saladoid people, who entered the Caribbean region at about 200 B.C., developed from two ceramic traditions earlier at about 2000 B.C.: the Ronquian Saladoid in the upper Río Orinoco region and the Barrancoid in the middle Río Orinoco region. It is believed that the Barrancoid pressured the Ronquian Saladoid towards the Caribbean coast where they developed their new ceramic sub-series called Cedrosan Saladoid, which is found throughout the Lesser Antilles to western Puerto Rico. Ronquian Saladoid ceramic style includes the use of curvilinear incision, strap handles, modeled lugs, and the very characteristic white-on-red painting. Characteristic of Barrancoid pottery is the use of elaborate figure modeling on the sides and ends of thicker ceramic vessels. Cedrosan Saladoid style incorporated all of these features to varying degrees, as well as the new stylistic attribute of zone-incised crosshatching. Two different styles emerged with the two different migratory routes along the Windward and Leeward Islands, called La Hueca (1125, 1127, 1131) and Hacienda Grande (1123), differentiated principally by the occurrence of zone-incised crosshatching with and without the occurrence of painted wares. It should be mentioned that accompanying both of these ceramic styles was the first appearance in the Caribbean of cassava griddles and the three-pointed stone idols known as *zemis*. The Saladoid peoples displaced the Ortoiroid as they migrated through the islands. Hacienda Grande peoples eventually broke through the Casimiroid frontier at the Mona Passage and began colonizing eastern Hispaniola. A problematic El Caimito style appears at this Saladoid-Casimiroid frontier between 200 B.C. and A.D. 600 (867), and may be the result of transculturation (422).

In the Lesser Antilles the Saladoid exploited forest and riverine resources more than the Preceramic Ortoiroid, who kept to the coastal areas. However, Saladoid site locations were never permanent and tended to shift from inland to coastal settings after initial occupations. They practiced agriculture, using river terraces for their gardens, and most likely made extensive use of manioc production and the baking of cassava bread. They made beads and ornaments with exotic lithics, showing evidence for participation in extensive trade networks.

By ca. A.D. 600 interaction across the Mona Passage between Hispaniola and Puerto Rico led to a variety of new ceramic styles, including Cuevas which evolved from Hacienda Grande. The Ostionan ceramic style, which is marked by simple modeling, a red slip, and the absence of zone-incised crosshatching ware, became more common at this point and spread throughout Puerto Rico and into Hispaniola. Finally, Meillac Ostionoid peoples, who had a new ceramic style incorporating crosshatching, simple applique work, and punctated lugs, moved from Hispaniola into Jamaica and Cuba, while Palmetto people, with their cruder plain and mat-impressed ceramics, migrated into the Bahamas. Rouse (422) suggests that the Casimiroid-Saladoid frontier may have been precipitated by Ostionoid adaptation to more stable island lifeways, refining their culture, and preparing them for final settlement of the larger islands of the Greater Antilles.

Hispano-Indian Contact: Textual Evidence

Early Spanish colonization has been relatively well documented. This is partially due to the nature of European-sponsored exploration into unknown lands, which demanded a legally accountable description of 'discovered' property. Furthermore, many early explorers took advantage of new paper-manufacturing and printing techniques, and were able to disseminate their work with great ease (409). Accounts by Girolamo Benzoni (163), Diego Alvarez Chanca (168), Christopher Columbus (174–181), Bartolomé de Las Casas (202–205), Pietro Martire d'Anghiera (162), Gonzalo Fernández de Oviedo y Valdés (213), and Ramón Pané (215), present impressive amounts of information concerning the geography, ethnography, and historical events in the Caribbean, and it is not surprising that documentary evidence has driven interpretations about the Caribbean in scholarly literature (143, 149, 227, 409).

However, even with the wealth of textual sources, interpreting historical accounts by European writers is complicated. Beyond the issues of intentional misrepresentation, selective or tendentious accounting, historical texts are fraught with fifteenth and sixteenth-century cultural biases that distort the distinction between accuracy and invention. There are also compounded biases that arise from processes of transcription and translation. Furthermore, Spanish texts need to be interpreted within their social context as part of a larger discourse of European colonial policy, not merely as objective descriptions of cultural reality. Finally, different 'true' interpretations of texts may exist according to different historically situated readings. Thus, when used as historical evidence, texts should be carefully evaluated against other texts and against archaeological, linguistic, geographical, or any other evidence available for their consistency and veracity. They need to be situated according to the social and historical positions of their authors, translators, as well as their readers.

Indian Cultures at Spanish Contact: The Taíno

Rouse (421, 422) has divided the Taíno by sociopolitical development into the following: the Classic Taíno in Puerto Rico,

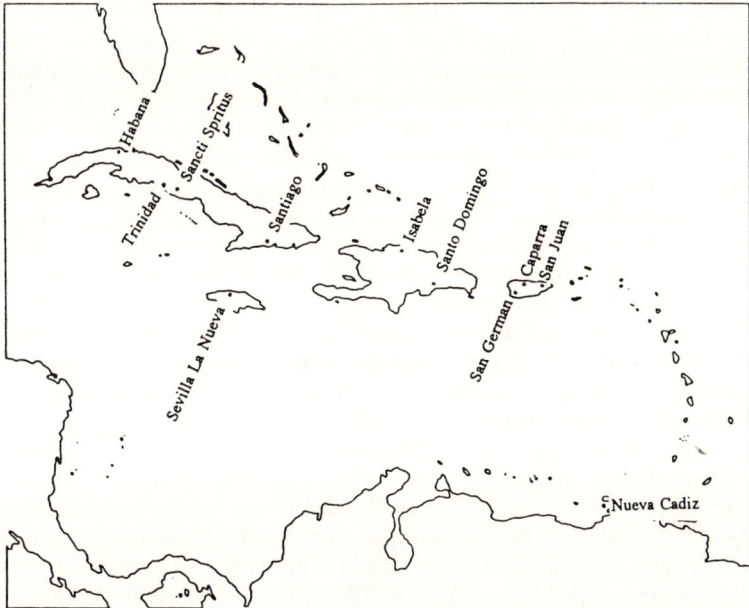

Figure 3. Map of Spanish colonial settlements within the Caribbean region, 1494–1515.

Source: I. Rouse, *The Taínos: Rise and Decline of the People Who Greeted Columbus.* New Haven: Yale University Press, 1992. Figure 37.

eastern and central Hispaniola, and eastern Cuba; the Western Taíno, formerly known as Sub-Taíno, in Jamaica, the Bahamas, and eastern and central Cuba; and the Eastern Taíno, also formerly known as Sub-Taíno, in the Virgin Islands and probably throughout the Lesser Antilles as far south as Guadeloupe. The Guanahatabey occupied western Cuba. The Island Carib were in the Lesser Antilles from Guadeloupe south to mainland South America.

While population estimates vary considerably, it is thought that as many as 3,000,000 Taíno lived on Hispaniola at the time of European contact. The Taíno were primarily cassava farmers, lived in nucleated villages with varying degrees of political cohesion, traveled by canoe to other islands on trading or raiding expeditions, spoke different dialects, and engaged in a myriad of distinctive religious and cultural behaviors. The tuber known as *yuca* or *manioc* served an important role in Taíno life. The Taíno used yuca as a starchy vegetable along with other foodstuffs, including sweet potato, maize, squash, beans, peanuts, and fruits including guayaba, guanabana, and pineapple. The bitter variety of yuca was grated, leeched, and toasted on ceramic griddles to produce a bread known as *casabe*. This bread could be stored for long periods of time without spoilage, and was a central part of the Taíno diet. It is not surprising that many religious ceremonies were devoted to the observance of yuca production and that important deity was called *Yucahu*, provider of yuca. A slash and burn or swidden technique of agriculture was used, together with the practice of mixing crops in elevated mounds called *conucos*. Fish, iguana, turtles, manatee, and the now extinct *jutia* also formed part of the Taíno diet.

The social organization of the Classic Taíno is well-known from documentary sources. The Spaniards recognized a feudal society of chieftains (*caciques*), nobility (*nitaíno*), and commoners (*naboria*). Land was partitioned into chiefdoms (*cacicazgos*) which probably had loose political and economic boundaries (409). The Taíno lived in permanent villages which are described in the historical literature as consisting of as many as 1,000 dwellings and some 5,000 persons. Two types of dwellings are reported, both manufactured of wood and thatch: a round common or public structure (*caney*), and a square or rectangular construction used by caciques (*bohio*). These buildings had earthen floors, rope hammocks for sleeping, and baskets for storage that were suspended from walls and ceiling.

The Taíno had a complex set of religious rituals and beliefs, including a pantheon of deities and mythologies. They communicated with these deities during dancing and cleansing ceremonies that incorporated the use of tobacco and an hallucinogenic snuff called *cohoba*. The Taíno also crafted physical representations of their deities, called *zemís*, which were reported to contain great spiritual power. *Zemís* appear as portable three-pointed stone sculpture, as modeled appliques on pottery vessels, in the form of cotton, shell, bone, and wooden idols, and represented as petroglyphs on large stone surfaces and in caves. Personal adornments of bone, shell, gold, and various alloys were also crafted with religious symbolism. Drums called *areitos* were used during dances and during the playing of a special ballgame. Ceremonial stools (*dujos*) were elaborately carved from mahogany wood and had important social and ritual functions.

The Taíno practiced a form of cranial modification and pierced their ears, lips, and septums. Tattooing is reported although body painting was probably more common. Hair was worn long in the back and short in the front. Facial and body hair was considered unsightly and was removed. Clothing consisted of cotton loin cloths for men and skirts for women.

Indian Cultures at Spanish Contact: The Carib

The early historical narratives for the Caribbean describe a male-dominated culture of battle-obsessed, bride-capturing man-eaters known as Carib Indians. The word 'cannibal' is a corruption of 'Caribal' or 'Carib' and has become synonymous with anthropophagy, or the consumption of human flesh. However, verifiable evidence for the practice of cannibalism is lacking (225, 312–315, 950, 1245). The genesis of these accounts of cannibalism may derive from a misunderstanding of a Taíno creation myth that involves the consumption of a son's flesh by the father (445), from the desire by Taíno storytellers to position the Spaniards against enemy factions on other islands to the east and south (409), or from some actual ritual associated with dead bodies or bones. Regardless, it is apparent that an artificial but meaningful distinction was created between the peaceful Arawaks (Taíno) and the man-eating Carib by the Europeans that was used to justify or rationalize the treatment of the aboriginal populations of the Caribbean by the Spaniards.

The term 'Carib' has remained well-established in the current scholarly literature despite the fact that linguistic evidence suggests that the groups of the Lesser Antilles spoke an Arawak dialect rather than a distinct Cariban language, and archaeological studies indicate that the material culture of the Lesser Antilles is within the range of variation known for earlier insular groups.

Rouse (422) suggests that the Carib were actually the Kalina, or Kalinga, a maritime trading culture of mainland origin who conquered the Igneri people of the Lesser Antilles and later developed locally. Unlike the Taíno, the Carib were patrifocal and Carib males went on frequent trading and raiding expeditions, used a creolized male-language, and lived in communal long houses. Although the Carib were yuca farmers, they depended more on fishing than did the Taíno.

Indian Responses to Contact and Conquest

Christopher Columbus and his three famous ships landed on the Bahamian island called Guanahani in 1492 (485, 486). After sailing around the Bahamas and the north coast of Cuba, one of the ships, the *Santa Maria*, ran aground on the north coast of modern Haiti. A fortification called La Navidad was constructed from the ship's wreckage and thirty-nine Spaniards remained on the island while Columbus and the remaining ships returned to Spain (975, 976). A year later, Columbus returned to find La Navidad destroyed and all of the men killed. A town was established further east at a site known as La Isabela (150, 905). Soon thereafter, the Spaniards began a plan of environmental exploitation and colonization. Forts, churches, and towns were built throughout the region and a new political order was imposed on the Caribbean landscape. Disease, warfare, and enslavement all contributed to the destruction of the Indian people; however, it appears that starvation, arising from the disruption of agricultural scheduling, may have resulted in the most damage (194, 399, 409).

While there is no doubt of the violence inherent to strategies of Spanish colonialism, it is important not to overlook the acculturative responses and transculturation that also occurred during this period (399). Archaeological sites of culture contact period in the Caribbean demonstrate shifts away from traditional lifeways, but also show acculturative responses to new social stresses. For example, Manuel García-Arévalo (150) has demonstrated how Taíno potters incorporated formal characteristics of European pottery such as jugs and plates into their ceramic inventories. José M. Cruxent (150) argues that the Spaniards similarly incorporated pottery made in local indigenous kilns during this formative period. European goods are often found in association with contact-period Taíno dwellings and burials (2). The Spaniards were also incorporating indigenous linguistic and dietary features (409). However, Kathleen Deagan (2) identifies the retention of Taíno symbolism on indigenous pottery well into the historic period, suggesting variations in the acculturation model and, possibly, resistance to it as well.

While the period of contact between Spaniards and indigenous populations was very brief, it left an indelible mark on the character of the Caribbean region. It is fair to say that the indigenous populations of the Caribbean became extinct as a cultural group although fragments of prehispanic lifeways have persisted, creolized in various dietary, architectural, medical, linguistic, genetic, religious, and artistic forms to the present (2, 150, 396, 422, 445, 978).

Resources for the Study of the Ancient Caribbean

Significant long-term interest in the archaeology and prehistory of the ancient Caribbean in the United States has been based at only a few important academic institutions, such as the Peabody Museum at Yale

University in New Haven, Connecticut, and the Florida Museum of Natural History, University of Florida, Gainesville. Both of these research institutions are associated with outstanding research library collections and excellent graduate programs in anthropology.

Museums and Research Collections

There are many museums, libraries, historical societies, and cultural centers in the Caribbean and elsewhere that have excellent collections of artifacts, books and journals, and manuscripts and maps pertaining to the prehistory and archaeology of the region. Many of these institutions are professionally organized and managed, and contain important archaeological site files and well-documented artifact collections that may serve as primary resources for archaeologically-based research.

This section lists many of the major museums and research facilities with scholarly interests in the archaeology and prehistory of the Caribbean region. Institutions in the United States are emphasized, keeping with the English-language focus of the volume. The extent of Caribbean collections in United States and European museums is unknown and difficult to determine. The results of an attempt by Robert A. Myers (376) to identify museums with archaeological collections from the Caribbean area has been useful. It is advisable to contact these museums to arrange a visit to examine specific collections.

CALIFORNIA

Robert H. Lowie Museum of Anthropology
Kroeber Hall
University of California, Berkeley
2620 Bancroft Way
Berkeley, California 94720

Founded in 1901, this general university anthropology museum possesses numerous objects from the Greater Antilles, especially Puerto Rico.

Museum of Cultural History
University of California, Los Angeles
Los Angeles, California 90024

The Museum has some 200–300 stone and shell tools from the Caribbean, chiefly from St. Kitts and Nevis.

CONNECTICUT

Peabody Museum of Natural History
Yale University
170 Whitney Avenue
New Haven, Connecticut 06511

Founded in 1866, the Peabody Museum at Yale University has extensive collections in anthropology and natural sciences. Yale University has for many years sponsored important archaeological research by Froelich Rainey, Irving Rouse, and others, in the Caribbean area. The Caribbean collections contain objects from throughout the region, and include excellent comparative lithic and ceramic collections.

FLORIDA

University of Central Florida Library
POB 25000
Orlando, Florida 32816

Includes the Bryant West Indies Collection, a scholarly special private collection on deposit to the library by William J. Bryant, containing books, journals, periodicals, serials, and original handicrafts, artifacts, and paintings from the West Indies and the Caribbean area which pertain to the history, geography, economic and social life of the area. There is a special focus on Haitian art. The collection consists of some 2,500 volumes and dates from 1709 to the present.

University of Florida Libraries
Gainesville, Florida 32611

Includes some 120,000 books, periodicals, and government documents pertaining to Latin America, with particular strengths on the Caribbean area and Brazil. The library catalog has been published as: University of Florida, Gainesville, Libraries, *Catalog of the Latin America Collection* (Boston: G.K. Hall, 1973. 13 v.; *First Supplement*, 1979. 7 v.).

Florida Museum of Natural History
University of Florida
Gainesville, Florida 32611

Founded in 1917 as the Florida State Museum, the Florida Museum of Natural History contains an excellent collection of prehistoric and historic period archaeological material from the West Indies.

ILLINOIS

Field Museum of Natural History
Roosevelt Road and Lake Shore Drive
Chicago, Illinois 60605

Founded by Marshall Field in 1893, houses an important anthropology collection as well as a library of 215,000 volumes.

MASSACHUSETTS

Peabody Museum of Archaeology and Ethnology
Harvard University
11 Divinity Avenue
Cambridge, Massachusetts 02138

The Museum works in close cooperation with the Department of Anthropology. Since its founding in 1866 more than 800 expeditions have been sent to every continent resulting in the addition of important collections of archaeology, ethnography, and physical anthropology. Extensive archaeological and ethnological holdings from the Greater and Lesser Antilles, especially from Barbados, Grenada, and Lesser Antilles. The annual reports of the Peabody Museum for the period 1868–1879 indicate the acquisition of shell implements from Barbados, stone implements from Granada, an elbow stone from Puerto Rico, and a collection of celts, axes, chisels and other stone implements, and a bamboo basket and sieve from various islands in the Caribbean region. In 1936 the Museum acquired the A. Godet collection of pottery from the West Indies, and in 1939 a collection of archaeological objects from Haiti from R.L. Pettigrew. Tozzer Library, with some 110,000 volumes, covers the entire field of anthropology. The library catalog has been published as: Harvard University, Peabody Museum of Archaeology and Ethnology Library, *Catalogue: Subjects* (Boston: G.K. Hall, 1963. 27 v.; *First Supplement*, 1970. 6 v.; *Second Supplement*, 1971. 3 v.; *Third Supplement*, 1975. 4 v.; *Fourth Supplement*, 1979. 4 v.); *Catalogue: Authors* (Boston: G.K. Hall, 1963. 26 v.; *First Supplement*, 1970. 6 v.; *Second Supplement*, 1971. 2 v.; *Third Supplement*, 1975. 3 v.; *Fourth Supplement*, 1979. 3 v.).

NEW JERSEY

Museum of Natural History
Princeton University
Princeton, New Jersey 08540

Founded in 1909, the Museum of Natural History at Princeton University possesses a few carved stone objects from Puerto Rico.

NEW YORK

American Museum of Natural History
Central Park West at 79th Street
New York, New York 10024

Founded in 1869, the American Museum of Natural History has in its anthropology collections an enormous amount of material from the West Indies in general, including celts from Jamaica.

Metropolitan Museum of Art
Fifth Avenue and 82 Street
New York, New York 10028

Founded in 1870, the Museum has several archaeological objects from the Caribbean region.

Museum of the American Indian, Heye Foundation
(National Museum of the American Indian, Smithsonian Institution)
Broadway at 155 Street
New York, New York 10032

The collections of the Museum of the American Indian, Heye Foundation, reflect a long standing interest in the Caribbean area. The Museum joined the Smithsonian Institution in sending Jesse W. Fewkes to the Caribbean where he conducted archaeological explorations on St. Vincent and Trinidad. Following Theodoor de Booy's earlier reconnaissance in eastern Cuba, Mark R. Harrington directed extensive excavations in that area. In 1931 Robert R. Bennett made additions to the collection through his work in shell middens at the western extremity of Cuba and in 1933 Godfrey J. Olsen conducted excavations on Haiti near Aux Cayes and on the Ilè la Vache. A comprehensive collection of over 2,000 pieces was obtained through an archaeological expedition to St. Croix under the direction of Lewis J. Korn and supported by Willard V. King, a trustee of the Museum (30, 31, 386).

Specific collections of interest include the following:

Cuba   pottery; celts, hammerstones, fetishes, amulets, mortars, cassava griddles, and weights; a wooden paddle and

	platter from a lake in Pinar del Río province; shell amulets; bone implements; European colonial objects.
Jamaica	pottery; stone mortars and a three-legged grinding stone.
Bahamas	pottery; celts, including a celt with its wooden handle intact from a cave on North Caicos Island; shell gouges; wooden *duhos* or seats.
Hispaniola	pottery, figurines, stamps; stone figurines or amulets, beads, pestles, celts, stone collars, *zemís* (three-pointed stones); shell and bone implements; wooden idol.
Puerto Rico	pottery; stone collars, elbow stones, celts, beads, *zemís*; a wooden *duho* or seat.
Virgin Islands	pottery; stone collar, *zemís*, axes and celts; bone objects, including handles and a swallow-stick, evidently thrust down the throat to induce vomiting; shell celts.
Anguilla	small general collection.
Antigua	stone celts.
Barbados	pottery; axes, celts, hookstone; large collection of shell celts and gouges.
Grenadines	*zemís*, celts, axes; shell celts.
Grenada	pottery; axes, adzes, *zemís*; shell celts.
Guadeloupe and Dominica	stone axes, *zemí*.
Martinique	celt and notched axe.
Montserrat	pottery, beads, decorative objects of amethyst, jade, carnelian, turquois, and rock crystal.
Nevis	stone axes and pestles.
St. Eustatius	small general collection.
St. Kitts	stone axes and pestles.
St. Lucia	stone axes, celts.
St. Martin	stone *zemí*.
St. Vincent	pottery; stone beads and amulets, notched axes, celts, stone dish, mortars and grinding platforms, *zemís*.
Tobago	celts, axes, *zemís*, plummet.
Trinidad	pottery; axes.

In addition to the archaeological material, the Museum has several small ethnographic collections from Yara village near Baracoa, Cuba, and from various families in the Maisi district, survivors of the Taíno. There are also ethnographic Carib collections from St. Vincent and Trinidad. The library catalog has been published as: Museum of the American

Indian, Heye Foundation, Huntington Free Library and Reading Room, *Dictionary Catalog of the American Indian Collection, Huntington Free Library and Reading Room* (Boston: G.K. Hall, 1977. 4 v.).

PENNSYLVANIA

Carnegie Museum of Natural History
Anthropology Center
POB 28, Meridian Station
Butler, Pennsylvania 16001

Includes a collection of coral celts from Barbados, stone celts from Jamaica and Puerto Rico, and shell and ceramics from San Salvador, Bahamas.

University Museum
University of Pennsylvania
33d and Spruce Streets
Philadelphia, Pennsylvania 19104–0657

Founded in 1887, the University Museum has extensive archaeological and ethnographic collections from the Old and New Worlds. The Caribbean material includes approximately 200 objects (small ceramic fragments, adornos, rim sherds, handles), including four intact vessels, mostly from Cuba, Puerto Rico and the Dominican Republic, and Haiti. Theodoor de Booy conducted archaeological research in Trinidad in 1915 for the University Museum.

RHODE ISLAND

Museum of Primitive Cultures
Columbia Street and Kingstown Road
Peace Dale, Rhode Island 02883

Two ancient clay heads from Santo Domingo.

WASHINGTON, DC

National Museum of Natural History
and National Museum of Man
Smithsonian Institution
Washington, DC 20560

Founded in 1846, it is the national depository of collections, containing over 119 million cataloged items; especially rich in the anthropology of the Americas, including the Caribbean. Bernardo Vega has examined the archaeological material at the Smithsonian Institution collected by Herbert Krieger from Hispaniola (729) and Otis T. Mason has described the Latimer Collection of pottery and lithics from Puerto Rico (1057). The library catalog of the National Anthropological Archives identifies materials pertaining to the Caribbean and has been published as: *Catalog to Manuscripts at the National Anthropological Archives, Department of Anthropology, National Museum of Natural History, Smithsonian Institution, Washington, DC* (Boston: G.K. Hall, 1975. 4 v.).

In addition to these North American museums and libraries, there are several museums with excellent archaeological collections in Europe and the Caribbean.

BAHAMAS

Bahamas Historical Society Museum
Elizabeth Avenue
P.O. N-1715
Nassau, Bahamas

Founded in 1959, contains a library with maps, prints, photographs, and archaeological site files.

BARBADOS

Barbados Museum and Historical Society
St. Ann's Garrison, St. Michael
Barbados

Includes collections illustrating the geology, prehistory, history, and natural history of the island; library of 3,000 volumes specializes in Barbadiana and West Indies (1185, 1186).

CUBA

Museo Antropológico Montané
Facultad de Biología
Universidad de La Habana
La Habana 4, Cuba

Founded in 1903, exhibits include objects relating to Cuban ethnography, the prehispanic cultures of Cuba and the Antilles, deriving from various archaeological expeditions; research and postgraduate courses; notable collections of Ciboney, Taíno and sub-Taíno pottery; library of 5,000 volumes (550, 551, 632, 638).

Museo Municipal Emilio Bacardi Moreau
Aguilera y Pio Rosado
Apartado 759
Santiago, Cuba

Founded in 1899, contains material relating to the archaeology of Cuba (724).

Museo 'Felipe Poey'
Capitolo Nacional
La Habana, Cuba

A natural history museum with extensive archaeological and ethnographic collections.

Museo Histórico de Guanabacoa
Martí 108
Guanabacoa, La Habana, Cuba

Extensive collection of nineteenth century and African-Cuba ethnographic materials, including a voodoo collection.

Museo Municipal Provincial de Mantanzas
Palacio de Junco
Calle de Milanés y Magdalena
Plaza de la Vigía
Mantanzas, Cuba

Founded in 1959, this museum has collections on the archaeology and ethnography of the Matanzas region.

Museo y Archivo Histórico Municipal de la Ciudad de La Habana
Oficina del Historiador
Palacio de los Capitanes Generales
Plaza Carlos Manuel Céspedes
La Habana, Cuba

Collection of historical objects from 1550 to the present.

CURAÇAO

Curaçao Museum
Van Leeuwenhoekstratt
Curaçao, Netherlands Antilles

Housed in an old Dutch quarantine station, includes an archaeological collection, as well as fine arts and historical objects; library pertaining to the Netherlands Antilles and the West Indies.

DOMINICAN REPUBLIC

Museo de las Casas Reales
Mercedes Las Damas
Apartado 2664
Santo Domingo, Dominican Republic

Founded in 1976, the buildings were once the headquarters of the colonial government; exhibits of objects from the period 1492–1821, including arms and armor, pottery, and items from shipwrecks; various aspects of the collection have been summarized by María Nieves Sicart and Eugenio Pérez Montás (727, 728).

Museo del Hombre Dominicano
Calle Pedro Henríquez Ureña
Plaza de la Cultura
Santo Domingo, Dominican Republic

Formerly the Museo Nacional, the Museo de Hombre Dominicano possesses an extensive collection of archaeological materials, including archaeological and ethnographic exhibits, pottery, lithics, wooden objects, amulets, skeletal remains; also a collection of historic objects, including weaponry, armor, maritime objects, religious objects, etc.; supports a library of some 4,000 volumes (725, 820).

Sala de Arte Prehispánico
Apartado 723
Santo Domingo, Dominican Republic

Founded in 1973 and operated by the García-Arévalo Foundation, studies and exhibits prehispanic Dominican culture; library has 6,000 volumes on the anthropology and history of Santo Domingo and the Caribbean.

GRENADA

Grenada National Museum
Young Street
St. George's, Grenada

Founded in 1976, contains a collection pertaining to the archaeology and prehistory of Grenada.

GUADELOUPE

Musée Edgar Clerc
Parc de la Rosette
97160 Le Moule, Guadeloupe

Founded in 1979, serves as an archaeological museum; contains a library with 800 volumes.

Musée L'Herminer
27 Rue Sadi-Carnet
Pointe-à-Pitre, Guadeloupe

Natural history museum with important archaeological and historical collections relating to the history of Guadeloupe.

Musée Schoelcher
26 Rue Peynier
Pointe-à-Pitre, Guadeloupe

The Musée Schoelcher, founded in 1883, has exhibits on African-American slavery and a library of 300 volumes on the history and art of Guadeloupe.

HAITI

Bureau Nationale d'Ethnologie de la République d'Haiti
Rue St. Honore et Ave. Magliore Ambroise
Place des Héros de l'Indépendance
BP 915
Port-au-Prince, Haiti

Founded in 1941, contains African and Haitian ethnographic and archaeological departments. An illustrated guide to the archaeological exhibits in the Musée du Bureau d'Ethnologie d'Haiti was prepared by Michel Auborg (940–942).

Musée National d'Haiti
Turgeau
Port-au-Prince, Haiti

Founded in 1938, contains collections pertaining to Haitian history, art, and culture.

Musée du Pantheon National
Place des Héros de l'Indépendance
Port-au-Prince, Haiti

Contains a collection of archaeological, historical, and ethnographic objects.

JAMAICA

Arawak Indian Museum
White Marl
St. Catherine, Jamaica

Includes a reconstruction of an indigneous village, and artifacts and other objects from nearby Sub-Taíno sites.

Institute of Jamaica
12–16 East Street
Kingston, Jamaica

Comprises the National Library and a number of cultural centers, including the Arawak Museum, Jamaica Folk Museum, Archaeological Museum, and the African-Caribbean Institute. The Reference Library of the Institute of Jamaica is especially strong for Jamaica and the English-speaking Caribbean; the library catalog has been published as: *The Catalogue of the West India Reference Library* (Millwood, New York: Kraus, 1980. 6 v.).

MARTINIQUE

Musée Departemental de la Martinique
9 Rue de la Liberté
97200 Fort de France Cedex, Martinique

Founded in 1970, this museum is devoted to the archaeology and prehistory of Martinique.

Musée du Père Pichon
Fort de France Seminary
97207 Fort de France, Martinique

PUERTO RICO

Caguana Indian Ceremonial Park and Museum
Calle del Santa Cristo de la Salud
Carrerera 11
Utuado, Puerto Rico

An Ostionoid burial ground associated with seven ball courts (*bateys*), two plazas, and petroglyphs; includes a replica of a Taíno village and a museum with excavated objects.

Centro de Estudios Avanzados de Puerto Rico y el Caribe
Del Cristo 255
Box 5–2265
San Juan, Puerto Rico 00902

The 5,000-volume library maintains an extensive collection on Caribbean prehistory and archaeology.

Instituto de Cultura Puertorriqueña
Apartado 4184
San Juan, Puerto Rico 00905

Founded in 1955, the Instituto de Cultura Puertorriqueña studies and preserves Puerto Rican historical and cultural patrimony and promotes the study of Puerto Rican culture.

Museum of Anthropology, History, and Art
University of Puerto Rico
Apartado 21908
Río Piedras, Puerto Rico

Contains exhibits of archaeological and historical objects.

TRINIDAD AND TOBAGO

National Museum and Art Gallery
117 Frederick Street
Port-of-Spain

Founded in 1898 as the Royal Victoria Institute, contains a collection pertaining to the archaeology and prehistory of Trinidad and Tobago.

VIRGIN ISLANDS

Christiansted National Historic Site
P.O. Box 160
Christiansted, St. Croix
United States Virgin Islands

Founded in 1952, the Christiansted National Historic Site is devoted to Danish colonial history in the West Indies, 1733–1917; includes also the Anderson Collection pertaining to the archaeology of the indigenous populations of the Virgin Islands.

DENMARK

Nationalmuseet
Prinsens Palae
Frederiksholms Kanal 12
1220 Copenhagen, Denmark

Includes the Guesde and Hatt collections as well as objects from Barbados, Cuba, Guadeloupe, Hispaniola, and the Virgin Islands. The Guesde Collection of material from Guadeloupe is described by Ernest T. Hamy and Otis T. Mason (1264). The Hatt Collection from the Virgin Islands is described by Ripley P. Bullen (1436).

FRANCE

Musée de l'Homme
Palais de Chaillot
Place du Trocadero
75116 Paris, France

Founded in 1878, the Musée de l'Homme has collections pertaining to the archaeology and ethnology of the world. The Caribbean holdings include celts from Hispaniola and Guadeloupe (387). The archaeological objects excavated by Eugène Revert from Martinique in the Musée de l'Homme are described by Raoul d'Harcourt (1283). The library has 250,000 volumes, 5,000 periodicals, and 1,000 microforms (1299, 1300).

GERMANY

Staatliche Museen Preussischer Kulturbesitz
1000 Berlin 30
Stauffenberstrasse 41
Berlin, Germany

The Museum für Völkerkunde has extensive ethnographic and archaeological collections, including axes and celts from Cuba and Jamaica as well as a cotton cordage and shell bead girdle from Hispaniola (726, 836).

SWEDEN

Folkens Museum-Etnografiska
S-115
27 Stockholm, Sweden

Founded in 1880, this museum has materials from around the world, including collections from Grenada and St. Vincent.

UNITED KINGDOM

British Museum
Great Russell Street
London, England WC1B 3DG

The anthropological materials are curated and displayed at the Museum of Mankind, 6 Burlington Gardens, W1X 2EX, London; Caribbean collections include archaeological specimens from Barbados, Jamaica, Nevis, St. Kitts, St. Vincent, Tobago, Trinidad, and the Virgin Islands (26, 27).

Horniman Museum and Library
London Road
Forest Hill
London, England SE23 3PQ

Founded in 1901, the Horniman Museum has important ethnographic collections from all parts of the globe, including the Caribbean.

Pitt-Rivers Museum
University of Oxford
South Parks Road
Oxford OX1 3PP

Founded in 1884, it is part of the School of Anthropology and Museum Ethnography at the University; teaching a research on the ethnology and archaeology of the world; Balfour Library of 29,000 volumes and 200 periodicals. A large collection of archaeological material from the West Indies, especially the Windward and Leeward Islands as well as Jamaica.

Salisbury and South Wiltshire Museum
The King's House
65 The Close
Salisbury, Wiltshire SPI 2DT

A few objects from Barbados, Grenada, and Haiti.

University Museum of Archaeology and Ethnology
Downing St.
Cambridge University
Cambridge, England CB2 3DZ

Founded in 1883, the University Museum of Archaeology and Anthropology has important collections worldwide, as well as extensive materials from the Greater and Lesser Antilles.

Literature of the Caribbean Past and Present

The number of books and journals pertaining to the ancient Caribbean is increasing rapidly. Since this volume is a brief bibliographic survey and guide to the literature of the region, considerable selectivity has been exercised so that works representative of important authors, archaeological sites, and general subject fields could be included.

Many works omitted from this guide can be easily located in bibliographies and other reference volumes useful to the study of the ancient Caribbean, such as:

Handbook of Latin American Studies. Gainesville. v. 1– , 1935 – . 1/yr.

An extensive annual annotated bibliography of the monographic and journal literature pertaining to Latin America, including the Caribbean region; beginning with v. 26, 1984, coverage alternates between the humanities (e.g., history and linguistics) and social sciences (e.g., archaeology and ethnography).

Baa, Enid M. 1970. *Theses on Caribbean Topics, 1778–1968*. San Juan: Institute of Caribbean Studies, University of Puerto Rico.

Commonwealth Caribbean Resource Centre. *Theses on the Commonwealth Caribbean, 1891–1973*. London, Ontario: Office of International Education, University of Western Ontario. 1975.

Hispanic American Periodicals Index. Los Angeles. v. 1— , 1974— . 1/yr.

Indexes some 200 journals published in Latin America and elsewhere; covers all major disciplines, including anthropology and related areas.

Mevis, Rene. 1974. *Inventory of Caribbean Studies: An Overview of Social Research on the Caribbean Conducted by Antillean, Dutch, and Surinamese Scholars in the Period 1945–1973; With an Index of Caribbean Specialties and a Bibliography*. Leiden: Caribbean Department, Royal Institute of Linguistics and Anthropology.

Nagelkerke, Gerard A. 1982. *Netherlands Antilles: A Bibliography, 17th Century-1980*. Leiden: Department of Caribbean Studies, Royal Institute of Linguistics and Anthropology. 422 p.

Survey, in Dutch, of books, articles, manuscripts, etc., relating to the Netherlands Antilles in the library of the Royal Institute of Linguistics and Anthropology (Koninklijk Instituut voor Taal-, Land-, en Volkenkunde) in Leiden, Netherlands.

In addition, the *Latin American Historical Dictionaries* series is especially useful since each volume contains a brief survey of the history of the country followed by a dictionary of people and subjects. Most volumes contain selective bibliographies. Titles pertaining to the Caribbean include:

Farr, K.R. 1973. *Puerto Rico and the U.S. Virgin Islands*. Latin American Historical Dictionaries, v. 9. Metuchen, New Jersey: Scarecrow. 148 p.

Gastmann, A. 1978. *French and Netherlands Antilles*. Latin American Historical Dictionaries, v. 18. Metuchen, New Jersey: Scarecrow. 162 p.

Lux, W. 1975. *British Caribbean*. Latin American Historical Dictionaries, v. 12. Metuchen, New Jersey: Scarecrow. 266 p.

Perosse, R.I. 1977. *Haiti*. Latin American Historical Dictionaries, v. 15. Metuchen, New Jersey: Scarecrow. 124 p.

Suchlicki, J. 1988. *Cuba*. Latin American Historical Dictionaries, v. 22. Metuchen, New Jersey: Scarecrow. 368 p.

Similarly, the *World Bibliographical Series* expects to provide coverage for every country in the world, each in a separate volume, with annotated entries dealing with history, geography, economics, politics, and with its peoples and their culture, customs, etc. Volumes pertaining to the Caribbean include:

Berleant-Schiller, Riva. 1991. *Montserrat*. World Bibliographical Series, v. 134. Oxford, England: CLIO Press. 102 p.

Boultbee, Paul G. 1989. *The Bahamas*. World Bibliographical Series, v. 108. Oxford, England: CLIO Press. 195 p.

———. 1991. *Turks and Caicos Islands*. World Bibliographical Series, v. 137. Oxford, England: CLIO Press. 97 p.

Cevallos, Elena E. 1985. *Puerto Rico*.World Bibliographical Series, v. 52. Oxford, England: CLIO Press. 193 p.

Chambers, Frances. 1983. *Haiti*. World Bibliographical Series, v. 39. Oxford, England: CLIO Press. 177 p.

———. 1986. *Trinidad and Tobago*. World Bibliographical Series, v. 74. Oxford, England: CLIO Press. 213 p.

Ingram, Kenneth E. 1984. *Jamaica*. World Bibliographical Series, v. 45. Oxford, England: CLIO Press. 369 p.

Moll, Verna P. 1991. *Virgin Islands*. World Bibliographical Series, v. 138. Oxford, England: CLIO Press. 210 p.

Myers, Robert A. 1987. *Dominica*. World Bibliographical Series, v. 82. Oxford, England: CLIO Press. 190 p.

Potter, Robert B. 1992. *St. Vincent and the Grenadines*. World Bibliographical Series, v. 143. Oxford, England: CLIO Press. 212 p.

———, and Graham M.S. Dann. 1987. *Barbados*. World Bibliographical Series, v. 76. Oxford, England: CLIO Press. 356 p.

Schoenhals, Kai. 1990. *Dominican Republic*. World Bibliographical Series, v. 111. Oxford, England: CLIO Press. 210 p.

———. 1990. *Grenada*. World Bibliographical Series, v. 119. Oxford, England: CLIO Press. 179 p.

JOURNALS

The results of recent research pertaining to the ancient Caribbean are published in several journals, including:

American Antiquity: A Quarterly Review of American Archaeology. Washington, DC: Society for American Archaeology. v. 1–, 193–. 4/yr.

A basic professional journal for the archaeology of the Americas; includes technical and other papers as well as obituaries, an interesting column on current research, and critical book reviews.

Archaeology. Boston: Archaeological Institute of America. v. 1–, 1948–. 6/yr.

Probably the best popular magazine of archaeology available, publishes short articles on archaeology throughout the world; includes a news section with brief notes of activities in the field, current museum exhibitions, and new discoveries.

Florida Anthropologist. Gainesville: Florida Anthropological Society. v. 1–, 1948–. 4/yr.

Journal of Field Archaeology. Boston: Boston University. v. 1– , 1974–. 4/yr.

Publishes articles that deal with reports of field excavation and survey throughout the world as well as studies of methodological and technical matters, scientific advances in archaeology, and larger interpretive issues.

Latin American Antiquity. Washington, DC: Society for American Archaeology. v. 1–, 1990–. 4/yr.

Publishes articles in English and Spanish dealing with archaeology and ethnohistory of Latin America, including the Caribbean region.

There are similarly many important Spanish-, French-, and German-language journals publishing the results of research pertaining to the ancient Caribbean, including:

Bahamas Historical Society, Journal. Nassau: Bahamas Historical Society. v. 1–, 1979–. 1/yr.

Barbados Museum and Historical Society, Journal. St. Ann's Garrison: Barbados Museum and Historical Society. v. 1–, 1933–. 1/yr.

Caribbean Journal of Science. Mayaguez, Puerto Rico: University of Puerto Rico. v. 1–, 1961–. 4/yr.

Caribbean Quarterly. Mona, Jamaica: University College of the West Indies. v. 1–, 1949–. 4/yr.

Caribbean Studies. Río Piedras, Puerto Rico: Instituto de Estudios del Caribe, Universidad de Puerto Rico. v. 1–, 1961–. 4/yr.

Casas Reales. Santo Domingo: Museo de las Casas Reales. v. 1–, 1976–. 3/yr.

Instituto de Cultura Puertorriqueña, Revista. San Juan: Instituto de Cultura Puertorriqueña. v. 1–, 1958–. 4/yr.

Jamaica Journal. Kingston: Institute of Jamaica. v. 1–, 1967–. 4/yr.

Museo del Hombre Dominicano, Boletín. Santo Domingo: Museo del Hombre Dominicano. v. 1–, 1972–. irreg.

Nieuwe West-Indische Gids/New West Indian Guide. Gravenhague: M. Nijhoff. v. 1–, 1960–. 4/yr.

Revista/Review Interamericana. Hato Rey, Puerto Rico: Inter-American University Press. v. 1–, 1970–. 4/yr.

Virgin Islands Archaeological Society, Journal. St. Thomas: Virgin Islands Archaeological Society. v. 1–, 1974–. 4/yr.

Arrangement and Content of the Bibliography

The Caribbean region has been the focus of intensive study for more than a century by European as well as North and Latin American scholars. The bibliography in the next section identifies some 1,450 annotated entries representative of this research.

Individual entries in the bibliography are arranged numerically and alphabetically by author according to island and broad subject area. Where known or imputed, the author is indicated. Where no author is entered, items are assumed to be anonymous and are arranged by title. Authorship is followed by title and publication information. Most entries have some annotation to indicate the subject or relative importance of the work.

Some of the annotations are evaluative and others simply report the contents of the work. We cannot claim that an exhaustive survey of the literature of the ancient Caribbean will be found in 1,450 entries. Within the limitation of length we have aimed for a judicious mix of the most significant, the most recent, and the unusual as well as those studies not represented in other reference works. We have given special attention to site reports.

The indexes provide access by personal name, place name, and subject. Index entries are given with their appropriate numerical prefixes. Headings used in constructing subject classifications are necessarily arbitrary and cannot serve the needs of all researchers equally well. They pertain more to personal research interests than to areas with which we are less familiar. However, they should prove adequate for providing access to most of the subject areas included in the bibliography.

Table 1. Radiocarbon Chronology of the Caribbean Region.

The chronology of the Caribbean region is relatively well documented as a result of an abundance of radiocarbon dates. The information presented in this table has been adapted from Rouse and Allaire (241). The chronology is based upon four 'ages':

Lithic: represents the beginning of chipped stonework to the appearance of groundstone or shell implements (Paleo-Indian);

Archaic: represents the appearance of groundstone or shell implements to the introduction of pottery (Meso-Indian);

Ceramic: represents the introduction of pottery to the appearance of European artifacts (Neo-Indian);

Historic: represents the appearance of European artifacts (Indo-Hispanic).

These 'ages' are further subdivided by 'series,' or technologically similar units, 'complexes' or local lithic and/or ceramic chronological units, and 'sites.'

Table 1 appears on pp. lxviii–lxxi.

Table 1

GREATER ANTILLES

Cuba	Dominican Republic

LITHIC

Series: Casimiroid
Complex: Mordán
Site: Mordán (2190–2610 B.C.)
Complex: Casimira

ARCHAIC

Series: Redondoid
Complex: Cayo Redondo
Site: La Vega del Palmar (A.D. 990)
Site: Mogote de la Cueva
(A.D. 330–A.D. 1300)
Complex: Guayabo Blanco
Site: Damajayabo (1300 B.C.)
Site: Residuario Fuenche
(2050 B.C.–120 B.C.)

Series: Casimiroid
Complex: El Porvenir
Site: El Porvenir (905–1030 B.C.)

CERAMIC

Series: Chicoid
Complex: Pueblo Viejo
Site: Esterito (A.D. 1360–1400)
Site: Laguna Limones (A.D. 1310)

Series: Meillacoid
Complex: Arroyo del Palo
Site: Arroyo del Palo
(A.D. 980–1190)
Site: Mejias (A.D. 930)
Complex: Bani
Site: Esterito (A.D. 1400–1450)
Site: Barajagua (A.D. 1360)
Site: Petrero del Mango
(A.D. 1140)
Site: Loma de la Forestal (A.D. 980)
Site: Aguas Gordas (A.D. 950)
Complex: (Meillacoid)
Site: El Morrillo (A.D. 1360)
Site: Damajayabo (A.D. 830)

Series: Chicoid
Site: Sonador (A.D. 1370–1470)
Site: Punta de Garza (A.D. 1300)
Site: La Llamada (A.D. 1220)
Site: Macao (A.D. 1025–1200)
Site: El Pleicito (A.D. 1085)
Site: Altos de Vireya (A.D. 1030)
Complex: Boca Chica
Site: La Caleta (A.D. 1280)

Series: Meillacoid
Site: López (A.D. 1050)
Site: El Carril (A.D. 920)
Site: Río Verde (A.D. 805–1025)

Series: Ostionoid
Site: La Caleta (A.D. 730–985)
Site: Macao (A.D. 825–980)
Site: Corrales (A.D. 860–870)
Site: Juan Dolio (A.D. 820)
Site: San Juan de la Maguana
(A.D. 695)
Complex: El Caimito
Site: El Caimito
(180 B.C.–A.D. 120)

GREATER ANTILLES

Haiti	Jamaica	Puerto Rico
Series: Casimiroid Complex: Cabaret		
Series: Casimiroid Complex: Couri		Complex: Cayo Cofesí Site: Cueva María de la Cruz (A.D. 30–40) Site: Cayo Cofresí (295–325 B.C.) Site: Caño Hondo (755–1060 B.C.)
Series: Chicoid Complex: Carrier Series: Meillacoid Complex: Meillac Series: Ostionoid Complex: Macady	Series: Meillacoid Complex: Fairfield Complex: White Marl Site: White Marl (A.D. 877–1490) Complex: Little River Site: Bottom Bay (A.D. 650)	Series: Chicoid Complex: Capá Site: Capá (A.D. 1270) Complex: Boca Chica Site: Cayito (A.D. 1250) Series: Ostionoid Complex: Ostiones Site: Punta Ostiones (A.D. 820–1050) Site: Villa Taina (A.D. 650–900) Site: Monserrate (A.D. 710) Series: Saladoid Complex: Cuevas Site: Montserrate (A.D. 510–590) Complex: Hacienda Grande Site: Hacienda Grande (A.D. 120–370) Complex: Santa Elena Site: Santa Elena (A.D. 890–1210)

Table 1 *(con't)*

LESSER ANTILLES

	Antigua	Barbados	Grenada

ARCHAIC	Complex: Jolly Beach
	   Site: Jolly Beach
	   (1775 B.C.)		

CERAMIC	Series: Elenoid
	   Complex: Freeman's Bay
	      Site: Freeman's Bay
	      (A.D. 1015–1470)
	   Complex: Marmora Bay
	      Site: Indian Creek
	      (A.D. 930–1105)
	
	Series: Saladoid
	   Complex: Mill Reef
	      Site: Indian Creek
	      (A.D. 445–950)
	   Complex: Indian Creek 2
	      Site: Indian Creek
	      (A.D. 185–510)
	   Complex: Indian Creek 1
	      Site: Indian Creek
	      (A.D. 35–160)
		Series: Suazoid
		   Complex: Peak Bay
		
		Series: Saladoid
		   Complex: Chancery Lane
		      Site: Chancery Lane
		      (A.D. 380)
			Series: Suazoid
			   Complex: Suazey
			      Site: Savanne Suazey
			      (A.D. 1400)
			
			Series: Saladoid
			   Complex: Salt Pond
			   Complex: Pearls
			   Complex: Black Point

	Saba-St. Eustatius	St. Kitts	St. Lucia

ARCHAIC		Complex: Sugar Factory
		   Site: Sugar Factory
		   (2123 B.C.)
			Series: Suazoid
			   Complex: Fannis
			      Site: Lavoute (A.D. 1240)

CERAMIC	Series: Elenoid
	   Complex: Bottom
	   Complex: Golden Rocks
		Series: Saladoid
		   Complex: Sugar Factory 2
		      Site: Sugar Factory
			Series: Troumassoid
			   Complex: Troumassé B
			      Site: Giraudy
			         (A.D. 710–830)
			      Site: Troumassé (A.D. 730)
			   Complex: Troumassé A
			      Site: Grande Anse
			         (A.D. 490)

LESSER ANTILLES

Grenadines   Guadeloupe   Martinique

Series: Suazoid
  Complex: Banana Bay
    Site: Banana Bay
    (A.D. 1230–1420)

Series: Elenoid
  Complex: Morel IV
  Complex: Morel III
    Site: Morel (A.D. 850)

Series: Saladoid
  Complex: Morel II
    Site: Morel (A.D. 550–570)
  Complex: Morel I
    Site: Morel (A.D. 170)

Series: Suazoid
  Complex: Macabou
  Complex: Paquemar
  Complex: Esperance
  Complex: Diamant
    Site: Grand Anse
    (A.D. 500)
    Site: Diamant
    (A.D. 460)
    Site: Vivé (A.D. 420)
  Complex: Vivé
    Site: Vivé
    (A.D. 220–225)
    Site: La Salle (A.D. 130)

Trinidad   Virgin Islands

Series: Ortoiroid
  Complex: Ortoire
    Site: Banwari Trace
    (600 B.C.–5250 B.C.)
    Site: Ortoire (800–810 B.C.)

Complex: Krum Bay
  Site: Arboretum (460 B.C.–A.D. 50)
  Site: Krum Bay (880–225 B.C.)
  Site: Grambokola Hill (835 B.C.)
  Site: Cancel Hill (870 B.C.)

Series: Guayabitoid
  Complex: Bontour

Series: Barrancoid
  Complex: Erin
    Site: Guayaguayare (A.D. 239–690)

Series: Saladoid
  Complex: Palo Seco
    Site: Palo Seco (180 B.C.–A.D. 470)
  Complex: Cedros
    Site: Cedros (190 B.C.–A.D. 100)

Series: Elenoid
  Complex: Magens Bay-Salt River
    Site: Hull Bay (A.D. 1220–1310)

Series: Saladoid
  Complex: Coralo Bay-Longford

BASIC LITERATURE OF THE ANCIENT CARIBBEAN

INTRODUCTION TO THE ANCIENT CARIBBEAN

General

1. Aleksandrenkov, E.G. 1976. *Indeitsy Antil'skikh ostrovov do evropeiskogo zavoevaniia.* Moskva: Nauka. 231 p.

2. Deagan, Kathleen A. 1988. The archaeology of the Spanish contact period in the Caribbean. *Journal of World Prehistory* 2(2):187–231. New York.

Synthesis of Spanish contact in the Caribbean, including patterns of cultural accommodation and responses to external influences; presents the results of recent research by the University of Florida on Hispaniola; a fine first source for Hispano-Indian contact studies in the Caribbean region.

3. Easby, Elizabeth K. 1972. Seafarers and sculptors of the Caribbean. *Expedition* 14(3):2–10. Philadelphia.

Popular summary of Caribbean prehistory with an emphasis on archaeological work prior to 1972.

4. Hostos, Adolfo de. 1941. *Anthropological Papers, Based Principally on Studies of the Prehistoric Archaeology and Ethnology of the Greater Antilles.* San Juan: Bureau of Supplies, Printing, and Transportation. 211 p.

Contents include: Notes on West Indian hydrology in its relation to prehistoric agriculture (pp. 30–53); Anthropomorphic carvings from the Greater Antilles (pp. 54–76); The *duho* and other wooden objects from the West Indies (pp. 77–84); Notes on the topography of certain wooden objects from the West Indies (pp. 85–87); The prehistoric art of the Antilles (pp. 88–107); Three-pointed stone *zemi* or idols from the West Indies: an interpretation (pp. 108–124); Antillean fertility idols and primitive ideas of plant fertilization elsewhere (pp. 125–131); Reptilian art-forms and sympathetic magic in the precolumbian Antilles (pp. 146–173).

5. Joyce, Thomas A. 1916. *Central American and West Indian Archaeology; Being An Introduction to the Archaeology of the States of Nicaragua, Costa Rica, Panama and the West Indies.* London: P.L. Warner; New York: G.P. Putnam's Sons; Freeport, New York: Books for Libraries Press, 1971. 270 p.

Useful for background information and as an introduction to and summary of excavations and discoveries prior to 1916; the latter portion of the volume deals with the archaeology and ethnography of the West Indies; coverage includes political organization, marriage and burial patterns, warfare, religious organization, food and housing, and dress.

6. Mattioni, Mario. 1972. La culture Arawak aux Antilles. *Archeologia* 45:30–33. Paris.

7. Ober, Frederick A. 1895. Aborigines of the West Indies. *American Philosophical Society, Proceedings* 9:270–313. Philadelphia.

Description of the Amerindians of the Greater and Lesser Antilles, their origins, contacts with Europeans, and their material culture.

8. Pichardo Moya, Felipe. 1956. *Los aborígenes de las Antillas.* México: Fondo de Cultura Económica. 140 p.

General synthesis of Caribbean prehistory.

9. Price-Mars, Jean. 1941. A propos des Caraibes: archéologie, ethnologie et linguistique. *Société d'Histoire et Géographie d'Haiti, Revue* 12(41):1–12. Port-au-Prince.

Review of the status of Carib and Arawak problems and argues for increased research in the region.

10. Rosny, Lucien J. de. 1886. *Les Antilles: études d'ethnographie et d'archéologie américaines.* Société d'Ethnographie, Mémoires, v. 2(6–7). Paris: Maisonneuve. 424 p.

11. Rouse, Irving. 1948. The West Indies: an introduction. In: *The Circum-Caribbean Tribes.* J.H. Steward, ed. pp. 495–496. Handbook of South American Indians, vol. 4. Bureau of American Ethnology, Bulletin 143. Washington, DC; New York: Cooper Square, 1963.

Together with 12 and 13, perhaps the classic and most often cited source on the Arawak and Carib populations of the Caribbean; as part of the Handbook of South American Indians compilations of culture histories, the insular Caribbean is treated as a site for indigenous peoples as if they still existed in situ; the work, although important, is descriptive and uncritical.

12. ———. 1948. The Arawak. In: *The Circum-Caribbean Tribes.* J.H. Steward, ed. pp. 507–546. Handbook of South American Indians, vol. 4. Bureau of American Ethnology, Bulletin 143. Washington, DC; New York: Cooper Square, 1963.

Basic survey article summarizing earlier sources for the ethnography of the Arawak; following brief discussions of archaeology, history, and sources, covers subsistence activities, settlement patterns, dress and adornment, transportation, social and political organization, life cycle, warfare, religion and shamanism, mythology, etc.

13. ———. 1948. The Carib. In: *The Circum-Caribbean Tribes.* J.H. Steward, ed. pp. 497–505. Handbook of South American Indians, vol. 4. Bureau of American Ethnology, Bulletin 143. Washington, DC; New York: Cooper Square, 1963.

Basic survey article summarizing earlier sources for the ethnography of the Carib; following brief discussions of archaeology, history, and sources, covers subsistence activities, settlement patterns, dress and adornment, transportation, social and political organization, life cycle, warfare, religion and shamanism, mythology, etc.; for a partial critique see D.M. Taylor, The interpretation of some documentary evidence on Carib culture (*Southwestern Journal of Anthropology* 5:379–392, 1949).

14. ———. 1962. The Intermediate Area, Amazonia, and the Caribbean Area. In: *Courses Towards Urban Life: Archaeological Considerations of Some Cultural Alternatives.* R.J. Braidwood and G.R. Willey, eds. pp. 34–59. Viking Fund Publications in Anthropology, no. 32. New York: Wenner-Gren Foundation for Anthropological Research.

Synthesis of the archaeology of the Caribbean area; includes chronological charts and lists of radiocarbon dates.

15. ———. 1964. Prehistory of the West Indies. *Science* 144(3618):499–513. Washington, DC.

Authoritative presentation of conclusions pertaining to when and how the Indians of the Caribbean region came to be where Columbus encountered them.

16.   ———. 1964. The Caribbean area. In: *Prehistoric Man in the New World*. J.D. Jennings and E. Norbeck, eds. pp. 389–417. Chicago: University of Chicago Press.

Summary of research and archaeological sequences of the West Indies and adjacent Venezuela.

17.   ———. 1977. Pattern and process in West Indian archaeology. *World Archaeology* 9(1):1–11. London.

Important consideration of normative and processual paradigms in Caribbean archaeology; Spanish translation: Patrones y procesos en la arqueología de las Antillas (*Museo del Hombre Dominicano, Boletín* 7(10):185–199, 1978).

18.   Willey, Gordon R. 1971. *An Introduction to American Archaeology: v. 2. South America*. Englewood Cliffs, New Jersey: Prentice-Hall. 559 p.

The Caribbean area (pp. 360–394) is considered as part of the South American tropical lowlands; includes an excellent discussion of cultural traditions, archaeological chronology, as well as summaries of the Northwest South American littoral tradition, Caribbean cultural tradition in Venezuela and Guyana, and the Caribbean cultural tradition in Trinidad and the West Indies.

Bibliography

19.   Chevrette, Valerie. 1971. *Annotated Bibliography of the Precolumbian Art and Archaeology of the West Indies*. Primitive Art Bibliographies, no. 9. New York: The Museum of Primitive Art. 18 p.

Bibliography of 275 items pertaining to the art and archaeology of the West Indies.

20.   Comitas, Lambros. 1977. *The Complete Caribbeana, 1900–1975: A Bibliographic Guide to the Scholarly Literature*. Millwood, New York: KTO Press. 4 v.

Perhaps the most important bibliographic work available for the Caribbean region. Lists some 17,000 unannotated references in a classified arrangement; coverage includes former colonies of Great Britain, France, the United States, and the Netherlands, as well as Belize in Central America, and Surinam, French Guiana, and Guyana on the South American coast; Haiti, Cuba, Puerto Rico, and the

Dominican Republic are excluded; see also: L. Comitas, *Caribbeana, 1900–1965: A Topical Bibliography* (Seattle: University of Washington Press, 1968. 909 p.) for coverage of some 7,000 books, reports, articles, theses, and government documents pertaining to the non-Hispanic Caribbean region.

21. Goodwin, R. Christopher, and Gus Pantel. 1978. A selected bibliography of physical anthropology in the Caribbean area. *Revista/Review Interamericana* 8(3):531–540. Hato Rey, Puerto Rico.

    See also: A.G. Pantel, A bibliography of physical anthropology in the Caribbean (*Universidad Central del Este, Anuario Científico* 2(2):163–177, 1977. San Pedro de Macorís).

22. Pagán Perdomo, Dato. 1978. Bibliografía sumaria sobre el arte rupestre del Caribe. *Museo del Hombre Dominicano, Boletín* 7(11):107–130. Santo Domingo.

    Bibliography of petroglyphs and rock art in the Caribbean.

23. Sued-Badillo, Jalil. 1977. *Bibliografía antropológica para el estudio de los pueblos indígenas en el Caribe.* Santo Domingo: Ediciones Fundación García-Arévalo. 579 p.

    Thorough bibliography of Caribbean anthropology and related fields; arranged by subject (general, archaeology, ethnography, geography, history, linguistics) and area; see also: C.R. Ewen, *The Archaeology of Spanish Colonialism in the Southeastern United States and the Caribbean* (Guides to the Archaeological Literature of the Immigrant Experience in America, no. 1. Washington, DC: Society for Historical Archaeology, 1990. 34 p.), for an excellent bibliographic guide to the literature of Spanish colonialism; includes a critical analysis of the literature pertaining to the early contact period of the region, missions, settlements and buildings, material culture and other specialized studies; includes some 400 unannotated references.

Museum Collections

24. Adderley, Augustus. 1886. *Colonial and Indian Exhibition: Handbook and Catalogue: The West Indies and British Honduras.* London: William Clowes.

    Catalog of Caribbean artifacts displayed at the London Exhibition of 1886.

25. Milanich, Jerald T., and Susan Milbraith, eds. 1989. *First Encounters: Spanish Explorations in the Caribbean and the United States, 1492–1570.* Gainesville: University of Florida Press; Florida Museum of Natural History. 222 p.

See also: A. Cummins, Exhibiting culture: museums and national identity in the Caribbean (*Caribbean Quarterly* 38(2–3):33–53, 1992) for an interesting discussion of the use of museums to exhibit, illustrate, and explain the history and development of the encounter of cultures; author argues the process of creolization is critical for an understanding of the development of a regional identity as well as the political and socioeconomic transformation of the Caribbean.

British Museum

26. Joyce, Thomas A. 1907. Prehistoric antiquities from the Antilles in the British Museum. *Royal Anthropological Institute of Great Britain and Ireland, Journal* 37:402–419. London.

Detailed description of important objects from the Caribbean in the British national collection; see also: *Piezas taínas de madera del Museo Britanico: Museo de Hombre Dominicano, Santo Domingo, República Dominicana, junio, 1979* (Santo Domingo: Museo del Hombre Dominicano, 1979. 17 p.).

27. ———. 1912. *A Short Guide to the American Antiquities in the British Museum.* London: British Museum. 52 p.

Horniman Museum

28. Quirik, Richard. 1902. Carib stone implements in the Horniman Museum. *The Reliquary and Illustrated Archaeologist* 1902:169–181. London.

Museo de América

29. Ramos Gomez, Luis J., and María Concepción Blasco Bosqued. 1975. Materiales líticos taínos del Museo de América. *Cuadernos Prehispanicos* 3:19–52. Valladolid.

Museum of the American Indian, Heye Foundation

30. Fewkes, Jesse W. 1922. A prehistoric island culture area of America. *Bureau of American Ethnology, Annual Report* 34:35–271. Washington, DC.

Detailed report based on visits to the Caribbean region in 1912–1913, to several European museums in 1913–1914, and an analysis of some 9,500 objects from the West Indies in the collection of the Museum of the American Indian, Heye Foundation.

31. Museum of the American Indian, Heye Foundation. 1922. *Guide to the Collections from the West Indies.* Museum of the American Indian, Heye Foundation, Indian Notes and Monographs, no. 32. New York. 38 p.

National Gallery of Art

32. Levenson, Jay A. 1991. *Circa 1492: Art in the Age of Exploration.* Washington, DC: National Gallery of Art. 671 p.

Catalog for an exhibition that opened on Columbus Day (October 12) at the National Gallery of Art in Washington, DC.

Smithsonian Institution

33. Viola, Herman J., and Carolyn Margolis, eds. 1991. *Seeds of Change: A Quincentennial Commemoration.* Washington, DC: Smithsonian Institution Press. 277 p.

Volume accompanies an exhibition at the Smithsonian Institution; text written by historians, anthropologists, and natural scientists.

History of Archaeological Research in the Caribbean

34. Blundell, M. 1962. First international conference for the study of pre-Columbian civilization in the Caribbean. *Antiquity* 36:135–136. London.

35. Geijskes, D.C. 1962. Het eerste Internationale Congres voor de Studie van de Prae-Columbiaanse Culturen in de Kleine Antillen. *Nieuwe Westindische Gids* 41(3):272–284. Gravenhague.

36. Ober, Frederick A. 1878. Report on a trip to the West Indies. *Smithsonian Institution, Annual Report* 1978:447. Washington, DC.

37. Rouse, Irving. 1977. Research objectives in Caribbean archaeology. *Caribe* 1:2–5. Santo Domingo.

Review of the development of Caribbean archaeology throughout the twentieth century; Spanish translation: I. Rouse, Objetivos de la investigación arqueológica en el Caribe (*Museo del Hombre Dominicano, Boletín* 7(11):11–15, 1978. Santo Domingo).

38. Watters, David R. 1976. Caribbean Prehistory: A Century of Researchers, Models, and Trends. M.A. thesis, Department of Anthropology, University of Nevada at Reno.

Biography

39. Fewkes, Jesse W. 1904. West Indian researches of J.W. Fewkes. *American Anthropologist* 6:363–364. Washington, DC.

40. Heye, George G. 1910. Forward [Theodoor de Booy, 1882–1919]. *Museum of the American Indian, Heye Foundation, Indian Notes and Monographs* 1(1):7–11. New York.

Theodoor de Booy was born in Hellevoetsluis, Netherlands, in 1882 and emigrated to the United States in 1906. He developed an interest in the archaeology of the Caicos Islands during a visit to the Bahamas in 1911. The following year de Booy was hired as a field explorer for the West Indies by the Museum of the American Indian, Heye Foundation. During his career he conducted archaeological surveys and excavations in the Bahamas (1912), Jamaica and the Dominican Republic (1913), Cuba (1914), the island of Margarita off the coast of Venezuela and in Trinidad (1915), and Puerto Rico, Martinique, and the Dominican Republic (1916). During 1916–1917 de Booy conducted archaeological investigations in the newly acquired Virgin Islands and the following year worked in the mountains of eastern Venezuela for the University Museum at the University of Pennsylvania, and the American Geographical Society.

Environment

41. Carbone, Victor A. 1980. The paleoecology of the Caribbean area. *Florida Anthropologist* 33(3):9–19. Gainesville.

Argues that study of cultural-environmental relationships in the Caribbean indicates a series of abrupt climatic shifts during the Holocene period.

42. Nicholson, Desmond V. 1976. The importance of sea-levels in Caribbean archaeology. *Virgin Islands Archaeological Society, Journal* 3:19–21. St. Thomas.

Discussion of the sea-level change and implications for Caribbean archaeology; argues that some archaeological sites will be found inland from the existing shoreline and others closer to the shore may be covered by sand and other sediments.

43. Sleight, Frederick W. 1965. Certain environmental considerations in West Indian archaeology. *American Antiquity* 31(2):226–231. Washington, DC.

44. Watters, David R. 1982. Relating oceanography to Antillean archaeology. *Journal of New World Archaeology* 5(2):3–12. Los Angeles.

Linguistics

45. Arrom, José J. 1973. Aportaciones lingüisticas al conocimiento de la cosmovisión taína. *Revista Eme-Eme* 8:3–17. Santo Domingo; Ediciones Fundación García Arevalo, 4. Santo Domingo: Fundación García Arevalo, 1974. 24 p.).

46. Granberry, J. 1986. West Indian languages: a review and commentary. *Virgin Islands Archaeological Society, Journal* 10:51–56. St. Thomas.

47. Taylor, Douglas M. 1948. Conversation and letter from the Black Caribs of British Honduras. *International Journal of American Linguistics* 14:99–107. Bloomington, Indiana.

48. ———. 1958. A case of reconstitution. *International Journal of American Linguistics* 24(4):323–324. Bloomington, Indiana.

49. ———. 1958. Lines by a Black Carib. *International Journal of American Linguistics* 24(4):324–325. Bloomington, Indiana.

50. ———. 1958. Use and disuse of languages in the West Indies. *Caribbean Quarterly* 5(12):67–77. Mona, Jamaica.

Survey article on West Indian languages with emphasis on constructions from French Creole and Island Carib.

51. ———. 1959. La catégorie du genre en caraibe insulaire. *Société de Linguistique de Paris, Bulletin* 54(1):201–207. Paris.

52. ———. 1959. Concerning the validity of some translations. *International Journal of American Linguistics* 25(1):70–71. Bloomington, Indiana.

53. ———. 1959. On function versus form in nontraditional languages. *Word* 15:485–498. New York.

54. ———. 1961. Disinheritance and adoption. *International Journal of American Linguistics* 27:187–188. Bloomington, Indiana.

55. ———. 1977. *Languages of the West Indies.* Baltimore: Johns Hopkins University Press. 278 p.

Includes detailed chapters on the phonology, grammar, and vocabulary of Island Carib, with texts in Arawak, Central American Island Carib, and Karina.

56. Zayas y Alfonso, Alfredo. 1914. *Lexicografía antillana: diccionario de voces usadas por los aborigines de las Antillas mayores y de algunas de las menores y consideraciones acerca de su significado y de su formación.* Habana: Imprenta El Siglo XX de A. Miranda. 487 p.

Important study of provincialisms, loan words, and indigenous influences in Caribbean Spanish.

Classification

57. Goeje, C.H. de. 1939. Nouvel examen des langues des Antilles avec notes sur les langues Arawak-Maipure et Caribes et vocabulaires Shebayo et Guayana (Guayane). *Société des Américanistes de Paris, Journal* 31:1–120. Paris.

58. Noble, G.K. 1965. Proto-Arawakan and its descendants. *International Journal of American Linguistics* 31(3):2–22. Bloomington, Indiana.

59. Taylor, Douglas M. 1945. Certain Carib morphological influences on Creole. *International Journal of American Linguistics* 11(3):140–155. Bloomington, Indiana.

Author argues the existence of historical, lexical, and phonological evidence for a hypothesis that Island Carib influenced the formation of Caribbean Creole.

60. ———. 1948. Loanwords in Central American Carib. *Word* 4:187–195. New York.

61. ———. 1951. Structural outline of Caribbean Creole. *Word* 7:43–59. New York.

62. ———. 1952. Sameness and differences in two Island Carib dialects. *International Journal of American Linguistics* 18:223–230. Bloomington, Indiana.

63. ———. 1953. A diachronic note on the Carib contribution to (Arawakan) Island Carib. *International Journal of American Linguistics* 20:28–33. Bloomington, Indiana.

64. ———. 1953. A note on some Arawak-Carib lexical resemblances. *International Journal of American Linguistics* 19:316–317. Bloomington, Indiana.

65. ———. 1954. A note on the Arawakan affiliation of Taíno. *International Journal of American Linguistics* 20:152–154. Bloomington, Indiana.

66. ———. 1954. A note on the status of Amuesha. *International Journal of American Linguistics* 20:240–241. Bloomington, Indiana.

67. ———. 1957. On the affiliation of Island Carib. *International Journal of American Linguistics* 23(4):297–302. Bloomington, Indiana.

68. ———. 1958. The place of Island Carib within the Arawakan family. *International Journal of American Linguistics* 24(2):153–156. Bloomington, Indiana.

69. ———. 1959. On dialectical divergence in Island Carib. *International Journal of American Linguistics* 25(1):62–67. Bloomington, Indiana.

70. ———. 1959. A possible Arawak-Carib blend. *International Journal of American Linguistics* 25:195–196. Bloomington, Indiana.

71. ———. 1960. Language shift or changing relationship? *International Journal of American Linguistics* 26(2):155–161. Bloomington, Indiana.

Theoretical discussion of relationship between Caribbean Creoles, and between them and their European mother languages, emphasizing structural similarities among the Creoles; includes examples from Dominican French Creole, Haitian Creole, Papiamentu and Sranan, the English Creole of Surinam.

72. ———. 1961. New languages for old in the West Indies. *Comparative Studies in Society and History* 3(3):277–288. London.

Overview of the creation of Creole languages in the region through the culture contacts among Amerindians, African slaves, and Europeans.

73. ———. 1961. A problem in relationship. *International Journal of American Linguistics* 27:284–286. Bloomington, Indiana.

74. ———. 1961. El Taíno en relación con el caribe insular y el lokono. *Instituto de Cultura Puertorriqueña, Boletín* 11:22–25. San Juan.

75. ———. 1962. Lexical borrowing in Island Carib. *Romance Philology* 16:143–152. Berkeley, California.

76. ———. 1962. Surinam Arawak as compared with different dialects of Island Carib. *Bijdragen Tot de Taal-, Land-, en Volkenkunde* 118(3):362–373. The Hague.

77. ———. 1963. The origin of West Indian Creole languages: evidence from grammatical categories. *American Anthropologist* 65(4):800–814. Washington, DC.

Historical Linguistics

78. Breton, Raymond. 1664. *Petit catechisme ou sommaire des trois premieres parties de la doctrine Chrestienne; traduit du François en la lengua de Caraibes insulaires.* Auxerre: Blainville. 70 p.

Raymond Breton, O.P., was born in 1609 and entered the Dominican Order in 1626. Between 1635 and 1655 he served as a missionary in the West Indies. He died at Caen, France, in January, 1679. In addition to the catechism, Breton also compiled the following: R. Breton, *Dictionnaire Caraibe-François, meslé de quantité de remarques historiques pour l'esclaircissement de la langue* (Auxerre: Gilles Bouquet, 1665. 480 p.; Leipzig: B.G. Trübner, 1892); *Dictionnaire François-Caraibe* (Auxerre: Gilles Bouquet, 1666. 415 p.; Leipzig: B.G. Trübner, 1900); *Grammaire Caraibe* (Auxerre: Gilles Bouquet, 1667. 136 p.); *Grammaire Caraibe, suivie du catéchisme* (Paris: Maisonneuve, 1878. 80, 56 p.); see also: Lady Chalmers, Note on Father Breton's Carib-French dictionary from the *Actes de la Société Philologique*, 1883 (*Timehri* 4:91–95, 1880. Georgetown).

79. Rochefort, César de. 1941. Remarques sur la langue Caraibe. *Société d'Histoire et Géographie d'Haiti, Revue* 12(41):13–20. Port-au-Prince.

Publication of an extract from *L'Histoire Naturelle et Morale des Iles Antilles* (Paris, 1666).

80. Taylor, Douglas M. 1959. Historical implications of linguistic data on the foods of the Island Carib. *International Congress of Americanists (33 session, San José, Costa Rica, 1958), Proceedings* 1:295–308. San José.

81. ———, and Berend J. Hoff. 1980. The linguistic repertory of the Island Carib in the seventeenth century: the men's language, a Carib pidgin? *International Journal of American Linguistics* 46(4):301–312. Bloomington, Indiana.

An interesting attempt to use linguistic evidence to support the traditional view of a Carib invasion of the Lesser Antilles.

82. Veloz Maggiolo, Marcio. 1973. Un vocabulario arauaco del siglo XVIII. *Museo del Hombre Dominicano, Boletín* 3:332–347. Santo Domingo.

Publication of an eighteenth-century manuscript in the Real Biblioteca de Madrid; see also: A. Jiménez Lambertus, Analisis antropologico fisico de un vocabulario arauaco del siglo XVIII (*Museo del Hombre Dominicano, Boletín* 9(13):245–253, 1980).

83. Williams, James. 1930. Christopher Columbus and aboriginal Indian words. *International Congress of Americanists (23 session, New York, 1928), Proceedings* 1:816–850. New York.

Phonology

84. Taylor, Douglas M. 1947. Phonemes of Caribbean Creole. *Word* 3(3):173–179. New York.

Phonemic analysis of Carib and French influences on Dominican Creole.

85. ———. 1951. The inflexional system of Island Carib. *International Journal of American Linguistics* 17:23–31. Bloomington, Indiana.

86. ———. 1951. Morphophonemics of Island Carib (Central American dialect). *International Journal of American Linguistics* 17:224–234. Bloomington, Indiana.

87. ———. 1955. Diachronic note on the consonantal system of Island Carib. *Word* 11:245–253. New York.

See also: D.M. Taylor, An additional note on the consonantal system of Island Carib (*Word* 11:420–423, 1955); D.M. Taylor, More on the consonantal system of Island Carib (*Word* 14:71–83, 1958).

88. ———. 1955. Phonemes of the Hopkins (British Honduras) dialect of Island Carib. *International Journal of American Linguistics* 21:233–241. Bloomington, Indiana.

89. ———. 1958. On the history of Island Carib consonantism. *International Journal of American Linguistics* 24(1):77–79. Bloomington, Indiana.

See also: D.M. Taylor, On the history of Island Carib consonantism (*International Journal of American Linguistics* 26:146–155, 1960); D.M. Taylor, On the history of Island Carib consonantism: a postscript (*International Journal of American Linguistics* 29:68–71, 1963).

90. ———. 1958. Some problems of sound correspondence in Arawakan. *International Journal of American Linguistics* 24(3):234–239. Bloomington, Indiana.

91.   ———. 1960. On consonantal correspondences in three Arawakan languages. *International Journal of American Linguistics* 26:244–252, 1960. Bloomington, Indiana.

92.   ———. 1961. Some remarks on teknonymy in Arawakan. *International Journal of American Linguistics* 27:76–80, 1961. Bloomington, Indiana.

93.   ———. 1969. Preliminary view of Arawak phonology. *International Journal of American Linguistics* 35:235–238. Bloomington, Indiana.

Grammar

94.   ———. 1952. The principal grammatical formatives of Island Carib. *International Journal of American Linguistics* 18:150–165. Bloomington, Indiana.

95.   ———. 1953. A note on the identification of some Island Carib suffixes. *International Journal of American Linguistics* 19:195–200. Bloomington, Indiana.

96.   ———. 1956. Island Carib II: word-classes, affixes, nouns and verbs. *International Journal of American Linguistics* 22(1):1–44. Bloomington, Indiana.

See also: D.M. Taylor, Island Carib III: locators, particles (*International Journal of American Linguistics* 22:138–150, 1956); D.M. Taylor, Island Carib IV: syntactic notes, texts (*International Journal of American Linguistics* 24(1):36–60, 1958); D.M. Taylor, Corrigenda to Island Carib I-IV (*International Journal of American Linguistics* 24(4):325–326, 1958).

97.   ———. 1958. Compounds and comparisons. *International Journal of American Linguistics* 24(1):77–79, 1958. Bloomington, Indiana.

See also: D.M. Taylor, Compounds and comparison again (*International Journal of American Linguistics* 26:252–256, 1960).

98.   ———. 1960. Some remarks on the spelling and formation of Taíno words. *International Journal of American Linguistics* 26(4):345–348. Bloomington, Indiana.

99.   ———. 1970. Arawak grammatical categories and translation. *International Journal of American Linguistics* 36(3):199–204. Bloomington, Indiana.

100.   ———. 1970. The postpositions of Arawak. *International Journal of American Linguistics* 36:31–37. Bloomington, Indiana.

101.   ———. 1976. The nominal plural in Arawak. *International Journal of American Linguistics* 42(4):371–374. Bloomington, Indiana.

Morphology

102.   ———. 1951. Sex-gender in Central American Carib. *International Journal of American Linguistics* 17:102–104. Bloomington, Indiana.

103.   ———. 1959. Homophony or polysemy? *International Journal of American Linguistics* 25:134–135. Bloomington, Indiana.

104.   ———. 1959. Morpheme mergers in Island Carib. *International Journal of American Linguistics* 25:190–195. Bloomington, Indiana.

Semantics

105.   Dick, K.C. 1977. Aboriginal and early Spanish names of some Caribbean, Circum-Caribbean islands and cays. *Virgin Islands Archaeological Society, Journal* 4:17–41. St. Thomas.

Investigation of indigenous etymology and early Spanish names in the Circum-Caribbean area.

106.   Holmer, Nils M. 1960–1961. Indian place names in South America and the Antilles. *Names* 8(3):133–149; 8(4):197–219; 9(1):37–52. Potsdam, New York.

107.   Taylor, Douglas M. 1952. A note on the derivation of the word *tobacco*. *American Anthropologist* 54:278–279. Washington, DC.

108.   ———. 1955. On the etymology of some Arawakan words for three. *International Journal of American Linguistics* 21(2):187–189. Bloomington, Indiana.

109.   ———. 1956. Spanish *huracán* and its congeners. *International Journal of American Linguistics* 22:275–276. Bloomington, Indiana.

110.   ———. 1957. Spanish *canoa* and its congeners. *International Journal of American Linguistics* 23(3):242–244. Bloomington, Indiana.

111.   ———. 1957. Spanish *hamaca* and its congeners. *International Journal of American Linguistics* 23(2):113–114. Bloomington, Indiana.

112.   ———. 1958. Carib, caliban, cannibal. *International Journal of American Linguistics* 24(2):156–157. Bloomington, Indiana.

113.   ———. 1980. A note on the derivation of the word *cayman*. *International Journal of American Linguistics* 46(1):47–48. Bloomington, Indiana.

114.   ———. 1980. Taíno burén *griddle* and its congeners. *International Journal of American Linguistics* 46(1):48–49. Bloomington, Indiana.

Vocabulary

115.   Coll y Toste, Cayetano. 1921. Vocabulario de palabras introducidas en el idioma español procedentes del lenguaje indo-antillano. *Boletin Historico de Puerto Rico* 7:294–320. San Juan.

See also: E. Narvaez Santos, *La influencia taína en el vocabulario ingles* (Barcelona: Ediciones Rumbos, 1960. 172 p.); E. Tejera, *Indigenismos* (Santo Domingo: Sociedad Dominicana de Bibliofilos, 1977. 2 v.), basically a Taíno-Spanish encyclopedia; Island-Arawakan place names and glosses are listed alphabetically and are defined, sourced, and compared with words in other languages.

116.   Perea, Juan Augusto. 1941. *Glosario etimológico taíno-espanōl, histórico y etnográfico*. Mayaguez: Tipografía Mayagus.

See also: C. Gaztamide Arrillaga, *El idioma indígena taíno en las Antillas* (San Juan, Puerto Rico: Ramallo, 1990. 111 p.)

Sociolinguistics

117.   Swadesh, Morris, and others. 1954. Time depths of American linguistic groupings. *American Anthropologist* 56(3):361–377. Washington, DC.

Considers Taylor's glottochronological date for the migration of the Arawak into the West Indies.

118.   Taylor, Douglas M. 1956. Language contacts in the West Indies. *Word* 12(3):399–414. New York.

Description of language borrowing between Carib-speaking men and Arawak-speaking women in Dominica.

119.   ———. 1956. Languages and ghost-languages of the West Indies. *International Journal of American Linguistics* 22(2):180–183. Bloomington, Indiana.

See also: D.M. Taylor, Languages and ghost-languages of the West Indies: a postscript (*International Journal of American Linguistics* 23(2):114–116, 1957).

120.   ———. 1957. Aji and batata. *American Anthropologist* 59:704–705. Washington, DC.

A comment on I.H. Burkill, Aji and batata as group-names within the species *Ipomea batatas* (*Ceiba* 4:227–240, 1957).

121. ———. 1957. Marriage, affinity and descent in two Arawakan tribes: a sociolinguistic note. *International Journal of American Linguistics* 23(4):284–290. Bloomington, Indiana.

122. ———. 1957. Ballyhoo. *International Journal of American Linguistics* 23(4):302–303. Bloomington, Indiana.

123. ———. 1958. Iwana-yuana *iquana*. *International Journal of American Linguistics* 24(2):157–158. Bloomington, Indiana.

124. ———. 1961. The dog, the opossum and the rainbow. *International Journal of American Linguistics* 27:171–172. Bloomington, Indiana.

125. ———. 1961. Grandchildren versus other semidomesticated animals. *International Journal of American Linguistics* 27:367–370. Bloomington, Indiana.

126. ———. 1961. Some Arawakan words for path, bone, hand: a semantic problem of reconstruction. *International Journal of American Linguistics* 27(4):365–367. Bloomington, Indiana.

127. ———. 1961. Some particular problems in the application of the 100–item lexicostatistic test list. *International Journal of American Linguistics* 27:30–41. Bloomington, Indiana.

128. ———. 1965. Tradition in Black Carib kinship terminology. *International Journal of American Linguistics* 31:286–292. Bloomington, Indiana.

Ethnography

129. Acosta Saignes, Miguel. 1953. *Zona circumcaribe: período indígena.* Instituto Panamericano de Geografía e Historia, Comisión de Historia, no. 60. México. 101 p.

Summary of contact-period ethnography of the Circum-Caribbean region, including the Antilles, northern South America, and Central America.

130. Ballet, J. 1875. Les Caraibes. *International Congress of Americanists (1 session, Nancy, 1875), Proceedings* 1:394–438. Nancy.

131. Blake, E. 1898. Aborigines of the West Indies. *Popular Science Monthly* 52(3):373–386.

132.   Mattioni, Mario. 1980. Finaltés culturelles de la recherche archéologique aux Antilles. In: *Cultural Traditions and Caribbean Identity: The Question of Patrimony.* S.J.K. Wilkerson, ed. pp. 139–156. Gainesville: Center for Latin American Studies, University of Florida.

Argues contemporary issues relating to geographical spheres of influence, cultural space, and ethnic order cannot be understood without considering the past; see also: J. Palacio, The sojourn toward self-discovery among Caribbean indigenous peoples (*Caribbean Quarterly* 38(2–3):55–72, 1992) for an analysis of the problems associated with situations where majority populations in the newly independent countries of the English-speaking Caribbean regard the indigenous populations as problems to be legislated, acculturated, assimilated, and integrated; author argues such events have led to a revindication of indigenous ancestry as well as the development of the Caribbean Organization of Indigenous Peoples.

133.   Valentine, Edith. 1953. West Indian cultural traditions. *Philadelphia Anthropological Society, Bulletin* 7(1):7–8. Philadelphia.

Ethnohistory

The primary historical sources pertaining to the indigenous populations of the Greater and Lesser Antilles are few in number when compared to the information available for Mesoamerica or Andean South America. A few references to the Ciboney may be found in the published works of Bartolomé de las Casas, Pietro Martire d'Anghiera, and Gonzalo Fernández de Oviedo y Valdes. The sources for the Taíno (Arawak) are concerned primarily with the Spanish colonization of the Greater Antilles and, for the island of Trinidad, in the context of Spanish and English attempts to locate El Dorado in the Guianas. The first protoethnography in the Americas took place on the island of Hispaniola when Columbus, during his second voyage, commissioned a friar named Ramón Pané to study the religion of the Arawak. Pané's report is the only primary ethnographic source available for the Arawak.

All of the early historians provide some information on the indigenous populations of the Greater Antilles, although most emphasize Hispaniola. The best information derives from those chroniclers who resided in Hispaniola during the early years of European colonization (e.g. Girolamo Benzoni, Christopher and Ferdinand Columbus, Bartolomé de Las Casas, and Gonzalo Fernández de Oviedo y Valdes). Subsequent historical accounts usually relied upon these original sources for their information. The information available for the Arawak on

Trinidad is less extensive and derives from writers who had early contact with the island (e.g., Sir Walter Drake).

Many of the writings of Columbus, his son, and other early explorers and historians as sources for the Taíno also contain some data on the Island Carib. The best material comes from the missionaries and other observers who had contact with the Island Carib between 1650 and 1700 when the Lesser Antilles were first being settled (e.g., Jean Baptiste Labat and Sieur de la Bord).

134.   Alegría, Ricardo E. 1978. El uso de la terminología etnohistórica para designar las culturas aborígenes de las Antillas. *Instituto de Cultura Puertorriqueña, Revista* 21(80):22–32. San Juan.

Discussion of ethnohistorical terms used in historical accounts; argues three indigenous groups existed at the time of contact: Archaic (nonagricultural Guanahatabeye); Arawak (Arawakan Igneri, Taíno, sub-Taíno, Ciboney, Lucayo); and Carib; see also: R.E. Alegría, *Las primeras noticias sobre los indios Caribes* (San Juan: Editorial Universidad de Puerto Rico; Centro de Estudios Avanzados de Puerto Rico y el Caribe, 1981. 89 p.).

135.   Arranz Márquez, Luis. 1979. *Emigración española a Indias: poblamiento y despoblación antillanos.* Santo Domingo: Fundación García Arévalo. 39 p.

136.   Boucher, Philip P. 1992. *Cannibal Encounters: Europeans and Island Caribs, 1492–1763.* Baltimore and London: Johns Hopkins University Press. 217 p.

Author examines the complex relationships between Europeans and indigenous populations of the Caribbean during the period 1492 to 1763; includes a basic narrative of events as well as an analysis of European imaging of Island Caribs; see also: P.P. Boucher, The Caribbean and the Caribs in the thought of seventeenth-century French colonial propagandists: the missionaries (*French Colonial Historical Society, Proceedings* 4:17–32) for an extended critique of the noble savage mirage; H.M. Beckles, Kalinago (Carib) resistance to European colonisation of the Caribbean (*Caribbean Quarterly* 38(2–3):1–14, 1992) states that the resistance of Arawaks and Caribs to European colonization must be viewed in terms of the pacification of 'wild ones' by conquerors or the defeat in battle of heathens or pagans who understood little of the blessing of Christian conversion; author argues for the need to redress the historical imbalance evident in the lack of "systematic accounts of anti-colonial and anti-slavery struggle."

137. Cortés, Vicenta. 1958. Los indios caribes en el siglo XVI. *International Congress of Americanists (32 session, Copenhagen, 1956), Proceedings* 1:726–731.

138. Dreyfus, Simone. 1977. Territoire et résidence chez les caraibes insulaires au XVIIème siècle. *International Congress of Americanists (42 session, Paris, 1976), Proceedings* 2:35–46. Paris.

139. Harris, W.R. 1904. The Caribs of Guiana and the West Indies. *Ontario Provincial Museum, Archaeological Report* 1903:139–145. Toronto.

140. Helms, Mary W. 1984. The Indians of the Caribbean and Circum-Caribbean at the end of the fifteenth century. In: *The Cambridge History of Latin America.* L. Bethell, ed. v. 1, pp. 37–57. Cambridge: Cambridge University Press.

141. Herrera Fritot, René. 1936. *Culturas aborígenes de las Antillas.* La Habana: Universidad de La Habana, Museo Antropológico Montané. 18 p.

142. Hostos, Adolfo de. 1952. Gods of the garden. *Américas* 4(1):16–18, 44. Washington, DC.

143. Hulme, Peter. 1986. *Colonial Encounters: Europe and the Native Caribbean, 1492–1797.* London; New York: Methuen. 348 p.

Author deconstructs the semi-historical/semi-mythological stories of Columbus, the Arawak, cannibalism, Prospero and Caliban, John Smith and Pocahontus, Robinson Crusoe and Friday, and Inkle and Yarico as part of a larger discourse of European colonialism. For similar studies by Hulme, see also: Columbus and the cannibals: a study of reports of anthropophagy in the journal of Christopher Columbus (*Ibero-Amerikanisches Archiv* 4:115–139, 1978); Chiefdoms of the Caribbean: review article (*Critique of Anthropology* 13(2):105–118, 1988); The rhetoric of description: the Amerindians of the Caribbean within the mode of European discourse (*Caribbean Studies* 23:35–49, 1990); P. Hulme and N.L. Whitehead, *Wild Majesty: Encounters with the Caribs From Columbus to the Present Day: An Anthology* (Oxford, England: Clarendon Press, 1992).

144. Rivet, Paul. 1913. Caribes ou Caraibes? *Société des Américanistes de Paris, Journal* 10:693–694. Paris.

145. Ross, Charlesworth. 1970. Caribs and Arawaks. *Caribbean Quarterly* 16(3):52–59. Mona, Jamaica.

146. Sauer, Carl O. 1966. *The Early Spanish Main.* Berkeley: University of California Press. 306 p.

A geographer's synthesis of the Spanish discovery and exploration of the Caribbean region to 1519; includes discussion of Columbus' explorations and the results of his mismanagement of Hispaniola; examines the effect on the native population of the Spaniard's destruction of the indigenous agricultural system.

147. Sheldon, William. 1820. Brief account of the Caraibs who inhabit the Antilles. *American Antiquarian Society, Transactions and Collections* 1:366–433. Worcester, Massachusetts.

148. Sued Badillo, Jalil. 1978. *Los Caraibes, realidad o fábula: ensayo de rectificación histórica*. Río Piedras: Editorial Antillana. 187 p.

Ethnohistoric, linguistic, and archaeological data are used to argue that there were no ethnic differences between the Island Carib and the Taíno and that these differences were a pure European fabrication to enslave indigenous populations; variability in aboriginal Caribbean cultures is seen as the result of regional adaptations to ecological conditions; see also: J. Sued Badillo, *Cristóbal Colón y la esclavitud del indio en las Antillas* (San Juan: Fundación Arqueológica, Antropológica, Histórica de Puerto Rico, 1983).

149. ———. 1992. Facing up to Caribbean history. *American Antiquity* 57(4):599–607. Washington, DC.

Author argues that the historiography of the Caribbean suffers from a failure to adequately discuss the economic processes imposed on the region; modern archaeologists have contributed little to the efforts of the Caribbean population to distance themselves from colonial historical misinterpretations.

150. Thomas, David H. 1990. *Archaeological and Historical Perspectives on the Spanish Borderlands*. Columbian Consequences, v. 2. Washington, DC: Smithsonian Institution Press. 586 p.

Contents include: K.A. Deagan, Sixteenth-century Spanish-American colonization in the southeastern United States and the Caribbean (pp. 225–250); J.M. Cruxent, The origin of La Isabela: first Spanish colony in the New World (pp. 251–259); C.R. Ewen, The rise and fall of Puerto Real (pp. 261–268); M. García-Arévalo, Transculturation in contact period and contemporary Hispaniola (pp. 269–280); J. Landers, African presence in early Spanish colonization of the Caribbean and the southeastern borderlands (pp. 315–327).

151. Todorov, Tzvetan. 1984. *The Conquest of America: The Question of the Other*. New York: Harper and Row. 274 p.

Argues that European failure to recognize the indigenous populations' humanity reduced them either to 'noble savages' or 'dirty dogs.'

152. Tyler, S. Lyman. 1988. *Two Worlds: The Indian Encounter With the Europeans, 1492–1509.* Salt Lake City: University of Utah Press. 258 p.

153. Wojciechowski, F.L. 1980. De Indianen van de Westindische Eilanden in de historische periode. *Nieuwe West-Indische Gids* 54(2):108–128. Gravenhague.

Collections of Documents

154. Cardenas Ruiz, Manuel. 1981. *Cronicas francesas de los indios caribes.* Río Piedras: Editorial Universidad de Puerto Rico; Centro de Estudios Avanzados de Puerto Rico y el Caribe. 624 p.

155. *Colección de los viajes y descubrimientos que hicieron por mar los españoles desde fines del siglo XV.* M. Fernández de Navarrete, ed. Madrid: Imprenta Real, 1825. 2 v.

Volume 1: Viajes de Colón, Almirantazago de Castilla; v. 2: Documentos de Colón y de las primeras poblaciones.

Figure 4. Stone amulet, El Lindero, Maisi, Cuba.

Source: M.R. Harrington, *Cuba Before Columbus*
Museum of the American Indian, Heye Foundation, Indian Notes and Monographs, no. 17. New York, 1921. Figure 85.

156. *Colección de documentos inéditos para la historia de España.* M. Fernández de Navarrete, M. Salvá, and P. Sainz de Baranda, eds. Madrid: Calero, 1842–1895. 112 v.

     Includes material concerning the colonial administration of Diego Columbus.

157. *Colección de documentos inéditos relativos al descubrimiento, conquista y colonización de las antiguas posesiones españolas en América y Oceania, sacados en su mayor parte del Real Archivo de Indias.* J.F. Pacheco, F. de Cardenas, and L. Torres de Mendoza, eds. Madrid: de Quivos, 1864–1884. 42 v.; Madrid: de Quivos, 1885–1932. 25 v.

     Publication of the texts of some 3,800 previously unpublished documents, mostly from the Archivo de Indias in Seville, relating to the exploration and colonial administration of the New World. E. Schäffer, *Indice de la Colección de documentos inéditos de Indias* (Madrid: Instituto Gonzalo Fernández de Oviedo, 1946. 2 v.) is an indispensible index to these volumes.

158. *Colección de los viajes y descubrimientos que hicieron por mar los Españoles desde fines del siglo XV; con varios documentos inéditos concernientes a la historia de la marina castellana y de los establecimientos Españoles en Indias.* M. Fernández de Navarrete, ed. Madrid, 1837–1880. 5 v.

     Contains the text of many historical and unpublished documents relating to the discovery of America.

159. *Documents Concerning English Voyages to the Spanish Main, 1569–1580.* I.A. Wright, trans. Hakluyt Society, v. 71. London, 1932. 348 p.

     See also: *Spanish Documents Concerning English Voyages to the Caribbean, 1527–1568: Selected From the Archives of the Indies at Seville.* I.A. Wright, trans. (Hakluyt Society, v. 72. London, 1928. 167 p.).

Archivo General de Indias, Seville

160. Rutimann, Hans, and M. Stuart Lynn. 1992. *Computerization Project of the Archivo General de Indias, Seville, Spain: A Report to the Commission on Preservation and Access.* Washington, DC: Commission on Preservation and Access. 20 p.

     Brief report on a project at the Archivo General de Indias to scan and produce a computerized image database for easier access to the collection of over 45 million documents, and 7,000 maps and other images.

Acosta, José de (fl. 1590)

161.   Acosta, José de. 1880. *The Natural and Moral History of the Indies.* C.R. Markham, ed. Hakluyt Society, nos. 60–61. London. 2 v.

For an earlier English language edition see José Acosta, *The Natvrall and Morall Historie of the East and West Indies; Intreating of the Remarkeable Things of Heaven, Of the Elements, Mettalls, Plants and Beasts Which Are Proper to That Country.* London: V. Sims, 1604. 590 p.

d'Anghiera, Pietro Martire (ca. 1455–1526)

A work of importance is *De Orbe Novo* by the Italian churchman and courtier, Pietro Martire d'Anghiera, also known as Peter Martyr, who is generally considered the first historian of the Americas. He was present in Barcelona when Columbus returned from the first voyage in 1493 and the following year began to write a history of the discovery and conquest of the Indies, ultimately published as *De Orbe Novo* in eight decades or sections. The first three decades of this work were published in Latin at Alcalá in 1516. The first complete edition of the eight decades to appear was that of 1530 at the same place. An excellent English edition in two volumes was edited by F.A. MacNutt and published at New York in 1912.

162.   d'Anghiera, Pietro Martire. 1912. *De Orbe Novo; The Eight Decades of Peter Martyr d'Anghera.* F.A. MacNutt, ed. New York; London: Putnam's Sons; New York: Burt Franklin, 1970. 2 v.

For an earlier English-language edition see Pietro Martire d'Anghiera, Pietro Martire, *The Decacdes of the Newe Worlde of West India; Conteynyng the Nauigations and Conquestes of the Spanyardes.* R. Eden, trans. London: William Powell, 1555.

Benzoni, Girolamo (1519–ca.1572)

Benzoni brought out at Venice in 1565 a superficial work, somewhat prejudicial to the Spaniards, entitled *La Historia del mundo novo*, an English translation of which was published in 1857. The work has been translated into several other languages. Benzoni went to the Americas at the age of twenty-two and stayed fourteen years collecting material.

163.   Benzoni, Girolamo. 1857. *History of the New World, by Girolamo Benzoni, Showing His Travels in America From A.D. 1541 to 1556.* W.H. Smyth, trans. Hakluyt Society, no. 21. London. 280 p.

Bouton, Jacques (fl. 1640)

164.   Bouton, Jacques. 1640. *Relation de l'establissement des François depuis l'an 1635, en l'isle de Martinique, l'une des Antilles de*

l'Amérique, des moeurs des sauvages, de la situation, et des autres singularitez de l'isla. Paris.

Bry, Theodore de (1528–1598)

165. Bry, Theodore de. 1976. *Discovering the New World; Based on the Works of Theodore de Bry.* M. Alexander, ed. New York: Harper and Row. 224 p.

166. Bucher, Bernadette. 1981. *Icon and Conquest: A Structural Analysis of the Illustrations of de Bry's Great Voyages.* Chicago: University of Chicago Press. 220 p.

167. *Catalog of the de Bry Collection of Voyages, in the New York Public Library.* New York: New York Public Library, 1904. 14 p.

Chanca, Diego Alvarez (fl. 1500)

168. Chanca, Diego Alverez. 1932. *Letter to the City of Sevilla.* C. Jane, trans. London: Hakluyt Society.

Spanish editions: Carta al cabildo de Sevilla (In: *Colección de los viajes y descubrimientos que hicieron por mar los Españoles desde fines del siglo XV* (M. Fernández de Navarette, ed. v. 1, pp. 198–224. Madrid, 1825); Carta del Dr. Chanca (In: *Cristobal Colon en Puerto Rico: llegada de los conquistadores españoles a Borinquen* (Sharon, Connecticut: Troutman Press, 1972).

169. Tio, Aurelio. 1966. *Dr. Diego Alvarez Chanca; estudio biografico.* San Juan: Instituto de Cultura Puertorriqueña, Universidad Interamericana de Puerto Rico. 450 p.

Charlevoix, Pierre François Xavier de (1682–1761)

An extensive account by Charlevoix of Haiti based largely upon the manuscript memoir of Jean Baptiste Le Pers (d. 1735) was published in four volumes at Amsterdam in 1723 under the title *Histoire de l'Ile espagnole ou de St. Domingue.*

170. Charlevoix, Pierre François Xavier de. 1977. *Historia de la isla Española o de Santo Domingo: escrita particularmente sobre las memorias manuscritos del Padre Jean Bautista Le Pers, jesuita, misionero en Santo Domingo y sobre los documentos originales que se conservan en el Depósito de la Marina.* Santo Domingo: Editorial de Santo Domingo. 2 v.

French edition: *Histoire de l'Isle Espagnole ou de S. Domingue, écrite particulièrement sur des mémoires manuscrits du P. Jean-Baptiste Le Pers,*

Jésuite, missionnaire à Saint Domingue & sur les pièces originales qui se con–servent au Dépot de la Marine (Paris: François Barois, 1731–1733. 4 v.).

Columbus, Christopher

The quincentennial anniversary of the arrival of Columbus in the Caribbean is being marked by many publishers with new books, some recounting the voyages of Columbus and some looking through centuries of history to comment on what the encounter between the Old and New Worlds has meant, especially to the indigenous inhabitants.

171.   Bedini, Silvio A., ed. 1992. *The Christopher Columbus Encyclopedia.* New York: Simon and Schuster; Houndmills, Basingstoke, England: Macmillan. 787 p.

This is a major published work of the Columbian Quincentenary by the former director of the Smithsonian National Museum of History and Technology. It is fully illustrated with hundreds of maps, drawings, and photographs, and contains some 350 signed original articles by leading scholars.

172.   Provost, Foster. 1991. *Columbus Dictionary.* Detroit: Omni-graphics. 142 p.

Basic reference to the people, events, circumstances, concepts, etc., associated with Columbus, especially during the years of his voyages, from 1492 to 1506.

173.   ———. 1991. *Columbus: An Annotated Guide to the Scholarship on His Life and Writings, 1750–1988.* Detroit: Omnigraphics. 225 p.

Excellent bibliography of some 800 annotated items pertaining to Columbus arranged by the following topics: Collections of sources, texts, and studies; Texts of primary documents; Studies of primary documents; Columbus's life; Columbiana; Bibliographies, and Columbus scholarship: questions, methods, achievement. Author and editor, persons and places, and topical indexes.

Diaries of Columbus' Voyages

174.   Columbus, Christopher. 1847. *Select Letters of Christopher Columbus, With Other Original Documents, Relating to His Four Voyages to the New World.* R.H. Major, trans. Hakluyt Society, v. 2. London. 240 p.

Includes English-language translations of accounts by Diego Alvarez Chanca and Diego Meudez.

175.   ———. 1870. *Select Letters of Christopher Columbus With Other Original Documents Relating to His Four Voyages to the New World.* R.H. Major, trans. Hakluyt Society, v. 43. London.

176.   ———. 1893. *The Journal of Christopher Columbus.* C. Jane, trans. Hakluyt Society, no. 86. London, 259 p.; London: Argonaut Press, 1930. 259 p.; New York: Bonanza Books, 1989. 227 p.

177.   ———. 1930. *The Voyages of Christopher Columbus, Being The Journals of His First and Third, And The Letters Concerning His First and Last Voyages, To Which Is Added The Account Of His Second Voyage Written by Andrés Bernáldez.* C. Jane, trans. London: Argonaut Press. 347 p.

178.   ———. 1930–1933. *Select Documents Illustrating the Four Voyages of Columbus, Including Those Contained in R.H. Major's Select Letters of Christopher Columbus.* C. Jane, trans. Hakluyt Society, no. 65, 70. London.

Vol. 1 includes the first and second voyages; and vol. 2, the third and fourth voyages.

179.   ———. 1969. *The Four voyages of Christopher Columbus; being his own log book, letters and dispatches with connecting narrative drawn from the life of the Admiral by his son Hernando Colon and other contemporary historians.* J.M. Cohen, trans. Harmondsworth: Penguin. 320 p.

180.   ———. 1987. *The Log of Christopher Columbus.* R.H. Fuson, trans. Camden, Maine: International Marine. 252 p.

Translation based on Las Casas' abstract of the log with additions from his *Historia* and Fernando Columbus' history of the Columbus family; see also: *Journal of First Voyage to America.* V.W. Brooks, ed. (Freeport, New York: Books for Libraries Press, 1971. 251 p.). This is possibly the best account of the landfall controversy.

181.   ———. 1990. *The Journal of the First Voyage; Diario del Primer Viaje, 1492.* B.W. Ife, trans. Warminster, England: Aris and Phillips. 259 p.

Text of the *diario*, in both Spanish and English, based on the extensive summary made by Bartolomé de Las Casas who was collecting material for use in his *History of the Indies*; translator distinguishes between passages that are summaries made by Las Casas and those that are direct quotes recorded by Las Casas from the original now lost journal.

Biographies of Columbus

182. Columbus, Ferdinand. 1959. *The Life of the Admiral Christopher Columbus By His Son Ferdinand*. B. Keen, trans. New Brunswick: Rutgers University Press. 316 p.

English translation based on Rinaldo Caddeo's *Le historie della vita e dei fatti di Cristoforo Colombo* (Milano: Alpes, 1930. 2 v.) of Ferdinand Columbus' *Historie* (1571) and a 1947 Spanish translation by Ramón Iglesia.

183. Fernández-Armesto, Felipe. 1991. *Columbus*. Oxford, New York: Oxford University Press. 218 p.

Important and possibly definitive historical biography of Columbus.

184. Morison, Samuel E. 1939. *The Second Voyage of Cristopher Columbus from Cadiz to Hispaniola and the Discovery of the Lesser Antilles*. Oxford: Clarendon Press. 112 p.

185. ———. 1942. *Admiral of the Ocean Sea: A Life of Christopher Columbus*. Boston: Little, Brown. 2 v.

Highly readable account of Columbus and his voyages, with emphasis on navigational matters; a condensed version was published as: *Admiral of the Ocean Sea, a Life of Christopher Columbus* (Boston: Little, Brown, 1942. 680 p.). Samuel Eliot Morison (1887–1976) has produced the standard works in English on Columbus, including: *Christopher Columbus, Mariner* (Boston: Little, Brown, 1955. 224 p.); *The Caribbean as Columbus Saw It* (Boston: Little, Brown, 1964. 252 p.), an account and photographic record of flights taken in 1963 to view all the locations visited by Columbus in the Caribbean; *The European Discovery of America: The Southern Voyages* (New York: Oxford University Press, 1974).

186. Perez, Alejandro R. 1987. *The Columbus Landfall in America and the Hidden Clues in His Journal*. Washington, DC: Abbe. 113 leaves.

187. Taviani, Paolo E. 1985. *Christopher Columbus: The Grand Design*. London: Orbis. 573 p.

Translation of *Cristoforo Colombo: la genesi della grande scoperta* (Novara: Istituto Geografico de Agostini, 1980. 2 v.)

188. ———. 1991. *Columbus, The Great Adventure: His Life, His Times, and His Voyages*. New York: Orion Books. 273 p.

Translation of: *I viaggi di Colombo: la grande scoperta* (Novara: Istituto Geografico de Agostini, 1984. 2 v.)

Assessments of Columbus' Work

189. Boff, Leonardo, and Virgil Elizondo, eds. 1990. *The Voices of the Victims, 1492–1992*. London: Concilium/SCM Press. 160 p.

190. Davidson, Basil, ed. 1992. *The Curse of Columbus*. Race and Class: A Journal of Black and Third World Liberation 33(3). London.

Collection of essays examining the Columbus Quincentenary against the historical record of the time of Columbus and since; contents include: B. Davidson, Columbus, the bones and blood of racism, examining the development of the New World through the use of chattel slavery; J. Carew examines the loss to the world of the great learning and cultural achievement of the Moors at the beginning of the Columbian era when thousands of books were burned and three million Moors and 300,000 Jews were expelled from Spain; M. Stevenson, Columbus and the war on indigenous peoples, explores the evolution of European thinking and terms and categories to justify the conquest and subordination of Native Americans; B. Ransby, Columbus and the making of historical myth; C. Searle, Unlearning Columbus, examines recent literature pertaining to Columbus.

191. Dyson, John. 1991. *Columbus: For Gold, God, and Glory*. New York: Simon and Schuster. 228 p.

Author, a Columbian apologist, was aboard a 1990 Atlantic crossing of the replica of the Columbus ship *Nina*; the route was mapped from the log of Columbus' 1492 voyage by Luis Miguel Coin Cuenca, a maritime historian.

192. Elkin, Judith Laikin. 1992. *Jews and the Encounter with the New World 1492/1992*. Ann Arbor, Michigan: The Jean and Samuel Frankel Center for Jewish Studies, University of Michigan. 16 p.

Useful background information to the historical significance of the Columbian Quincentenary and the expulsion of the Jews from Spain; see also: S. Wiesenthal, *Sails of Hope: The Secret Mission of Christopher Columbus* (New York: Macmillan, 1973. 248 p.) and M. Keyserling, *Christopher Columbus and the Participation of the Jews in the Spanish and Portuguese Discoveries* (North Hollywood, California: Carmi House Press, 1989. 189 p.) for an examination of Columbus' relations with the Jews.

193.   Russell, Jeffrey B. 1991. *Inventing the Flat Earth: Columbus and Modern Historians.* New York: Praeger. 117 p.

194.   Sale, Kirkpatrick. 1990. *The Conquest of Paradise: Christopher Columbus and the Columbian Legacy.* New York: Knopf. 543 p.; London: Hodder and Stoughton, 1990. 384 p.

Interesting revisionist historical attempt to present both sides of the Hispano-Indian encounter; see also: R. Nettleford, Surviving Columbus: Caribbean achievements in the encounter of worlds, 1492–1992 (*Caribbean Quarterly* 38(2–3):97–117, 1992) for an analysis of the role of Columbus in carrying out the 'civilizing' mission of Europe among the 'lesser races' of the world.

195.   Wilford, John N. 1991. *The Mysterious History of Columbus: An Exploration of the Man, the Myth, the Legacy.* New York: Knopf. 318 p.

Lively account by the science editor of *The New York Times* portrays Columbus as a combination of superstitition and deep religious devotion to the Virgin Mary.

Coppier, Guillaume (ca. 1600–1670)

A work dealing largely with the natives of the West Indies, and particularly with the Caribs, entitled *Histoire et voyage des indies occidentales* published at Lyons in 1645. An English volume dealing with the West Indies and with many other parts of the Americas appeared at London in 1655 under the initials N.N. and the title *America: Or An Exact Description of the West Indies.*

196.   Coppier, Guillaume. 1645. *Histoire et voyage des Indes Occidentales.* Lyon: I. Hvgvetan. 182 p.

Herrera y Tordesillas, Antonio de (ca. 1549–1625)

Antonio de Herrera y Tordesillas was born in 1559 and served as the official historian to Philip II, III, and IV. Among the most important general histories of the seventeenth century which dealt with the Hispanic world was Herrera's *Historia general.* This work appeared at Madrid in eight volumes in four between 1601 and 1615. The work was based upon considerable documentary research since the author had been commissioned by Philip II to write the treatise. Certain parts are taken from Bartolomé de Las Casas. An English edition by John Stevens was printed at London in 1725 and 1726 in six volumes. The best Spanish edition was published in eight volumes at Madrid in 1725.

197. Herrera y Tordesillas, Antonio de. 1725–1726. *The General history of the vast continent and islands of America, commonly called the West Indies, from the first discovery thereof; with the best accounts the people could give of their antiquities; collected from the original relations sent to the kings of Spain.* J. Stevens, trans. London.

La Borde, Sieur de (fl. 1704)

198. La Borde, Sieur de. 1886. History of the origin, customs, religion, wars, and travels of the Caribs, savages of the Antilles in America. *Timehri* 5(2):224–254. Georgetown.

An abridged version, Voyage qui content un relation exacte de l'origine, moeurs, coutumes, réligion, guerres et voyages des Caraibes, sauvages des isles Antilles de l'Amerique, faite par le Sieur de la Borde, employé à la conversion des Caraibes (In: *Voyage ou Nouvelle Decouverte.* L. Hennepin, ed. pp. 517–604. Amsterdam, 1704).

Labat, Jean Baptiste (1663–1738)

199. Labat, Jean Baptiste. 1724. *Nouveau voyage aux isles de l'Amerique, contenant l'histoire naturelle de ces pays, l'origine, les moeurs, la religion et le gouvernement des habitans anciens et modernes.* The Hague. 2 v.

200. ———. 1931. *The memoirs of Père Labat, 1693–1705.* J. Eaden, trans. London.

201. Young, Everild. 1965. *The Pirates Priest: The Life of Père Labat in the West Indies, 1693–1705.* London: Jarrolds. 200 p.

Las Casas, Bartolomé de (1474–1566)

Bartolomé de Las Casas was born at Seville in 1474 and died at 92 in Madrid. Before he became a Dominican priest, Las Casas went to Hispaniola in 1500 to make his fortune at the urging of his father amd uncle, who had gone there as colonists on Columbus' second voyage in 1494. He became distressed by the mistreatment of the native population and decided to dedicate his life to improving their lot. He was ordained a Dominican priest in 1510 and, in addition to campaigning to abolish slavery, engaged in many activities on behalf of the Indians, including an attempt to establish a model colony for them in 1520/21. He later became bishop of Chiapas, México, and made long visits to Spain attempting to change official policy regarding native Americans. His *Historia de las Indias*, written between 1527 and 1563, provides one of the best sources of information on the ill treatment of the indigenous population. Las Casas' published attack on Spain's cruelty and rapacity toward the Indians, the *Apologetica Historia* (1530), was translated and gave rise to the 'Black Legend,' an account of Spanish cruelties in the New World. Publication of his books was at first forbidden but after a lapse of some twelve years these tracts were finally published.

Las Casas was one of the most important writers of history of the sixteenth century. His chief works, which because of their nature are not always trustworthy, are the *Brevíssima relación de la destrucción de las Indias* (Sevilla, 1552), *Historia de las Indias* (Madrid, 1875–1870), and *Historia apologética de las Indias* (Madrid, 1867). A great number of editions of these volumes were subsequently published in many languages, particularly by the French and Dutch who used the books as propaganda against Spain.

202. Las Casas, Bartolomé de. 1971. *History of the Indies.* A. Collard, trans. New York: Harper and Row. 302 p.

First publication of the history of the Spanish occupation of the Western Hemisphere through 1520, written over the period ca. 1527–1561; some recent Spanish-language editions include: *Historia de las indias.* Madrid: Imprenta de M. Ginesta, 1875–1876. 5 v.; *Historia de las indias.* J.M. Vigil, ed. México, 1877. 2 v.; *Historia de las Indias.* Madrid, 1927. 3 v.; *Historia de las Indias.* A. Millares Carlo, ed. México: Fondo de Cultura Economica, 1951. 3 v.

203. ———. 1909. *Apologética historia de las indias.* Nueva Biblioteca de Autores Españoles, v. 14. Madrid: Bailly, Bailliere e Hijos. 704 p.

Other editions include: *Apologética historia sumaria.* México: Universidad Nacional Autónoma de México, Instituto de Investigaciones Históricas, 1967.

204. ———. 1974. *The Devastation of the Indies: a brief account.* H. Briffault, trans. New York: Seabury Press. 182 p.; Baltimore: Johns Hopkins University Press, 1992. 138 p.

For other English translations of *Brevisima relacion de la destrucción de las Indias* see: *The Spanish Colonie; or, brief chronicle of the actes and gestes of the Spaniardes in the West Indies, called the Newe World* (London: William Brome, 1583; Ann Arbor: University Microfilms, 1966); *The Tears of the Indians; being an historical and true account of the cruel massacres and slaughters of above twenty millions of innocent people; committed by the Spaniards in the islands of Hispaniola, Cuba, Jamaica, etc.* (Stanford:

Academic Reprints, 1953. 134 p.), a reproduction of an English edition of 1656; *Popery truly display'd in its bloody colours, or, a faithful narrative of the horrid and unexampled massacres, butcheries, and all manner of cruelties, that hell and malice could invent, committed by the popish Spanish party on the inhabitants of West-India* (London: R. Hewson, 1689. 80 p.); *An Account of the First Voyages and Discoveries Made By The Spaniards in America; Containing the most exact relation hitherto publish'ed, of their unparallel'd cruelties on the Indians, in the destruction of above forty millions of people* (London: J. Darby, 1699. 248 p.); recent Spanish language editions: *Brevisima relacion de la destruccion de las Indias* (México: Secretaria de Educacion Publica, 1945. 89 p.).

205. ———. 1974. *In Defense of the Indians: the defense of the Most Reverend Lord, Don Fray Bartolomé de las Casas, of the Order of Preachers, late Bishop of Chiapa, against the persecutors and slanderers of the peoples of the New World discovered across the seas.* S. Poole, trans. DeKalb: Northern Illinois University Press. 385 p.

206. Hanke, Lewis. 1951. *Bartolomé de las Casas.* The Hague: M. Nijhoff. 102 p.

207. MacNutt, Francis A. 1909. *Bartholomew de las Casas.* New York: G.P. Putnam's Sons. 472 p.

208. Wagner, Henry R. 1967. *The Life and Writings of Bartolomé de las Casas.* Albuquerque: University of New Mexico Press. 310 p.

Monardes, Nicolás (ca. 1512–1588)

An important work of an historical nature dealing with the medicinal plants of the New World was first published at Sevilla in 1565. It was published in many other languages, the first English edition being that at London in 1596, which was titled *Joyful News Out of the New Found World*.

209. Monardes, Nicolás. 1574. *Primera y segunda y tercera partes de la historia medicinal de las que se traen de nuestras Indias Occidentales, que sirven en medicina; tratado de la piedra bezaar, y de la yerba escuerconera.* Sevilla

English translations: *Joyfull Newes out of the New Found Worlde; Wherein are Declared the rare and singular Vertues of diuers Herbs, Trees, Plantes, Oyles, and Stones, with their applications, as well to the use of Phisicke, as of Chirurgery.* London, 1580; London, 1596; London, 1925. 2 v.;

Amsterdam: Theatrum Orbis Terrarum; New York: Da Capo Press, 1970. 109 leaves).

The author was a noted Spanish physician living in Seville. In this work he describes the medicines and herbs carried back to Europe from the West Indies and the uses to which they were put by the Indians. It contains a long account of tobacco and is the earliest notice of its use in Spain.

Múñoz, Juan Bautista (1745–1799)

Múñoz was named Cosmógrafo Mayor de Indias by Carlos III in 1770. His important collection of documents including transcripts of documents pertaining to the Spanish administration of the Antilles is maintained today in the Real Academia de la Historia in Madrid.

210.   *Catalogo de la coleccion de don Juan Bautista Muñoz.* Madrid, 1954–1956. 3 v.

211.   Marte, Roberto. 1981. *Santo Domingo en los manuscritos de Juan Bautista Muñoz.* Santo Domingo: Ediciones Fundación García Arévalo. 573 p.

Collection of manuscript sources pertaining to the history of the Dominican Republic.

212.   Murgas Sanz, Vicente. 1960. *Puerto Rico en los manuscritos de don Juan Bautista Muñoz.* Río Piedras: Ediciones de la Universidad de Puerto Rico. 419 p.

Oviedo y Valdes, Gonzalo Fernández de (1478–1557)

Among the earliest and most frequently quoted of the histories concerning the Indies is that by Oviedo y Valdes, whose *Historia general y natural de las Indias* was published at Sevilla in 1535. Oviedo, the official chronicler of the Indies, derived many of the facts for his history from direct observation since he spent twenty-four years in the Americas.

213.   Oviedo y Valdés, Gonzalo Fernández de. 1851–1855. *Historia general y natural de las Indias, islas y tierra firme de la mar oceano.* J. Amador de los Rios, ed. Madrid. 4 v.

Selected other Spanish-language editions include: *Historia general y natural de las Indias* (Biblioteca de Autores Españoles, v. 117–121. Madrid, 1959. 5 v.); *De la Natural Hystoria de las Indias* (Chapel Hill: University of North Carolina Press, 1969. 116 p.) a facsimile edition of an early edition.

214.   Turner, Daymond. 1967. *Gonzalo Fernández de Oviedo y Valdes; An Annotated Bibliography*. Chapel Hill: University of North Carolina Press. 61 p.

Pané, Ramón (d. 1571)

A Jeronymite priest who accompanied Columbus on the second voyage. He was responsible for the first conversion and baptism of a Native American in September, 1496, some three years after Fray Bernal Buil had been charged with the task of converting the Indians of Hispaniola. Pané is seen by some as the founder of American anthropology with his excellent account of Taíno religion.

215.   Bourne, Edward G. 1906. Ramón Pané: treatise on the antiquities of the Indians of Haiti, which he as one who knows their language diligently collected by the command of the Admiral. *American Antiquarian Society, Proceedings* 17:318–348. Worcester, Massachusetts.

Other Spanish-language editions include: *Relación de Indias, 1496* (A. Wildner-Fix, ed. Buenos Aires: Ene Editorial, 1954. 69 p.); *Relación acerca de las antiguedades de los indios; el primer tratado escrito en América* (J.J. Arrom, ed. México: Siglo Veintiuno, 1974. 125 p.; 1987. 125 p.; 1988. 92 p.); *Relación acerca de las antigüedades de los indios* (H.E. Polanco Brito, ed. Santo Domingo: Ediciones de la Fundación Corripio, 1988. 163 p.).

216.   Deive, Carlos E. 1976. Fray Ramón Pané y el nacimiento de las etnografía americana. *Museo del Hombre Dominicano, Boletín* 6:133–156. Santo Domingo.

217.   Laurencich Minelli, Laura. 1991. Diffusione e censura nell'Italia cinquecentesca dell'opera di Fra' Ramón Pané. *L'Universo, Supplemento* 1:60–67. Firenze.

Raleigh, Sir Walter (1552–1618)

218.   Raleigh, Sir Walter. 1596. *The Discoverie of the Large, Rich and Beavtifvl Empyre of Gviana* (London: Robert Robinson, 1596; reprinted: Cleveland: World, 1966; Amsterdam: Theatrum Orbis Terrarum, 1968. 112 p.).

Other English-language editions include: *The Discoverie of the Large and Beautiful Empire of Guiana* (V.T. Harlow, ed. London: The Argonaut Press, 1928. 182 p.); *The Discovery of the Large, Rich, and Beautiful Empire of Guiana* (R.H. Schomburgk, ed. Hakluyt Society, no. 3, 1848. London. 240 p.).

Rochefort, Charles de (b. 1605)

A French description of the West Indies is entitled *Histoire naturelle et morale des isles Antilles de l'Amérique* and was published in Rotterdam in 1658. Other editions have appeared in Dutch and German.

219.   Rochefort, César de. 1658. *Histoire naturelle et morale des Iles Antilles de l'Amérique, enrichie de plusieurs belles figures des raretés les plus considerables, qui y sont d'écrites avec un vocabulaire caraibe.* Rotterdam: Chez Arnould Leers. 12, 527, 12 p.

Historical Archaeology

220.   Deagan, Kathleen A. 1987. *Artifacts of the Spanish Colonies of Florida and the Caribbean, 1500–1800.* Washington, DC: Smithsonian Institution Press. 212 p.

Important reference guide to ceramics, glassware, and beads frequently found in Spanish colonial sites; includes material from Havana in Cuba; La Isabela, Concepción de la Vega, Convento de San Francisco, and Santo Domingo sites in the Dominican Republic; Puerto Real and Bayahá in Haiti; Sevilla Nueva in Jamaica; and Caparra, La Perla, and El Morro in Puerto Rico as well as the

Figure 5.
Shell amulet, Batey Cacata, La Romana, Dominican Republic.

Source: M.A. García Arévalo, *Los signos en el arte Taíno*
Santo Domingo: Fundación García-Arévalo, 1989.

Concepción, Tolosá, and *Guadalupe* wrecks off the coast of the Dominican Republic.

Majolica Pottery

221.   Goggin, John. 1968. *Spanish Majolica in the New World: Types of the Sixteenth to Eighteenth Centuries.* Yale University Publications in Anthropology, no. 72. New Haven. 240 p.

An excellent overview of majolica pottery found in archaeological contexts throughout the colonial Americas; Caribbean examples are from Cuba, Dominican Republic, Jamaica, Puerto Rico, and Trinidad; see also: R. Lister, Tentative outline of Majolica traditions in colonial Spanish America (*Revista Dominicana de Antropología e Historia* 4(7–8):141–146, 1974) for an identification and definition of five majolica pottery traditions: late fifteenth-sixteenth century Caribbean; late sixteenth century to present Mexican; mid-sixteenth to mid-seventeenth century Guatemala; late sixteenth and early seventeenth century Panama; and eighteenth and nineteenth century Andean; J.E. Vaz and J.M. Cruxent, Determination of the provenience of Majolica pottery found in the Caribbean using its gamma-ray induced thermoluminescence (*American Antiquity* 40(1):71–82, 1975. Washington, DC), argue that majolica pottery was widespread in contact and colonial period sites of the Caribbean and Mesoamerica and South America and suggest thermoluminescence has applicability in determining origins of majolica; J.M. Cruxent and J.E. Vaz, Provenience studies of majolica pottery: Type Ichtucknee Blue on Blue (In: *Archaeological Essays in Honor of Irving B. Rouse.* R. Dunnell and E. Hall, eds. pp. 343–374. The Hague: Mouton, 1978), use thermoluminescence to demonstrate that majolica found in archaeological contents in Hispaniola and Venezuela was imported from Seville (Spain) and pieces from Panama and Azua, Dominican Republic, were exported from Albisola, Italy.

Olive Jar Pottery

222.   Goggin, John. 1960. *The Spanish Olive Jar: An Introductory Study.* Yale University Publications in Anthropology, no. 62. New Haven. 37 p.

Typology of the Spanish olive jar based upon stratigraphic studies and seriation within the Caribbean area; see also: S.R. James, Reassessment of the chronological and typological framework of the Spanish olive jar (*Historical Archaeology* 22(1):43–66, 1988. Washington, DC).

Cultural Evolution and Society

The archaeological chronology for the Caribbean region has been synthesized by Irving Rouse, Louis Allaire, and others (14, 15, 240, 241), into three principal ages, or temporal and spatial units defined by technological developments.

Lithic Age

Remains from this period, referred to as Casimiroid, appear first in the Greater Antilles and suggest human occupation in the region may date as early as 5000 B.C. The Casimiroid were highly skilled in the working of flint and in the earliest complex, Casimira, they produced only irregular chunks and flakes. By the final complex, Cabaret, these people were manufacturing projectile points made from flakes by trimming one side at the base in order to produce a crude stem for hafting (412). Shell refuse has been found in association with the middle and most recent complexes. Cruxent and Rouse (412) have theorized that Casimiroid peoples derived from Central America through the chain of mid-Caribbean islets and reefs that extend from Nicaragua, through Jamaica, to Hispaniola.

Archaic Age

The earliest remains of the Archaic Age come from Trinidad where they are assigned to an Ortoiroid series, which began about 5000 B.C. In Hispaniola the Casimiroid peoples developed into the Archaic Age technology by acquiring stone grinding, probably from the Ortoiroid peoples. Redondoid series in Cuba was characterized by shell gouges, possibly originating in Florida.

Ceramic Age

Pottery reached the Caribbean area by the end of the third millennium B.C. in the form of a Saladoid series, which was established at that time only in the middle Río Orinoco area. During the 2000–1000 B.C. millenium the Saladoid peoples expanded downstream into the lower Río Orinoco area. At the same time a Barrancoid series was developing in the middle Río Orinoco. The Barrancoid moved downstream during the first millennium B.C., pushing the Saladoid of the lower Río Orinoco out through the delta to the coast and adjacent islands. The movement of pottery-using cultures into the Antilles was a continuation of the original Saladoid movement into the Río Orinoco valley. After the Saladoid people of the lower Río Orinoco passed through the delta to the adjacent coast and islands and adapted to maritime environment, they were able to proceed to the Lesser Antilles, which they occupied quickly during the first centuries A.D. They developed to a climax about A.D. 600 with the help of Barrancoid influences from the mainland. Thereafter they declined, giving way toward the close of the first millennium to a Troumassoid series in the Windward Islands and an Elenoid series in the Leeward Islands. The Troumassoid series was succeed by a Suazoid series during the second millennium A.D.

The original Saladoid migrants reached the Virgin Islands and Puerto Rico during the first centuries A.D. They underwent an immediate process of decline and, by about A.D. 600, gave way to an Ostionoid series in which the decline was gradually reversed. The new series survived in western Puerto Rico and the Dominican Republic until A.D. 1000 but several centuries earlier influenced the Elenoid series farther east and the Meillacoid series farther west. Meillacoid evidently shows influences from the previous Archaic Age complexes.

Cultural Evolution and Development

223. Bullen, Ripley P. 1970. Pottery, radiocarbon dates, and sea level rises. *International Congress of Anthropological and Ethnological Sciences (8 session, Tokyo and Kyoto, 1968), Proceedings* 3:168–169. Tokyo.

224. ———. 1977. Culture change, radiocarbon dates, and trade in the Antilles. *International Congress of Americanists (41 session, México City, 1974), Proceedings* 3:600–607. México.

Previous archaeological research, radiocarbon dates, and ceramic information are used to identify significant differences in the ceramic histories of the Greater and Lesser Antilles; includes a discussion of commerce, isolation, ceremonialism, and population expansion.

225. Davis, Dave D., and R. Christopher Goodwin. 1990. Island Carib origins: evidence and nonevidence. *American Antiquity* 55(1):37–48. Washington, DC.

Authors challenge Louis Allaire's disconnection of Suazey pottery and Island Carib culture; also reject the possibility that Kalina culture is the ancestor of the Island Carib and argue that interactions and transculturation account for cultural similarities.

226. Fewkes, Jesse W. 1915. Prehistoric culture centers in the West Indies. *Washington Academy of Sciences, Journal* 5(12):436–443. Washington, DC.

227. Keegan, William F., ed. 1991. *Earliest Hispanic/Native American Interactions in the Caribbean.* Spanish Borderlands Sourcebooks, no. 13. New York: Garland. 383 p.

Reprint collection of important essays pertaining to Caribbean prehistory organized in four sections: Caribbean cultures at contact, Caribbean ethnohistory, Historical demography, and Consequences of contact; contents include: S. Lovén, Immigrations and Indian elements in the West Indies, 1935 (pp. 3– 85); I. Rouse, Whom did Columbus discover in the West Indies?, 1987 (pp. 89–87); J.W. Fewkes, Selection from *The Aborigines of Porto Rico and Neighboring Islands*, 1907 (pp. 97–169); E.G. Bourne, Columbus, Ramón Pané and the beginnings of American anthropology, 1906 (pp. 170–208); J.H. Steward and L.C. Faron, Selections from *Native Peoples of South America*, 1959 (pp. 209–236); A.E. Figueredo and S.D. Glazier, A revised aboriginal ethnohistory of Trinidad, 1978 (pp. 237–240); W.C. Sturtevant, Taíno agriculture, 1961 (pp. 241–254); S.F. Cook and W. Borah, The aboriginal population of Hispaniola, 1971 (pp. 256–290); D. Henige, On the contact population of Hispaniola: history as higher mathematics, 1978 (pp. 291–311); C.O. Sauer, Organization of the Indies, 1502–1509, 1966 (pp. 315–328); K. Deagan, The archaeology of the Spanish contact period in the Caribbean, 1988 (pp. 329–375); J. Granberry, Spanish slave trade in the Bahamas, 1509–1530: an aspect of the Caribbean pearl industry, 1979–1981 (pp. 376–383).

228. Keegan, William F., and J.M. Diamond. 1987. Colonization of islands by humans: a biogeographical perspective. *Advances in Archaeological Method and Theory* 10:49–92. Orlando.

Authors examine why, how, and when humans colonize islands and discuss environmental factors, competition for resources, and various social factors to develop a model of insular colonization and migration.

229. Kennedy, James. 1854. *On the Probable Origin of the American Indians With Particular Reference to that of the Caribs.* Edinburgh and London: Williams and Norgate.

230. Mattioni, Mario. 1969. Etude des migrations arawak et caraibe aux antilles sur la base de 4 ans de fouilles archéologiques. *International Congress of Americanists (38 session, Stuttgart-München, 1968), Proceedings* 1:309–316. Stuttgart.

231.   Oramas, Luis R. 1947. Los caribes invasores del territorio autóctono arauaco. *Sociedad de Ciencias Naturales La Salle, Memoria* 7:201–204. Caracas.

232.   Rouse, Irving. 1958. The inference of migrations from anthropological evidence. In: *Migrations in New World Culture History.* R.H. Thompson, ed. pp. 63–68. Tucson: University of Arizona Press.

233.   ————. 1985. Arawakan phylology, Caribbean chronology, and their implications for the study of population movement. In: *La Esfera de interación de la cuenca del Orinoco: Festschrift a Marshall Durbin.* Caracas: Instituto Venezolano de Investigaciones Científicas.

234.   ————. 1986. *Migrations in Prehistory: Inferring Population Movement From Cultural Remains.* New Haven: Yale University Press. 202 p.

235.   Willey, Gordon R. 1974. Un modelo de difusion-aculturación. *Museo del Hombre Dominicano, Boletín* 5:73–92. Santo Domingo.

Chronology

236.   Alegría, Ricardo E. 1948. La población aborígen antillana y su relación con otras áreas de América. *Congreso de Historia Municipal Interamericano, Actas y Documentos* 3:233–246. San Juan.

Archaeological and historical definition of major culture complexes: Archaic, Arawak, and Ciboney.

237.   Cosculluela, José A. 1946. Sincronísmo de las culturas indo-antillanas. *Revista de Arqueología y Etnología* 1(3):27–51. La Habana.

Correlation of chronological sequences throughout the West Indies.

238.   Pina Peña, Plinio F. 1971. Los períodos cronológicos de las culturas aborígenes. *Revista Dominicana de Arqueología y Antropología* 1(1):165–179. Santo Domingo.

239.   Pina Peña, Plinio F. 1976. Notas sobre determinación de edades por el método del carbono 14. *Museo del Hombre Dominicano, Boletín* 6:35–40. Santo Domingo.

240.   Rouse, Irving, and Ricardo E. Alegría. 1978. Radiocarbon dates from the West Indies. *Revista/Review Interamericana* 8(3):495–499. Hato Rey, Puerto Rico.

241.   ———, and Louis Allaire. 1978. Caribbean. In: *Chronologies in New World Archaeology*. R.E. Taylor and C.W. Meighan, eds. pp. 431–481. New York: Academic Press.

Important article establishing a chronological framework for the entire Caribbean region; includes summaries of archaeological complexes in the Río Orinoco region, Venezuelan llanos, Caribbean mountains, coastal region, and the Lesser and Greater Antilles; complete listing of radiocarbon dates up to 1977; Spanish translation: Cronologia del Caribe (*Museo del Hombre Dominicano, Boletín* 8(12):59–117, 1979).

242.   ———, José M. Cruxent, and John M. Goggin. 1958. Absolute chronology in the Caribbean area. *International Congress of Americanists (32 session, Copenhagen, 1956), Proceedings* 1:508–515. Copenhagen.

Author discusses seventeen radiocarbon dates obtained from archaeological sites in Trinidad and eastern Venezuela as a check upon Douglas Taylor's glottochronological date for the migration of the Arawak into the Antilles.

243.   Vescelius, Gary S. 1980. A cultural taxonomy for West Indian archaeology. *Virgin Islands Archaeological Society, Journal* 10:36–39. St. Thomas.

Circum-Caribbean Theory

244.   Evans, Clifford. 1955. New archaeological interpretations in northeastern South America. In: *New Interpretations of Aboriginal American Culture History: 75 Anniversary Volume.* pp. 82–94. Washington, DC: Anthropological Society of Washington.

Refutation of the Circum-Caribbean theory as it pertains to Brazil and the Guianas; author argues that the mouth of the Amazon was a peripheral region where Circum-Caribbean culture penetrated late.

245.   Meggers, Betty J. 1954. Environmental limitation on the development of culture. *American Anthropologist* 56(5):801–824. Washington, DC.

Argues that environmental limitation prevented Tropical Forest Culture from evolving into Circum-Caribbean culture in lowland South America.

246.   ———, and Clifford Evans. 1978. Lowland South American and
the Antilles. In: *Ancient Native Americans.* J.D. Jennings, ed. pp.
543–591. San Francisco: Freeman.

247.   ———. 1977. Las tierras bajas de Suramérica y las Antillas.
Estudios Arqueológicos 1977:11–69. Quito.

Summary of archaeological knowledge west of Cuba to Tierra
del Fuego; includes consideration of population movements and
diffusion vectors through time and the southern lowlands of South
America, coastal band of the Amazon, Venezuela, and the Antilles.

248.   ———. 1979. *Aspectos arqueológico de las tierras bajas de Suramerica
y las Antillas.* Santo Domingo: Universidad Autonoma de Santo
Domingo, Centro Dominicano de Investigaciones Antro-
pologicas. 40 p.

249.   Rouse, Irving. 1953. The Circum-Caribbean theory, an
archaeological test. *American Anrthropologist* 55(2):188–200.
Washington, DC.

Refutation of the Circum-Caribbean theory propounded by
Julian H. Steward as it applies to Venezuela and the Antilles; it was
developed as a hypothesis to stimulate work on the culture history of
the area; the theory assumes the following: 1. the original settlement
of the Caribbean region by marginal or hunting-gathering people; 2.
spread of Indians northward from the central Andes, introducing
Circum-Caribbean culture which is characterized by intensive
agriculture, social stratification, and a priest-temple-idol cult; and 3.
degeneration of some of the Circum-Caribbean tribes to a Tropical
Forest level, with simpler slash-and-burn agriculture and a lack of
both social stratification and the priest-temple-idol cult; archaeology
suggests that Tropical Forest culture preceded Circum-Caribbean
culture in the area, contrary to the theory; Spanish translation: La
teoría del circumcaribe sometida a prueba arqueológica (*Ciencias
Sociales* 5(25):24–35, 1954, Washington, DC).

See also: Theodore Stern, A note on Rouse's The Circum-
Caribbean theory, an archaeological test, with a reply by Rouse
(*American Anthropologist* 56(1):106–108, 1954), which challenges
Loven's hypothesis that the Antillian ball-game originated in
Mesoamerica, as elaborated by Rouse; Stern favors an origin among
the Otomac of the Upper Río Orinoco.

Preceramic

250.   Alegría, Ricardo E. 1955. La tradición cultural arcaica antillana. In: *Miscelánea de Estudios Dedicados a Fernando Ortíz*. pp. 43–62. La Habana: Ucar García.

Summary of archaeological and ethnographic evidence for Preceramic populations in the West Indies; argues all belong to a single Archaic tradition ultimately derived from Florida

251.   Dávila, Ovidio. 1984–1985. Poblamiento aborigen precerámico en las Antillas. *Cuadernos Prehispánicos* 11:5–49. Valladolid.

252.   Kozlowski, Janusz K. 1978. In search of the evolution pattern of the Preceramic cultures of the Caribbean. *Museo del Hombre Dominicano, Boletín* 9(13):61–79. Santo Domingo.

Argues previous classificatory systems applied to Caribbean archaeology are inadequate; Palaeoindian and Mesoindian are modes of adaptation.

253.   Pina Peña, Plinio, Marcio Veloz Maggiolo, and Manuel García Arévalo. 1974. *Esquema para una revision de nomenclatura arqueológicas del poblamiento precerámico en las Antillas*. Santo Domingo: Ediciones Fundación García-Arévalo. 16 p.

Classification of archaeological materials in the Caribbean region.

254.   Raggi Ageo, Carlos M. 1971–1972. Posibles rutas de poblamiento de las Antillas en Paleo-Indio. *Revista Dominicana de Arqueología y Antropología* 2(2–3):152–160. Santo Domingo.

255.   Rouse, Irving. 1960. The entry of man into the West Indies. In: *Papers in Caribbean Anthropology*. S.W. Mintz, ed. pp. 3–26. Yale University Publications in Anthropology, no. 61. New Haven; New Haven: HRAF Press, 1970.

Author discusses three hypotheses concerning the migration of the Meso-Indians into the islands of the Caribbean; concludes that the Palaeo-Indians were probably limited to the mainland and Trinidad, and that colonization of the islands took place during the Meso-Indian period, when the coastal Indians turned from big-game hunting to collecting sea food as subsistence strategies.

256.   Veloz Maggiolo, Marcio, and Bernardo Vega. 1982. The Antillean Preceramic: a new approximation. *Journal of New World Archaeology* 5(2):33–44. Los Angeles.

257.   ————. 1987. Modos de vida en el precerámico antillano. *Revista Española de Antropología Americana* 16:135–145. Madrid.

258.   Willey, Gordon R. 1977. The Caribbean Preceramic and related matters in a summary perspective. *Puerto Rican Symposium on Archaeology (1 session, Santurce, 1976), Proceedings* 1:1–9. Santurce.

Commentary on papers presented at the First Puerto Rican Symposium on Archaeology held in 1976.

Relationships with Mesoamerica and Central America

259.   Estevez-Weber, Leda. 1968. Current status of Taíno prehistory. *International Congress of Anthropological and Ethnological Sciences (8 session, Tokyo and Kyoto, 1968), Proceedings* 3:184–186.

Review of pre-1965 archaeological research in the Greater and Lesser Antilles; argues Preceramic (Ciboney) populations of Hispaniola probably came from Central America and another group may have come from Venezuela but there is no evidence to indicate movement from Florida before ca. A.D. 1200.

260.   Evans, Clifford, and Betty J. Meggers. 1977. Some potential contributions of Caribbean archaeology to the reconstruction of New World prehistory. In: *Puerto Rican Symposium on Archaeology (1 session, 1976, Santurce), Proceedings* 1:25–33. Santurce.

Authors argue that there was probably direct contact between Central America and the Greater Antilles.

261.   Morales Patiño, P. 1949. Los Mayas de Honduras y los indígenas antillanos precolombinos. *Tzunpame* 7(6–7):9–40. San Salvador, El Salvador.

Author finds little evidence for prehispanic contact although Spaniards took Indians from both directions in historic times; concludes Central American-type grinding platforms (*metates*) found archaeologically on Cuba were historic introductions.

262.   Rouse, Irving. 1966. Mesoamerica and the eastern Caribbean area. In: *Archaeological Frontiers and External Connections*. G.F. Ekholm and G.R. Willey, eds. pp. 234–242. Handbook of Middle American Indians, v. 4. Austin: University of Texas Press.

Interesting summary of information pertaining to prehispanic connection between the Caribbean area and Mesoamerica to the west; summarizes documentary evidence of contact, objects of foreign origin, and cultural similarities in subsistence patterns, religious organization, the ball game, and prerogatives of political office, and so forth.

263.   Torres de Arauz, Reina, and Marcia A. de Arosemena. 1973. Influencia mesoamericana en la zona circuncaribe. *Boletín Bibliográfico de Antropología America* 36(45):125–136. México.

Summary of evidence for cultural contacts between Mesoamerica and the Circum-Caribbean area.

Relationships with North America

264.   Bullen, Ripley P. 1974. Were there Pre-Columbian culture contacts between Florida and the West Indies: the archaeological evidence. *Florida Anthropologist* 27(4):149–160. Gainesville.

265.   ———. 1977. Did Paleolithic, Archaic, or Formative man enter the Antilles from Florida? *International Congress of Americanists (41 session, México City, 1974), Proceedings* 3:592–599. Mexico.

Terminological review of Palaeolithic, Archaic, and Formative as applied in North America; argues that Palaeolithic, Archaic, or Formative people did not enter the West Indies from Florida.

266.   Chapman, Charlotte G. 1927. *The Northern and Southern Affiliations of Antillean Culture.* American Anthropological Association, Memoir no. 35. Menasha, WI. 60 p.

267.   Griffin, John W. 1943. The Antillean problem in Florida archaeology. *Florida Historical Quarterly* 22(2):86–91. Gainesville.

268.   Holmes, William H. 1874. Caribbean influence in the prehistoric art of southern states. *American Anthropologist* 7(1):71–79. Washington, DC.

269.   Rouse, Irving. 1949. The Southeast and the West Indies. In: The *Florida Indian and His Neighbors.* J.W. Griffin, ed. pp. 117–137. Winter Park, Florida: Inter-American Center, Rollins College.

Comparison of archaeological traditions known from the southeastern United States and the West Indies; author concludes there was little diffusion from south to north through the islands and the primary movement may have been southward by the Ciboney of Florida into the Greater Antilles.

270.   ———. 1951. *A Survey of Indian River Archaeology, Florida.* Yale University Publications in Anthropology, no. 44. New Haven. 296 p.

Argues some Preceramic remains in east Florida may be related to the Ciboney cultures of Cuba.

271.   ———. 1958. Archaeological similarities between the Southeast and the West Indies. In: *Florida Anthropology.* C.H. Fairbanks, ed. pp. 3–14. Florida Anthropological Society, Florida Anthropology, Publication 5; Florida State University, Department of Anthropology, Notes in Anthropology 2. Gainesville.

Summary of research on the problem; Rouse concludes that there is greatest evidence of cultural contact between the Southeast and the Antilles on a Marginal or Archaic level of development, less on a Tropical Forest or pre-Formative level, and least connection on the Circum-Caribbean or Formative level.

272.   Sturtevant, William C. 1960. *The Significance of Ethnological Similarities Between Southeastern North America and the Antilles.* Yale University Publications in Anthropology, Publication no. 64. New Haven. 58 p.

Author reviews archaeological and ethnographic similarities between southeastern North America and the West Indies and concludes there is little evidence of cultural contact.

273.   Willey, Gordon R. 1949. *Archaeology of the Florida Gulf Coast.* Smithsonian Institution, Miscellaneous Collections, v. 113. Washington, DC. 599 p.

Includes a brief summary of Preceramic and ceramic relationships between Florida and the West Indies; discusses similarities between Weeden Island pottery in northwest Florida and the Carrier ceramic styles in Haiti and eastern Cuba.

Relationships with South America

274.   Callaghan, Richard T. 1990. Mainland Origins of the Preceramic Cultures of the Greater Antilles. Ph.D. dissertation, Department of Anthropology, University of Calgary. 301 p.

Investigation of the mainland origins of the Preceramic cultures of the Greater Antilles and the capabilities of watercraft indigenous to the Caribbean Sea and the Gulf of Mexico; results indicate that the Venezuela/Colombia region has the greatest chance of successful accidental drift or intentional voyages to the Greater Antilles.

275.   Moscoso, Francisco. 1987. Etapas históricas de la sociedad tribal en las Antillas. *Dédalo* 25:99–136. Milan.

Argues Antillean prehistory is associated with Venezuelan Palaeo/ Archaic traditions in terms of migrations and sociopolitical complexity.

276.   Oliver, José R. 1989. The Archaeological, Linguistic, and Ethnohistorical Evidence for the Expansion of Arawakan into Northwestern Venezuela and Northeastern Colombia. Ph.D. dissertation, Department of Anthropology, University of Illinois, Urbana. 781 p.

Using archaeological, linguistic, and ethnohistorical information, author constructs a model of prehistoric and protohistoric expansion by Arawak-speaking populations into northwestern Venezuela and northeastern Colombia; it is argued that an early proto-Arawakan group expanded from the central Amazon into the confluence of the Orinoco-Apure River (Amazonian Polychrome Tradition), subsequently expanding northward into the Maracaibo Basin and, by 1200–900 B.C., into the Lower Magdalena and Rancheria valleys in northeastern Colombia (Macro-Tocuyanoid Tradition), eventually surviving until after the conquest in the Lower Guajira as Onoto, Paraujano, and Guajiro.

An intermediate proto-Maipuran expansion may have taken place ca. 1500 B.C. resulting in the Caquetto; expansion moved westward along the Apure and north into the Cojedes River and by A.D. 700–800, two distinct archaeological traditions emerged. The Tierroid Tradition colonized the Barquisimeto and Yaracuy valleys and the Dabajuroid Tradition expanded into the Yaracuy Valley where it spread along coastal Venezuela, and eventually into Aruba, Curaçao, and Bonaire by A.D. 900. The process of expansion was interrupted by the Spanish conquistadores.

277.   Osgood, Cornelius B. 1942. Prehistoric contact between South America and the West Indies. *National Academy of Sciences, Proceedings* 28(1):1–4. Washington, DC.

Preliminary publication of evidence for ceramic connections between Venezuela and the West Indies; Spanish-language translation:

C.B. Osgood, Contacto prehistórico entre Sud America y las Antillas (*Acta Venezolana* 1:285–290, 1946; *Universidad de Santo Domingo, Instituto de Antropología, Boletín* 9:1–6, 1971).

278. Rouse, Irving. 1951. Prehistoric Caribbean culture contact as seen from Venezuela. *New York Academy of Sciences, Transactions* 13(8):342–347. New York.

279. ———. 1961. Archaeology in lowland South America and the Caribbean, 1935–1960. *American Antiquity* 27(1):56–62. Washington, DC.

280. ———, and José M. Cruxent. 1959. Venezuela and its relationships with neighboring area. *International Congress of Americanists (33 session, San José, 1958), Proceedings* 1:173–183. San José, Costa Rica.

281. Sanoja Obediente, Mario. 1965. Venezuelan archaeology looking toward the West Indies. *American Antiquity* 31(2):232–236. Washington, DC.

Summary of the archaeology of eastern and western Venezuela; author argues that events in Venezuela impacted groups in the Lesser Antilles.

282. ———, and Iraida Vargas Arenas. 1977. Las culturas alfareras temporanas del Oriente de Venezuela y sus relaciones con las área andina nuclear y las Antillas. *Puerto Rican Symposium on Archaeology (1 session, Santurce, 1976), Proceedings* 1:139–147. Santurce.

Discussion of the radiocarbon chronology in eastern Venezuela and the Barrancoid and Ronquin Saladeroid traditions; argue that early ceramic cultures of the Orinoco are marginal variants of the earlier South American Formative period.

283. Taylor, Douglas M., and Irving Rouse. 1955. Linguistic and archaeological time depth in the West Indies. *International Journal of American Linguistics* 21:105–115. Bloomington, Indiana.

Revision of Douglas Taylor's glottochronological date for the migration of the Arawak into the West Indies to A.D. 150 and application of this date by Rouse to Period II in the archaeological sequence.

284. Wagner, Erika, ed. 1984. *Relaciones prehispánicas de Venezuela.* Caracas: Asociación Venezolana de Arqueología; Asociación Venezolana Para el Avance de la Ciencia. 87 p.

Collection of papers presented at the Simposio Relaciones Prehispánicas e Indohispánicas de Venezuela con Areas Circunvecinas, held in Caracas, 1983.

Economic Organization

285. Boomert, Aad. 1987. Gifts of the Amazons: 'green stone' pendants and beads as items of ceremonial exchange in Amazonia and the Caribbean. *Anthropológica* 67:33–54. Caracas.

Subsistence Patterns

286. Arrom, José J. 1972. Manatí: el testimonio de los cronistas y la cuestion de su etomología. *Museo del Hombre Dominicano, Boletín* 2:33–38. Santo Domingo.

287. Brown, William L. 1953. Maize of the West Indies. *Tropical Agriculture* 30(7–9):141–170. Trinidad.

Classification of varieties of maize in the West Indies into eight races; author suggests one variety may have spread prehispanically from México to Cuba.

288. Keegan, William F. 1982. A biological introduction to the prehistoric procurement of the *Strombus gigas*. *Florida Anthropologist* 35(2):76–88. Gainesville.

Description of the spatial distribution and meat removal techniques associated with the queen conch.

289. Keegan, William F. 1987. Diffusion of maize from South America: the Antillean connection reconsidered. In: *Emergent Horticultural Economies of the Eastern Woodlands*. W.F. Keegan, ed. pp. 329–344. Southern Illinois University, Center for Archaeological Investigations, Occasional Paper, 7. Carbondale.

290. Krasniewicz, L. 1978. Prehistoric ethnobotany and West Indian archaeology. *Virgin Islands Archaeological Society, Journal* 5:36–37. St. Thomas.

291. Krieger, Herbert W. 1942. Aboriginal land utilization and food economy in the Antilles. *American Scientific Congress (8 session, Washington, DC, 1940), Proceedings* 2:141–142. Washington, DC.

292. Pérez de la Riva, Francisco. 1952. La agricultura indoantillana: su aporte a los cultivos y alimentación del hombre. *Revista de Arqueología y Etnología* 7(13–14):228–286. La Habana.

Includes illustrations of cassava graters, metates, and zemís from archaeological contexts.

293. Siegel, Peter E., ed. 1989. *Early Ceramic Population Lifeways and Adaptive Strategies in the Caribbean*. British Archaeological Reports, International Series, v. 506. Oxford, England. 418 p.

Most of the papers were prepared originally for a symposium held in 1988 at the fifty-third annual meeting of the Society for American Archaeology in Phoenix; contents include: B.F. Morse, Saladoid remains and adaptive strategies in St. Croix, Virgin Islands (pp. 29–42); A.R. Jones, Dating of excavation levels using animal remains: a proposed scheme for Indian Creek (pp. 43–56); P.L. Drewitt, Prehistoric ceramic population lifeways and adaptive strategies on Barbados, Lesser Antilles (pp. 179–118); W.F. Keegan, Transition from a terrestrial to a maritime economy: a new view of the crab/shell dichotomy (pp. 119–128); D.R. Watters and I. Rouse, Environmental diversity and maritime adaptations in the Caribbean area (pp. 129–144); L. Allaire, Volcanic chronology and the early Saladoid occupation of Martinique (pp. 147–168); A.H. Versteeg, Internal organization of a pioneer settlement in the Lesser Antilles: the Saladoid Golden Rock site on St. Eustatius, Nertherlands Antilles (pp. 171–192); P.E. Siegel, Site structure, demography, and social complexity in the early Ceramic Age of the Caribbean (pp. 193–245); M. Rodríguez, Zoned incised crosshatch (ZIC) ware of early Precolumbian Ceramic Age sites in Puerto Rico and Vieques Island (pp. 249–266); P.G. Roe, Grammatical analysis of Cedrosan Saladoid vessel form categories and surface decoration: aesthetic and technical styles in early Antillean ceramics (pp. 267–382); I. Rouse, Peoples and cultures of the Saladoid frontier in the Greater Antilles (pp. 383–403); A.C. Roosevelt, Discussion of early Ceramic population lifeways and adaptive strategies in the Caribbean (pp. 407–418).

294. Smith, Hale G. 1951. The ethnological and archaeological significance of *zamia*. *American Anthropologist* 53:238–244. Washington, DC.

295. Sturtevant, William C. 1969. History and ethnography of some West Indian starches. In: *The Domestication and Exploitation of Plants and Animals*. P.J. Ucko, ed. pp. 177–199. Chicago: Aldine.

296. ———. 1971. Taíno agriculture. In: *Evolution of Horticultural Systems in Native South America: Causes and Consequences*. J. Wilbert, ed. pp 69–82. Caracas: Sociedad de Ciencias Naturales.

297. Veloz Maggiolo, Marcio. 1971–1972. Las Antillas precolombinas ecología y población. *Revista Dominicana de Arqueología y Antropología* 2(2–3):165–169. Santo Domingo.

298. ———. 1978. Variantes productivas de los agricultores precolombinos antillanos. *Museo del Hombre Dominicano, Boletín* 7(11):177–183. Santo Domingo.

Discussion of prehispanic subsistence strategies in the Antilles, including proto-agriculture, tropical and prototheocratic modes of production.

299. ———, Marcio, and Gus Pantel. 1988–1989. Modo de vida de los recolectores en la arqueología del Caribe. *Boletín de Antropología Americana* 18:149–167, 19:83–117. Santo Domingo.

300. Wing, Elizabeth S. 1989. Human exploitation of animal resources in the Caribbean. In: *Symposium on the Biogeography of the West Indies.* C.A. Woods, ed. pp. 137–152. Gainesville: Sandhill Crane Press.

301. ———, and Elizabeth Reitz. 1982. Prehistoric fishing communities of the Caribbean. *Journal of New World Archaeology* 5(2):13–32. Los Angeles.

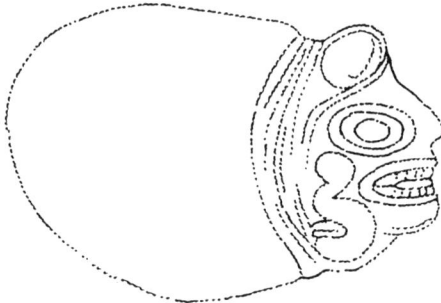

Figure 6. Anthropomorphic celt, Rodríguez-Ferrer Collection, Cuba. A celt is an ungrooved stone axe blade, usually of stone or shell, and used as a ceremonial object as well as a woodworking implement.

Source: M.R. Harrington, *Cuba Before Columbus,* Museum of the American Indian, Heye Foundation, Indian Notes and Monographs, no. 17. New York, 1921. Figure 2.

302. ———, and S. Scudder. 1983. Animal exploitation by prehistoric peoples living on a tropical marine edge. In: *Animals and Archaeology: 2. Shell Middens, Fishes, and Birds.* C. Grigson and J. Clutton-Brock, eds. pp. 197–210. British Archaeological Reports, International Series, no. 183. Oxford.

Demography

303. Dobyns, Henry F. 1966. Estimating aboriginal American population. *Current Anthropology* 7:395–416. Chicago.

Author estimates the indigenous population of the Caribbean to have been 440,000–550,000; see also: H.F. Dobyns, *Native American Historical Demography* (Bloomington: Indiana University Press, 1976).

304. Henige, David. 1978. On the contact population of Hispaniola: history as higher mathematics. *Hispanic American Historical Review* 58(2):217–237.

Attempts to demonstrate that recent estimates of the population of Hispaniola are futile; rejects estimates of Sherburne Cook and Woodrow Borah, The aboriginal population of Hispaniola (*Essays in Population History*, pp. 376–410. Berkeley: University of California Press, 1971), William M. Denevan, *Native Populations of the Americas in 1492* (Madison: University of Wisconsin Press, 1976), and Henry Dobyns, *Native American Historical Demography* (Bloomington: Indiana University Press, 1976); see also: E.A. Zambardino, Critique of David Henige's On the contact population of Hispaniola: history as higher mathematics (*Hispanic American Historical Review* 58(4):700–708, 1978) and David Henige's reply (*Hispanic American Historical Review* 58(4):709–712, 1978).

305. Rosenblat, Angel. 1967. *La población de América en 1492: viejos y nuevos cálculos.* México: Colegio de México. 100 p.

Physical Anthropology

306. Crosby, Alfred W. 1972. *The Columbian Exchange: Biological and Cultural Consequences of 1492.* Westport, Connecticut: Greenwood. 268 p.

Discussion of the interchange of Old and New World organisms and the subsequent changes in global ecology, especially epidemic diseases, food crops, and animals.

307.   Goodwin, R. Christopher. 1978. The history and development of osteology in the Caribbean area. *Revista/Review Interamericana* 8(3):463–494. Hato Rey, Puerto Rico.

308.   Im Thurn, E.F. 1887. On the races of the West Indies. *Royal Anthropological Institute of Great Britain and Ireland, Journal* 16:190–196. London.

309.   Pina Peña, Plinio F. 1972. Las deformaciones intencionales del cuerpo humano en las Antillas. *Museo del Hombre Dominicano, Boletín* 1:9–19. Santo Domingo.

310.   Rosny, Lucien J. de. 1884–1885. *De la mort et des funérailles chez les anciens Caraibes.* Archives de la Société Américaine de France, 3. Paris.

311.   Stewart, T. Dale. 1939. Negro skeletal remains from Indian sites in the West Indies. *Man* 39:49–51. London.

Cannibalism

312.   Arens, William. 1979. *The Man-Eating Myth: Anthropology and Anthropophagy.* New York: Oxford University Press. 185 p.

Author attacks the notion of cannibalism, calling it a myth generated to enslave or oppress a hostile 'other.' See also: N. Whitehead, Carib cannibalism: the historical evidence (*Journal de la Société des Américanistes* 70:69–87, 1984) for a reexamination of the historical evidence for South American Carib cannibalism. Whitehead argues that Spanish accusations of cannibalism must be considered in the context of state propaganda since cannibals were the sole American Indians subject to enslavement.

313.   Moore, Richard B. 1973. Carib cannibalism: a study in anthropological stereotyping. *Caribbean Studies* 13(3):117–135. Río Piedras, Puerto Rico.

314.   Salas, Julio C. 1920. *Los indios caribes: estudio sobre el origen del mito de la antropofagia.* Madrid: Editorial América. 235 p.

315.   Tannahil, Reay. 1975. *Flesh and Blood: A History of the Cannibal Complex.* New York: Stein and Day. 203 p.

Geophagy

316.   Veloz Maggiolo, Marcio. 1971–1972. Sobre un posible caso de geofagia en las Antillas precolombinas. *Revista Dominicana de Arqueología y Antropología* 2(2–3):128–146. Santo Domingo.

Political Organization

317. Alegría, Ricardo E. 1951. Origin and diffusion of the term *cacique*. In: *Acculturation of the Americas: Proceedings and Selected Papers of the XXIX International Congress of Americanists*. S. Tax, ed. pp. 313–315. Chicago: University of Chicago Press.

318. Helms, Mary W. 1980. Succession to high office in pre-Columbian Circum-Caribbean chiefdoms. *Man* 15:718–731. London.

Sixteenth-century historical evidence indicates sociopolitical solidarity of ruling groups in Circum-Caribbean chiefdoms (Muisca and Cauca Valleys in Colombia and the Taíno) was based on close female relatives the *cacique*, providing genealogical legitimacy and fulfilling roles as regents.

319. Mattioni, Mario. 1980. Finaltés culturelles de la recherche archéologique aux Antilles. In: *Cultural Traditions and Caribbean Identity: The Question of Patrimony*. S.J.K. Wilkerson, ed. pp. 139–156. Gainesville: Center for Latin American Studies, University of Florida.

Argues contemporary issues relating to geographical spheres of influence, cultural space, and ethnic order cannot be understood without considering the past.

320. Sears, William H. 1954. The sociopolitical organization of pre-Columbian cultures on the Gulf coastal plain. *American Anthropologist* 56(3):339–346. Washington, DC.

Argues that a class-stratified social system on the Gulf coastal plain in the southeastern United States was a local development stimulated from the Antilles before the late Arawak expansion.

321. Sued Badillo, Jalil. 1985. Las cacicas indoantillanas. *Instituto de Cultura Puertorriqueña, Revista* 87:17–26. San Juan.

Discussion of the role of women in mainland and insular Arawakan cultures; census data from 1514 list more than 35 *cacicas* (female lords) or some fifteen percent of the 409 *caciques*, suggesting matrilineality remained strong after contact.

Warfare

322. Alegría, Ricardo E. 1974–1976. El uso de gases nocivos como arma bélica por los indios taínos y caribes de las Antillas. *Société*

des Américanistes de Paris, Journal 63:302–308. Paris; Revista Española de Antropologia Americana 8:171–179, 1978. Madrid.

Ethnohistoric evidence supports argument that poison gas (Capsicum annum and C. frutescens) was used as a weapon by both the Taíno and Carib.

Religious Organization

Mythology

323. Arrom, José J. 1975. Mitología y artes prehispánicas de las Antillas. México: Siglo Veintiuno Editores; Fundación García Arévalo. 191 p.

324. Jiménez Lambertus, Abelardo. 1987. Mitología y genética. Museo del Hombre Dominicano, Boletín 20:13–16. Santo Domingo.

Cohoba

325. Wassen, S. Henry. 1964. Some general viewpoints in the study of native drugs especially from the West Indies and South America. Ethnos 29(1–2):97–120. Stockholm.

Cults

326. Royo Guardia, Fernando. 1947. El culto de cráneos y los cemíes de algodón entre los antillanos precolombinos. Revista de Arqueología y Etnología 2(4–5):143–155. La Habana.

Social Organization

327. Diaz Polanco, Hector. 1974. El proceso de acumulación capitalista y la esclavitud en las Antillas. Revista Dominicana de Antropología e Historia 4(7–8):106–133. Santo Domingo.

Settlement Patterns

328. Rouse, Irving. 1956. Settlement patterns in the Caribbean area. In: Prehistoric Settlement Patterns in the New World. G.R. Willey, ed. pp. 165–172. Viking Fund Publications in Anthropology, no. 23. New York: Wenner-Gren Foundation for Anthropological Research.

Classification of Caribbean cultures according to Julian H. Steward's three levels of development, Marginal, Tropical Forest, and Circum-Caribbean.

Material Culture

Art

329.   García-Arevalo, Manuel Antonio. 1977. Los pasadores y orejeras entre las culturas aborígenes del período ceramista antillano: aspectos tipológicos. *International Congress of Americanists (41 session, México, 1974), Proceedings* 3:615–631. México.

Historical and archaeological data are used to construct a typology of ear plugs and their uses.

330.   Helms, Mary W. 1986. Art styles and interaction spheres in Central America and the Caribbean: polished black wood in the Greater Antilles. *Journal of Latin American Lore* 12(1):25–43. Los Angeles.

Author examines the use of polished black wood objects as they played a role in sociopolitical definitions in the Greater Antilles; historical evidence suggests that the objects had important religious and social connotations; they were often crafted with zemi representations on them in the form of stool (duhos) and were affiliated with class stratification; also published in *Chiefdoms in the Americas*. R.D. Drennan and C.A. Uribe, eds. pp. 67–84 (Lanham, Maryland: University Press of America, 1987).

331.   Kay-Willock, Katheryne. 1977. Animistic art in the Antilles. *Virgin Islands Archaeological Society, Journal* 4:42–43. St. Thomas.

332.   Keegan, William F. 1981. Artifacts in Archaeology: A Caribbean Case Study. M.A. thesis, Department of Anthropology, Florida Atlantic University. 132 p. Boca Raton.

Theoretical examination of categories of artifact analysis and the generation of a developmental sequence including: selection of raw materials; construction techniques; artifact use and function; and formation of the archaeological record; author also uses *Strombus gigas* shell artifacts from the Caribbean to demonstrate the utility of the artifact development sequence as a theoretical concept.

333.   Sainte-Croix de la Roncière, Georges. 1937. L'art primitif chez les caraibes. *Société d'Etudes Guadeloupéennes, Bulletin* 1:11–18. Pointe-à-Pitre.

334.   Tavares, Julia. 1978. *Cultura y arte precolombino del Caribe*. Santo Domingo: Museo del Hombre Dominicano.

335.   Wilkerson, S. Jeffrey K. 1980. The question of Caribbean patrimony. In: *Cultural Traditions and Caribbean Identity: The Question of Patrimony*. S.J.K. Wilkerson, ed. pp. 3–16. Gainesville: Center for Latin American Studies, University of Florida.

Discussion of the implications and importance of cultural patrimony for national and regional identity in the Caribbean.

Petroglyphs and Pictographs

336.   Booy, Theodoor H.N. de. 1917. Indian petroglyphs in the Antilles. *Forward* 36:17–18. Philadelphia.

337.   Bouge, L.J. 1948. Objets lithiques et pétroglyphes des Antilles à l'origine, à l'arrivée de C. Colomb, après la conquete. *International Congress of Americanists (28 session, Paris, 1947), Proceedings* 1:587–598. Paris.

Author concludes that deeply engraved petroglyphs are of prehispanic Arawak origin but that *zemís* and other ceremonial stone objects are not prehispanic.

338.   Dubelaar, C.N. 1986. *South American and Caribbean Petroglyphs*. Koninklijk Instituut voor Taal-, Land- en Volkenkunde, 3. Dordrecht; Riverton, NJ: Foris. 249 p.

Geographical classification and description of petroglyphs in South America and the Caribbean.

339.   Hellinga, W.G. 1954. Pétroglyphes Caraibes: problème sémiologique. *Lingua* 2:121–135. Amsterdam.

340.   Pinart, Alphonse. 1893. Note sur les pétroglyphes et antiquités des Grandes et Petites Antilles. *Bureau of American Ethnology, Annual Report* 10:136–140. Washington, DC.

Sculpture

341.   Alegría, Ricardo E. 1981. *El uso de la incrustación en la escultura de los indios antillanos*. San Juan de Puerto Rico: Centro de Estudios Avanzados de Puerto Rico y el Caribe; Fundación García-Arevalo. 79 p.; *Seminario Americanista de la Universidad Casa de Colón* 9:5–32, 1981. Valladolid, Spain.

Crustation as an artistic technique appeared first in Puerto Rico ca. A.D. 120 (Saladoid) and spread throughout the Antilles to historic times.

342. Caro Alvarez, José A. 1977. *Cemís y trigonolitos*. Barcelona: Artes Gráficas Pareja.

343. Josselin de Jong, J.P.B. de. 1924. A natural prototype of certain three-pointed stones. *International Congress of Americanists (21 session, The Hague, 1924), Proceedings* 1:43–45. The Hague.

Pottery

344. Allaire, Louis A. 1984. A reconstruction of early historic Island Carib pottery. *Southeastern Archaeology* 3(2):121–133. Gainesville.

Analysis of protohistoric Island Carib pottery.

345. Rouse, Irving. 1940. Some evidence concerning the origins of West Indian pottery-making. *American Anthropologist* 42(1):49–80. Washington, DC.

Spanish translation: Alguna evidencia acerca de los orígenes de la alfarería antillana (*Revista de Arqueología y Etnología* 3(6–7):196–226, 1948. La Habana).

346. ———. 1966. Caribbean ceramics: a study in method and theory. In: *Ceramics and Man*. F.R. Matson, ed. pp. 88–103. Viking Fund Publications in Anthropology, no. 41. New York: Wenner-Gren Foundation for Anthropological Research.

Theoretical discussion of ceramic types and modes in the classification of pottery from eastern Venezuela and the West Indies.

Lithics

347. Figueredo, Alfredo E. 1974. Ancient West Indian arrowheads. *Museum of the American Indian, Heye Foundation, Indian Notes* 10(2):59–61. New York.

348. Im Thurn, E.F. 1884. Notes on West Indian stone implements and other Indian relics. *Timehri* 1:257–271; 2(2):2352–264; 3)(3–4):103–137. Georgetown.

349. Lee, James W. 1962. Arawak stone artifacts. *Scientific Research Council of Jamaica, Information Bulletin* 2(4):70–72. Kingston.

350. Pantel, A. Gus. 1988. Precolumbian Flaked Stone Assemblages in the West Indies. Ph.D. dissertation, Department of Anthropology, University of Tennessee, Knoxville. 262 p.

Author examines the history of the development of West Indian lithic research and proposes a classification scheme based on technological processes; data used derives from Cuba, Jamaica, Haiti, the Dominican Republic, Puerto Rico, and the Virgin Islands.

351. Rouse, Irving. 1942. Flint tools of the West Indies. *American Scientific Congress (8 session, Washington, DC, 1940), Proceedings* 2:129. Washington, DC.

A note on some crude, Palaeolithic-type, flint tools.

Groundstone

352. Booy, Theodoor H.N. de. 1916. Certain similarities in amulets from the northern Antilles. *Holmes Anniversary Volume.* pp. 24–30. Washington, DC.

353. Fewkes, J. Walter. 1903. Precolumbian West Indian amulets. *American Anthropologist* 5:679–691. Washington, DC.

354. ———. 1909. An Antillean statuette with notes on West Indian religious beliefs. *American Anthropologist* 11(3):348–358. Washington, DC.

355. Hostos, Adolfo de. 1923. Anthropomorphic carvings from the Greater Antilles. *American Anthropologist* 25:525–558. Washington, DC.

356. Mead, Charles W. 1916. The distribution of an Arawak pendant. *Holmes Anniversary Volume.* pp. 316–319. Washington, DC.

357. Sellon, Michael. 1973. Exploring the enigmatic tri-point. *Museum of the American Indian, Heye Foundation, Indian Notes* 9(2):51–64. New York.

Classification of shell and stone three-pointed objects from the Antilles; summarizes relevant theories of de Hostos, Lovén, and Olsen.

358. Sued Badillo, Jalil. 1977. La industria lapidaria pretaína en las Antilles. *International Congress of Americanists (41 session, México, 1974), Proceedings* 3:717–724. México; *Revista/Review Interamericana* 8(3):429–462, 1978.

Chronological and distributional study of green stone amulets and other examples of lapidary industries in the Caribbean.

Celts

359. Booy, Theodoor H.N. de. 1915. Certain West-Indian superstitions pertaining to celts. *Journal of American Folklore* 28(107):76–82; *Museum of the American Indian, Heye Foundation, Contributions* 2(3):78–82, 1915–1916. New York.

360. Desmaisons, Henri. 1942. Haches dites Caraibes et pics néolithiques des mineurs marocains dans les exploitations de sel gmme. *Société Préhistorique Française, Bulletin* 39:228–229. Paris.

361. Fewkes, Jesse W. 1915. Engraved celts from the Antilles. *Museum of the American Indian, Heye Foundation, Contributions* 2(2):1–12. New York.

362. Gibbs, G.J. 1877. Stone celts in the West Indies and in Africa. *Smithsonian Institution, Annual Report* 1876:308. Washington, DC.

363. Goggin, John M., and Irving Rouse. 1948. A West Indian ax from Florida. *American Antiquity* 13(4):323–325. Washington, DC.

Description of an apparent West Indian chopping implement acquired by prehistoric Florida Indians.

Metalwork

364. Rivet, Paul. 1923. L'orfèvrerie précolombienne des Antilles, des Guyanes et du Venezuela, dans ses rapports avec l'orfèvrerie et la métallurgie des autres régions américaines. *Société des Américanistes de Paris, Journal* 15:183–213. Paris.

Basketry

365. Lindblom, Karl G. 1937. An old African basket from the West Indies in the Stockholm Museum. *Ethnos* 2:367–368. Stockholm.

Wood

366. McKusick, Marshall B. 1960. *Aboriginal Canoes in the West Indies.* Yale University Publications in Anthropology, no. 63. New Haven. 11 p.

Intellectual Life

Astronomy

367.   Robiou-Lamarche, Sebastián. 1990. Island Carib mythology and astronomy. *Latin American Indian Literatures Journal* 6(1):36–54. Beaver Falls, PA.

Navigation

368.   Purroy y Furillos, Maria del Carmen. 1966. La navegación en la vida primitiva de la Antillas. *Revista Española de Indigenismo* 7–8:5–8. Madrid.

New Directions

369.   *International Congress for the Study of Pre-Columbian Cultures in the Lesser Antilles (1 session, Fort-de-France, July 3–7, 1961), Proceedings.* R.P. Bullen, ed. Fort de France, Martinique: Société d'Histoire de la Martinique, 1963–1964. 96, 141 p.

Contents include: W.G. Haag, A comparison of Arawak sites in the Lesser Antilles (pp. 9–37); I. Rouse, The developement of pre-Columbian art in the West Indies (pp. 39–56); J. Petitjean-Roget, The Caribs as seen through the dictionary of Reverend Breton (pp. 43–68); R. Pinchon, The archaeological problem in Martinique: a general view (pp. 75–79); R. Pinchon, The different forms of pottery in the Arawak civilization (pp. 80–84); R. Pinchon, The different forms of pottery in the Arawak civilization (pp. 89–94); F. Olsen, Arawak campsites on Antigua (pp. 95–106); R.P. Bullen, Krum Bay, a Preceramic workshop in the Virgin Islands (pp. 107–126).

370.   *International Congress for the Study of Pre-Columbian Cultures in the Lesser Antilles (2 session, St. Ann's Garrison, Barbados, July 24–28, 1967), Proceedings.* R.P. Bullen, ed. St. Ann's Garrison, Barbados: Barbados Museum and Historical Society, 1968. 146 p.

Contents include: J. Petitjean-Roget, Méthodes suives pour la différentiation des niveaux au Diamant: quelques mots sur la typology (pp. 1–8); B.J. Meggers, The theory and purpose of ceramic analysis (pp. 9–20); R.L. Vanderwal, Archaeological classification (pp. 21–30); R.P. Bullen and A.K. Bullen, Salvage archaeology at Caliviny [sic] Island, Grenada: a problem in typology (pp. 31–43); A.K. Bullen, Field comments on the skull excavated in 1967 at Caliviny [sic]

Island, Grenada, West Indies (pp. 44–46); E. Clerc, Sites précolombiens de la côte nord-est de la Grand-Terre de Guadeloupe (pp. 47–60); J. Petitjean-Roget, Etude d'un horizon Arawak et proto-Arawak à la Martinique a partir du niveau II du Diamant (pp. 61–68); M. Mattioni, Symbolisme de la décoration des poteries Arawak (pp. 69–80); R.P. Bullen, Some Arawak ceramic variations between Grenada, Barbados, St. Lucia, and eastern Trinidad (pp. 81–86); W.G. Haag, The Lesser Antilles: their ecological setting and function as a diffusion route (pp. 87–92); C. Evans, The lack of archaeology on Dominica (pp. 93–102); E.S. Wing, Aboriginal fishing in the Windward Islands (pp. 103–107); M. Sanoja, Ethnohistorical evaluation of zoological remains from two archaeological sites in western Venezuela (pp. 108–114); P. Vérin, Carib culture in colonial times (pp. 115–120); W.G. Haag, The identification of archaeological remains with ethnic groups (pp. 121–124); J. Petitjean-Roget, Etude d'un horizon Caraibe à la Martinique a partir de niveau III du Diamant (pp. 125–133); R.P. Bullen and A.K. Bullen, Barbados archaeology, 1966 (pp. 134–144).

371. *International Congress for the Study of Pre-Columbian Cultures in the Lesser Antilles (3 session, St. George's, Grenada, July 7–11, 1969), Proceedings.* R.P. Bullen, ed. St. George's, Grenada: Grenada National Museum, 1970. 154 p.

Contents include: M. Mattioni and R.P. Bullen, A chronological chart for the Lesser Antilles (pp. 1–3); H. Theuvenin, R.P. Bullen, and M. Sanoja O., Terminologie utilisée pour la description des poteries des Petites Antilles, équivalence des termes Anglais, Espagnols, et Français (pp. 4–7); J. Petitjean-Roget, Essai de taxonomie des ensembles reconstitués (pp. 8–14); J. Petitjean-Roget, Etude des ensembles reconstitués de la Martinique (pp. 15–26); M. Barbotin, Les sites archéologiques de Marie-Galante, Guadeloupe (pp. 27–44); A.K. Bullen, Case study of an Amerindian burial with grave goods from Grande Anse, St. Lucia (pp. 45–60); A.K. Bullen and R.P. Bullen, The Lavoutte Site, St. Lucia: a Carib ceremonial center (pp. 61–86); J. Petitjean-Roget, Etude des tessons (pp. 87–94); C.A. Hoffman, Implications from the Mill Reef, Antigua; Sugar Factory, St. Kitts; and Palmetto Grove, San Salvador, sites (pp. 95–106); I. Vargas and M. Sanoja, The Orinoco Project: preliminary report, 1968–1969 (pp. 107–113); E. Kirby, The pre-Columbian stone monuments of St. Vincent, West Indies (pp. 114–128); W.G. Haag, Stone artifacts in the Lesser Antilles (pp. 129–138); M.D. Mattioni, Etude théorique des couches archéologiques aux Petites

Antilles sur la base des migrations Arawak et Caraibe (pp. 139–146);
R.P. Bullen, The archaeology of Grenada, West Indies, and the spread
of ceramic people in the Antilles (pp. 147–152).

372. *International Congress for the Study of Pre-Columbian Cultures in the
Lesser Antilles (4 session, Reduit Beach, St. Lucia, July 26–30, 1971),
Proceedings.* R.P. Bullen, ed. Castries, St. Lucia: St. Lucia
Archaeological and Historical Society, 1973. 216 p.

Contents include: M. Veloz Maggiolo, P. Pina, E. Ortega, and
B. Vega, Antillean pictographs and petroglyphs: patterns and
procedures which can be applied in the study of their location in time
(pp. 1–8); C.A. Hoffman, Petroglyphs on Crooked Island, Bahamas
(pp. 9–12); R.P. Bullen, Petroglyphs of the Virgin Islands and Puerto
Rico (pp. 13–16); C.K. Laurie and D.L. Matheson, The petroglyphs
of St. Kitts, West Indies (pp. 17–20); E. Clerc, Petroglyphs on
Guadeloupe (pp. 21–24); M. Mattioni, Communication sur les
petroglyphes de la Martinique (pp. 25–32); C. Jesse, Petroglyph and
rock-cut basins at Dauphin, St. Lucia (pp. 33–34); F. Olsen,
Petroglyphs of the Caribbean Islands and Arawak deities (pp. 35–46);
W.J. Kennedy, A comparison of certain Costa Rican petroglyph
designs with those from adjacent area (pp. 47–56); J. de Abate, A key
to the interpretation of the petroglyphs of the Orinoco (pp. 57–64);
R.P. Bullen, Petroglyphs in Guayana (p. 65); R.P. Bullen, Further
comments on Antillean petroglyphs (pp. 65–68); C. Jesse, Pre-
Columbian stone artifacts put to strange uses (pp. 68–72); E. Clerc,
Les trois-pointes des sites précolombiens de la Côte Nord-Est de la
Grand-Terre de la Guadeloupe (pp. 73–81); R.P. Bullen, Stone
specimens from St. Barthelemy (pp. 82–83); M. Mattioni, L'outillage
lithique d'un site du nord-est de la Martinique (pp. 84–89); C. Jesse,
The Caribs in St. Lucia after A.D. 1605 (pp. 90–93); F. Olsen, Did the
Ciboney precede the Arawaks in Antigua? (pp. 94–102); M. Veloz
Maggiolo, E. Ortega, P. Pina Peña, and B. Vega, Three stone artifact
sites in the Dominican Republic (pp. 103–109); R.P. Bullen, Krum
Bay, a Preceramic workshop on St. Thomas (pp. 110–114); P. O'B.
Harris, Preliminary report on Banwari Trace, a Preceramic site in
Trinidad (pp. 115–125); A.H.T. Ahmad Dawud, Greencastle Hill,
Antigua: a possible megalithic monument of a prehistoric civilization
(pp. 126–129); C.M. Raggi Ageo, Posibles rutas de poblamiento de
las Antillas en el Paleo-Indio (pp. 130–139); M. Barbotin, Tentative
d'explication de la forme et du volume des haches précolombiennes
de Marie-Galante et de quelques autres pierres (pp. 140–150); J.
Petitjean-Roget and H. Petitjean-Roget, Recherche d'une méthode

pour l'étude de la décoration des céramiques précolombiennes de la Martinique (pp. 151–156); J. Petitjean-Roget and H. Petitjean-Roget, Etude comparative des tessons graves ou incises (pp. 157–173); J. Petitjean-Roget and H. Petitjean-Roget, Etude de la décoration des vases précolombiens de la Martinique (pp. 174–180); F. Olsen, On the trail of the Arawaks: when did they arrive in Trinidad? (pp. 181–191); R.P. Bullen and A.K. Bullen, Stratigraphic tests at two sites on Guadeloupe (pp. 192–196); R.P. Bullen, A.K. Bullen, and I.A.E. Kirby, Dating the Troumassee decorated cylinder: a horizon style (pp. 197–198); A.K. Bullen, R.P. Bullen, and E.M. Branford, The Giraudy Site, Beane Field, St. Lucia (pp. 199–214).

373. *International Congress for the Study of Pre-Columbian Cultures in the Lesser Antilles (5 session, Antigua, July 22–28, 1973), Proceedings.* R.P. Bullen, ed. Antigua, Antigua Archaeological Society; Antigua National Trust, 1974. 178 p.

Contents include: R.C. Goodwin and J.B. Walker, Salvage archaeology at Villa Taína, Puerto Rico (pp. 1–10); F. Olsen, The Arawak ball court at Antigua and the prototype *zemi* (pp. 11–12); E.H.J. Boerstra, Preliminary report on the 1971 Ceru Noka excavations, Aruba, Netherlands Antilles (pp. 13–20); M. Mattioni, Essai sur les concordances archéologiques du Venezuela à la Martinique (pp. 21–27); J.F. Turene, Le gisement de Pointe Gravier, Guyane Française (pp. 28–34); C.M. Raggi, Los indios luchahios en las Antillas Menores (pp. 35–47); R.P. Bullen and A.K. Bullen, Inferences from cultural diffusion to Tower Hill, Jamaica, and Cupercoy Bay, St. Martin (pp. 48–60); I.A.E. Kirby, The Cayo pottery of St. Vincent: a pre-Calivigny series (pp. 61–64); D.D. Davis, Some notes concerning the Archaic occupation of Antigua (pp. 65–71); J.P. Duprat, Les thèmes de décoration de la poterie Arawak (pp. 72–81); H. Petitjean-Roget, La savane des pétrifications (Martinique): un gisement de l'age lithique (pp. 82–93); R.P. Bullen, Certain petroglyphs of the Antilles (pp. 94–109); P.O'B. Harris, Summary of Trinidad archaeology (pp. 110–116); L. Allaire, Paquemar revisited (pp. 117–126); E. Clerc, Le travail du coquillage dans les sites précolombiens de la Grand-Terre de Guadeloupe (pp. 127–132); J. Gautier, Etude de pates ceramiques de la Martinique pré-Colombienne (pp. 133–139); D.W. Pike and A.G. Pantel, The first flint workshop found in Puerto Rico (pp. 140–142); C.A. Hoffman, Multilinear evolution in the prehistoric West Indies (pp. 143–152); C.E. Rotenberg, Introducing the pre-Columbian cultures of the Virgin Islands to the present day inhabitants (pp. 153–154); E.M.

Branford, The role of the Congress in the Caribbean (pp. 155–156); O.D. Lara, Centre d'histoire économique et sociale des Antilles (p. 157); L. Allaire, An archaeological reconnaissance of St. Kitts, Leeward Islands (pp. 158–161); M. Mattioni and R.P. Bullen, Pre-Columbian dogs in the Lesser and Greater Antilles (pp. 162–165); I. Rouse, The Indian Creek excavations (pp. 166–176).

374. *International Congress for the Study of Pre-Columbian Cultures in the Lesser Antilles (6 session, Pointe-a-Pitre, Guadeloupe, July 6–12, 1975), Proceedings.* R.P. Bullen, ed. Pointe à Pitre, Guadeloupe: Central University Antilles-Guayane; Department of History and Archaeology, U.E.R., 1976. 316 p.

Contents include: R.P. Bullen and A.K. Bullen, Culture areas and climaxes in Antillean prehistory (pp. 1–10); M. Mattioni, Les grandes familles des formes du Saladoide Insulaire au site de vive a la Martinique (pp. 11–13); I.A.E. Kirby, The pre-Hispanic peopling of the Antilles (pp. 14–20); P. Arnoux, Anse Marguerite Dit Gros Cap, Guadeloupe (pp. 21–27); R.P. Bullen and A.K. Bullen, Three stratigraphic tests along the eastern shore of Trinidad (pp. 28–34); I. Rouse, The Saladoid sequence on Antigua and its aftermath (pp. 35–41); E. Clerc, Remarques sur quelques pierres a trois-pointes provenant des gisements précolombiens de la côte N.E. de Grande-Terre de Guadeloupe (pp. 42–45); L. Sutty, Further excavations at Chatham Midden, Union Island, The Grenadines (pp. 54–65); L. Sutty, Archaeological excavations at Miss Pierre, Union Island, the Grenadines (pp. 66–75); J. Petitjean-Roget, A propos des platines a manioc (pp. 76–81); R.E. Alegría, The use of noxious gas as a weapon of war by the Taínan and Carib Indians of the Antilles (pp. 82–86); S. Dreyfus, Remarques sur l'organisation socio-politique des Caraïbes insulaires au XVIIème siecle (pp. 87–97); D.V. Nicholson, Precolumbian seafaring capabilities in the Lesser Antilles (pp. 98–105); M. Sanoja O., La tradición barrancoide del bajo Orinoco (pp. 106–116); I. Rouse, J.M. Cruxent, F. Olsen, and A.C. Roosevelt, Ronquin revisited (pp. 117–122); I. Vargas Arrenas, La Gruta, un nuevo sitio ronquinoide en Orinoco medio (pp. 123–124); E.H.J. Boerstra, Burying the dead in pre-Columbian Aruba (pp. 125–133); A. Boomert, Pre-Columbian raised fields in coastal Surinam (pp. 134–144); P.O'B. Harris, Excavation report on the ceramic site of Golden Grove, Tobago (pp. 145–157); D. Groene, Note sur le site de Kormontibo, Guayane Française (pp. 158–164); H. Petitjean-Roget and D. Roy, Site archeologique du Rorota, Guyane (pp. 165–174); M. Mattioni, La symbolique dans les cultures précolombiennes des Petites Antilles (pp. 175–176); H. Petitjean-Roget, Note sur le motif de la Grenouille dans l'art Arawak des Petites Antilles (pp. 177–182); H. Petitjean-Roget, Le thème de la chauve-souris frugivore dans l'art Arawak des Petites Antilles (pp. 182–186); K. Kay, A survey of Antillean sculptured stone (pp. 187–199); B. Vega, Comparison of newly found cave drawings in Santo Domingo with petroglyphs and pictographs in the Caribbean region (pp. 200–212); R.J. Devaux, Petroglyphs recently discovered at Stonefield, St. Lucia (p. 213); I.A.E. Kirby, A newly found petroglyphic rock on St. Vincent (p. 214); H. Petitjean-Roget, Note sur quelques petroglyphes des Antilles (pp. 215–220); A. Pollak-Eltz, Venezuelan petroglyphs: a survey (pp. 221–231); J.M. Gross, The Archaic period of the Virgin Islands: new investigations (pp. 232–238); B.E. Tilden, The Arboretum Complex: a Preceramic culture of the Virgin Islands (pp. 239–246); A.E. Figueredo, Cano Hondo, un residuario preceramico en la Isla de Vieques (pp. 247–252); A.G. Pantel, Progress report and analysis, Barrera-Mordan Complex, Azua, Dominican Republic (pp. 253–257); D.V. Nicholson, An Antigua shell midden with ceramic and Archaic components (pp. 258–263); D.V. Nicholson, Artifact types of Preceramic Antigua (pp. 264–268); J. Ortiz, Excavations at the Preceramic Cerrillo Site, southwest Puerto Rico (pp. 269–271); M. Pons Alegría, Saladoid incense-burners from the site of El Convento, Puerto Rico (pp. 272–275); E. Ortega, M. Veloz Maggiolo, and P. Pina, El Caimito: un antiguo complejo ceramista de las Antillas Mayores (pp. 276–282); M. Veloz Maggiolo, E. Ortega, M. Sanoja, and I. Vargas, Preliminary report on archaeological investigations at El Atajadizo, Dominican Republic (pp. 283–294); F. Luna Calderón, Preliminary report on the Indian cemetery El Atajadizo, Dominican Republic (pp. 295–303); M.J. Roobol and J.W. Lee, Petrography and source of some Arawak rock artifacts from Jamaica (pp. 304–313); D.W. Eichholz, A potential archaeo-astronomical horizon at Las Flores, Puerto Rico (p. 314).

375.   *International Congress for the Study of Pre-Columbian Cultures in the Lesser Antilles (7 session, Caracas, July 11–16, 1977), Proceedings.* J. Benoist and F.M. Mayer, eds. Montreal: Université de Montreal, Centre de Recherches Caraïbes, 1978. 349 p.

Contents include: S.J.K. Wilkerson, Ripley Pierce Bullen, 1902–1976 (pp. 1–8); I.A.E. Kirby, Fr. Bullen and the amateurs (p. 9); A.K. Bullen, Bibliography of Rilpey P. Bullen (pp. 11–25); L. Arvelo B., Tucuragua, un yacimiento aruquinoide del Orinoco medio (pp. 27–37); A.E. Figueredo, Prehistoric ethnozoology of the Virgin Islands (pp. 39–45); P. Harris, A revised chronological framework for ceramic Trinidad and Tobago (pp. 47–63); I.A.E. Kirby, Some notes of interest to the archaeology of the Antilles (pp. 65–67); I.A.E. Kirby and J. Wall, A unique Barrancoid pot-stand (p. 69); F.N. de Galicia, Bañador: un sitio arqueológico del bajo Orinoco (pp. 71–80); H. Petitjean-Roget, Reconnaissance archéologique à l'Ile de la Dominique (West Indies) (pp. 81–97); H. Petitjean-Roget, Note sur un vase Arawak trouvé à la Martinique (pp. 99–115); H. Petitjean-Roget, Note descriptive de la collection d'objets lithiques de la librairie publique de Roseau-Dominique (W.I.) (pp. 117–135); D. Roy, Découverte du site de jarre Indien (Guyane)(pp. 137–147); H. Petitjean-Roget, Découverte du site de Gros-Montagne (Guyane) (149–155); M. Sanoja, Proyecto Orinoco: excavación en el sitio arqueológico de los Castillos de Gayana, Territorio Federal Delta Amacuro, Venezuela (pp. 157–168); L. Sickler Robinson, Modified oliva shells from the Virgin Islands: a morphological study (pp. 169–187); K.T. de Ruiz, Comparación estilistica entre la cerámica de Lagunillas, Estado Zulia y Santa Ana, Estado Trujillo, Venezuela nor-occidental (pp. 189–194); L.A. Sutty, A study of shells and shelled objects from six Pre-Columbian sites in the Grenadines of St. Vincent and Grenada (pp. 195–210); I. Vargas Arenas, Puerto Santo: un nuevo sitio arqueológico en la costa oriental de Venezuela (pp. 211–220); I. Vargas and M. Sanoja, Comparaciones entre la arqueología del bajo y medio Orinoco (pp. 221–229); J. Winter, A note on Bahamian griddles (pp. 231–236); J. Winter, Preliminary work from the McKay site on Crooked Island (pp. 237–242); M.E. Escardo, Who were the inhabitants of the Virgin Islands at the time of Columbus' arrival? (pp. 245–257); A.E. Figuerdo and S.D. Glazier, A revised aboriginal ethnohistory of Trinidad (pp. 259–262); M.A. García Arévalo, Influencias de la dieta indo-hispánica en la cerámica taína (pp. 263–277); S.D. Glazier, Trade and warfare in protohistoric Trinidad (pp. 279–282); C.J.M.R. Gullick, Black Carib origins and early society (pp. 283–290); M. Mattioni, Problèmes de l'évolution des groupes ethniques Amerindiens de la Guyane française et de la défense de leurs valeurs culturelles (pp. 291–296); M. Mattioni, Essai sur la contribution apportée par le texte de Ramon Pané a la connaissance des groupes ethniques d'Hispaniola (pp. 297–303); F. Moscoso, Tributo y formación de clases en la sociedad de los taínos de las Antillas (pp. 305–323); R.A. Myers, Ethnohistorical vs. ecological considerations: the case of Dominica's Amerindians (pp. 325–341); C.S. Rotenberg, Conservation of archaeological sites (pp. 343–344); E. Wagner, Problematica de la destrucción arqueológica y la etica del arqueologo (pp. 345–349).

376. *International Congress for the Study of Pre-Columbian Cultures in the Lesser Antilles (8 session, St. Kitts, July 30–August 4, 1979), Proceedings.* S.M. Lewenstein, ed. Arizona State University, Anthropological Research Papers, no. 22. Tempe, 1980. 623 p.

Contents include: F. Olsen, The Arawaks, their art, religion, and science (pp. 3–42); R.C. Goodwin, Demographic change and the crab-shell dichotomy (pp. 45–68); J. Walker, Analysis and replication of lithic artifacts from the Sugar Factory Pier site, St. Kitts (pp. 69–79); C. Angulo Valdes, Concheros tardios en el norte de Colombia (pp. 80–87); A.H. Versteeg, Prehistoric cultural ecology of the coastal plain of Suriname (pp. 88–97); V.A. Carbone, Some problems in cultural paleoecology in the Caribbean area (pp. 98–126); E.R. Lundberg, Old and new problems in the study of Antillean aceramic traditions (pp. 131–138); M. Sanoja Obediente, Los recolectores tempranos del golfo de Paria, Estado Sucre, Venezuela (pp. 139–150); D.V. Armstrong, Shellfish gatherers of St. Kitts: a study of Archaic subsistence and settlement patterns (pp. 152–167); M.J. Roobol and A.L. Smith, Archaeological implications of some radiocarbon dating on Saba and St. Kitts (pp. 168–176); D. Pagán Perdomo, Aspectos zooarqueologicos y geograficos en el arte rupestre de Santo Domingo (pp. 179–186); L. Sickler Robinson, The crab motif in aboriginal West Indian shellwork (pp. 187–194); H. Petitjean-Roget, Faragunaol: zemi du miel chez les taïnos des Grandes Antilles (pp. 195–205); R.O. Rimoli, Restos de fauna en el sitio arqueologico de Escalera Abajo, Puerto Rico (pp. 210–213); M. Faught, Better than tree rings? (pp. 214–217); A.E. Dittert, E.S. Sipe, and R.C. Goodwin, The conservation of shell and shell artifacts: archaeological contexts (pp. 218–235); E.S. Wing and S. Scudder, Use of animals by the prehistoric inhabitants of St. Kitts, West Indies (pp. 237–244); E.S. Sipe, J.P. Collins, A.E. Dittert, and R.C. Goodwin, The preservation and study of prehistoric coral and coral artifacts: a preliminary study from St. Kitts, West Indies (pp. 246–263); A.R. Jones, Animal food and human population at Indian Creek, Antigua (pp. 264–273); I. Vargas Arenas, La tradición cerámica pintada del oriente de Venezuela (pp. 276–289); F. Nieves de Galicia, Población prehispanica de la region de Cupira: sector oriental de la Ensenada de Higuerote (Venezuela) (pp. 290–306); C.A. Hoffman, The outpost concept and the Mesoamerican connection (pp. 307–316); S. Levin, A computer-cataloging system for pre-Columbian Antillean ceramics in United States museums (pp. 320–330); R.J. Ruppé, Sea-level rise and Caribbean prehistory (pp. 331–337); D.R. Watters and R. Scaglion, Utility of a transect survey technique in Caribbean prehistoric studies:

applications on Barbuda and Montserrat (pp. 338–347); P.F. Thall and R.C. Goodwin, Seriation and clustering of archaeological excavation units from potsherd frequencies: the case of the St. Kitts Sugar Factory Pier site (pp. 348–362); A.G. Pantel, Canejas Cave site excavations, Fort Buchanan Military Reservation, San Juan, Puerto Rico (pp. 363–393); D.V. Nicholson, The atlatl spur: a newly identified artifact from the Lesser Antilles (pp. 394–405); S.M. Lewenstein, Analyzing chipped stone artifacts: the study of lithic technology, function and exchange (pp. 406–425); R.E. Alegría, Etnografía taína y los conquistadores (pp. 430–446); S.D. Glazier, A note on shamanism in the Lesser Antilles (pp. 447–454); A. Jiménez Lambertus, Analisis antropológico fisico de un vocabulario arauaco del siglo XVII (pp. 456–463); C.J.M.R. Gullick, Island Carib traditions about their arrival in the Lesser Antilles (pp. 464–472); R.A. Myers, Archaeological materials from Dominica in North American and European museums (pp. 473–480); M.I. Gullick, Changing Carib cookery (pp. 481–487); B. Vega, Metals and the aborigines of Hispaniola (pp. 488–497); L.A. Chanlatte-Baik, La Hueca Vieques: nuevo complejo cultural agroalfarero en la arqueología antillana (pp. 501–522); P. Harris, Excavation report: Lovers Retreat Period IV, Tobago (pp. 524–552); M. Mattioni, Salvage excavations at the Fond-Brule site (northeast coast of Martinique) (pp. 553–566); L. Sutty, A further study of the Troumassee cylinder and its place in Arawak society (pp. 567–576); M. Pons Alegría, The use of masks, spectacles, and eye-pieces among the Antillean aborigines (pp. 578–591); I.A.E. Kirby, The Carib incursion into the Greater Antilles (pp. 593–596); J.W. Lee, Jamaican redware (597–609).

377. *International Congress for the Study of Pre-Columbian Cultures in the Lesser Antilles (9 session, Santo Domingo, 1981), Proceedings.* L. Allaire and F.H. Mayer, eds. Montréal: Centre de Recherches Caraïbes, Université de Montréal, 1983. 574 p.

Contents include: I. Rouse, Diffusion and interaction in the Orinoco Valley and on the coast (pp. 3–13); M. Sanoja, Tipología de concheros preceramicos del noreste de Venezuela (pp. 15–26); L. Allaire and M. Mattioni, Boutbois et le Godinot: deux gisemernts aceramiques de la Martinique (pp. 27–38); L. Hurtado de Mendoza, Algunos ensamblajes liticos de Costa Rica y su ubicación cronologico-cultural (pp. 39–56); I. Vargas Arenas, Nuevas evidencias de sitios saladoides en la costal oriental de Venezuela, el sitio Playa Grande (S9)(pp. 57–71); L.A. Chanlatte Baik, Sorce-Vieques: climax cultural

del Igneri y su participacion en los procesos socioculturales antillanos
(pp. 73–95); A. Boomert, The Saladoid occupation of Wonotobo
Falls, western Surinam (pp. 97–120); M. Pons Alegría, Las figuras de
barro de la cultura Saladoide de Puerto Rico (pp. 121–129); F. Nieves
de Galicia, Ocupaciones ceramistas de la llanada barlovonteña:
consideraciones en torno a la investigación arqueologica de la costa
centro-oriental de Venezuela (pp. 131–144); L. Sutty, Liaison
Arawak-Caliviny-Carib between Grenada and St. Vincent, Lesser
Antilles (pp. 145–153); J. Winter and J. Stipp, Preliminary
investigations of the Minnis/Ward site, San Salvador, Bahamas (pp.
155–162); M. Rodríguez López and V. Rivera, Sitio "El Destino,"
Vieques, Puerto Rico: informe preliminar (pp. 163–172); E.H.J.
Boerstra, Some of the soil marks in the Tanki Flip excavation, Aruba,
Netherlands Antilles: the ditches (pp. 173–182); H. Petitjean-Roget,
Evolution et décadence de l'art funéraire des sites pré- et post-
Colombiens de la Baie de l'Oyapock (pp. 183–199); O.M. Finseca
Zamora, Historia de las investigaciones en la region de Guayabo (pp.
201–218); M.J. Snarskis, Casas precolombinas en Costa Rica: una
visita diacronica (pp. 219–238); J. Walker, Use-wear analysis of
Caribbean flaked stone tools (pp. 239–247); J.M. Cruxent, la tecnica
de talla levalloisiense en Panama y Venezuela (pp. 249–256); P.O'B.
Harris, Antillean axes/adzes: persistence of an Archaic tradition (pp.
257–290); H. Peñalver Gomez, Protectores genitales de las pobladores
precolombinos que habitaron la cuenca del lago de Valencia,
Venezuela (pp. 291–299); R.C. Goodwin and P.F. Thall, Production
step measures and prehistoric Caribbean ceramics: an exploratory
survey (pp. 301–323); R.E. Alegría, La incrustación en la escultura
aborigen antillana (pp. 325–347); D. Slozinski and G. Slozinski, Notes
sur la Grotte du Morne Rita à Capesterre de Marie-Galante (pp. 349–
361); C. Toutouri, La roche gravée de l'Inipi, Guyane Française (pp.
363–374); C.N. Dubelaar, The distribution of Im Thurn's elaborate
type petroglyphs in South America (pp. 375–397); C.E. Montcourt
de Kosan, Caracteristicas craneologicas de los indígenas precolombinos
de Caño Rico, estado Aragua, Venezuela (pp. 399–407); C.H.
Fairbanks and R.A. Marrinan, The Puerto Real Project, Haiti (pp.
409–417); K. Deagan, Spanish Florida as part of the Caribbean colonial
sphere (pp. 419–429); D.V. Armstrong, The Drax Hall slave
settlement: site selection procedures (pp. 431–442); M. Posnansky,
Towards an archaeology of the Black diaspora (pp. 443–450); J.C.
Eichholz, A Spanish colonial lime kiln (pp. 451–457); A. de Prato-
Perelli, Relations existant au début de la colonisation esapagnole
entre los populations Caribes des Petits Antilles et celles de Venezuela

(pp. 459–483); F. Moscoso, Parentesco y clase en los cacicazgos taínos: el caso de los naborias (pp. 485–494); P.J. Moreno, Los Guajiros y su historia (pp. 495–503); J. Tattersall, A standardised simplified spelling system applied to interpreting the Taíno and Island Carib languages (pp. 505–509); H. Petitjean-Roget, De l'origine de la famille humaine ou contribution à l'étude des pierres à trois-pointes des Antilles (pp. 511–530); D.R. Watters, Assessing the ocean's roles in Antillean prehistory (pp. 531–541); S.W. Mitchell, Archaeological significance of shell growth in the bivalve *Codakia orbicularis* (Linnaeus) (pp. 543–554); S.D. Glazier, Antique maps and the study of Caribbean prehistory (pp. 555–570); R.V. Taylor, Archaeological events in Barbados (pp. 571–574).

378.   *International Congress for the Study of Pre-Columbian Cultures in the Lesser Antilles (10 session, 1983), Proceedings.* L. Allaire and F.H. Mayer, eds. Montréal: Centre de Recherches Caraïbes, Université de Montréal, 1985. 477 p.

Contents include: I. Rouse and C. Moore, Cultural sequence in southwestern Haiti (pp. 3–21); M. Rodriguez, Cultural resources survey at Camp Santiago, Salinas, Puerto Rico (pp. 23–44); B.R. Johnston and E.R. Lundberg, Archaeological survey of the United States Virgin Islands: a preliminary report (pp. 45–59); J.B. Haviser, An inventory of prehistoric resources on St. Eustatius, Netherlands Antilles (pp. 61–81); J. Winter, J. Granberry, and A. Liebold, Archaeological investigations within the Bahamas archipelago (pp. 83–92); A. Boomert, The Guayabitoid and Mayoid series: Amerindian culture history in Trinidad during late prehistoric and protohistoric times (pp. 93–148); P.G. Roe, A preliminary report on the 1980 and 1982 field seasons at Hacienda Grande (12 PSJ7–5), Puerto Rico: overview of site history, mapping, and excavations (pp. 151–180); J.B. Walker, A preliminary report on the lithic and osteological remains from the 1980, 1981, and 1982 field seasons at Hacienda Grande (12 PSJ7–5) (pp. 181–224); L. Chanlatte-Baik, Asentamiento poblacional Agro-1, complejo cultural La Hueca, Vieques, Porto Rico (pp. 225–250); Y.M. Narganes Storde, Restos faunisticos vertebrados de Sorce, Vieques, Puerto Rico (pp. 251–264); P.O'B. Harris, A comparison of three Bontour period sites, Trinidad (pp. 265–286); F. Luna Calderón, Antropologia y paleopatologia de los pobladores del Soco (pp. 287–294); M. Mattioni, Réaction osseuse, suite a blessure, sur humerus d'homme précolombien de la Martinique (pp. 295–296); L. Allaire, Changements lithiques dans l'archéologie de la Martinique (pp. 299–310); E. Ortega and J.G. Guerrero, El complejo litico de la cordillera, las grandes puntas especializadas y su relación con los modos de vida preagroalfareros en la prehistoria de Santo Domingo (pp. 311–334); A. Almeida, La Escuela de Cerámica Campesina e Indigena del Instituto Agrario en Venezuela (pp. 335–342); J.W. Lee, A pre-Columbian gold artifact from Jamaica (pp. 434–345); E.R. Lundberg, Observations on *Strombus columella* fragments: cautionary notes and experimental microwear analysis (pp. 347–361); M. Burac, L'apport de l'archéologie a la géographies des Petites Antilles (pp. 363–367); M. Schvoerer, P. Guibert, F. Bechtel, M. Mattioni, and J. Evin, Des hommes en Martinique vingt siècles avant Christophe Colomb? (pp. 369–397); L. Sutty, An early ceramic effigy bottle from Chatham Pasture, Union Island in the Grenadines (pp. 401–407); E.H.J. Boerstra, A limestone human figure from Taki Leendert, Aruba, Netherlands Antilles (pp. 409–420); C.N. Dubelaar, A comparison between petroglyphs of the Antilles and of northeastern South America (pp. 421–435); D. Pagán Perdomo, Apuntes sobre el arte rupestre prehispánico de Santo Domingo: discusión acerca de una hipothesis de identificación cultural del arte rupestre antillano (pp. 437–447); P. Caesar and M. Caesar, On the petroglyphs of St. John, U.S. Virgin Islands (pp. 449–454); H. Petitjean-Roget, Mythes et origine des maladies chez les taínos: les zemis Bugia et Aiba (Badraima) et Corocote (pp. 455–477).

379. *International Congress for Caribbean Archaeology (11 session, San Juan, 1985), Proceedings.* A.G. Pantel, ed. Report of the Institute of Archaeology and Anthropology of the Netherlands Antilles, no. 4. Curaçao: Institute of Archaeology and Anthropology of the Netherlands Antilles, 1987. 133 p.

Contents include: A.H. Versteeg, Methods and preliminary results on an archaeological salvage project on St. Eustatius, Netherlands Antilles (pp. 1–23); J.B. Haviser, Prehistoric human remains on Curaçao (pp. 24–50); J. Tacoma, Skeletal remains from De Savaan region, Curaçao (pp. 51–63); E.N. Ayubi, The study of the aesthetic aspects of the precolumbian pottery of Aruba, Curaçao and Bonaire (pp. 64–92); W. Nagelkerken, Preliminary report on the wine bottles of Orange Bay, St. Eustatius (pp. 93–122); N.F. Barka, The potential for historical archaeological research in the Netherlands Antilles (pp. 123–133).

380. *International Congress for Caribbean Archaeology (12 session, Cayenne, French Guiana, 1987), Proceedings.* L.S. Robinson, ed. Martinique: International Association for Caribbean Archaeology, 1991. 401 p.

Contents include: A. Zucchi, El Negro-Casiquiare-Alto Orinoco como ruta conectiva entre el Amazonas y el norte de Suramerica (pp. 1–34); A.H. Versteeg, Saladoid houses and functional areas around them: the Golden Rock site on St. Eustatius, Netherlands Antilles (pp. 35–44); M. Rodríguez and V. Rivera, Puerto Rico and the Caribbean pre-Saladoid "crosshatch connection" (pp. 45–51); J.-F. Durand and H. Petitjean-Roget, A propos d'un collier funéraire; Morel, Guadeloupe: les Huecoids sont-ils un mythe? (pp. 53–72); L.A. Sutty, A preliminary inventory and short essay on ceramic and stone artifacts from recent excavations on Grenada and in the southern Grenadines (pp. 73–85); P.E. Siegel and D.J. Bernstein, Sampling for site structure and spatial organization in the Saladoid: a case study (pp. 87–107); P.E. Siegel and P.G. Roe, The Maisabel Archaeological Project: a long term multi-disciplinary investigation (pp. 109–115); L.C. Budinoff, An osteological analysis of the human burials recovered from Maisabel: an early site on the north coast of Puerto Rico (pp. 117–133); M.R. Khudabux, G.J.R. Maat, and A.H. Versteeg, The remains of prehistoric Amerindians of the 'Tingi Holo Ridge' in Suriname: a physical anthropological investigation of the Versteeg Collection (pp. 135–151); J. Winter, A multiple Lucayan burial from New Providence, Bahamas (pp. 153–161); S. Hackenberger, An abstract of archaeological investigations by the Barbados Museum, 1986 (pp. 163–173); P.L. Drewett and M.H. Harris, The archaeological survey of Barbados: 1985–87 (pp. 175–202); M.D. Caesar, P.D. Caesar, and E.R. Lundberg, The Calabash Boom site, St. John, USVI: preliminary report (pp. 203–215); M. Barbotin, Les gisements de la Guadeloupe et les grandes lignes de leur classement chronologique (pp. 217–226); J.B. Haviser, A summary of Amerindian cultural geography research on Curaçao, Netherlands Antilles (pp. 227–240); H. Petitjean-Roget, 50 sites de montagnes en Guyane française: contribution a l'inventaire des sites archeologiques d'Emile Abonnenc (pp. 241–258); P. Harris, Amerindian Trinidad and Tobago (pp. 259–269); J.-P. Moreau, Nouvelles donnees sur les Indiens Caraibes recueillies par un filibuster français ayant sejourne onze mois a la Martinique en 1619 (pp. 271–283); J. Petitjean-Roget and A. Petitjean-Roget, Regards sur le cannibalisme (pp. 285–295); F.R. Thomas, Adaptation and exchanges on coral islands: data from the Bahamas and Oceania (pp. 297–316); P.G. Roe, The petroglyphs of Maisabel: a study in methodology (pp. 317–370); J. Winter and M. Gilstrap, Preliminary results of ceramic analysis and the movements of populations onto the Bahamas (pp. 371–386); M. Schvoerer and P. Guibert, Test d'anciennete par thermoluminescence sur deux documents presumes d'origine Amerindienne (pp. 387–401).

381. *International Congress for Caribbean Archaeology (13 session, Willemstad, Curaçao, 1989), Proceedings*. Willemstad, Curaçao: Archaeological-Anthropological Institute of the Netherlands Antilles, 1991.

Contents include: E.R. Lundberg, Interrelationships among Preceramic complexes of Puerto Rico and the Virgin Islands; C. Moore, Cabaret: lithic workshop sites in Haiti; A.H. Versteeg, Three Preceramic sites in Aruba; S.D. Glazier, Impressions of aboriginal technology: the case of the Caribbean canoe; C.L. Hoffman and M.L.P. Hoogland, The later prehistory of Saba, N.A.: the settlement site of Kelbey's Ridge (A.D. 1300–1450); N. Douglas, Recent Amerindian finds on Anguilla; A.K. Cody, From the site of Pearls, Grenada: exotic lithics and radiocarbon dates; M. Rodríguez, Arqueología de Punta Candelero, Puerto Rico; Y.M. Narganes Storde, Secuencia cronológica de dos sitios arqueológicos de Puerto Rico (Sorcé, Vieques y Tecla, Guayanilla); J.B. Haviser, Preliminary results from test excavations at the Hope Estate Site (SM-026), St. Martin; I. Rouse, Ancestries of the Taínos: Amazonian or Circum-Caribbean?; L. Allaire, Understanding Suazey; J. Tacoma, Precolumbian human skeletal remains from Curaçao, Aruba, and Bonaire; P.G. Roe, The best enemy is a defunct, drilled and decorative enemy: human corporeal art (frontal bone pectorals) in pre-Columbian Puerto Rico.

GREATER ANTILLES

382. *La Cultura taína*. Madrid: Comisión Nacional Para la Celebración del V Centenario del Descubrimiento de América, 1983. 182 p.

Results of the first Seminario Sobre la Situación de la Investigación de la Cultura Taína, held in April, 1983, at the Museo Arqueologico Nacional de Madrid and organized by the Comisión Nacional del Quinto Centenario del Descubrimiento and the Museo Arqueologico Nacional de Madrid; contents include: A.G. Pantel, Orígenes y definición de la cultura taína: sus antecedentes technológicos en el precerámico (pp. 9–13); M. Veloz Maggiolo, Para una definición de la cultura taína (pp. 15–21); M. Sanoja Obediente, El origen de la sociedad taína y el formativo suramericano (pp. 37–47); J. Alcina Franch, La cultura taína como sociedad de transición entre los niveles tribal y de jefaturas (pp. 69–80); M. García Arévalo, El murciélago en la mitología y el arte taíno (pp. 109–117); F.J. Arnáiz Márquez, El mundo religioso taíno visto por la fe católica española (pp. 141–154).

383. Espinola, Vera B. 1973. Aboriginal inhabitants of the island of Hispaniola. *Chesopiean* 11(2–3):63–73. Norfolk, Virginia.

384. Krieger, Herbert W. 1930. Aborigines of the ancient island of Hispaniola. *Smithsonian Institution, Annual Report* 1929:473–506. Washington, DC.

Description of Arawak culture on Hispaniola at the time of the Spanish discovery of the New World in 1492; includes discussion of travel and trade routes, cultural diffusion, population distribution, habitations, weapons, food resources, agriculture, hunting and fishing, implements, and decorative objects, religious objects, clothing, metals, and pottery.

Herbert W. Krieger (1889–1970) was affiliated with the Department of Anthropology of the Smithsonian Institution's United States National Museum. Much of his professional life involved museum administration and the study of artifact collections at the Smithsonian Institution. His major Caribbean fieldwork was carried out in the Greater Antilles, the Bahamas, and the Virgin Islands, during 1928–1937 and 1947–1952.

385.   Lovén, Sven. 1935. *Origins of the Taínan Culture, West Indies.* Göteborg: Elanders Boktryckeri Aktiebolag. 696 p.

First comprehensive study of the Arawaks of the Greater Antilles, dealing with their material culture and domestic and social life; a fundamental treatise on the Taíno, the Arawak-speaking group on Hispaniola at the time of Columbus; a revised second edition of Lovén's *Uber die Wurzeln der Tainischen Kultur* (Göteborg, 1924).

Museum Collections

386.   Caro Alvarez, J.A. 1972. Una escultura taína excepcional en el Museo del Indio Americano. *Museo del Hombre Dominicano, Boletín* 1:5–7. Santo Domingo.

387.   Lehmann, Henri. 1951. Un *duho* de la civilisation Taíno au Musée de l'Homme. *Société des Américanistes de Paris, Journal* 40:153–161. Paris.

Description of a carved wooden stool probably from Hispaniola in the collection of the Musée de l'Homme.

388.   Oldman, William O. 1943. *The Oldman Collection of Polynesian Artifacts: Tahiti, Austral, and Cook Groups.* Polynesian Society, Memoirs, no. 15. Wellington, New Zealand.

Description of a carved seat (*dujo*) and a wooden bowl from a cave on Hispaniola (pp. 45–46).

389.   Ripley, George. 1980. El cemí taíno de algodón. *Museo del Hombre Dominicano, Boletín* 9(13):115–124. Santo Domingo.

Investigation of a cotton *zemí* now in Turin, Italy; concludes it probably represented an important personage in the *cohoba* ceremony.

History of Archaeological Research

390.   Fewkes, Jesse W. 1904. Preliminary report on an archaeological trip to the West Indies. *Smithsonian Institution, Miscellaneous Collections* 45(129):112–133. Washington, DC.

Account of excavations in Puerto Rico and description of objects from Puerto Rico and the Dominican Republic.

391. Morales Patiño, Oswaldo, Fernando Royo García, Luis Cabrera Torrens, Leandro de Ona, and Justo S. Cabrera. 1952. La expedición científica cubana: Jamaica, Haiti, Puerto Rico e Islas Virgenes. *Revista de Arqueología y Etnología* 7:93–202. La Habana.

Ethnohistory

392. Alegría, Ricardo E. 1976. *Las relaciones entre los taínos de Puerto Rico y los de la Española.* Instituto Montecristeño de Arqueología, Boletín no. 2. Montecristi; *Museo del Hombre Dominicano, Boletín* 6:117–121, 1976. Santo Domingo.

393. Alegría, Ricardo E. 1978. *Apuntes en torno a la mitología de los indios taínos de las Antillas Mayores y sus orígenes suramericanos.* Santo Domingo: Centro de Estudios Avanzados de Puerto Rico y el Caribe; Museo del Hombre Dominicano. 179 p.; 2 ed. Santo Domingo: Centro de Estudios Avanzados de Puerto Rico y el Caribe; Museo del Hombre Dominicano, 1986. 178 p.

Discussion of four Taíno mythological themes in early historical sources; themes pertain to creation of man; origin of women, divine twins, and great flood.

394. Alegría, Ricardo E. 1985. Christopher Columbus and the treasure of the Taíno Indians of Hispaniola. *Jamaica Journal* 18(1):2–11. Kingston.

Description of artifacts received by Columbus from the Taíno between 1490 and 1495; Spanish edition: *Cristóbal Colón y el tesoro de los indios taínos de la Española.* Santo Domingo: Fundación García-Arévalo, 1980. 48 p.

395. Allaire, Louis A. 1987. Some comments on the ethnic identity of the Taíno-Carib frontier. In: *Ethnicity and Culture.* R. Auger, M.F. Glass, S. MacEachern, and P.H. McCartney, eds. pp. 127–133. Proceedings of the Chacmool Annual Conference, no. 18. Calgary.

396. Anderson-Córdova, Karen. 1990. Hispaniola and Puerto Rico: Indian Acculturation and Heterogenity, 1492–1550. Ph.D. dissertation, Department of Anthropology, Yale University, New Haven. 358 p.

An ethnohistorical examination of the acculturation of the Native Americans of Hispaniola and Puerto Rico between 1492 and 1550; in particular, the study explores the social and cultural transformations that occurred as a result of contact with Europeans, the significance of the contribution of immigration and emigration to the historic Native American population, and whether the responses to contact with the Spanish were different among various indigenous groups.

397.   Cassa, Roberto. 1974. *Los taínos de La Española*. Colección Historia y Sociedad, no. 11. Santo Domingo: Editora de la Universidad Autónoma de Santo Domingo. 272 p.

Summary of Taíno ethnohistory pertaining to the island of Hispaniola; considers subsistence patterns, technology, social and economic systems, religious beliefs, and ceremonialism.

398.   Coscullela, Juan A., and María Elena Cosculluela. 1947. *Prehistoria documentada: Cuba y Haiti*. Grupo Guamá, Contribución no. 12. La Habana: Lex. 88 p.

Examination of the indigenous groups of late-fifteenth century Cuba and Hispaniola.

399.   Deagan, Kathleen A. 1985. Spanish-Indian interaction in sixteenth-century Florida and Hispaniola. In: *Cultures in Contact: The European Impact on Native Cultural Institutions in Eastern North America, A.D. 1000–1800*. W.W. Fitzhugh, ed. pp. 281–318. Washington, DC: Smithsonian Institution Press.

400.   Garcia Valdes, Pedro. 1948. The ethnology of the Ciboney. In: *The Circum-Caribbean Tribes*. J.H. Steward, ed. pp. 503–505. Handbook of South American Indians, vol. 4. Bureau of American Ethnology, Bulletin 143. Washington, DC; New York: Cooper Square, 1963.

401.   Keegan, William F. 1989. Creating the Guanahatabey (Ciboney): the modern genesis of an extinct culture. *Antiquity* 63(239):373–379. London.

402.   Moscoso, Francisco. 1980. Las Guaizas: apuntes para el estudio del trueque entre los taínos. *Museo del Hombre Dominicano, Boletín* 9(14):75–86. Santo Domingo.

Guaízas are part of a material complex of objects with symbolic/magical importance produced by tributary artisans.

403.   Moya Pons, Frank. 1971. *La Española en el siglo XVI, 1493–1520: trabajo, sociedad y política en el economía del oro*. Colección

Estudios, 10. Santiago: Universidad Católica Madre y Maestra. 367 p.

Includes coverage of the encomienda and repartimiento systems (1500–1508), the colonial administration of Diego Colón (1509–1511), the religious, economic, and political organization of the colony (1512–1514), the repartimiento of 1514, the government by Jeronymite clergy (1516–1519), and the beginnings of the sugar economy; also includes a tabular demographic summary of the 1514 repartimiento arranged by Spaniards and Indians (caciques, naborias, indios de servicio, niños, and viejos); see also: F. Moya Pons, The politics of forced Indian labour in La Española, 1493–1520 (*Antiquity* 66:130–139, 1992) for an excellent overview of early Spanish settlement on Hispaniola; the repartimiento and encomienda systems are discussed and an important census document from 1514 is analyzed.

404. Moya Pons, Frank. 1972. La sociedad taína. *Revista Eme Eme* 1972:3–32. Santo Domingo; Santiago: Universidad Católica Madre y Maestra, 1973. 22 p.

Brief historical account of the Taíno of the Greater Antilles.

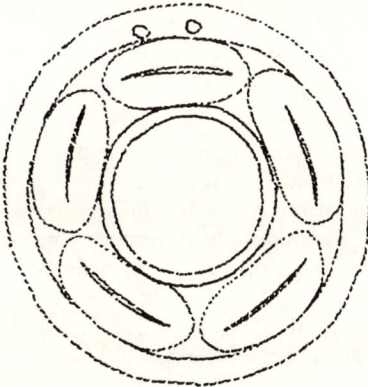

Figure 7.
Shell pendant, El Lindero, Maisi, Cuba.

Source: M.R. Harrington, *Cuba Before Columbus*,
Museum of the American Indian, Heye Foundation, Indian Notes and
Monographs, no. 17. New York, 1921. Figure 86.

405.   Moya Pons, Frank. 1984. The Taínos of Hispaniola: the island's first inhabitants. *Caribbean Review* 13(4):20–23, 47. Miami.

An important synthesis of the current knowledge pertaining to the indigenous inhabitants of the island of Hispaniola; includes description of lifeways, social organization, political organization, religion, and art of the Taíno Indians.

406.   Pina Chevalier, Téodulo. 1942. Apuntes acerca de los indios de la Isla Española. *América Indígena* 2(1):39–40. México.

Brief summary of the elimination of the native population of Hispaniola; traces of indigenous population survive in place names and in the importance of archaeological remains.

407.   Roth, H. Ling. 1887. The aborigines of Hispaniola. *Royal Anthropological Institute of Great Britain and Ireland, Journal* 16:247–286. London.

408.   Taylor, Robert B. 1989. *Indians of Middle America: An Introduction to the Ethnology of México, Central America, and the Caribbean.* Manhattan, Kansas: Lifeway Books. 304 p.

An historical ethnographic reconstruction of the Taíno is found on pp. 260–271.

409.   Wilson, Samuel M. 1990. *Hispaniola: Caribbean Chiefdoms in the Age of Columbus.* Tuscaloosa: University of Alabama Press. 170 p.

Examination of the early years of the contact period in the Caribbean and in narrative form reconstructs the social and political organization of the Taíno; detailed description of the interactions between the Taíno and the Spaniards, with attention given to the structure and operation of Taíno chiefdoms; an excellent use of archaeology and ethnohistory to construct a context within which to understand the Taíno and their responses to the Spaniards; publication of: *The Conquest of the Caribbean Chiefdoms: Sociopolitical Change on Prehispanic Hispaniola* (Ph.D. dissertation, Department of Anthropology, University of Chicago, 1986).

410.   Wilson, Samuel M. 1990. Columbus, my enemy. *Natural History* 12:44–49. Washington, DC.

Description of the initial conflict on Hispaniola between the Spaniards and the Taíno leader Guarionex, and the subsequent invasion of the Greater Antilles by Christopher Columbus and his brother, Bartolomé.

Historical Archaeology

411. Guerrero, José, and Marcio Veloz Maggiolo. 1988. *Los inicios de la colonización en América: la arqueología como historia*. San Pedro de Macorís: Universidad Central del Este. 117 p.

Cultural Evolution and Society

Cultural Evolution and Development

412. Cruxent, José M., and Irving Rouse. 1969. Early man in the West Indies. *Scientific American* 221(5):42–52.

Summary of the history of twentieth-century archaeological research in Haiti and the Dominican Republic; authors argue for the settlement of Hispaniola by Palaeo-Indians more than 7,000 years ago and reconstruct migration routes and cultural sequences on the island; detailed illustrations of artifacts, a map of archaeological sites, and a chronological chart of migrations and settlements in the West Indies; Spanish translation: El hombre primitivo en las Indias Occidentales (*Revista Dominicana de Arqueología y Antropología* 1(1):151–164, 1971. Santo Domingo).

413. Kozlowski, Janusz K. 1974. *Preceramic Cultures in the Caribbean*. Prace Acheológiczne, 20. Krakow: Panstwowe Wydawn. Naukowe, Oddz. w Krakowie. 114 p.

Important summary of blade technology of Cuba and adjacent areas.

414. Moscoso, Francisco. 1981. The Development of Tribal Society in the Caribbean. Ph.D. dissertation, Department of Anthropology, State University of New York at Binghamton, 1981. 470 p.

A theoretical analysis of the transition from tribal to class society in the Caribbean using information pertaining to the Taíno of the Greater Antilles; study includes a theoretical examination of the archaeology and anthropology of the Caribbean region, an archaeological reconstruction of the evolution of Caribbean society, and finally, an historical reconstruction of the development of Taíno chiefdoms; published as: *Tribú y clases en el Caribe antiguo* (San Pedro de Macorís, 1986. 518 p.); see also: Tributo y formación de clases en la sociedad de los taínos de las Antillas (*Revista Dominicana de Antropología e Historia* 6(8–9):89–113, 1977–1979).

415. Pina Peña, Plinio. 1971. Los períodos cronológicos de las culturas aborígenes en las Antillas Mayores. *Revista Dominicana de Arqueología y Antropología* 1(1):165–179. Santo Domingo.

416. ———, Marcio Veloz Maggiolo, and Manuel García Arévalo. 1974. *Esquema para una revisión de nomenclatura arqueológicas del poblamiento precéramico en las Antillas.* Santo Domingo: Fundación García Arévalo/Museo del Hombre Dominicano.

Authors propose a chronological sequence consisting of three traditions (Palaeo-Archaic, Archaic, and Ceramic) and five subtraditions.

417. Rimoli, Renato O. 1975. Prueba zooarqueologica del contacto del hombre precolombino de Cuba con la Española. *Cuadernos Prehispánicos* 3:99–101. Valladolid.

418. Rouse, Irving. 1946–1947. La arqueología de las Antillas Mayores. *Acta Venezolana* 2:36–45. Caracas.

419. ———. 1951. Areas and periods of culture in the Greater Antilles. *Southwestern Journal of Anthropology* 7(3):248–265. Albuquerque.

Establishes three major areas and four major periods of culture in the Greater Antilles; indicates that Ciboney (Preceramic) were land oriented whereas Arawak (Ceramic) were maritime oriented.

420. Rouse, Irving. 1982. Ceramic and religious development in the Greater Antilles. *Journal of New World Archaeology* 5(2):45–55. Los Angeles.

421. ———. 1989. Peopling and repeopling of the West Indies. In: *Biogeography of the West Indies: Past, Present, and Future.* C.A. Woods, ed. pp. 119–135. Gainesville: Sandhill Crane Press.

422. ———. 1992. *The Taínos: Rise and Decline of the People Who Greeted Columbus.* New Haven: Yale University Press. 211 p.

Using archaeological and ethnohistorical information to reconstruct fifteenth-century Taíno society; discussion of the antecedents of the Taíno, the voyages of Columbus, events of European contact with the Taíno, and early Spanish perceptions of Taíno art and religion.

Subsistence Patterns

423. Roumain, Jacques. 1942. *Contribution a l'étude de l'ethnobotanique precolombienne des Grandes Antilles.* Bureau d'Ethnologie de la République d'Haiti, Bulletin no. 1. Port-au-Prince. 72 p.

Systematic botanical identification of plants mentioned in early sources or known from archaeological contexts; includes table of Taíno, vernacular, and scientific designations.

Demography

424. Danubio, Maria E. 1987. The decline of the Taínos: critical revision of the demographical-historical sources. *International Journal of Anthropology* 3(2):241–248.

425. ———. 1991. L'impatto demografico della colonizzazione ad Hispaniola. *L'Universo, Supplemento* 1:28–32. Firenze.

426. Rosenblat, Angel. 1976. The population of Hispaniola at the time of Columbus. In: *The Native Population of the Americas in 1492.* W.M. Denevan, ed. pp. 43–66. Madison: University of Wisconsin Press.

Physical Anthropology

427. Morales Patiño, Oswaldo. 1952. El médico-hechicero entre las tribus indoamericanas. *Congreso Histórico Municipal Interamericano (5 session, Ciudad Trujillo, 1952), Memoria* 1:133–147. Ciudad Trujillo.

Political Organization

428. Vega, Bernardo. 1987. *Los cacicazgos de la Hispaniola.* 2 ed. Santo Domingo: Fundación Cultural Dominicana. 88 p.

Religious Organization

429. Arrom, Juan J. 1990. Presuntos ritos atribuidos a los indígenas de Cuba, de Jamaica y Puerto Rico. *Museo del Hombre Dominicano, Boletín* 23:119–126. Santo Domingo.

Discussion of marriage rituals in Cuba as well as human sacrifice and the ball game in Jamaica and Puerto Rico, using historical sources.

430.   Caro Alvarez, José A. 1977. *La cohoba*. Santo Domingo: Museo del Hombre Dominicano. 29 p.

Brief discussion of the cohoba ceremony with illustrations of *zemís*, *duhos*, and vomit spatulas assoiciated with this ritual; see also, M.A. García Arevalo, *Las espatulas vomicas sonajeras de la cultura taína* (Museo del Hombre Dominicano, Colección Investigaciones, no. 4. Santo Domingo, 1976. 55 p.).

431.   Hostos, Adolfo de. 1965. Plant fertilization by magic in the Taíno area of the Greater Antilles. *Caribbean Studies* 5(1):3–5. Río Piedras, Puerto Rico.

432.   Morales Patiño, Oswaldo. 1937. La religion de los indígenas antillanos. *Congreso Histórico Municipal Interamericano (1 session, La Habana, 1937), Actas y Documentos* 1:292–332. La Habana.

Mythology

433.   Arrom, José J. 1971. El mundo mítico de los taínos. *Revista Dominicana de Arqueología y Antropología* 1:181–200. Santo Domingo.

Discussion of a 1525 manuscript by German Pérez de Oliva which identifies and describes three Arawak deities; important for the identification of archaeological figures from the eastern West Indies.

434.   ———. 1972. De como se poblaron las Antillas: glosas etnolinguisticas a un ciclo mítico taíno. *Instituto de Cultura Puertorriqueña, Revista* 15(57):1–8. San Juan.

Commentary on a Taíno myth.

435.   ———. 1973. Mitos taínos en las letras de Cuba, Santo Domingo y México. *Museo del Hombre Dominicano, Boletín* 3:285–299. Santo Domingo.

436.   ———. 1980. Taíno mythology: notes on the supreme being. *Latin American Literary Review* 8(16):21–37. Pittsburgh.

Author examines the meaning of the 'supreme being' (*Yucahu Bagua Maorocoti*) in Taíno mythology and contends that the tri-cornered *zemí* is a representation of the supreme being; see also, G. Crespo, *How the Sea Began: A Taíno Myth* (New York: Clarion Books, 1993) for a retelling of a story collected by Ramón Pane in which a gourd containing the bow and arrow of the great departed hunter Yayael produces a torrent of water that becomes the world's ocean.

437. Deive, Carlos E. 1978. Los Taínos y la leyenda de las Amazonas. *Museo del Hombre Dominicano, Boletín* 7(10):253–270. Santo Domingo.

438. Fernández Méndez, Eugenio. 1979. *Arte y mitología de los indios taínos de las Antillas Mayores.* San Juan: Ediciones CEMI. 109 p.

Discussion of the art and mythology of the Taíno; author explores relationship of Taíno cosmology with that of the Intermediate Area and Mesoamerica; see also, E. Fernández Mendez, *Art and Mythology of the Taíno Indians of the Greater West Indies* (San Juan, Puerto Rico: El Cerni, 1972. 95 p.).

439. García Arévalo, Manuel A. 1984. Murciélago en la mitología y el arte taíno. *Museo del Hombre Dominicano, Boletín* 19:45–55. Santo Domingo.

440. López-Baralt, Mercedes. 1976. *El mito taíno: raíz y proyecciones en la Amazonia continental.* Buenos Aires: Ediciones Huracán; Río Piedras, Puerto Rico: Ediciones Huracán, 1990. 108 p.

Examination of relationships in the mythology of insular and mainland Arawak; see also, M. López-Baralt, *El mito taíno: Levi-Strauss en las Antillas* (Río Piedras, Puerto Rico: Ediciones Huracán, 1985. 158 p.).

441. Morales Patiño, Oswaldo. 1946. La mítica indoantillana del tabaco. *Revista de Arqueología y Etnología* 1(1):57–88. La Habana.

442. Orsini Luiggi, Sadi. 1974. *Canto al cemí: leyendas y mitos taínos.* San Juan de Puerto Rico: Instituto de Cultura Puertorriqueña. 80 p.

443. Pérez Memén, Fernando. 1987. Pensamiento mítico taíno en comparación con el de las viejas culturas orientales: los origenes de nuestra idea del mundo. *Museo del Hombre Dominicano, Boletín* 20:121–133. Santo Domingo.

444. Stevens-Arroyo, Antonio M. 1984. A Taíno tale: a mythological statement of social order. *Caribbean Review* 13(4):24–26. Miami.

Using an interpretive methodology from the study of comparative religion, including Levi-Strauss's structural analyses of South American mythology and Jungian psychology, author presents an excellent and readable reconstruction of Taíno mythology and social structure; probably the most detailed examination of Taíno mythology, religion, and world view.

445.   ———. 1988. *Cave of the Jagua: The Mythological World of the Taínos.* Albuquerque: University of New Mexico Press. 282 p.

446.   Vega, Bernardo. 1987. *Santos, shamanes y zemís.* Santo Domingo: Fundación Cultural Dominicana.

Cohoba

447.   Alcina Franch, José. 1982. Religiosidad, alucinógenos y patrones artísticos taínos. *Museo del Hombre Dominicano, Boletín* 10(17):103–118. Santo Domingo.

Author argues that Taíno art was influenced by hallucinogens used in religious rituals (*cohoba*).

Ball Game

448.   García Goyco, Isvaldo. 1984. *Influencias mayas y aztecas en los taínos de las Antillas Mayores: el juego de pelota al arte y la mitología.* San Juan, Puerto Rico: Ediciones Xibalbay. 130 p.

The Caribbean ball game was described by Oviedo y Valdés shortly after the conquest (213). It was played in courts or plazas by two teams of players pitted against each other. A heavy ball was bounced and kept in the air, without the use of hands or feet. As in Mesoamerica, this was done by striking the ball with the hips. Gordon F. Ekholm (1100) has argued that the so-called stone collars either represent or were devices that were worn around the hips of the players for protection on striking the ball. Other stones, the elbow stones, appear to represent only the bosses and decorated sections of complete collars. Ekholm has also argued that three-pointed stones may have been related to the game as well. According to Ekholm, one side was lashed to a wooden belt and the three-pointed stone served as a striking point of the belt similar to the boss of the stone collars.

The hypothesis is of interest since it indicates an extraordinary integration of most of the Taíno or Chicoid subtradition high art with the ball game. This together with the importance of the plazas or courts in the major sites would seem to elevate the status of the game to the primary ceremonial-religious and social integrative force in protohistoric Caribbean society. In addition, this interpretation of the stone paraphernalia would help throw light on the historical origins of the game in the West Indies. Ekholm argues for a direct relationship between the islands and Mesoamerica. Rouse (1056) argues that the presence of the three-pointed stones offers an early beginning for one of the central themes in Caribbean art.

449. Russell, A.D. 1926. Stone collars and elbow stones. *Man* 26:213–216. London.

Material Culture

Art

450. Arrom, José Juan. 1988. *El murcielago y la lechuza en la cultura taína*. Santo Domingo: Ediciones Fundación García-Arevalo. 59 p.

Study of the significance of bats and owls in Taíno art, especially pottery.

451. Fernández Méndez, Eugenio. 1972. *Art and Mythology of the Taíno Indians of the Greater West Indies*. San Juan: Ediciones El Cemí. 95 p.

Author explores the similarities of art forms and mythology of the West Indies to those of Mesoamerica; argues diffusion is evident in mythology, Taíno art and symbolism, deities, and the ball game.

452. García-Arevalo, Manuel A. 1989. *Los signos en el arte taíno*. Santo Domingo: Fundación García-Arevalo. 39 p.

Study of symbolism in Taíno art.

453. Herrera Fritot, René. 1952. Arqueotipos zoomorfos en las Antillas Mayores. *Revista de Arqueología y Etnología* 7:215–226. La Habana.

Survey of zoomorphic and anthropomorphic designs in the archaeology of the Greater Antilles; in Cuba they are associated with Taíno assemblages.

454. Jiménez Lambertus, Abelardo. 1978. Representación simbólica de la tortuga mítica en el arte cerámico taíno. *Museo del Hombre Dominicano, Boletín* 7(11):63–76. Santo Domingo.

Discussion of the importance of the turtle in Taíno mythology and material culture

455. Salazar, Tula. 1990. El diseño taíno y su integración en los proyectos artesanales. *Museo del Hombre Dominicano, Boletín* 23:129–140. Santo Domingo.

456. Torres, Constantino M. 1988. *Taíno; los descubridores de Colón; exposición del 17 de noviembre de 1988 al 31 de julio de 1989*. Santiago de Chile: Museo Chileno de Arte Precolombino. 47 p.

Exhibition of Taíno antiquities sponsored by the Banco Exterior S.A. Chile and the Embassy of Spain.

457.   Vega, Bernardo. 1987. *Arte neotaíno*. Santo Domingo: Fundación García-Arévalo.

Pottery

458.   Bullen, Ripley P. 1959. Similarities in pottery decoration from Florida, Cuba, and the Bahamas. *International Congress of Americanists (33 session, San Jose, 1958), Proceedings* 2:107–110. San Jose.

Argues that West Indies and Florida cultures developed independently.

459.   Cartagena Portalatin, Aida. 1972. *Dos técnicas cerámicas indoantillanas: diagnóstico de orígén de los yacimientos de las Antillas Mayores*. Santo Domingo: Universidad Autonoma de Santo Domingo, Facultad de Humanidades, Instituto Dominicano de Antropología. 22 p.

Summary description of prehispanic pottery from Haiti and Dominican Republic.

Cordage and Textiles

460.   Alfan Núñez, Reina E. 1973. La industria textil y la cordelería aborigen en la isla Española. *Museo del Hombre Dominicano, Boletín* 3:92–104. Santo Domingo.

Intellectual Life

Astronomy

461.   Allaire, Louis. 1981. The Saurian pineal eye in Antillean art and mythology. *Journal of Latin American Lore* 7(1):3–22. Los Angeles.

462.   Robiou-Lamarche, Sebastián. 1983. Del mito al tiempo sagrado: un posible calendario agrícola-ceremonial taíno. *Museo del Hombre Dominicano, Boletín* 11(18):117–140. Santo Domingo.

Author argues that the sun and moon, Pleiades, Orion, and Venus, were important in Taíno mythology; ceremonial plazas and artifacts from several locations suggest that a complex agricultural-ceremonial calendar was operative in Taíno society.

463.   ———. 1984. Astronomy in Taíno mythology. *Archaeoastronomy* 7(1–4):110–115.

464.   ———. 1987. Panorama de la astronomía indígena en las Antillas. *Museo del Hombre Dominicano, Boletín* 14(20):83–91. Santo Domingo.

Discussion of astronomical symbolism is Taíno mythology and possibility of the use of a solar calendar based on archaeological features at ceremonial sites in Puerto Rico and the Dominican Republic.

465.   ———. 1988. Astronomía primitiva entre los taínos y los caribes de las Antillas. In: *New Directions in American Archaeoastronomy.* A.F. Aveni, ed. pp. 121–141. British Archaeological Reports, International Series, v. 454. Oxford, England.

466.   ———. 1989. Mitología y astronomía Caribe según los cronistas Franceses y el Dictionaire Caraibe-Francais del Padre Raymond Breton (1665). *Museo del Hombre Dominicano, Boletín* 22:199–222. Santo Domingo.

Calendar

467.   Escabi Agostini, Petro C. 1985. Pintadera calendaria antillana. *Revista de Ciencias Sociales* 24(1–2):291–298. Río Piedras, Puerto Rico.

Illustration of a Taíno clay stamp, possibly a precolumbian calendrical device; author infers a calendar of 19 months and 359 days.

BAHAMAS

(Capital: Nassau)

The Bahamas is an archipelago of some 700 islands, 2,000 cays (keys), and innumerable reefs, scattered over 1,200 km of the Atlantic Ocean. The archipelago extends from about 80 km east of the southern coast of Florida past the northern coast of Cuba to within 112 km of Haiti. Most of the islands are narrow and rocky with shallow soil. The climate is subtropical and tropical and temperate zone forests grow side by side. Some original pine forests still exist on Abaco, Andros, and Grand Bahama islands.

Although Columbus made his landfall on San Salvador (Watling Island) in 1492, Spain made no use of the Bahamas except to enslave and deport the Arawak-speaking inhabitants.

General

468. Booy, Theodoor H.N. de. 1912. Lucayan remains on the Caicos Islands. *American Anthropologist* 14(1):81–105. Washington, DC.

Summary of excavations on the island of Providenciales, Ambergris Cay, North Caicos Island, and Grand Caicos Island.

469. Granberry, Julian. 1953. A Survey of Bahamian Archaeology. M.A. thesis, Department of Anthropology, University of Florida, Gainesville.

470. Keegan William F. 1992. *The People Who Discovered Columbus: The Prehistory of the Bahamas.* Gainesville: University Press of Florida. 279 p.

Author provides a historical reconstruction of the population movement into the Bahamas, a description of the islands during early Taíno settlement, and an analysis of the social organization, subsistence systems, and demography of the Lucayans at the time of the arrival of the Spaniards. A good overview of Caribbean prehistory is provided.

Figure 8.
Shell pendant, Finca Caridad, Maisi, Cuba.

Source: M.R. Harrington, *Cuba Before Columbus,*
Museum of the American Indian, Heye Foundation, Indian Notes and
Monographs, no. 17. New York, 1921. Figure 62.

471.   Richards, Douglas G. 1988. Archaeological anomalies in the
Bahamas. *Journal of Scientific Exploration* 2:181–201.

Bibliography

472.   Granberry, Julian. 1988. *A Bibliography of Bahamian Prehistory.* 2
ed. Nassau: Bahamas Archaeological Team. 14 p.

Bibliography of published works on Bahamian archaeology and
prehistory to 1988.

Museum Collections

473.   Keegan, William F., Dave D. Davis, and Herman J. Viola. 1992.
Beachhead in the Bahamas. *Archaeology* 45(1):44–59. New York.

Discussion of Christopher Columbus' landing on Watling Island
and the subsequent destruction of the Taíno, as well as a future

exhibition at the Smithsonian Institution's National Museum of
Natural History featuring the transfer of plants, animals, diseases, and
people resulting from the events of 1492.

History of Archaeological Research

474.   Granberry, Julian. 1956. The cultural position of the Bahamas in
        Caribbean archaeology. *American Antiquity* 22(2):128–134.
        Washington, DC.

        Discussion of archaeological surveys carried out in the Bahamas
between 1887 and 1955.

475.   ———. 1980. A brief history of Bahamian archaeology. *Florida
        Anthropologist* 33(3):83–93. Gainesville.

        Description of archaeological research conducted in the Bahamas,
Turks, and Caicos Islands since the late 1880s.

476.   Keegan, William F. 1988. New directions in Bahamian
        archaeology. *Bahamas Historical Society, Journal* 10:3–8. Nassau.

        Examination of the types of archaeological study needed in the
Bahamas, including studies in colonization, pottery, and subsistence
patterns.

Environment

477.   Mitchell, Steven W., and William F. Keegan. 1987.
        Reconstruction of the coastline of the Bahamas Islands in 1492.
        American Archaeology 6(2):88–96. Albuquerque.

Ethnohistory

478.   Córdova, Efrén. 1968. La encomienda y la desaparición de los
        indios en las Antillas Mayores. *Caribbean Studies* 8(3):23–49. Río
        Piedras, Puerto Rico.

479.   Granberry, Julian. 1979–1981. Spanish slave trade in the
        Bahamas, 1509–1530: an aspect of the Caribbean pearl industry.
        Bahamas Historical Society, Journal 1:14–15, 2:15–17, 3:17–19.
        Nassau.

        Examination of the role of Lucayan Indians in the pearl industry
centered on the island of Cubagua, off the northwest coast of
Venezuela.

480.   Keegan, William F. 1984. Columbus and the City of Gold. *Bahamas Historical Society, Journal* 6:34–39. Nassau.

481.   ———, and Steven W. Mitchell. 1987. The archaeology of Christopher Columbus' voyage through the Bahamas. *American Archaeology* 6(2):102–108. Albuquerque.

482.   Rouse, Irving. 1987. Whom did Columbus discover in the West Indies? *American Archaeology* 6(2): 83–87. Albuquerque.

483.   Varnhagen, Francisco A. de. 1864. La verdadera Guahani de Colon. *Universidad de Chile, Anales* 24:1–20.

484.   Williams, John A. 1987. Searching for a name and a theme. *American Archaeology* 6(2):113–118. Albuquerque.

Reflections on the significance of the Columbian Quincentennial.

Historical Archaeology

485.   De Vorsey, Louis, and John Parker. 1985. *In the Wake of Columbus: Islands and Controversy*. Detroit: Wayne State University. 231 p.

Collection of articles and texts dealing with the Columbus landfall in the Bahamas; contents include: J. Parker, The Columbus landfall problem (pp 1–28); P. Verhoog, Columbus landed on Caicos (pp. 29–34); O. Dunn, Columbus's first landing place (pp. 33–50); R.H. Fuson, The diario de Colon, a legacy of poor transcription, translation, and interpretation (pp. 51–75); J.E. Kelley, In the wake of Columbus on a portolan chart (pp. 77–111); A.B. Molander, A new approach to the Columbus landfall (pp. 113–149); R.H. Power, The discovery of Columbus's island passage to Cuba, October 12–27, 1492 (pp. 151–172); O. Dunn, The diario, or journal, of Columbus's first voyage (pp. 173–231).

Some selected additional literature pertaining to the landfall of Columbus include: T.H.N. de Booy, On the possibility of determining the first landfall of Columbus by archaeological research (*Hispanic American Historical Review* 2:55–61, 1919); E. Doran, This Columbus-Caicos confusion (*Professional Geographer* 13(4):32–34, 1961); R.H. Fuson, Caicos: site of Columbus's landfall (*Professional Geographer* 13(2):6–9, 1961); R.H. Fuson, Caicos, confusion, conclusion (*Professional Geographer* 13(5):35–37, 1961); J. Judge,

Where Columbus found the New World (*National Geographic Magazine* 170(5):566–599, 1986); E.A. Link and M.C. Link, *A New Theory on Columbus's Voyage Through the Bahamas* (Smithsonian Institution, Miscellaneous Collections, no. 135. Washington, DC, 1958); L. Marden, The first landfall of Columbus (*National Geographic Magazine* 170:572–577, 1986); A.B. Molander, Columbus landed here, or did he? (*Américas* 33:3–7, 1981); J.B. Murdock, The cruise of Columbus in the Bahamas, 1492 (*U.S. Naval Institute, Proceedings* April:449–486, 1884); A.R. Pérez, *The Columbus Landfall in America and the Hidden Clues in His Journal* (Washington, DC: Abbe, 1987).

486. Gerace, Donald T., ed. 1987. *Columbus and His World: Proceedings of the First San Salvador Conference.* Fort Lauderdale: College Center of the Finger Lakes, Bahamian Field Station. 359 p.

Proceedings of the first San Salvador Conference held in 1986 contains a variety of essays by historians and archaeologists; the majority are concerned with arguments about the identity of Columbus, the site of his first landfall, and his psychological makeup; contents include: C. Varela, Florentines' friendship and kinship with Christopher Columbus (pp. 33–43); D.C. West, Scholarly encounters with Columbus's Libro de las Profecías (pp. 45–56); F. Provost, Columbus's seven years in Spain (pp. 57–68); C.R. Phillips, Spanish ships in the Age of Discovery (pp. 69–98); G. Ferro, Columbus and his sailings (pp. 99–113); C.A. Charlier, Value of the mile (pp. 115–120); J.E. Kelley, The navigation of Columbus (pp. 121–140); A.B. Molander, Egg Island is the landfall (pp. 141–171); R.H. Fuson, The Turks and Caicos Islands as possible landfall sites (pp. 173–184); M. Obregón, Columbus's first landfall: San Salvador (pp. 185–195); P.A. Taviani, Why we are favorable for Watlings (pp. 197–212); D.T. Gerace, Additional comments relating to Watlings Island to San Salvador (pp. 229–235); C.A. Hoffman, Archaeological investigations at the Long Bay Site, San Salvador, Bahamas (pp. 237–245); R.H. Brill, I.L. Barnes, S.S.C. Tong, E.C. Joel, and M.J. Murtaugh, Laboratory studies of some European artifacts excavated on San Salvador Island (pp. 247–292); I. Rouse, Origin and development of the Indians discovered by Columbus (pp. 293–311); J. Winter, San Salvador in 1492: its geography and ecology (pp. 313–320); R. Rose, Lucayan lifeways at the time of Columbus (pp. 321–339); K.A. Deagan, Initial encounters: Arawak responses to European contact at the En Bas Saline Site, Haiti (pp. 341–359).

Cultural Evolution and Society

Cultural Evolution and Development

487.   Hoffman, Charles A. 1967. Bahama Prehistory: Cultural Adaptation to an Island Environment. Ph.D. dissertation, Department of Anthropology, University of Arizona, Tucson. 153 p.

488.   Keegan, William F. 1985. Dynamic Horticulturalists: Population Expansion in the Prehistoric Bahamas. Ph.D. dissertation, Department of Anthropology, University of California, Los Angeles. 376 p.

The prehistory of the Bahamas is used to examine the spatial expansion of a growing population; resource supply and changes in production are identified using ethnohistorical, ecological, and archaeological sources of evidence; changes in supply are linked to changes in demand, documented with settlement pattern evidence for spatial expansion and population growth; author concludes that the population of the Bahamas grew rapidly, spread quickly at low densities, and that production expanded in a predicted direction.

489.   ———, and Steven W. Mitchell. 1986. Possible allochthonous Lucayan Arawak artifact distributions: Bahama Islands. *Journal of Field Archaeology* 13(3):255–258. Boston.

Rootgrafting and historical redistribution of artifact-bearing deposits are seen as significant for accurate settlement pattern and exchange network reconstruction.

490.   Rouse, Irving. 1980. The concept of series in Bahamian archaeology. *Florida Anthropologist* 33(3):94–98. Gainesville.

Discussion of the series concept in Caribbean prehistory using examples from Bahamian archaeology.

491.   Sears, William H., and Shaun O. Sullivan. 1978. Bahamas prehistory. *American Antiquity* 43(1):3–25. Washington, DC.

Excavations indicate Antillean Lucayans migrated to the central Bahamas at A.D. 800–1000 in search of concentrations of crystalline salt and shellfish; authors argue that cultural expansion throughout the Bahamas was primarily limited by temperature and rainfall requirements of manioc agriculture.

Economic Organization

492.   Daggett, Richard E. 1980. The trade process and the implications of trade in the Bahamas. *Florida Anthropologist* 33(3):143–151. Gainesville.

Examination of the various types of prehispanic commerce and their impact in the Bahamas.

Subsistence Patterns

493.   Keegan, William F. 1986. The ecology of Lucayan fishing practices. *American Antiquity* 51(4):816–825. Washington, DC.

Synthesis of ecological, archaeological, ethnographic, and historical evidence for prehistoric fishing practices in the Bahama archipelago; see also, W.F. Keegan, Lucayan fishing practices: an experimental approach (*Florida Anthropologist* 35(4):146–161, 1982), for a discussion of Lucayan subsistence living and fishing practices; author replicates fishing practices using Haitian-style basketry fish traps; includes a list of fish species captured in tidal flat and reef environments.

494.   ———, and Michael J. De Niro. 1988. Stable carbon and nitrogen isotope ratios used to study coral reef and terrestrial components of prehistoric Bahamian diet. *American Antiquity* 53(2):320–336. Washington, DC.

Reconstruction of terrestrial and marine coastal diets by the prehispanic Lucayan Taíno.

495.   Maynard, Charles J. 1893. Traces of the Lucayan Indians in the Bahamas. In: *Contributions to Science*, v. 2, pp. 23–34. Newtonville, Massachusetts.

Discussion of water wells and hand axes used by Lucayans to remove conch meat from its shell.

Demography

496.   Krieger, Herbert W. 1937. The Bahama Islands and their prehistoric population. *Smithsonian Institution, Explorations and Fieldwork* 1936:893–98. Washington, DC.

Physical Anthropology

497.   Brooks, William K. 1889. On the Lucayan Indians. *National Academy of Sciences, Memoirs* 4(2): 1–9. Washington, DC.

Brief introduction to Lucayan Indians and examination of three Lucayan skulls.

498.   Keegan, William F. 1982. Lucayan cave burials from the Bahamas. *Journal of New World Archaeology* 5(2):57–65. Los Angeles.

Information on skeletal collections from Freeport and six other islands in the Bahamas is used to reconstruct Lucayan mortuary practices; includes a summary of twenty-two skeletal remains now housed at the Yale Peabody Museum.

Social Organization

499.   ———, and Morgan D. Maclachlan. 1989. Evolution of avunculocal chiefdoms: a reconstruction of Taíno kinship and politics. *American Anthropologist* 91(3):613–630. Washington, DC.

Examination of prehistoric settlement systems of the Lucayan Taíno of the Bahamas; study involves archaeological consideration of Taíno kinship, and the politics and evolution of avunculocal chiefdoms; see also: M. Maclachlan and W.F. Keegan, Archaeology and ethno-tyrannies (*American Anthropologist* 92:1011–1013, 1990).

Material Culture

Art

500.   Booy, Theodoor H.N. de. 1913. Lucayan artifacts from the Bahamas. *Museum of the American Indian, Heye Foundation, Contributions* 1(1):1–7. New York; *American Anthropologist* 15(1):1–7, 1913. Washington, DC.

Description of a wooden paddle from Mores Island, a cay on the Little Bahama Bank; petroglyphs found in a cave on Rum Cay; a wooden stool (*duho*) from a cave at Spring Point on Acklins Island; and a ceremonial celt from Mariguana Island.

Regional and Site Reports

Andros Island

501.   Goggin, John M. 1939. An anthropological reconnaissance of Andros Island, Bahamas. *American Antiquity* 5(1):21–26. Washington, DC

Report on archaeological and ethnographic work done on Andros Island; no Lucayan sites were found and it was concluded that the island was sparsely populated in prehistoric times.

Fehling

502.   Keegan, William F., and Neil E. Sealey. 1988. A preliminary archaeological survey of the Fehling Site (An-1), Andros, Bahamas. *Florida Museum of Natural History, Miscellaneous Project Report Series*, no. 40. Gainesville. 14 p.

Report on a surface survey at the Fehling Site; author notes a high frequency of decorated and other imported ceramics.

Bimini Island

503.   Granberry, Julian. 1957. An anthropological reconnaissance of Bimini, Bahamas. *American Antiquity* 22(4):378–381. Washington, DC.

Results of an archaeological survey of Bimini in 1955 in search of pre-ceramic, pre-Arawak sites.

Cat Island

504.   MacLaury, James C. 1968. Archaeological Investigations on Cat Island, Bahamas. M.A. thesis, Department of Anthropology, Florida Atlantic University, Boca Raton.

505.   MacLaury, James C. 1970. Archaeological investigations on Cat Island, Bahamas. *University of Florida, Contributions of the Florida State Museum: Social Sciences* 16:27–50. Gainesville.

Cat Island was first inhabited between A.D. 1000 and 1500; shell, lithic, and pottery artifacts described in this monograph were excavated from eighteen different sites.

Crooked Island

506.   Keegan, William F. 1988. Archaeological investigations on Crooked and Acklins Islands, Bahamas: a preliminary report of the 1987 field season. *Florida Museum of Natural History, Miscellaneous Project Report Series*, no. 36. Gainesville.

Gordon Hill
507.   Granberry, Julian. 1978. The Gordon Hill site, Crooked Island, Bahamas. *Virgin Islands Archaeological Society, Journal* 6:32–44. St. Thomas.

Report on Froelich G. Rainey's 1934 excavation on the island and argues that Rainey's findings provide a basis for reconstructing Bahamian cultural history.

Eleuthera Island

508.   Sullivan, Shaun D. 1974. Archaeological Reconnaissance of Eleuthera, Bahamas. M.A. thesis, Department of Anthropology, Florida Atlantic University, Boca Raton. 73 p.

Results of an archaeological reconnaissance of Eleuthera, Harbor Island, and St. George's Cay; some 15 open village sites were found on Eleuthera; examination of material culture from surface collections and excavation, as well as settlement patterning, suggests little stratification and a relatively unproductive economic system.

Highborn Cay

509.   Smith, Roger C., Donald Keith, and Denise Lakey. 1985. The Highborn Cay wreck: further exploration of sixteenth-century Bahamian shipwreck. *International Journal of Nautical Archaeology and Underwater Exploration* 14(1):63–72. London.

Summary of research at a sixteenth-century Spanish wreck at Highborn Cay, Bahamas.

New Providence Island

Clifton Pier Rockshelter
510.   Winter, John. 1978. The Clifton Pier Rockshelter, New Providence, Bahamas. *Virgin Islands Archaeological Society, Journal* 6:45–48. St. Thomas.

Rum Cay

511.   Maynard, Charles J. 1890. Some inscriptions found in Hartford Cave, Rum Cay, Bahamas. In: *Contributions to Science*, v. 1, pp. 167–171. Newtonville, Massachusetts.

San Salvador Island

512. Mann, John C. 1986. Composition and origin of material in precolumbian pottery, San Salvador Island, Bahamas. *Geoarchaeology* 1(2):183–194. New York.

Thin section and x-ray defraction techniques are used to investigate the origins of Bahamian soil as well as clay and quartz bonds in shell temper.

513. Wing, Elizabeth S. 1969. Vertebrate remains excavated from San Salvador Island, Bahamas. *Caribbean Journal of Science* 9(102):25–28. Mayaguez, Puerto Rico.

Identification of fish and other bones from San Salvador Island; most of the fish identified are associated with coral reefs.

Long Bay

514. Hoffman, Charles A. 1987. The Long Bay Site, San Salvador. *American Archaeology* 6(2):97–101. Albuquerque.

Author reports on Long Bay, a Taíno village on the west coast of San Salvador Island, the site where Columbus first set foot in the New World; material culture recovered included a coin (ca. 1471–1474), European ceramics, glass beads, and metal buckles.

Palmetto Grove

515. Hoffman, Charles A. 1970. The Palmetto Grove Site on San Salvador, Bahamas. *University of Florida, Contributions of the Florida State Museum: Social Sciences* 16:1–26. Gainesville.

Summary report on archaeological investigations on San Salvador Island conducted to study relationships between prehistoric cultures and their environments; description of lithics, coral, bone, shell, and ceramics dating to A.D. 750–1200.

Pigeon Creek

516. Rose, Richard. 1982. The Pigeon Creek site, San Salvador, Bahamas. *Florida Anthropologist* 35(4):129–145. Gainesville.

Author presents results of investigations from the Pigeon Creek site, including chronology, ceramics, settlement, and subsistence.

TURKS AND CAICOS ISLANDS

(Capital: Grand Turk)

Geographically, these islands, of which there are about 30, are part of the Bahamas and lie at the southeast of the archipelago, 145 km north of the Dominican Republic and 725 km northeast of Jamaica. The total area of the Turks and Caicos Islands is about 275 sq km. The most important is Grand Turk, which is about 10.5 km long and 2.5 km wide. Grand Turk and Salt Cay, about 11 km to the southwest, are the only inhabited Turks Islands. They are separated from the Caicos group by a deep water channel, 35 km across. The islands are low, flat, and barren, their only vegetation bushes and stunted trees. They were visited about 1512 by Ponce de León but were never settled by the Spanish. Their first regular visitors were Bermudians in search of salt.

Cultural Evolution and Society

Cultural Evolution and Development

517. Sullivan, Shaun D. 1981. Prehistoric Patterns of Exploitation and Colonization in the Turks and Caicos Islands. Ph.D. dissertation, Department of Anthropology, University of Illinois, Urbana. 460 p.

An archaeological and environmental survey of the Turks and Caicos Islands by the author resulted in the identification of 43 prehistoric sites; analysis indicated the existence of two prehistoric cultural periods: the Antillean Period (ca. A.D. 750–950) was characterized by seasonal exploitation of the islands by Arawak from the Greater Antilles; the Lucayan Period (ca. A.D. 950–1500) was characterized by the establishment of large permanent villages and the development of intra-village social stratification; see also: M.A. Tromans, Temporal and Spatial Analysis of Two Antillean Period Sites, Middle Caicos, British West Indies (M.A. thesis, Florida Atlantic University. 89 p.).

107

Material Culture

Lithics

518. Campbell, Melfort. 1877. [Stone implements from Honduras and Turks and Caicos Islands exhibited.] *Royal Anthropological Institute of Great Britain and Ireland, Journal* 6:37–40. London.

Groundstone

519. Mason, Otis T. 1877. Jadeite celts from Turks and Caicos Islands, also two low wooden stools. *American Naturalist* 11:626. Chicago.

Regional and Site Reports

520. Sullivan, Shaun D. 1980. An overview of the 1976 to 1978 archaeological investigations in the Caicos Islands. *Florida Anthropologist* 33(3):94–98. Gainesville.

Summary of a site survey in Turks and Caicos; most sites date from A.D. 750–900; other sites had imported (Meillacoid) ceramics and one site was planned, exhibiting plazas, ball court, and distinct residential zones.

Molasses Reef Wreck

521. Keith, Donald H. 1987. The Molasses Reef Wreck. Ph.D. dissertation, Texas A & M University, College Station, Texas.

522. Keith, Donald H., J.A. Duff, S.R. James, T.J. Oertling, and J.J. Simmons. 1984. The Molasses Reef wreck, Turks and Caicos Islands, B.W.I.: a preliminary report. *International Journal of Nautical Archaeology and Underwater Exploration* 13:45–63.

523. Keith, Donald H., and J.J. Simmons. 1985. Analysis of hull remains, ballast and artifact distribution of a sixteenth-century shipwreck: Molasses Reef, British West Indies. *Journal of Field Archaeology* 12(4):411–424. Boston.

Report on excavation of a sixteenth-century Spanish shipwreck in the Turks and Caicos Islands.

CUBA
(Capital: La Habana)

Cuba, measuring 1,200 km in length and 40–290 km in width, is the largest island in the Caribbean Sea. It commands the main entry to the Gulf of Mexico and is less than 160 km south of the Florida Keys. The Isle of Pines and more than 1,600 keys and small islands are clustered around Cuba proper. The unusually varied terrain is mountainous and the Sierra Maestra and smaller parallel ranges dominate the eastern provinces of Oriente and Camagüey.

When Columbus landed on the island of Cuba in October 1492 it was inhabited by some 200,000 Ciboney and the Taíno-speaking Arawak Indians. Diego Velázquez, acting under authority granted by the Spanish Crown, brought the island under effective control by 1513 and, by 1515, seven Spanish towns had been founded. Cuba prospered until the 1550s. Considerable gold was found in the first few years, and farming was developed. The Spaniards applied the *encomienda* (a system of forced labor and tribute) to the Indians to make them work. Although this system, and the conquest itself, killed many, it was the diseases of the Europeans that most rapidly decimated the population.

General

524. Alvarez Conde, José. 1949. Fomento: nuevo centro de hallazgos arqueológicos indígenas. *Revista Trimestre* 3(2):1–20. La Habana.

   Report on the excavation of a midden (Ciboney) and cave burial (Guayabo Blanco) in central Cuba.

525. Alvarez Conde, José. 1956. *Arqueología indocubana*. La Habana: Junta Nacional de Arqueología y Etnología. 329 p.

   Illustrated overview of Cuban archaeology; includes biographical summaries.

526. Brinton, Daniel G. 1898. The archaeology of Cuba. *American Archaeologist* 10:253–256. Columbus, Ohio.

527. Coscullela, José A. 1922. La prehistoria de Cuba. *Sociedad Cubana de Historia Natural Felipe Poey, Memorias* 5:11–50. La Habana.

528.   ———. 1952. Puntos fundamentales de la prehistoria de Cuba. *Congreso Histórico Municipal Interamericano (1 session, La Habana, 1952), Actas y Documentos* 1:203–246.

529.   *Cuba arqueológica.* Santiago de Cuba: Editorial Oriente, 1978. 271 p.

530.   Dacal Mouré, Ramón, and Manuel Rivero. 1986. *Arqueología aborigen en Cuba.* La Habana: Editorial Gente Nueva. 176 p.

531.   Fewkes, Jesse W. 1904. Prehistoric culture of Cuba. *American Anthropologist* 6:585–598. Washington, DC.

532.   Guarch, José M. 1987. *Arqueología de Cuba: métodos y sistemas.* La Habana: Editorial Ciencias Sociales. 112 p.

533.   Harrington, Mark R. 1921. *Cuba Before Columbus.* Museum of the American Indian, Heye Foundation, Indian Notes and Monographs, no. 17. New York. 2 v.; *Cuba antes de Colón.* Colección de libros cubanos, v. 32. La Habana: Editora Cultural, 1935. 290 p.

Excellent and standard work on Cuban archaeology; contents include a summary of the history of archaeological research on Cuba (Miguel Rodríguez Ferrer, A. Poey, Ephraim G. Squier, Luis Montané, Carlos de La Torre, Stewart Culin, Jesse W. Fewkes, and Jose A. Coscullela), survey of private and museum collections of archaeological materials; and syntheses of the author's researches near Jauco, Monte Cristo and Ovando, Gran Tierra de Maya, village sites and caves at La Patana, Santiago, Pinar del Río, Portales de Guane, Remates, Cabo San Antonio, and the Viñales district.

534.   Herrera Fritot, René. 1946. Tres notas para la arqueología indocubana: Asas-sonajeros. *Revista de Arqueología y Etnografía* 1:37–51. La Habana.

535.   ———. 1956. Los complejos culturales indo-cubanos basados en la arqueología. *Instituto Nacional de Cultura, Revista* 1(2):16–21, 42–45. La Habana.

Illustrated summary of Cuban archaeology written in celebration of the opening of the Hall of Antillean Archaeology in the Palacio de Bellas Artes.

536.   Krieger, Herbert W. 1933. The early Indian cultures of Cuba. *Smithsonian Institution, Explorations and Fieldwork* 1932:49–52. Washington, DC.

537.   Morales Patiño, Oswaldo. 1939. *Dos ensayos arqueológicos: estudios de investigación científica; en Cuba, cienfuegos 1930–1931 en México, Yucatán, Valle de México, Oaxaca, dic. y enero 1939.* La Habana: Cultural S.A. 46 p.

538.   Morales Patiño, Oswaldo. 1952. Los indígenas en los primeros municipios cubanos. *Revista de Arqueología y Etnología* 7(13–14):368–387. La Habana.

539.   Núñez Jiménez, Antonio. 1963. *Cuba con la mochila al hombro.* La Habana: Unión de Escritores y Artistas de Cuba. 410 p.

Collection of essays describing various archaeological research in Cuba, including Arawak caves, mounds and village sites, and Ciboney remains.

540.   Poey, A. 1853. Cuban antiquities; a brief description of some relics founds in the island of Cuba. *American Ethnological Society, Transactions* 3:193–302. New York.

541.   Rivero de la Calle, Manuel. 1966. *Las culturas aborígenes de Cuba.* La Habana: Editorial Universitaria. 194 p.

Popularly written general account of prehistory of Cuba.

542.   Royo Guardia, Fernando. 1940. Algunas consideraciones sobre los ciboneyes. *Sociedad Cubana de Historia Natural Felipe Poey, Memorias* 14(2):107–111. La Habana.

543.   Tabio, Ernesto E., and Estrella Rey. 1979. *Prehistoria de Cuba.* 2 ed. Ciudad de La Habana: Editorial de Ciencias Sociales. 234 p.

Excellent summary of Cuban archaeology reviewed in five sequential periods (Ciboney [Guayabo Blanco and Cayo Redondo], Mayarí, Subtaíno, and Taíno); revision of: *Prehistoria de Cuba.* La Habana: Departamento de Antropología, Academia de Ciencias de Cuba, 1966. 280 p.

Museum Collections

544.   Herrera Fritot, René. 1942. Falsificaciones de objetos aborígenes cubanos. *Sociedad Cubana de Historia Natural, Memorias* 16(1):13–38. La Habana.

Colección Fornaguera

545.   La Colección Fornaguera. *Revista de Arqueología y Etnología* 3(6–7):99–107, 1949. La Habana.

Colección García Feria

546.   García Castañeda, José A. 1940. Asiento pesquero, colección García Feria. *Revista de Arqueología* 1(4):56–60. La Habana.

547.   García Castañeda, José A. 1942. *La Colección arqueológica García Feria y las colecciones arqueologicas privadas.* Holguín: Museo García Feria. 11 p.

Colección García y Grave de Peralta

548.   Morales Patiño, Oswaldo, and Fernando Royo García. 1949. La colección del Sr. Fernando García y Grave de Peralta (Santiago de Cuba). *Revista de Arqueología y Etnología* 4(8–9):98–110. La Habana.

Illustrated description of objects collected by García y Grave de Peralta.

Museo Guama

549.   Morales Patiño, Oswaldo. 1948. Ejemplares únicos y ejemplares escasos de la arqueología indocubana en el Museo Guamá. *Revista de Arqueología y Etnología* 3(6–7):55–90. La Habana.

Museo Montané

550.   Herrera Fritot, Rene. 1940. Un nuevo dujo taíno en las colecciones del Museo Antropológico Montané, de la Universidad de la Habana; descripción y estudio comparativo. *Revista de Arqueología* 1(4):26–31. La Habana.

551.   Stépánek, Paval. 1966. El Museo Antropológico Montané en La Habana. *Terra Ameriga* 2(3):30–32. Genoa.

Description of four wood and stone carvings.

History of Archaeological Research

552.   Cosculluela, José A. 1946. Prehistoric cultures of Cuba. *American Antiquity* 12(1):10–18. Washington, DC.

Review of archaeological history of Cuba.

553.   Cosculluela, José A. 1951. Cuatro años en la Ciénaga de Zapata. *Revista de Arqueología y Etnología* 6(12):31–168. La Habana.

Republication of an important report describing the author's three years work as an engineer in the Ciénaga de Zapata where he excavated several sites, including the shell mound at Guayabo Blanco.

554.   Febres Cordero G., Julio. 1950. Balance del indigenismo en
       Cuba. *Revista de la Biblioteca Nacional* 1(4):61–204. La Habana.
       Evaluative summary of research on ancient Cuba.

555.   García y Grave de Peralta, Fernando. 1938–1952. Excursiones
       arqueológicas. *Revista de Arqueología* 1(1):20–31; 1(3):23–31;
       2(4):32–51; 2(5):35–67; 4(8–9):48–97; 5(10–11):35–67; 7(13–
       14):36–98; 7(15–16):31–92. La Habana.
       Summary of archaeological investigations in eastern Cuba.

556.   García Molina, José A. 1988. El grupo Guamá en la cultura
       cubana. *Temas* 16:137–157.

Historical examination of the Guamá Group, an organization
created in the first half of the twentieth century to undertake
archaeological research in Cuba.

557.   García Robiou, Carlos. 1942. Estado actual de la arqueología en
       Cuba; sugestiones para su desenvolvimiento ulterior. *American
       Scientific Congress (8 session, Washington, DC, 1940), Proceedings*
       2:139–140. Washington, DC.

558.   García Valdés, Pedro. 1947. Una contribución más al estudio de
       la prehistoria de Cuba. *Revista de Arqueología y Etnología* 2(4–
       05):169–179. La Habana.

559.   Morales Patiño, Oswaldo. 1947. Arqueología cubana: resumen
       de actividades durante el año 1946. *Revista de Arqueología y
       Etnología* 2(4–5):5–32. La Habana.

Continued by: Arqueología cubana: compendio cronológico de
actividades sobre arqueología y etnología durante el año 1947 en
Cuba (*Revista de Arqueología y Etnología* 3(6–7):5–36, 1948);
Arqueología cubana: resumen de actividades durante el año de 1948
(*Revista de Arqueología y Etnología* 4(8–9):5–48, 1948); Arqueología
cubana: relación de actividades durante el año 1949 (*Revista de
Arqueología y Etnología* 5(10–11):5–34, 1950); Arqueología cubana;
relación de actividades durante el año 1950 (*Revista de Arqueología y
Etnología* 7(13–14):8–35, 1951); Arqueología colonial cubana;
resumen de actividades durante el año 1951 (*Revista de Arqueología y
Etnología* 7(15–16):5–30, 1952).

560.   Ortiz, Fernando. 1922. *Historia de la arqueología indocubana*. La
       Habana: Imprenta El Siglo XX. 109 p.

A fundamental, although dated, work on the archaeology of Cuba; F. Ortiz, *Historia de la arqueología indocubana* (2 ed. Colección de Libros Cubanos, v. 33. La Habana: Editorial Cultural, 1936. 457 p.)

Biography

561. Alvarez Conde, José. 1951. *Carlos de la Torre; su vida y su obra.* La Habana: El Siglo XX. 233 p.

Biography of an important Cuban nationalist and educator; includes an account of an 1890 trip to collect archaeological materials in Puerto Rico and eastern Cuba.

562. Morales Patiño, Oswaldo. 1951. Cosculluela. *Revista de Arqueología y Etnología* 6(12):16–27. La Habana.

Biography of José A. Coscullela, an important Cuban archaeologist.

Environment

563. Aguayo, C. Guillermo. 1950. Observaciones sobre algunos mamíferos cubanos extinguidos. *Sociedad Cubana de Historia Natural Felipe Poey, Boletín* 1(3):121–134. La Habana.

Review of evidence for the association of extinct sloths and insectivores with the Indians of Cuba; author suggests that the Indians may have been responsible for the extinction of these mammals.

564. Alvarez Conde, José. 1951. *Los perezosos cubanos; sus relaciones con el indio.* La Habana: La Milagrosa. 16 p.

Summary of research on ground sloths of Cuba; argues that Ciboney hunted these animals and were extinct by Taíno times.

565. ———. 1961. *Historia de la geografía de Cuba.* La Habana: Junta Nacional de Arqueología y Etnología. 574 p.

A summary of Cuban archaeology and ethnography is presented on pp. 91–161.

566. Pichardo Moya, Felipe. 1950. Presencia en Cuba de un monstruo prehístorico. *Bohemia* 42(7):8–9, 138–139. La Habana.

Association of the bones of an ancient sloth with Native American remains in central Cuba.

Ethnography

Over the years meetings with small numbers of indigenous people in Cuba and Puerto Rico have been reported. Miguel Rodríguez Ferrer encountered Indian communities on the eastern tip of Cuba in 1847 and José Martí claimed to have lived with some indigenous groups in Cuba in 1895. Although the Taíno were destroyed as a functional social group, there survive a few hundred people in the Baraboa region of Cuba as well as in the mountainous regions of western Puerto Rico whose ancestry retains strong indigenous characteristics.

567.   Azcuy Alon, Fanny. 1941. *Psicografía y supervivencias de los aborígenes de Cuba*. La Habana: Cardenasa. 101 p.

568.   Bachiller y Morales, Antonio. 1883. *Cuba primitiva: origen, lenguas, tradiciones e historia de los indios de las Antillas Mayores y las Lucayas*. 2 ed. La Habana: Libreria de Miguel de Villa. 399 p.

569.   Barreal Fernández, I. 1970. Tendencias sincreticas de los cultos populares en Cuba. *International Congress of Anthropological and Ethnological Sciences (7 session, Moscow, 1964), Proceedings* 8:84–88. Moscow.

570.   Barreiro, José. 1989. Indians in Cuba. *Cultural Survival Quarterly* 13(3):56–60. Cambridge, Massachusetts.

An interesting report on indigenous populations in the mountains of the Oriente region of Cuba from Baracoa on the southern coast to Pico Turquino, the highest mountain in Cuba; research by Manuel Rivero de la Calle identified some 1,000 people with Arawak physical characteristics; see also, S. Culin, The Indians of Cuba (*Free Museum of Science and Art, Bulletin* 3:125–226, 1902. Philadelphia).

571.   Dominguez, Lourdes. 1978. La transculturación en Cuba (s. XVI-XVII). *Cuba Arqueológica* 33:50. La Habana.

572.   Mestre, Aristides. 1925. *La antropología en Cuba y el conocimiento de nuestros indios (1894–1925)*. La Habana: Imprenta El Siglo XX. 55 p.

573.   ———. 1936. *La medicina de los indios de Cuba*. La Habana: Seoane y Fernández. 21 p.

574.   Morales Coello, Julio. 1941. Los indígenas de Cuba. *Revista de Agricultura y Ganadería* 6(6):314–320. La Habana.

Brief history of the Indians of Cuba since the conquest; concludes there are no pure Indians left in Cuba.

575.   Ortiz, Fernando. 1948. La música y los areítos de los indios de Cuba. *Revista de Arqueología y Etnología* 3(6–7):115–189. La Habana.

Use of historical sources on Cuban music to identify Native American and African-introduced factors.

576.   Pichardo Moya, Felipe. 1945. *Los indios de Cuba en sus tiempos históricos.* Academia de la Historia de Cuba, Publicación no. 170. La Habana. 52 p.

Brief account of Cuban Native Americans from contact until extinction in the early twentieth century; archaeological evidence is used to examine population and acculturation.

577.   Rey, Estrella. 1969. *Las peculiaridades de la disintegración de las comunidades primitivas cubanas.* Academia de Ciencias de la República de Cuba, Serie Antropologica, no. 5. La Habana. 22 p.

Excellent historical archaeological study of the disintegration of Native American cultures on Cuba.

Ethnohistory

578.   Azcárate y Rosell, Rafael. 1937. *Historia de los indios de Cuba.* Historia cubana, 1. La Habana: Editorial Trópico. 254 p.

579.   Cancela Femenías, Pedro. 1952. Algo más sobre la encomienda del Padre Las Casas. *Revista de Arqueología y Etnología* 7(15–16):247–249. La Habana.

Description of two shell deposits found during a search of Las Casas' encomienda.

580.   Dacal Mouré, Ramón. 1980. De los Ciboneyes del Padre Las Casas a los Ciboneyes de 1966. *Universidad de La Habana* 211:6–41. La Habana.

Review of definitional confusion associated with the Ciboney; lists characteristic features of 42 Ciboney sites.

581.   Davis, Dave D. 1974. The strategy of early Spanish ecosystem management in Cuba. *Journal of Anthropological Research* 30(4):294–314. Albuquerque.

582.   Guarch Delmonte, José M. 1978. *El Taíno de Cuba: ensayo de reconstrucción etno-histórica.* La Habana: Academia de Ciencias de Cuba, Instituto de Ciencias Sociales. 263 p.

   See also: J.M. Guarch Delmonte, *Ensayo de reconstrucción etnohistórica de taíno de Cuba* (Academia de Ciencias de la República de Cuba, Instituto de Arqueología, Serie Arqueoloica, no. 4. La Habana, 1973. 58 p.).

   Ethnohistorical reconstruction of Taíno culture of Cuba.

Historical Archaeology

583.   Domínguez, Lourdes. 1984. *Arqueología colonial cubana: dos estudios.* La Habana: Ciencias Sociales. 124 p.

584.   Morales Patiño, Oswaldo. 1952. Donde estuvo la encomienda del Padre Las Casas. *Revista de Arqueología y Etnología* 7(15–16):239–242. La Habana.

   Attempt to locate the site of the encomienda of Bartolomé de Las Casas at the mouth of the Arimao River near Cienfuegos.

585.   Payarés, Rodolfo. 1968. *La Casa de Filomeno en Nueva Paz.* Academia de Ciencias de Cuba, Departamento de Antropología, Serie Granja 17 de Mayo, no. 6. La Habana. 24 p.

Cultural Evolution and Society

Cultural Evolution and Development

586.   Berlin, Heinrich. 1940. Relaciones precolombinas entre Cuba y Yucatán. *Revista Mexicana de Estudios Antropológicos* 4:141–160. Mexico.

587.   Dacal Mouré, Ramón. 1971–1972. El estudio de los grupos amerindios tempranos en el archipiélago Cubano. *Revista Dominicana de Arqueología y Antropología* 2(2–3):147–151. Santo Domingo.

588.   García Castañeda, José A. 1941. Asientos taínos localizados en el cacicato de Bani. *Revista de Arqueología* 3(5):18–22. La Habana.

589. Hahn, Paul G. 1961. A Relative Chronology of the Cuban Nonceramic Tradition. Ph.D. dissertation, Department of Anthropology, Yale University, New Haven. 327 p.

590. Morales Coello, Julio, René Herrera Fritot, and Fernando Royo Guardia. 1940. Las esferas líticas como base de una nueva cultura aborigen cubana. *Universidad de La Habana* 28–29:93–104. La Habana; *American Scientific Congress (8 session, Washington, DC, 1940), Proceedings* 2:131–138. Washington, DC, 1942.

591. Morales Patiño, Oswaldo. 1950. La antiguedad de los asientos indocubanos. *Revista de Arqueología y Etnología* 5(10–11):115–133. La Habana.

Survey of the various methods of determining the age of dwelling sites and a critique of Rouse's *Archaeology of the Maniabón Hills, Cuba.*

592. ———. 1952. Los complejos o grupos culturales indocubanos. *Revista de Arqueología y Etnología* 7(15–16):259–267. La Habana.

Illustrated traits lists for Complejo I (Guayabo Blanco), Complejo II (Cayo Redondo), and Complejo III (Baní and Pueblo Viejo).

593. Ortiz Fernández, Fernando. 1943. *Las cuatro culturas indias de Cuba.* Biblioteca de Estudios Cubanos, v. 1. La Habana: Arellano. 176 p.; *Acta Americana* 2(1–2):79–84, 1944. Washington, DC.

Scholarly review of past theories about native cultures and a synthesis and interpretation of recent archaeological and ethnographic information; see also: F. Ortiz Fernández, Nuevas teorias sobre las culturas indias de Cuba (*Revista Bimestre Cubana* 52(1):5–17, 1942. La Habana).

594. Pichardo Moya, Felipe. 1945. *Caverna, costa y meseta; interpretaciones de arqueología indocubana.* Biblio. de Historia, Filosofía y Sociología, 17. Habana. 175 p.

General analysis of Cuban prehistory.

595. Tabío, Ernesto E. 1951. La cultura más primitiva de Cuba precolombina. *Revista de Arqueología y Etnología* 7(13–14):117–157. La Habana.

Comparison of two Ciboney cultures of Cuba (Guayabo Blanco and Cayo Redondo). Guayabo Blanco and Cayo Redondo are Preceramic cultures distinguished by shell implements (553, 696, 694).

In Guayabo Blanco these are shell vessels made from conchs and in Cayo Redondo they include gouges, celts, and cups. Rough groundstone tools are found at both and Cayo Redondo has preshaped stone pendants similar to those of the Couri cultures of Haiti. It is uncertain how early these complexes may date. A radiocarbon date in available for Cayo Redondo and it falls in the tenth century A.D. However, historic sources suggest that Cayo Redondo-type cultures continued in far western Cuba until the sixteenth century. This part of the Caribbean never became agricultural and pottery was not utilized. The Spaniards referred to these people as 'wild men' and 'cave dwellers,' the Ciboney.

596. ———, José M. Guarch Delmonte, and Lourdes Dominguez. 1977. La antigüedad del hombre preagroalfarero temprano en Cuba. *International Congress of Americanists (41 session, Mexico, 1974), Proceedings* 3:725–732. Mexico.

Discussion of evidence for the antiquity of human occupation in Cuba; radiocarbon dates for the early Mesoindian site of Cueva Funche and Río Levisa are discussed.

597. Vasil'evskii, Ruslan S. 1986. *Arkheologiia Kuby/Arqueología de Cuba.* Novosibirsk: Isd-vo Nauka, Sibirskoe otd-nie. 172 p.

Collection of essays by Russian and Cuban archaeologists pertaining to the initial population of Cuba as well as the sub-Taíno and Taíno; Spanish summaries.

598. Vivanco, Julian. 1950. *Los indios palafíticos de Cuba y los jujuos o metates.* La Habana: Imprenta Belascoain. 16 p.

Attempt to prove that the Taíno, and not Ciboney, constructed pile dwellings of Cuba.

599. Vivanco, Julián. 1952. *Indología cubana.* Habana: Editorial Sol de Cuba. 20 p.

Author theorizes about the origin of the three Cuban cultures.

Demography

600. Pérez de la Riva, Juan. 1972. Desaparación de la población indígena cubana. *Universidad de La Habana* 196–197:61–84. La Habana.

Physical Anthropology

601.   Gates, R. Ruggles. 1954. Studies in race crossing: VI. The Indian remnants in eastern Cuba. *Genetica* 27:65–96. Dordrecht.

602.   ———. 1955. Indian remnants in eastern Cuba. *International Congress of Americanists (30 session, London, 1952), Proceedings* 1:248. London.

603.   Ginzburg, Vul'f V. 1967. Antropologicheskaia kharakteristika drevnikh aborigenov kuby. *Sbornik muzeia antropologii i etnografii* 24:180–278. Leningrad.

604.   Pospisil, Milan F. 1971. Physical anthropological research on Indian remains in eastern Cuba. *Current Anthropology* 12(2):229. Chicago.

605.   ———, and M. Rivero de la Calle. 1968. Estudio de los cráneos aborígenes de Cuba no ceramista. *International Congress of Anthropological and Ethnological Sciences (7 session, Moscow, 1964), Proceedings* 3:87–98. Moscow.

Anthropometric study of 28 Preceramic skulls from Cuba.

606.   Rivero de la Calle, Manuel. 1962. Deformación craneana en los aborigines de Cuba; estudio comparativo. *International Congress of Anthropological and Ethnological Sciences (6 session, Paris, 1960), Proceedings* 1:251–260. Paris

607.   ———. 1971. La estatura en los aborígenes de Cuba del grupo no ceramista; datos métricos y morfológicos de sus huesos largos. *Revista Dominicana de Arqueología y Antropología* 1(1):239–249. La Habana.

608.   ———. 1972. *Paleopatología de los aborígenes de Cuba.* Serie Espeleológica y Carsológica, no. 32. La Habana. 28 p.

609.   ———. 1978. De la antropología fisica de Cuba. *Universidad de La Habana* 207:43–52.

610.   ———. 1988. Estudio antropológico de los huesos del antiguo Convento de Santa Clara, Habana Vieja. *Documentos* 1:1–9.

611.   Zayas Bazan y Perdomo, Héctor. 1946. La medicina de los Indocubanos. *Sociedad de Geografía e Historia de Guatemala, Anales* 31:99–116. Guatemala.

Religious Systems

612. Morales Patiño, Oswaldo. 1946. La mítica indoantillana del tabaco. *Revista de Arqueología y Etnología* 2(1):57–75. La Habana.

Caves

613. Núñez Jiménez, Antonio. 1960. La espeleología en Cuba, esquema histórico. *Junta Nacional de Arqueología y Etnología, Revista* 4:39–103. La Habana.

Summary of cave explorations from ancient times; includes a discussion of the role of caves in the Cuban Revolution.

614. Tabio, Ernesto E. 1970. *Arqueología espeleológica de Cuba.* Academia de Ciencias de la República de Cuba, Serie Espeleológica y Carsológica, no. 27. La Habana. 91 p.

Burial Patterns

615. Alvarez Conde, José. 1952. *Las cavernas funerarias de Cayo La Aguada.* La Habana. 34 p.

Account of the discovery of Taíno burials in caves off the north coast of Cuba.

616. Royo Guardia, Fernando. 1940. Entierros aborígenes en Cuba. *Sociedad Cubana de Historia Natural Felipe Poey, Memorias* 14(1):39–43. La Habana.

617. ———. 1940. Túmulos aborígenes en Cuba. *Revista de Arqueología.* 1(4):52–55. La Habana.

Material Culture

Art

618. Alvarez Conde, José. 1960. El arte precolombino en Cuba. *Junta Nacional de Arqueología y Etnología, Revista* 1960:105–128. La Habana.

619. Domínguez González, Lourdes S. 1978. Reflexiones sobre el arte de los aborígenes cubanos. *Revolución y cultura* 76:32–33. La Habana.

620. Herrera Fritot, René. 1950. Arqueotipos zoomorfos en las Antillas Mayores. *Sociedad Cubana de Historia Natural Felipe Poey, Boletín* 1(3):140–149. La Habana.

Brief survey of the occurrence and kinds of zoomorphic and anthropomorphic designs in the archaeology of the Greater Antilles; author notes that they are limited to the latest of the three known cultural complexes; includes material from Cuba and the Dominican Republic.

621.   Ortiz, Fernando. 1947. *El Huracán, su mitología y sus símbolos.* México: Fondo de Cultura Económica. 686 p.

Scroll and other designs on several sculptures from Cuba are seen to be related to the circular movement of the hurricane or cyclone.

Petroglyphs and Pictographs

622.   Núñez Jiménez, Antonio. 1970. *Caguanes pictográficos.* Academia de Ciencias de la República de Cuba, Serie Espeleológica y Carsológica, no. 16. La Habana. 72 p.

Description of pictographs in the Caverna de las Pictografías, Cueva del Pirata, Cueva de los Chivos, and Cueva del Lago.

623.   ———. 1975. *Cuba: dibujos rupestres.* La Habana: Instituto Cubano del Libro, Editorial de Ciencias Sociales. 503 p.

Description of pictographs and cave paintings from some 48 caves and grottos in Cuba.

624.   ———. 1986. Arte rupestre de Cuba: las pictografías de las cuevas del Indio y de los Portales en la Sierra de Cubitas. *Centro Camuno di Studi Preistorici, Bolletino* 23:123–132.

Pottery

625.   Bullen, Ripley P., and D.D. Laxson. 1954. Some incised pottery from Cuba and Florida. *Florida Anthropologist* 7(1):23–26. Gainesville.

Pottery from the Glades culture of southern Florida is compared with Sub-Taíno pottery from Cayo Ocampo, Cuba.

626.   Dacal Mouré, Ramón. 1972. Notas sobre las figurinas araucas de la prehistoría cubana. *Universidad de La Habana* 196–197:85–117. La Habana.

627.   García Castañeda, José A. 1940. Notas arqueológicas: burenes marcados con dibujos. *Sociedad Cubana de Historia Natural, Memorias* 14(3):253–255. Holguin.

See also: J.A. García Castañeda, Los burenes marcados (*Revista de Arqueología y Etnología* 4–5:161–167, 1947).

628.   Guarch Delmonte, José M. 1972. *La cerámica taína de Cuba.* Academia de Ciencias de la República de Cuba, Instituto de Arqueología, Serie Arqueología, no. 2. La Habana. 78 p.

Discussion of Taíno ceramics in Cuba.

629.   Navarro Betancourt, Ernesto. 1973. *Motivos de arte en la cerámica indocubana.* Universidad de La Habana, Escuela de Ciencias Biológicas, Museo Antropológico Montañé, Publicación 4. La Habana. 41 p.

Consideration of incised line motifs on precolumbian ceramics of Cuba.

Lithics

630.   Dacal Mouré, Ramón. 1966. *Método experimental para el estudio de artefactos líticos de culturas antillanas no-cerámicas.* Academia de Ciencias de la República de Cuba, Serie Antropológica, no. 1. La Habana. 26 p.

Discussion of analytical approaches to pre- or nonceramic materials from western Cuba.

631.   Guarch Delmonte, José M. 1973. *El ajuar no-cerámico de los Taínos de Cuba.* Academia de Ciencias de la República de Cuba, Instituto de Arqueología, Serie Arqueología, no. 3. La Habana. 42 p.

Discussion of the nonceramic material culture of the Taíno.

632.   Kozlowski, Janusz K. 1975. *Las industrias de la piedra tallada de Cuba en el contexto del Caribe.* Academia de Ciencias de la República de Cuba, Instituto de Arqueología, Serie Arqueología, no. 5. La Habana. 34 p.

Classification of lithic artifacts based on the collections at the University of Oriente, Montané Museum of Havana University, and Institute of Archaeology.

Groundstone

633.   García Castañeda, Jose A. 1943. *Las hachas petaloides.* Notas del Museo García Feria, Cuaderno 1. Holguín: Impresos Sánchez. 41 p.

634.   Herrera Fritot, René. 1964. *Estudio de las hachas antillanas: creación de índices axiales para las petaloides.* La Habana: Departamento de Antropología, Comisión Nacional de la Academia de Ciencias. 146 p.

Excellent descriptive and classificatory analysis of stone axe and celt forms from the West Indies; see also, R. Herrera-Fritot, *Revisión de las hachas de ceremonia de la cultura taína: presentación de nuevos ejemplares del Museo Montané* (La Habana: Museo Antropológico Montané, Universidad de La Habana, 1938. 47 p.).

635.   Miguel Alonso, Orencio. 1946. Fases constructivas del hacha petaloide. *Revista de Arqueología y Etnología* 1(3):5–10. La Habana.

636.   Trelles Duelo, L. 1936. El metate no es utensilio indo-cubano. *Sociedad Cubana de Historia Natural, Memoria* 10(3):195–198. La Habana.

Metalwork

637.   Miguel Alonso, Orencio. 1950. Discovery of a pre-Columbian gold figurine in Cuba. *American Antiquity* 15(4):340–341. Washington, DC.

Description of a gold figurine in Central or South American style found near an Indian village site in eastern Cuba; Spanish translation: El primer ídolo de oro pre-colombino encontrado en Cuba (*Revista de Arqueología y Etnología* 7(13–14):166–169, 1952. La Habana).

Shell

638.   Dacal Mouré, Ramón. 1978. *Artefactos de concha en las comunidades aborígenes cubanas.* Universidad de La Habana, Museo Antropológico Montañé, Publicación 5. La Habana. 114 p.

Classificatory and functional analysis of some 955 shell artifacts from Cuba in the Museo Antropológico Montañé.

Regional and Site Reports

639. Conte, Antonio. 1973. Exploradores. *Cuba Internacional* 5:50–53. La Habana.

Report on the excavation of prehistoric cultures in Cayo Blanco.

640. García Castañeda, José A. 1939. Asiento de Ochiles. *Revista de Arqueología* 1(3):47–56. La Habana.

Summary descriptive report on archaeological discoveries.

641. Martínez Arango, Felipe. 1977. Arqueología de Los Ciguatos. *International Congress of Americanists (41 session, Mexico, 1974), Proceedings* 3:647–673. Mexico.

Summary of excavations at the multicomponent (Sub-Taíno/Taíno) Los Ciguatos site.

642. Miguel Alonso, Orencio. 1949. Descubrimiento y excavación de un montículo funeral en el potrero El Porvenir. *Revista de Arqueología y Etnografía* 4(8–9):175–194. La Habana.

Report on excavation of a sub-Taíno midden containing burials and European trade items.

643. Silva, Adolfo. 1979. Arqueología en el Valle de Cubitas. *Bohemia* 71:90–93. La Habana.

644. Torres Valdes, Pastor, and M. Rivero de la Calle. 1970. *La Cueva de la Santa*. Academia de Ciencias de la República de Cuba, Serie Espeleólogica y Carsológica, no. 13. La Habana. 42 p.

Camagüey Province

645. Mysterious mound in Camaguey, Cuba. *El Palacio* 32:261–262, 1932. Santa Fe, New Mexico.

646. Pichardo Moya, Felipe, 1939. Informe sobre sitios de población indios en la provincia de Camagüey. *Revista de Arqueología* 1(3):45–46. La Habana.

647. ———, 1939. Zonas indo-arqueológicas en Camagüey. *Revista de Arqueología* 1(3):39–44. La Habana.

Preliminary partition of Camagüey into four archaeological zones.

648.   ———. 1948. Los caneyes del sur de Camagüey, 1843–1943. *Revista de Arqueología y Etnología* 3(6–7):37–54. La Habana

Critical discussion and interpretation of funerary mounds found in southern Cuba; see also: F. Pichardo Moya, El primer caney explorado en Cuba (In: *Miscelánea de estudios dedicados a Fernando Ortiz*. v. 2, pp. 1217–1223. La Habana: Sociedad Económica de Amigos del País, 1956) for an account of the archaeological work of Miguel Rodríguez Ferrer in the mounds of southern Camagüey during the nineteenth century.

649.   ———. 1960. Mapa indoarqueológico de Camagüey. *Junta Nacional de Arqueología y Etnología, Revista* 4:7–38.

Important history of archaeological research in Camagüey Province.

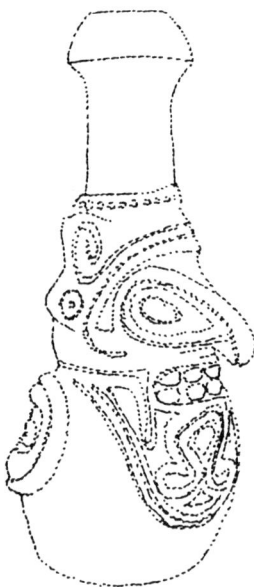

Figure 9. Zoomorphic ceramic vessel from La Cucama, Distrito Nacional, Dominican Republic.

Source: M.A. García Arévalo, *Los signos en el arte Taíno* (Santo Domingo: Fundación García-Arévalo, 1989.

650. Rivero de la Calle, Manuel, and Antonio Nuñez Jiménez. 1958. *Excursiones arqueológicas y Camagüey.* La Habana: Universidad Central de las Villas, Departamentos Investigaciones Antropológicas e Investigaciones Geográficas. 62 p.

Report on a cave with painted pictographs in the Cerro de Tubaquey and a village site with a possible ball court in the Lomas de Guaney, both in north central Cuba.

Caney del Castillo
651. Guarch Delmonte, José M., and Rodolfo Payares. 1964. *Excavación en el Caney del Castillo.* La Habana: Academia de Ciencias de la República de Cuba, Departamento de Antropología. 35 p.

Description of Meso-Indian (Cayo Redondo Complex) mound site in Camagüey Province; includes burial deposits.

La Finca de Dos Marías
652. Smith, Hale G. 1954. Excavations at La Finca de Dos Marías, Camagüey, Cuba. *Florida Anthropologist* 7(1):19–21. Gainesville.

Summary report on excavations at a single-component, sub-Taíno site near Jatibonico, Camaguey Province, Cuba.

Jardines de la Reina

653. Pichardo Moya, Felipe. 1950. Los Jardines de la Reina. *Bohemia* 42(22):28–29, 111–112. La Habana.

Summary of the archaeology and ethnohistory of the islands on the south coast of Cuba.

La Habana Province

Cueva de García Robiou
654. Núñez Jiménez, Antonio. 1961. La caverna del sol. INRA 2(3):58–67. La Habana.

Description of pictographs in Ciboney style from the Cueva de García Robiou in Havana Province.

655. Núñez Jiménez, Antonio. 1964. *Cuevas y pictografías.* La Habana: Edición Revolucionaria. 146 p.

Illustrated account of the pictographs of Cueva García Robiou and Cueva de Ambrosio.

Isla de Pinos

656.   Bucan Academy of Sciences reports on archaeological fieldwork. *Current Anthropology* 15(1):66, 1974. Chicago.

Brief report on excavations of Preceramic sites in southeastern Isla de Pinos, Bahía Hondo, and later sites in the Banes region; grave goods from Cuevas IV de Punta del Este (Isla de Pinos) suggest an occupation ca. 4000–5000 B.C.; gold pendant is found at Esterito site in Banes region and radiocarbon dated to ca. A.D. 1400–1450.

657.   Herrera Fritot, René. 1938. Las pinturas rupestres y el ajuar ciboney de Punta del Este, Isla de Pinos. *Revista de Arqueología* 1(2):40–60. La Habana.

Summary discussion of painted designs and shell artifacts from a cave on Isla de Pinos.

658.   ———. 1939. Discusión sobre el posible origen de las pictografías de Punta del Este, Isla de Pinos. *Sociedad Cubana de Historia Natural Felipe Poey, Memorias* 13(5):307–314. La Habana.

659.   ———. 1939. Informe sobre una exploración arqueológica a Punta del Este, Isla de Pinos, realizada por el Museo Antropológico Montané de la Universidad de La Habana; localización y estudio de una cueva con pictografías y restos de un ajuar aborigen. *Universidad de la Habana* 20–21:25–59. La Habana. 37 p.

660.   Núñez Jiménez, Antonio. 1947. Nuevos descubrimientos arqueológicos en Punta del Este, Isla de Pinos. *Universidad de La Habana* 12(73–75):213–247. La Habana.

Description of simple pictographs in several caves; see also: A. Núñez Jiménez, El archipiélago de las cavernas (*INRA* 1(5):46–55, 1960) for a discussion of painted pictographs on the gallery ceiling of the Cueva de la Isla, Punta del Este, Isla de Pinos and an illustration of a painted pictograph from the Cueva de Ramos in Punta de Caguanas, north of Las Villas; A. Núñez Jiménez, Descubrimiento de pictografías en Caleta Grande, Isla de Pinos (*Universidad de La Habana* 82–87:357–365, 1950) provides an illustrated account of the discovery of painted pictographs on the Isle of Pinos.

661. Royo Guardia, Fernando. 1939. El misterio secular de la Cueva de Punta del Este. *Sociedad Cubana de Historia Natural Felipe Poey, Memorias* 13(5):38–41. La Habana.

662. ———, and Oswaldo Morales Patiño. 1948. Colección Felix Duarte, Batabanó, Provincia de La Habana. *Revista de Arqueología y Etnología* 3(6–7):91–98. La Habana.

Illustrated inventory of an archaeological collection from Isla de Pinos.

Jibacoa

663. Royo Guardia, Fernando. 1946. Exploración arqueológica en Jibacoa, Provincia de La Habana. Contribuciones del Grupo Guamí, Antropología, no. 7. *Sociedad Cubana de Historia Natural Felipe Poey, Memorias* 18(1):81–100. la Habana.

La Habana Vieja

664. Dominguez, Lourdes. 1981. Arqueología del sitio colonial Casa de la Obrapia o de Calvo de la Puerta, Habana Vieja. *Santiago* 41:63–82. La Habana.

665. Núñez Lemus, H. 1981. Investigación arqueológica en El Morro de La Habana. *Bohemia* 73:90–91. La Habana.

Santa Fe

666. Pérez de Acevedo, Roberto. 1951. *Minero de la fauna extinguida de Cuba en Santa Fe, Habana.* La Habana: Instituto Cubano de Arqueología. 63 p.

Report on investigation of a rock shelter near Santa Fe, Habana Province, Cuba; Ciboney deposits overlay bones of extinct fauna.

Las Villas Province

667. Alvarez Conde, José. 1971. *Revisión indoarqueológica de la provincia de Las Villas.* La Habana: Junta Nacional de Arqueología y Etnología. 175 p.

Important summary of sites and excavations in Las Villas province.

Caguanas

668. Rivero de la Calle, Manuel. 1960. Caguanas: nueva zona arqueológica de Cuba. *Islas* 2(3):727–808. Santa Clara, Cuba.

Report on an important archaeological site with elaborate dance and ball courts near Caguanas on the northeast coast of Las Villas province; includes description of pictographs, refuse and burial sites, and skeletal remains.

Guamuhaya

669.   Morales Patiño, Oswaldo. 1949. Guamuhaya: estudio arqueológico de esta región indocubana; revisión del llamado Hombre del Plurial. *Revista de Arqueología y Etnología* 4(8–9):111–174. La Habana.

Survey of the archaeology and ethnohistory of the southeastern part of Las Villas province; argues that Plurial Man is associated with Guanajatabey material culture and not Palaeo-Indian.

La Jutia Cave

670.   Alvarez Conde, José. 1954. Huesos marcadaos en la isla de Cuba. *Sociedad Cubana de Historia Natural Felipe Poey, Memorias* 22(4):383–388. La Habana.

Description of incised human bones from La Jutia cave site near Fomento in Las Villas Province; possible suggestion of cannibalism among the Ciboney.

Matanzas Province

Canimar

671.   Febles Dueñas, Jorge. 1982. *Estudio tipológico y tecnológico del material de piedra tallada del sitio arqueológico Canimar I, Matanzas, Cuba.* La Habana: Academia de Ciencias de Cuba. 51 p.

Technical and typological analysis of lithics from Canimar I site, Matanzas, Cuba.

Carbonera

672.   Herrera Fritot, René, and Manuel Rivero de la Calle. 1954. *La cueva funeraria de Carbonera, Matanzas.* La Habana: Sociedad Espeleológica de Cuba. 45 p.

Descriptive excavation summary of a Ciboney cave site on the north coast of Cuba.

Cayo Jurajuría
673. ———. 1970. *Exploración arqueológica inicial en Cayo Jorajuria, Matanzas.* Academia del Ciencias de la República de Cuba, Departmento de Antropología, Serie Antropológica, no. 6. La Habana. 20 p.

Results of site survey on Cayo Jurajuría near Playa Menéndez; includes food remains, shell celts, chert chips, and red ochre.

Cueva de la Palma
674. Rivero de la Calle, Manuel. 1981. Pendientes aborígenes cubanos. *Biblioteca Nacional Jose Martí, Revista* 72(23)1,3:49–59. La Habana.

Report on shell and carved sea lion (*Monachus tropicalis*) pendants in a Ciboney burial at Cueva de la Palma, Cubre Alta, Matanzas.

Oriente Province

675. Fierrozala Bermúdez, Gustavo, and Manuel Rivero de la Calle. 1970. *Notas sobre la expedición arqueológica y geológica realizada en la región de Maisí, Oriente.* Academia de Ciencias de la República de Cuba, Instituto de Arqueología, Serie Ciencias Biológicas, no. 11. La Habana. 5 p.

676. García Castañeda, José A. 1938. Asiento Yayal. *Revista de Arqueología* 1(1):44–58. La Habana.

Holquín burial mounds and discussion of shell, lithic, and ceramic artifacts.

677. García Castañada, José A. 1949. La transculturación indo-española en Holguín. *Revista de Arqueología y Etnología* 4(8–9):195–205. La Habana.

Historical review of Spanish-Indian contact in Holguín, eastern Cuba; results of historic sites archaeology used to determine the degree of transculturation.

678. Guarch Delmonte, José M. 1972. *Excavaciones en el extremo oriental de Cuba.* Academia de Ciencias de la República de Cuba, Instituto de Arqueología, Serie Arqueología, no. 1. La Habana. 53 p.

Summary of archaeological research at some 22 sites in the eastern portion of Oriente Province, Cuba; includes discussion of geography and previous archaeological investigations in the region.

679. Martínez Arango, Felipe. 1976. Arqueología de Maisi II. *Museo del Hombre Dominicano, Boletín* 4(8):11–34. Santo Domingo.

680. ———. 1982. *Registro de todos los sitios arqueológicos investigados por la Sección Arqueológica Aborigen de la Universidad de Oriente.* Mexico: Litográfica Machado. 41 p.

Inventory and description of 134 archaeological sites in Oriente Province, Cuba.

681. Núñez Jiménez, Antonio. 1950. Un viaje arqueológico a Mayarí. *Carteles* 39:43–45.

Illustrated report on excavations in Ciboney and Taíno sites.

682. Posposil, Milan F. 1976. *Indian Remains From the Oriente Province, Cuba.* Bratislava: Univerzita Komenskeho. 225 p.

683. Utset, Bernardo. 1951. Exploraciones arqueológicas en la región sur de Oriente. *Revista de Arqueología y Etnología* 7(13–14):99–116. La Habana.

Illustrated description of Ciboney (Complejo II) sites on the south shore of eastern Cuba; argues Ciboney culture survived into historic times.

Aguas Verdes

684. Artiles, Milagros, and Ramón Dacal. 1973. *Moluscos marinos y terrestres presentes en el sitio arqueológico Aguas Verdes, Nibuján, Oriente, Cuba.* Universidad de La Habana, Centro de Información Científica y Técnica, Serie Ciencias, 9. Antropología y Prehistoria, 2. La Habana. 41 p.

Description of mollusc remains from Aguas Verdes and Cueva Funche.

685. Kozlowski, Janusz K. 1972. *Industria litica de Aguas Verdes, Baracoa, Oriente, Cuba.* Universidad de La Habana, Centro de Información Científica y Tecnica, Ciencias, ser. 9: Antropología y Prehistoría, no. 1. La Habana. 11 p.; *Museo del Hombre Dominicano, Boletin* 3:300–309. Santo Domingo, 1973.

Description of the blade industry from Baracoa.

Arroyo del Palo

686. Tabio, Ernesto E., and J.M. Guarch. 1966. *Excavaciones en Arroyo del Palo, Mayarí, Cuba.* La Habana: Departamento de Antropología, Academia de Ciencias de la República de Cuba. 82 p.

Report on the excavation of Arroyo del Palo, a rock shelter in eastern Cuba radiocarbon dated to A.D. 1000; includes preceramic Ciboney lithic and shell components and pottery appears related to Meillac deposits from Hispaniola.

Banes

687. Morales Patiño, Oswaldo. 1952. Estudio comparativo del pendiente efigie de oro encontrado en Banes. *Revista de Arqueología y Etnología* 7(13–14):166–227. La Habana.

Excellent study of a gold pendant found in eastern Cuba; similar objects found in Costa Rica, Panama, and Colombia.

Bayamo

688. Azcárate y Rosell, Rafael. 1938. El misterio del idolo de Bayamo. *Revista de Arqueología* 1(1):10–11. La Habana.

689. Dacal Mouré, Ramón, and Ernesto Navarro. 1972. *El idolo de Bayamo.* Universidad de La Habana, Museo Antropológico Montané, Publicación, no. 3. La Habana. 37 p.

Description of a *zemí* known as the Idolo de Bayamo from the archaeological collection at the Universidad de La Habana.

Caimanes

690. Boytel Jambu, Fernando. 1947. El residuario de Cayo Caimanes. *Revista de Arqueología y Etnología* 2(4–5):185–191. La Habana.

691. Navarrete Pujol, Ramón. 1983. El sitio cubano de Caimanes III. *Museo del Hombre Dominicano, Boletín* 11(18):111–113. Santo Domingo.

Report on the Caimanes III site near Santiago de Cuba; radiocarbon dated at 1745 B.C.

Casanova

692. Rodríguez, Alexis, Aurelio Sánchez Agramonte, Gilberto Silva, Justo Salvador Cabrera, and Rafael Cepero. 1952. Exploración

arqueológica a ventas de Casanova, Contramaestre, Oriente. *Revista de Arqueología y Etnología* 7(15–16):227–238. La Habana.

Summary report on excavations at a sub-Taíno village.

Damajayabo

693. Martínez Arango, Felipe. 1963. Superimposición cultural en Damajayabo, Oriente de Cuba. *Revista Mexicana de Estudios Antropológicos* 19:105–122. Mexico; La Habana: Instituto del Libro, 1968. 125 p.

Report on Damajayabo, a multicomponent Ciboney (Preceramic) and Sub-Taíno (Ceramic) site southeast of Santiago de Cuba.

694. Ruiz Lafont, Aurelio. 1968. *Un presunto horno de alfarería aborigen en Damajayabo.* Santiago de Cuba: Universidad de Oriente. 24 p.

Excavation of a presumed kiln or paved area at the site of Damajayabo.

La Patana Cave

695. Harrington, Mark R. 1951. The idol of the cave. *Natural History* 60(7):312–317, 335. New York.

Account of the exploration of a cave at La Patana, Cabo Maisí, Cuba; remains include pottery, petroglyphs, and a *zemí*.

Maníabon Hills

696. Rouse, Irving. 1942. *Archaeology of the Maníabon Hills, Cuba.* Yale University Publications in Anthropology, no. 26. New Haven. 84 p.

The results of a surface survey in eastern Cuba and descriptions of material obtained from local archaeologists.

Mejías

697. Guarch Delmonte, José M., and Milton Pino. 1968. *Excavaciones en Mejías, Mayarí, Cuba.* Academia de Ciencias de la República de Cuba, Departamento de Antropología, Serie Antropología, no. 3. La Habana. 31 p.

Report on excavations at Mejías, a Mayarí period site with pottery similar to Arroyo del Palo.

698. Pino, Milton. 1970. *La dieta y el ajuar aborigén en el sitio Mejías, Mayarí, Cuba.* Academia de Ciencias de la República de Cuba, Departamento de Antropología, Serie Antropológica, no. 4. La Habana. 38 p.

Sardinero

690. Trincado Fontán, M. Nelsa, Lilecta Castellanos Castellanos, and Gloria Sosa Montalvo. 1973. *Arqueología de Sardinero.* Santiago: Instituto Cubano del Libro, Sección Editorial Oriente. 131 p.

Description of lithic, shell, bone, and ceramic material from the multicomponent site of Sardinero (Archaic and Subtaíno).

Pinar del Río Province

691. García Valdés, Pedro. 1947. Una contribución más al estudio de la prehistoria de Cuba; resultado de una exploración arqueológica a Río del Medio, Biajaca y Cocuyo, en la región pinareña. *Revista de Arqueología y Etnología* 2(4–5):169–184. La Habana.

692. García Valdés, Pedro. 1949. Nuevas exploraciones arqueológicas en la provincia de Pinar del Río. *Revista de Arqueología y Etnología* 4(8–9):206–226. La Habana.

Report on the excavation of two Ciboney (Cayo Redondo) middens in western Cuba.

693. Tabio, Ernesto E., and Rodolfo Payarés. 1968. *Sobre los cafetales coloniales de la Sierra del Rosario.* Academia de Ciencias de la República de Cuba, Departamento de Antropología, Serie Pinar del Río, no. 17. La Habana. 82 p.

Cayo Redonda

694. Osgood, Cornelius. 1942. *The Ciboney Culture of Cayo Redonda, Cuba.* Yale University Publications in Anthropology, no. 25. New Haven. 65 p.

Detailed analysis of material from one of the earliest known sites in the West Indies.

695. Pérez de Acevedo, Roberto. 1957. *El respetable e inequietante Arcaico II cubano.* La Habana. 286 p.

Author proposes a theory of prehispanic migration across the Atlantic to account for the Cayo Redondo culture of Cuba.

Cueva de Enrique

696.   Dacal, Ramón, and Milton Pino. 1968. *Excavaciones en la Cueva de Enrique, Península de Guanahacabibes.* Academia de Ciencias de la República de Cuba, Departamento de Antropología, Serie Pinar del Río, no. 16. La Habana. 26 p.

Summary of the excavation of a nonceramic habitation cave in western Cuba.

Cueva Funche

697.   Dacal Mouré, Ramón. 1970. *Excavaciones en Cueva Funche, artefactos e instrumentos.* Academia de Ciencias de la República de Cuba, Serie Espeleológica y Carsológica, no. 11. La Habana. 22 p.

698.   Guarch, José M. 1970. *Excavaciones en Cueva Funche, Guanahacabibes, Pinar del Río, Cuba.* Academia de Ciencias de la República de Cuba, Serie Espeleológica y Carsológica, no. 10. La Habana. 20 p.

699.   Pino, Milton. 1970. *La dieta de los aborígenes de Cueva Funche, Guanahacabibes, Pinar del Rio, Cuba.* Academia de Ciencias de la República de Cuba, Serie Espeleológica y Carsológica, no. 12. La Habana. 29 p.

Guanahacabibes

700.   Dacal Mouré, Ramón. 1968. *Introducción a la arqueología de la península de Guanahacabibes, Cuba.* Academia de Ciencias de la República de Cuba, Departamento de Antropología, Serie Pinar del Río, no. 14. La Habana. 11 p.

Summary of archaeological research in southwestern Cuba.

Pinar del Río

701.   García Castañeda, José A. 1938. Pinar del Río: exploraciones arqueológicas. *Revista de Arqueología* 1(2):62–72. La Habana.

Report on an archaeological survey of Pinar del Río and other sites.

702.   García Valdés, Pedro. 1939. Pinar del Rio, exploración arqueológica en Ceja del Negro. *Revista de Arqueología* 1(3):32–38. La Habana.

See also, P. García Valdés, *La civilización taína en Pinar del Río: trabajo de ingreso* (La Habana: Imprenta El Siglo XX, 1989. 83 p.).

703. García Valdés, Pedro. 1949. *Las Esferolitias; estudio etnológico y arqueológico.* Pinar del Río, Cuba. 52 p.

     Speculative review of the discovery of stone spheres in western Cuba.

Soroa

704. Herrera Fritot, René. 1970. *El yacimiento arqueológico de Soroa, Pinar del Río.* Academia del Ciencias de la República de Cuba, Serie Espeleológica y Carsológica, no. 9. La Habana. 18 p.

Vega del Palmar

705. González Muñoz, Antonio. 1952. El mound de la Vega del Palmar: exploración del 5 de marzo de 1951. *Revista de Arqueología y Etnología* 7(15–16):243–245. La Habana.

     Description of a Ciboney refuse and burial site.

706. González Muñoz, Antonio, and Ignacio Avello. 1946. Asiento Cantabria: descubrimiento del residuario de cultura alfarera más occidental de Cuba. *Revista de Arqueología y Etnología* 1(3):11–19. La Habana.

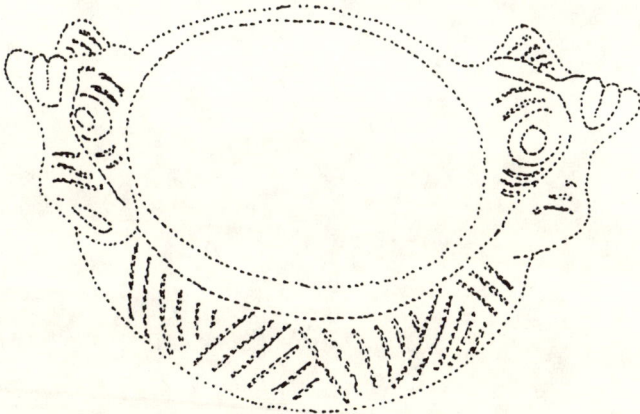

Figure 10. Ceramic vessel, Dominican Republic.

Source: M.A. García Arévalo, *Los signos en el arte Taíno,* Santo Domingo: Fundación García-Arévalo, 1989. Figure 4.

DOMINICAN REPUBLIC

(Capital: Santo Domingo)

The Dominican Republic occupies the eastern two-thirds of the island of Hispaniola, the other third being Haiti. The Dominican Republic takes its name from Santo Domingo, its capital city, which was founded in 1496. Hispaniola, second only to Cuba in size among the Caribbean Islands, was the first to be settled by the Spaniards; Santo Domingo is the oldest permanent European settlement in the New World. The city became an important center of colonial administration, but the island itself was neglected in favor of other, richer lands. The terrain of the Dominican Republic is dominated by a central mountain chain and several lesser ranges. Despite the island's subtropical location, it enjoys a predominately comfortable climate, well suited for agricultural production.

Columbus landed on the island of Hispaniola in December, 1492. His flagship, the *Santa Maria*, ran aground on what is now the north coast of Haiti, forcing him to construct a small fort, called Navidad, to protect the sailors who could not be accommodated on the remaining two ships for the return voyage to Spain. When he returned in 1493 with several shiploads of settlers, he found that the seemingly friendly Arawak Indians had destroyed the fort and killed its occupants. A temporary peace was reestablished but the Spaniards' lust for gold and silver could not be satisfied unless the Indians could be forced to relinquish their freedom and work for the Europeans. Late in 1493, Columbus' companions established the first colony in the New World at La Isabela (near present Puerto Plata) on the north coast of Hispaniola, but early in 1496 this site was abandoned for a healthier and better protected harbor on the south coast. Here the Spaniards established Santo Domingo (originally Santiago de Guzman), the administrative capital of their colonizing operations in the Caribbean. Within fifty years, virtually all of the native population of Hispaniola, an estimated 100,000, was exterminated through mistreatment and disease.

General

707.   Abbott, William L. 1922. Archaeological collecting in the Dominican Republic. *Smithsonian Institution, Explorations and Fieldwork* 1921:83–92. Washington, DC.

William L. Abbott (1860–1936) was a collector of natural history specimens who traveled to the Greater Antilles, East Africa, Kashmir, Malaya, and the East Indies. Between 1916 and 1923 he worked in Haiti and the Dominican Republic and his ethnological collections were donated to the Smithsonian Institution, Peabody Museum of Archaeology and Ethnology at Harvard University, and other museums. His collections, photographs, and personal notes were used by Otis T. Mason and others at the Smithsonian Institution for publications and exhibits. Abbott also financed the work of Herbert W. Krieger in the Caribbean during 1928–1932.

708.   Alberti Bosch, Narciso. 1912. *Apuntes para la prehistoria de Quisqueya.* La Vega: Imprenta El Progeso. 148 p.

Important summary descriptions for several prehistoric sites, including Angelina, Constanza, Cueva de Guacapa, Cueva El Peñon de La Sabana, Cueva El Pozo del Indio, Cueva Hernan de Alonso, El Circo de San Juan, Haitisis, Samana, Mao, and Yuboa.

709.   Boyrie Moya, Emile de. 1954. L'archéologie indigène et coloniale dans la République Dominicaine. *La Revue Française* 6(56):52–56. Paris.

Summary of indigenous and colonial archaeology in the Dominican Republic.

710.   Boyrie Moya, Emile de. 1957. La posición cultural de Santo Domingo en la arqueología indo-antillana. *Revista Clío: Organo de la Academia Dominicana de la Historia* 25(112):401–436. Santo Domingo.

711.   Despradel i Batista, Guido. 1939–1940. Apuntes sobre arqueología quisqueyana. *Archivo General de la Nación, Boletín* 2(2):109–117; 2(3):227–235; 2(4):366–376; 3(5):116–124. Ciudad Trujillo.

712.   Didiez Burgos, Ramón J. 1974. *Guanahani y Mayaguan: las primeras isletas descubiertas en el Nuevo Mundo.* Santo Domingo: Sociedad Dominicana de Geografía. 424 p.

713.   Estrada Torres, Aristides. 1973. Conceptos del pueblo taíno sobre la cabeza. *Museo del Hombre Dominicano, Boletín* 3:73–80. Santo Domingo.

714.   García Arévalo, Manuel A. 1988. *Indigenismo, arqueología e identidad nacional.* Santo Domingo: Museo del Hombre Dominicano; Fundación García Arévalo. 39 p.

See also, M.A. García Arévalo, La arqueología Indo-Hispano en Santo Domingo. In: *Unidades y variedades: Ensays en homenaje a José M. Cruxent.* pp. 77–127. Caracas: Centro de Estudios Avanzados.

715.   Jiménez Lambertus, Abelardo. 1984. Guácara de los Cacaos y la Cueva de la Laguna. *Museo del Hombre Dominicano, Boletín* 19:105–119. Santo Domingo.

716.   Krieger, Herbert W. 1930. Prehistoric inhabitants of the Dominican Republic. *Smithsonian Institution, Explorations and Fieldwork* 1929:157–166. Washington, DC.

717.   Krieger, Herbert W. 1931. Prehistoric Santo Dominican kitchen-middens, cemeteries, and earthworks. *Smithsonian Institution, Explorations and Fieldwork* 1930:145–156. Washington, DC.

718.   Ortega, Elpidio J. 1971. Dos informes arqueológicos. *Revista Dominicana de Arqueología y Antropología* 1(1):21–55. Santo Domingo.

719.   Palm, Erwin W. 1947. Antiquities of Dominica and Santo Domingo: a correction. *Man* 47:51–52. London.

720.   Tavares, Julia. 1978. *Guide to Caribbean Prehistory.* Santo Domingo: Editora Taller.

721.   Veloz Maggiolo, Marcio. 1972. *Arqueología prehistórica de Santo Domingo.* Singapore; New York: McGraw-Hill Far Eastern Publishers. 384 p.

Important summary of the archaeology and prehistory of the Dominican Republic by a leading Dominican scholar; includes a summary of the history of archaeological research in the Caribbean area, evaluation of historical sources, synthesis of Dominican and Caribbean archaeology, formal analysis of pottery and lithics, and ethnographic connections between the Caribbean and coastal South America.

722.   Veloz Maggiolo, Marcio. 1980. *Vida y cultura en la prehistória de Santo Domingo.* San Pedro de Macorís: Universidad Central del Este. 169 p.

Disparate collection of articles covering Hispaniola's prehispanic population, economic organization, art, agriculture, historical reconstruction of the sweet potato in the Antilles, development of Antillean archaeology, and the use of archaeological materials as sources for historical research

Museum Collections

723.   *Catálogo de los objetos que presenta la República Dominicana á la Exposición Histórico-Americana de Madrid.* Madrid, 1892. 14 p.

724.   Scott, John F. 1985. *The Art of the Taíno from the Dominican Republic.* Gainesville: University Gallery, College of Fine Arts, University of Florida/University Presses of Florida. 48 p.

Brief gallery catalog written for an exhibition of some ninety pieces of Taíno art from the Dominican Republic in the art gallery of the University of Florida at Gainesville, the Bicardi Museum at Miami, and the Metropolitan Museum of Art at New York in 1985; includes a good summary on the history of the Taíno Indians; see also: H. Soto Ricart, Universidad de la Florida organizó exposición arte taíno (*Ahora* 28(1118):34–37, 1988).

Museo del Hombre Dominicano
(Museo Nacional de la República Dominicana)

725.   Ortega, Elpidio, and Plinio Pina Peña. 1972. Un vaso inhalador de la colección del Museo Nacional, República Dominicana. *Museo del Hombre Dominicano, Boletín* 2:18–24. Santo Domingo.

Objects are generally similar to examples from Puerto Rico and Grenada.

Museum für Völkerkunde

726.   Schweeger-Hefel, Annemarie. 1951–1952. Ein rätselhaftes Stück aus der alten Ambraser Sammlung. *Archiv für Völkerkunde* 6–7:209–228. Vienna.

Description of a cotton cordage and shell bead girdle in the Museum für Völkerkunde in Vienna.

Museo Arqueológico Regional de Altos de Chavon

727.   García Arévalo, Manuel A. 1982. *Museo Arqueológico Regional, Altos de Chavon.* La Romana: Ediciones Museo Arqueológico Regional de Altos de Chavon. 127 p.

Museo de las Casas Reales

728. Pérez Montás, Eugenio. 1976. First scenario of the New World: Museum of the Casas Reales. *Américas* 28(10):s1–s12. Washington, DC.

See also, M. Nieves Sicart, Piezas cerámicas conservadas en los depósitos del departamento de ceramología histórica del Museo de las Casas Reales (*Casas Reales* 5(11):89–97, 1980. Santo Domingo).

Smithsonian Institution

729. Vega de Boyrie, Bernardo. 1973. Material pre-cerámico de la Hispaniola en el Instituto Smithsonian. *Museo del Hombre Dominicano, Boletín* 3:55–63. Santo Domingo.

An interesting examination of archaeological material from Hispaniola collected by Herbert Krieger and Jesse W. Fewkes.

History of Archaeological Research

730. Barret, P. 1931. Expédition archéologique à la République Dominicaine. *Société des Américanistes de Paris, Journal* 23:469. Paris.

731. Boyrie Moya, Emile de. 1960. Cinco años de Arqueología dominicana. *Universidad de Santo Domingo, Anales* 26(93–96):33–86. Santo Domingo.

732. Hatt, Gudmund. 1932. Notes on the archaeology of Santo Domingo. *Geografisk Tidschrift* 35(1–2):1–8. Copenhagen.

Important early account of fieldwork in the Dominican Republic; Spanish translation: G. Hatt, Notas sobre la arqueología de Santo Domingo (*Museo del Hombre Dominicano, Boletín* 7(11):221–240, 1978. Santo Domingo).

733. Pérez Sánchez, Félix M. 1978. Exploradores e investigadores de la arqueología Quisqueyana. *Museo del Hombre Dominicano, Boletín* 7(11):198–210. Santo Domingo.

734. Veloz Maggiolo, Marcio. 1973. *Los poblamientos aborígenes de la isla Española*. Museo del Hombre Dominicano, Papeles Ocasionales, no. 7. Santo Domingo. 30 p.

An interesting review of the history of the archaeology of the Dominican Republic and the Preceramic period; summarizes generally arguments made in his *Arqueología prehistórica de Santo*

Domingo (Singapore; New York: McGraw-Hill Far Eastern Publishers, 1972).

Biography

735.   Ortega, Elpidio. 1974. Emile de Boyrie Moya: pionero de la arqueología en la región noroeste de la República Dominicana. *Instituto Montecristeño de Arqueología, Boletín* 1:34–44. Monte Cristi.

Environment

736.   Flint, Jacques. 1963. Des cavernes de la partie espagnole de l'Ile de Saint-Domingue (République Dominicaine). *Société des Américanistes de Paris, Journal* 51:103–108. Paris.

737.   Rímoli, Renato O. 1980. Informe preliminar sobre el proyecto paleofáuna de cuevas y abrigos rocosos en la Republica Dominicana. *Museo del Hombre Dominicano, Boletín* 9(13):165–169. Santo Domingo.

   Presents results of investigations in several locations, including Escalera Abajo (Puerto Plata province), Rancho La Guardia (Elias Piña province), Cueva de Pomier (San Cristobal province), Cueva de las Marvillas (San Pedro Macorís province), and Cueva Berna (Altagracia province).

738.   Vega, Bernardo. 1980. Quinientos años de cambio ecológico en Santo Domingo. *Museo del Hombre Dominicano, Boletín* 9(13):153–158. Santo Domingo.

   First published in *Revista Helios* (1(2):27–29, 1973), an historical summary of the ecological devastation in Santo Domingo during the last 500 years.

Ethnography

739.   Deive, Carlos E. 1979. Notas sobre la cultura dominicana. *Museo del Hombre Dominicano, Boletín* 8(12):293–305. Santo Domingo.

   Summary of contributions to Dominican culture by the Taíno, black slaves from the United States, fugitive slaves from Haiti, black workers from the English-speaking Caribbean and Haiti.

740.   Schomburgk, Robert. 1851. Ethnological researches in Santo Domingo. *Ethnological Society of London, Journal* 3:114–122. London.

Schomburgk was a German natural scientist and served as British consul in the Dominican Republic. He arrived in 1849 and wrote the first archaeological report for the Caribbean region in which he described the ceremonial plaza at San Juan de la Maguana, cave art in the southeastern part of the country, and indigenous burials in the central mountains. This report was actually a letter written by Schomburgk to Prince Albert, husband of Queen Victoria of England, and forwarded to the Ethnological Society of London; see also: R.H. Schomburgk, Visit to the valley of Constanza (*The Athenaeum* 1291:797–799, 1852); D. Pagan Perdomo, *Sir Robert H. Schomburgk: notas críticas a su obra etnológica en Santo Domingo* (Santo Domingo: Museo del Hombre Dominicano, 1985. 96 p.) for a critical evaluation of Schomburgk's contributions. Spanish translation: Investigaciones etnológicas en Santo Domingo (*Archivo General de la Nación, Boletín* 5:164–169, 1942. Ciudad Trujillo; *Museo del Hombre Dominicano, Boletín* 7(11):211–220, 1978).

741. Vega de Boyrie, Bernardo, Carlos Dobal, Carlos E. Deive, Ruben Silié, José del Castillo, and Frank Moya Pons. 1981. *Ensayos sobre cultura dominicana.* Santo Domingo: Museo del Hombre Dominicano. 245 p.

Dominican scholars discuss various influences upon the culture of their country in a series of lectures at the Museo del Hombre Dominicano in Santo Domingo; contents include: B. Vega, La herencia indígena en la cultura dominicana de hoy (pp. 9–53); M. Veloz Maggiolo, Comentarios a la conferencia La herencia indígena en la cultura dominicana de hoy (pp. 55–59); C. Dobal, Herencia española en la cultura dominicana de hoy (pp. 61–104); C.E. Deive, La herencia africana en la cultura dominicana actual (pp. 105–141); R. Silié, El hato y el conuco: contexto para el surgimiento de la cultura criolla (pp. 143–168); J. del Castillo, Las inmigraciones y su aporte a la cultura dominicana (finales del siglo XIX y principios del siglo XX) (pp. 169–210); F. Moya Pons, Modernización y cambios en la República Dominicana (pp. 211–245).

742. Veloz Maggiolo, Marcio. 1969. Remanentes culturales indígenas y africanos en Santo Domingo. *Revista Dominicana de Antropología e Historia* 4(7–8). Santo Domingo.

Ethnohistory

743. Moya Pons, Frank. 1992. *Manual de historia dominicana.* 9 ed. Santiago: Universidad Católica Madre y Maestre.

Chapter 1 provides a useful summary material pertaining to Taíno society.

744. Peña Batlle, Manuel A. 1948. *La Rebelión de Bahoruco*. Ciudead Trujillo: Impresora Dominicana. 162 p.

Study of the rebellion of the *cacique* Enriquillo against the Spaniards.

745. Rodríguez Demorizi, Emilio. 1971. *Nueva Dominicos y las encomiendas de indios de la Isla Española*. Academia Dominicana de la Historia, v. 30. Santo Domingo.

746. Tavares K., Juan T. 1977. *Los Indios de Quisqueya*. Santo Domingo: Editora de Santo Domingo. 61 p.; Santo Domingo: Taller, 1988. 63 p.

Historical Archaeology

747. Manón Arredendo, Manuel J. 1978. Importancia arqueológica de los ingenios indohispánicos de las Antillas. *Museo del Hombre Dominicano, Boletín* 7(10):139–172. Santo Domingo.

Discussion of the need for archaeological studies of sixteenth- and seventeenth-century sugar mills and factories in the Antilles.

748. Peguero Guzmán, Luis A. 1989. Algunas consideraciones sobre la arqueología de Cimarronaje. *Museo del Hombre Dominicano, Boletín* 22:163–177. Santo Domingo.

General synthesis of African-American archaeology in the Dominican Republic.

Architecture

749. Boyrie Moya, Emile de. 1955. Las ruinas de una torre redonda en la Punta Torrecilla. *Universidad de Santo Domingo, Anales* 20(73–76):149–154. Ciudad Trujillo.

750. Palm, Erwin W. 1955. *Los monumentos arquitectónicos de La Española*. Barcelona: Edit. Seix Barral Hnos; Ciudad Trujillo: Universidad de Santo Domingo. 2 v.

See also: E.W. Palm, *Arquitectura y arte colonial en Santo Domingo* (Santo Domingo: Universidad Autónoma de Santo Domingo, 1974. 251 p.) for an interesting collection of essays on the colonial art and architecture of Santo Domingo and the ruins of Jacagua, the ancient Santiago de los Caballeros.

751. Rosemberg, J.C. 1971–1972. The plaza in a town in the Dominican Republic. *Revista Dominicana de Arqueología y Antropología* 2(2–3):161–165. Santo Domingo.

Pottery

752. Cruxent, José M., and J. Edward Vaz. 1980. Hidroceramicos mexicanos en la República Dominicana. *Casas Reales* 6:23–85. Santo Domingo.

753. Ortega, Elpidio J. 1972. Estudio tipológico de diferentes pipas de los siglos XVII al XX. *Museo del Hombre Dominicano, Boletín* 2:45–72. Santo Domingo.

Underwater Archaeology

754. Borrell B., Pedro J. 1980. *Arqueología submarina en la República Dominicana.* Santo Domingo: Comisión de Rescate Arqueológico Submarino, Grupo de Investigaciones Submarinos. 138 p.

Description of the underwater salvage archaeology program in the Dominican Republic; contains an account of the salvage operation off the coast of Samaná of the eighteenth-century Spanish galleons *Nuestra Señora de Guadalupe* and *Conde de Tolosa*; see also: P.J. Borrell B., El rescate del galeón Concepción en aguas dominicanas (*Geomundo* 2:384–403, 1979); P.J. Borrell B., *Historia y rescate del galeón Nuestra Señora de la Concepción* (Santo Domingo: Museo Casas Reales, 1983); P.J. Borrell B., *The Quicksilver Galleons* (Santo Domingo: Museo Casas Reales, 1983).

Cultural Evolution and Society

Cultural Evolution and Development

755. Morbán Laucer, Fernando. 1979. Cronología de radiocarbono (C-14) para la isla de Santo Domingo. *Museo del Hombre Dominicano, Boletín* 8(12):147–159. Santo Domingo.

756. Veloz Maggiolo, Marcio. 1972. Resumen tipológico de los complejos relacionables con Santo Domingo. *Museo del Hombre Dominicano, Boletín* 1:21–60. Santo Domingo.

757.   ———. 1979. Notas sobre modelos de ocupación prehistórica en la isla de Santo Domingo. *Museo del Hombre Dominicano, Boletín* 8(12):49–57. Santo Domingo.

Archaic

758.   ———. 1980. *Las sociedades arcaicas de Santo Domingo.* Santo Domingo: Museo del Hombre Dominicano; Fundación García-Arévalo. 100 p.

Preceramic

759.   Ortega, Elipdio J., Marcio Veloz Maggiolo, and Fernando Luna Calderón. 1973. Informe sobre tres nuevos pre-cerámicos de la República Dominicana. *Museo del Hombre Dominicano, Boletín* 3:105–134. Santo Domingo.

Description of two Preceramic sites on the southeastern coast at Madrigales and La Isleta (San Pedro de Macorís province) and one on the north coast at Estero Hondo (Puerto Plata province).

760.   Veloz Maggiolo, Marcio, and Elpidio Ortega. 1973. *El Precerámico de Santo Domingo: nuevos lugares y su posible relación con otros puntos del area Antillana.* Museo del Hombre Dominicano, Papeles Occasionales, no. 1. Santo Domingo, 62 p.

Presentation of new information on the Preceramic Period in the Dominican Republic including site summaries for Sanate in Altagracia province, Mordan in Azua province, Honduras del Oeste in the Distrito Nacional, Batey Negro, El Caimito, El Porvenir, Hoyo de Tor, and Sabaneta de Juan Dolio in San Pedro de Macorís province, and Tavera in Santiago province.

761.   Veloz Maggiolo, Marcio, and Elpidio Ortega. 1976. The Preceramic of the Dominican Republic: some new finds and their possible relationships. *Puerto Rican Symposium on Archaeology (1 session, Santurce, P.R., 1976), Proceedings* 1:147–201. Santurce.

Important review of archaeological work pertaining to the Preceramic conducted between 1970–1975.

762.   Veloz Maggiolo, Marcio, Elpidio Ortega, and Plinio Pina P. 1977. Las hallazgos precerámicos en Santo Domingo y sus posibles relaciones en el área. *International Congress of Americanists (41 session, México. 1974), Proceedings* 3:738–755. México.

Consideration of the Preceramic of the Dominican Republic and its relationships with contemporary cultures in the Lesser and Greater

Antilles; authors identify two early Preceramic traditions based upon lithic assemblages which converge with a later culture; the earliest may be as early as 5500 B.C. in Trinidad (Banwari-Trace; St. John; Poonah Road), 3100 B.C. in Cuba (Cayo Redondo), and 2600 B.C. in the Dominican Republic (El Porvenir); a second tradition appears ca. 3200 B.C. in Cuba (Levisa), and ca. 2600–2000 B.C. in the Dominican Republic (Mordan); a third tradition related to the Maicuare culture in Venezuela appears in Cuba at 2000 B.C. (Guayabo Blanco) and in the Dominican Republic at 1250 B.C. (La Isleta)

Ceramic

763. Rimoli, Renato O., and Joaquín Nadal. 1983. *El horizonte ceramista temprano en Santo Domingo y otras Antillas*. Santo Domingo: Editoria de la Universidad Autónoma de Santo Domingo. 353 p.

    Excellent synthesis of existing knowledge pertaining to early ceramic complexes in Cuba and the Dominican Republic; authors argue that early ceramics are not linked to Saldero expansion from South America.

764. Veloz Maggiolo, Marcio, Elpidio Ortega, and Angel Caba Fuentes. 1981. *Los modos de vida Meillacoides y sus posibles orígenes: un estudio interpretativo*. Santo Domingo: Museo del Hombre Dominicano. 433 p.

    Archaeological analysis of Río Joba on the north coast and Río Verde (Cutupu) in the La Vega valley, two sites with similar ceramic assemblages but different settlement and economic patterns.

765. Veloz Maggiolo, Marcio, Elpidio Ortega, and Plinio Pina Peña. 1973. Fechas de radiocarbón para el período ceramista en la República Dominicana. *Museo del Hombre Dominicano, Boletín* 3:138–198. Santo Domingo.

Subsistence Patterns

766. Boyrie Moya, Emile de, Marguerita K. Krestensen, and John M. Goggin. 1957. Zamia starch in Santo Domingo: a contribution to the ethnobotany of the Dominican Republic. *Florida Anthropologist* 19(3–4):17–40. Gainesville.

767. Pina Peña, Plinio F. 1988. Construyeron nuestros aborígenes canales de riego? *Museo del Hombre Dominicano, Boletín* 21:87–90. Santo Domingo.

768.   Rimoli, Renato O. 1971. Restos alimenticios en los yacimientos arqueológicos de la República Dominicana. *Revista Dominicana de Arqueología e Antropología* 2(2–3):68–78. Santo Domingo.

769.   ————. 1972. La hutía y su importancia en la dieta del indio antillano. *Museo del Hombre Dominicano, Boletín* 2:39–44. Santo Domingo.

770.   ————. 1974. Prueba zooarqueológica del tránsito del hombre precolombino de Cuba hacia la Hispaniola. *Revista Dominicana de Antropología y Historia* 4(7–8):19–27. Santo Domingo.

Summary descriptions of zoological materials found in association with archaeological materials in Cuba and the Dominican Republic.

771.   ————. 1982. Estudio comparativo de la dieta en sitios precolombinos de la Española. *Museo del Hombre Dominicano, Boletín* 10(17):141–148. Santo Domingo.

Reconstruction of prehistoric diet inferred from ecological and archaeological data taken from two Chicoid sites, El Soso and Sitio Dumet.

772.   Tavares, Julia. 1978. Notas etnológicas sobre el cazabe. *Museo del Hombre Dominicano, Boletín* 7(11):147–176. Santo Domingo.

773.   Vega Boyrie, Bernardo. 1980. Herencia taína: nuestros corrales de pesca. *Museo del Hombre Dominicano, Boletín* 9(13):315–320. Santo Domingo.

Description of fishing traps used in Laguna de Rincón and other lakes in Cabral, Barahona province, and a discussion of possible archaeological correspondences.

774.   ————. 1978. El lambí en muestra cultura prehispánica. *Museo del Hombre Dominicano, Boletín* 7(10):173–183. Santo Domingo.

Discussion of the prehispanic importance of *Strombus gigas* shellfish; uses included as a food source, musical instrument, material for utilitarian implements, ornaments, and as a magico-religious item.

775.   Veloz Maggiolo, Marcio. 1976–1977. *Medioambiente y adaptación humana en la prehistoria de Santo Domingo*. 2 ed. Santo Domingo: Ediciones de Taller. 2 v.

Based on differences in production and subsistence strategies, author attempts to revise the concepts, nomenclature, and cultural schemes established for the study of the Ciboney; analysis of material culture and environment which produced the initial typology of the Paleoarchaic and Archaic for the Caribbean; included are useful summaries for the following preagricultural sites: Banwari-Trace in Trinidad (5500–3500 B.C.); Jolly Beach in Antigua (1800 B.C.); Krum Bay in St. Thomas, Virgin Islands (450–225 B.C.), Maria de la Cruz in Puerto Rico (40–30 B.C.); Cayo Cofresi in Puerto Rico (325–295 B.C.); Cueva del Ferrocarril near Samana in the Dominican Republic (A.D. 785); Madrigales-Serralles-El Porvenir sequence for the Dominican Republic (2050–905 B.C.); Barrera area with the Mordan-Casimira sequence in the Dominican Republic (2610–2165 B.C.); La Isleta in the Dominican Republic (1250 B.C.); Hoyo del Toro in the Dominican Republic (1950–650 B.C.); Couri in Haiti; Cordillera Central in the Dominican Republic (ca. 850 B.C.); Cayo Redondo in Cuba (A.D. 990); Guayabo Blanco in Cuba (2000–1000 B.C.); Damajayabo in Cuba (1250 B.C.); Ortoire, Levisa in Cuba (3190–1510 B.C.); agricultural sites in the Dominican Republic summarized include: El Caimito (180 B.C.-A.D. 125), Musiepedro (305 B.C.), Los Corrales (A.D. 645–720), Punta de Garza (A.D. 1245–1300), La Cucana (A.D. 880–910), Atajadizo and Guayabal phases at Yuma (A.D. 840; A.D. 1015), Río Verde in the Vega Real (A.D. 825–850), El Carrill (A.D. 930), and La Union (A.D. 1435).

776. Veloz Maggiolo, Marcio, and Renato Rimoli. 1975. Estudio preliminar sobre restos alimenticios y poosibles medioambientes en el precerámico de Santo Domingo. *Revista Ciencia* 2(1):75–90. Santo Domingo; *International Congress of Americanists (41 session, México, 1974), Proceedings* 3:756–771, 1977. México.

Preliminary study of microenvironments and dietary reconstructions during the Preceramic and modern times.

Demography

777. Moya Pons, Frank. 1979. *Datos para el estudio de la demografía aborigen en Santo Domingo.* Jahrbuch für Geschichte von Staat, Wirtschaft und Gesellscahft Lateinamerikas, no. 16. Cologne; Vienna: Böhlau Verlag. 435 p.

Author doubts the extinction of Taíno population was the result of diseases introduced by the Spaniards in the sixteenth century; most Taínos committed suicide because they were unwilling to endure the mistreatment which was inflicted upon them by the Spaniards; see also: F. Moya Pons, Datos para el estudio de la demografía aborigen en Santo Domingo (*Museo del Hombre Dominicano, Boletín* 6:72–92, 1976) and Nuevas consideraciones sobre la historia de la población dominicana: curvas, tasas y problemas (*Museo del Hombre Dominicano, Boletín* 7:131–160, 1976).

Physical Anthropology

778. Drusini, Andrea G., and Fernando Luna Calderón. 1991. Antropología física dei taíno di Hispaniola. *L'Universo, Supplemento* 1:24–27. Firenze.

779. Drusini, Andrea C., F. Businaro, and F. Luna Calderon. 1987. Skeletal biology of the Taíno: a preliminary report. *International Journal of Anthropology* 2:247–253.

780. Estrada Torres, Arístedes. 1990. La sífilis en la historia de nuestra isla. *Museo del Hombre Dominicano, Boletín* 23:107–118. Santo Domingo.

See also, A. Estrada Torres, *Evidencias patologicas en algunas obras taínas* (Azua: Editora Taller, 1978. 29 p.).

781. García-Godoy, Franklin. 1980. Caries dental en craneos primitivos de la isla Santo Domingo. *Museo del Hombre Dominicano, Boletín* 9(13):235–243. Santo Domingo.

Examination of more than one hundred skulls from the Dominican Republic indicates a low incidence of dental caries and a high incidence of extraction.

782. Luna Calderón, Fernando. 1982. Antropología y paleopatología de Cueva Maria Sosa, Boca de Yuma, provincia La Altagracia. *Museo del Hombre Dominicano, Boletín* 17:1489–167. Santo Domingo.

783. ———. 1988. Enfermedades en las osamentas indígenas de la isla de Santo Domingo. *Museo del Hombre Dominicano, Boletín* 21:79–83. Santo Domingo.

784. Jiménez Lambertus, Abelardo. 1978. En torno al cráneo ciguayo descrito por el Dr. Alejandro Llenas en 1890. *Museo del Hombre Dominicano, Boletín* 7(10):239–252. Santo Domingo.

785. Jiménez Lambertus, Abelardo. 1978. Paleopatología osea columnar en esqueletos indígenas precolombinos de la isla de Santo Domingo. *Museo del Hombre Dominicano, Boletín* 9:113–124. Santo Domingo.

786. Morbán Laucer, Fernando. 1980. Anomalias buco-dentarias en los aborígenes de la Hispaniola. *Acta de Odontología Pediatrica* 1(1):1–54.

787. Morbán Laucer, Fernando. 1987. Características de los dientes de grupos raciales prehistóricos y su presencia actual. *Museo del Hombre Dominicano, Boletín* 14(20):17–45. Santo Domingo.

788. Morbán Laucer, Fernando. 1988. Enfermedades en las osamentas indígenas de la isla de Santo Domingo. *Museo del Hombre Dominicano, Boletín* 21:79–83. Santo Domingo.

789. Pina Peña, Plinio. 1972. Las deformaciones intencionales del cuerpo humano en las Antillas. *Museo del Hombre Dominicano, Boletín* 1:5–7. Santo Domingo.

Religious Organization

790. Arrom, Juan José. 1988. Lechuza: motivo recurrente en el arte religioso taíno y el folklore hispanoamericano. *Museo del Hombre Dominicano, Boletín* 21:71–76. Santo Domingo.

Burial Patterns

791. Alberti Bosch, Narciso. 1932. Sepulturas indígenas de Santo Domingo. *Revista Bimestre Cubana* 29(2):219–235. La Habana; *Museo del Hombre Dominicano, Boletín* 8(12):327–344, 1979. Santo Domingo.

First published in the Cuban journal *Bimestre* in 1932, this essay is valuable for important descriptions of cave burials at Saona, Constanza, Puerto Plata, Samaná, and Cotuí as well as the first excavations in La Caleta, Punta Garza, and Ingenio Cristóbal Colón. Alberti was born in Cataluña, Spain, and emigrated to Cuba in 1875 as physician.

792. Morbán Laucer, Fernando A. 1979. *Ritos funerarios: acción del fuego y medio ambiente en las osamientas precolombinas.* Academia de Ciencias de la República Dominicana, Comisión de Arqueología, v. 1. Santo Domingo: Editora Taller. 157 p.

Historical and archaeological evidence is used in a discussion of the use of fire as part of religious mortuary ritual among various cultures on Hispaniola; discusses secondary burials and other practices associated with inhumation.

793. Veloz Maggiolo, Marcio. 1973. La Athebeanenequen: evidencia de sacrificio humano en los taínos. *Museo del Hombre Dominicano, Boletín* 3:64–69. Santo Domingo.

Review of archaeological evidence for human sacrifice at the La Cucama site.

794.   Veloz Maggiolo, Marcio, Elpidio Ortega, and Renato Rimoli, and Fernando Luna Calderón. 1973. Estudio comparativo y preliminar de los cementerios neo-indios: La Cucama y La Unión, República Dominicana. *Museo del Hombre Dominicano, Boletín* 3:11–47. Santo Domingo.

Figure 11. Bone vomit spatula with ornithomorphic design.
Vomit spatulas were used to induce vomiting associated with *cohoba*,
an hallucinogenic snuff used in ritual contexts.

Source: M.A. García Arévalo, *Los signos en el arte Taíno*, Santo Domingo: Fundación García-Arévalo, 1989. Figure 9.

Deities

795. Veloz Maggiolo, Marcio. 1970. Los trigonolitos antillanos: aportes para un intento de reclasificación e interpretación. *Revista Española de Antropología Americana* 5:317–339. Madrid.

Discussion of three-pointed stones as representations of the Arawak supreme deity, Yocahu.

Cohoba

796. Veloz Maggiolo, Marcio. 1971. El rito de la cohoba entre los aborígenes antillanos. *Revista Dominicana de Arqueología e Antropología* 1(1):201–208. Santo Domingo.

Ball Game

797. Veloz Maggiolo, Marcio. 1972. Tres modalidades del juego de pelota entre los aborígenes americanos. *Museo del Hombre Dominicano, Boletín* 2:25–32. Santo Domingo.

Settlement Patterns

798. Bullen, Ripley P., and Adelaide K. Bullen. 1973. Settlement patterns and environment in [pre-] Columbian eastern Dominican Republic. *Museo del Hombre Dominicano, Boletín* 3:315–324. Santo Domingo.

Description of thirty-three archaeological sites found in the La Romana region of eastern Dominican Republic.

799. Veloz Maggiolo, Marcio, and Elpidio Ortega. 1976. La fotografía aérea como experiencia en la prospección de lugares arqueológicos precolombinos y coloniales en la República Dominicana. *Instituto Montecristeño de Arqueología, Boletín* 2:35–40. Monte Cristi.

Material Culture

Art

800. García Arévalo, Manuel A. 1977. *El arte taíno de la República Dominicana.* Santo Domingo21: Museo del Hombre Dominicano. 64 p.

See also, O. Montas, *Arte taíno* (Santo Domingo: Banco Central de la Republica Dominicana, 1985. 231 p.).

801. García Arévalo, Manuel. 1988. Precisiones acerca de los signos en el arte taíno. *Museo del Hombre Dominicano, Boletín* 21:3–22. Santo Domingo.

802. Herrera Fritot, René. 1947. Tres tipos de objetos indoarqueológicos de Santo Domingo. *Revista de Arqueología y Etnología* 2(4–5):125–135. La Habana.

803. Morbán Laucer, Fernando. 1988. El murciélago: sus representaciones en el arte y la mitología precolombina. *Museo del Hombre Dominicano, Boletín* 21:37–57. Santo Domingo.

804. Morbán Laucer, Fernando. 1989. Arte, falsificación, saqueo y destrucción II Congreso Nacional de Arqueología Jose Antonio Caro Alvarez, 1988. *Museo del Hombre Dominicano, Boletín* 22:51–63. Santo Domingo.

805. Suro, Darío. 1950. El mundo mágico taíno: amuletos, espátulos y majaderos. *Cuadernos Hispanoamercanos* 17:259–264.

   Commentary on the art of the Taíno, as found in the Dominican Republic.

806. Suro, Darío. 1966. Of artists and owls: Taíno sculpture. *Américas* 18(3):21–28. Washington, DC.

   Illustrated account on Taíno art from Hispaniola.

807. Veloz Maggiolo, Marcio. 1977. *Arte indígena y economía en Santo Domingo.* Santo Domingo: Ediciones Cohoba.

808. Wirz, Paul. 1947. Uber einige Ton- und Steinobjekte aus Santo Domingo. *Verhandlungen der naturforschenden Gesellschaft in Basel* 58:80–107. Basel.

   Description of two effigy vessels and other objects from the Dominican Republic.

Petroglyphs and Pictographs

809. Morbán Laucer, Fernando A. 1970. *Pintura rupestre y petroglífos en Santo Domingo.* Santo Domingo: Universidad Autónoma de Santo Domingo, Facultad de Humanidades, Instituto de Investigaciones Antropológicas. 233 p.

   Study of pictographs and petroglyphs discovered by a research team from the Institute of Anthropological Research at the Autonomous University of Santo Domingo.

810. Morbán Laucer, Fernando A. 1979. *El arte rupestre de la República Dominicana: petroglífos de la Provincia de Azua.* Santo Domingo: Fundación García Arévalo. 93 p.

Illustrated monograph on rock art in the Dominican Republic; includes discussion of general features and motifs and techniques used, and petroglyphs in Azua province.

811. Pagán Perdomo, Dato. 1978. *Arte rupestre en el area del caribe; inventario de sitios de arte rupestre en República Dominicana y bibliografía sumaria del area.* Santo Domingo: Editora Taller. 80 p.

See also, P. Pagán Perdomo, Inventario del arte rupestre en Santo Domingo (*Museo del Hombre Dominicano, Boletín* 8(12:119–135, 1979).

812. ———. 1980. Aspectos zooarqueológicos y geográficos en el arte rupestre de Santo Domingo. *Museo del Hombre Dominicano, Boletín* 9(13):49–60. Santo Domingo.

Description of seventy-seven examples of rock art displaying zoomorphic motifs found in the Dominican Republic.

813. ———. 1982. Aspectos ergológicos e ideología en el arte rupestre de la Isla de Santo Domingo. *Museo del Hombre Dominicano, Boletín* 10(17):55–94. Santo Domingo.

List of selected cultural elements depicted in petroglyphs and pictographs.

814. ———. 1984. Apuntes sobre el arte rupestre prehispánico de Santo Domingo (discusión acerca de una hipótesis del arte rupestre antillano). *Museo del Hombre Dominicano, Boletín* 19:95–103. Santo Domingo.

815. ———. 1987. Estudio del arte rupestre en el contexto de la arqueología como ciencia social. *Museo del Hombre Dominicano, Boletín* 20:61–67. Santo Domingo.

816. Vega de Boyrie, Bernardo. 1976. *Pictografías.* Santo Domingo: Museo del Hombre Dominicano. 44 p.

Illustrated discussion of pictographs found in cave sites throughout the Dominican Republic, including Cueva del Ferrocarril on the south coast of Samaná Bay, Cueva de Borbón north of San Cristobal, and Cueva de las Maravillas east of San Pedro de Macorís; author argues areas with petroglyphs possess magical or ritual importance and pictographs are not simply works of art.

817.   Veloz Maggiolo, Marcio. 1970. Informe sobre una posible metodología para la interpretación y posible identificación de las pinturas rupestres antillanas. *Revista Española de Antropología Americana* 5:317–340. Madrid.

818.   ———, Plinio Pina Peña, Elpidio Ortega, and Bernardo Vega. 1971–1972. El Quehacer rupestre antillano: modo de realización y patrones aplicables al estudio de su ubicación en el tiempo. *Revista Dominicana de Arqueología y Antropología* 2(2–3):111–127. Santo Domingo.

Pottery

819.   Booy, Theodoor H.N. de. 1915. Pottery from certain caves in eastern Santo Domingo, West Indies. *American Anthropologist* 17(1):69–97. Washington, DC.

820.   Diaz Niese, Rafael. 1945. *La alfarería indígena dominicana.* Santo Domingo: Editorial La Opinión. 34 p.

Descriptive classification of Boca Chica style and Taíno pottery bottles in the Museo Nacional, Ciudad Trujillo.

821.   Estrada Torres, Aristides. 1967. *Cerámica propociatoria entre nuestros indígenas.* Universidad Autónoma de Santo Domingo, Instituto Dominicano de Investigaciones Antropológicas, 1. Santo Domingo. 16 p.

Illustrated description of anthropomorphic and zoomorphic effigy clay vessels with evidence of possible pathologies.

822.   Herrera Fritot, René. 1952. Vasos-efigies indígenas de la República Dominicana: primera parte, formas anchas y bajas. *Congreso Histórico Municipal Interamericano (5 session, Ciudad Trujillo, 1952), Memorias* 1:89–132. Ciudad Trujillo.

Classification and description of effigy vessels in Dominican collections; author argues these are the outstanding products of Taíno ceramics and are probably associated with the cult of the *zemis.*

823.   Jiménez Lambertus, Abelardo. 1978. Representación simbólica de la tortuga mítica en el arte cerámico taíno. *Museo del Hombre Dominicano, Boletín* 7(11):63–76. Santo Domingo.

824.   Krieger, Herbert W. 1931. *Aboriginal Indian Pottery of the Dominican Republic.* Smithsonian Institution, Bulletin, no. 156. Washington, DC. 165 p.

825.   Veloz Maggiolo, Marcio. 1972. Algunas formas de Asa-Estribio en Santo Domingo. *Museo del Hombre Dominicano, Boletín* 2:120–129. Santo Domingo.

Pottery Technology

826.   Cartagena Portalatin, Aida. 1972. *Dos técnicas cerámicas indoantillanas: diagnóstico de origen de los yacimientos de las Antillas Mayores.* Universidad de Santo Domingo, Instituto de Antropología, Boletin 10. Santo Domingo. 22 p.

Figurines

827.   Morbán Laucer, Fernando A. 1980. Los figurines de arcilla en la prehistoria. *Museo del Hombre Dominicano, Boletín* 9(13):81–115. Santo Domingo.

Discussion of clay figurines found in the Dominican Republic and the New World.

Whistles

828.   Boyrie Moya, Emile de. 1952. Aparición en la isla de Santo Domingo de los primeros silbatos modulados indígenas, tipo ocarino, encontrados en las Antillas. *Congreso Histórico Municipal Interamericano (5 session, 1952, Ciudad Trujillo), Memorias* 1:187–188. Ciudad Trujillo.

Description of two clay whistles from a Taíno site.

Lithics

829.   Veloz Maggiolo, Marcio, and Carlos Alberto Martin. 1983. Las técnicas unifaciales de los yacimientos del Jobo y sus similitudes con el Paleo-Arcaico antillano. *Museo del Hombre Dominicano, Boletín* 11(18):13–37. Santo Domingo.

Summary of similarities and differences of unifacially worked lithic artifacts from El Jobo in Venezuela and early lithic industries of the Paleo-Archaic in the Antilles.

Groundstone

830.   Baztan Rodrígo, Francisco J. 1971. Los amuletos precolombinos de Santo Domingo. *Revista Dominicana de Arqueología y Antropología* 2(2–3):196–227. Santo Domingo.

831.   Fewkes, Jesse W. 1891. On zemes from Santo Domingo. *American Anthropologist* 4(2):167–175. Washington, DC.

Metalwork

832.   Vega de Boyrie, Bernardo. 1979. *Los metales y los aborígenes de la Hispaniola*. Santo Domingo: Ediciones Museo del Hombre Dominicano. 63 p.

Anaylsis of gold, copper, silver, brass, and copper-silver alloys found in the Dominican Republic; author traces the distribution of these metal artifacts and draws several possible conclusions regarding their origin.

Cordage and Textiles

833.   Biscione, Marco. 1991. Lo zemi del Museo Pigorini: problemi di interpretazione. *L'Universo, Supplemento* 1:77–84. Firenze.

834.   Masali, Melchiorre, and Gabriella Erica Pia. 1991. I materiali taíno del Museo di Antropología di Torino: lo zemi di cotone. *L'Universo, Supplemento* 1:885–900. Firenze.

835.   Vega de Boyrie, Bernardo. 1971. Descubrimiento de la actual localización del único zemí de algodón antrillano aún existente. *Revista Dominicana de Arqueología y Antropología* 2(2–3):88–110. Santo Domingo.

836.   ———. 1973. Un cinturon tejido y una careta de madera de Santo Domingo, del período de transculturación taíno-español. *Museo del Hombre Dominicano, Boletín* 3:199–226. Santo Domingo.

Illustrated account of a cotton belt in the Museum für Völkerkunde in Vienna and a wooden mask in the Luigi Pigorini Museum in Rome.

Intellectual Life

Music

837.   Lizardo, Fradique. 1975. *Instrumentos musicales indígenas dominicanos*. Santo Domingo: Ediciones Cultura Nacional. 105 p.

Regional and Site Reports

838.   Jiménez Lambertus, Abelardo, Renato O. Rimoli, and Joaquín E. Nadal. 1980. Exploraciones espeleológicas y arqueológicas en los parajes La Tina (provincia La Vega), El Cigual y Monte Bonito (provincia Azua). *Museo del Hombre Dominicano, Boletín* 9(14):123–146. Santo Domingo.

839.   Morbán Laucer, Fernando. 1976. Informe arqueológico preliminar del extremo sureste de la isla de Santo Domingo y la Saona. *Museo del Hombre Dominicano, Boletín* 6:13–27. Santo Domingo.

840.   Ortega, Elpidio J., and José Guerrero. 1981. *Estudio de cuatro nuevos sitios paleoarcaicos de la Isla de Santo Domingo.* Santo Domingo: Museo del Hombre Dominicano. 226 p.

Authors provide excellent description and analysis of lithics excavated from four Palaeo-Archaic Preceramic sites in the Dominican Republic: El Curro, Las Salinas, Los Toros, and Canade de Palma.

841.   Veloz Maggiolo, Marcio, and Elpidio Ortega. 1980. Nuevos hallazgos arqueológicos en la costa norte de Santo Domingo. *Museo del Hombre Dominicano, Boletín* 9(13):11–48. Santo Domingo.

Report on a reconnaissance of the north coast provinces of Espaillat, María Trinidad Sanchez, and Puerto Plata which yielded sixteen archaeological sites.

Altagracía Province

842.   Veloz Maggiolo, Marcio, Iraida Vargas Arenas, Mario Sanoja, and Fernando Luna Calderón. 1976. *Arqueología de Yuma, República Dominicana.* Santo Domingo: Taller. 346 p.

Report on excavations at El Atajadizo, a multicomponent site near San Rafael del Yuma, southeastern Dominican Republic; two phases have been radiocarbon dated at A.D. 540, A.D. 840, and A.D. 1015. The site of Musiepedro is dated at 305 B.C.; includes a description of 33 ceramic types at El Atajadizo and ten at Musiepedro.

Cuadro de Piedras

843.   Guerrero, José G. 1981. Dos plazas indígenas y el poblado de Cotubanamá, Parque Nacional del Este. *Museo del Hombre Dominicano, Boletín* 10(16):13–30. Santo Domingo.

Discussion of the Parque Nacional del Este and suggestion that Cuadro de Piedras, a site within the park, may have been the residence of the cacique Cotubanama.

Cueva de Berna

844.   Veloz Maggiolo, Marcio, Elpidio Ortega, Joaquin Nadal, Fernando Luna Calderon, and Renato O. Rimoli. 1977.

Arqueología de Cueva de Berna. San Pedro de Macorís: Universidad Central del Este. 99 p.

Report on excavations at preceramic Cueva de Berna, radiocarbon dated at 1890–1255 B.C.; site was evidently occupied for some 600 years by marine gatherers and later served as a ceremonial locus; authors suggest similarities between Cueva de Berna and Banwari-Trace in Trinidad.

El Atajadizo

845.   Informe preliminar de las investigaciones realizadas en El Atajadizo, República Dominicana. *Museo del Hombre Dominicano, Boletín* 7:7–63, 1976. Santo Domingo.

846.   Jeldes, Fidel, and Shirley Hall. 1976. Restos alimenticos de la zona de Atajadizo-Yuma. *Museo del Hombre Dominicano, Boletín* 7:107–119. Santo Domingo.

847.   Luna Calderón, Fernando. 1976. Informe preliminar del cementerio indígena de El Atajadizo, República Dominicana. *Museo del Hombre Dominicano, Boletín* 7:67–95. Santo Domingo.

848.   Pagan Perdomo, Dato. 1976. Reconocimiento de las cavernas del area del paraje El Atajadizo. *Museo del Hombre Dominicano, Boletín* 7:99–104. Santo Domingo.

El Macao

849.   Borrell Bentz, Pedro J. 1979. Buceando tras los taínos. *Museo del Hombre Dominicano, Boletín* 8(12):137–145. Santo Domingo.

Report on the underwater investigation of cave sites near El Macao, Dominican Republic.

850.   Veloz Maggiolo, Marcio, and Elpidio Ortega. 1972. Excavaciones en Macao, República Dominicana. *Museo del Hombre Dominicano, Boletín* 2:157–175. Santo Domingo.

Sanate Abajo

851.   Chanlatte Baik, Luis A. 1978. Informe: Sanate-Higüey. *Museo del Hombre Dominicano, Boletín* 7(10):133–138. Santo Domingo.

Summary of excavations by the Museo del Hombre Dominicano in a sixteenth-century sugar processing facility near Sanate Abajo, municipality of Higüey, Altagracia province; see also: J.A. Caro Alvarez, Introducción (*Museo del Hombre Dominicano, Boletín* 7(10):45–49, 1978); D. Pagán Perdomo, Descripción geografica (*Museo del Hombre Dominicano, Boletín* 7(10):51–52, 1978); and L. Chanlatte Baik,

Informe sobre el yacimiento prehispánico (*Museo del Hombre Dominicano, Boletín* 7(10):53–74, 1978).

852. Fortuna, Luis. 1978. Análisis polínico de Sanate Abajo. *Museo del Hombre Dominicano, Boletín* 7(10):125–130. Santo Domingo.

An ecological reconstruction based upon results of a palynological study of Sanate Abajo, an Ostionoid site in the Dominican Republic.

853. Fortuna, Luis. 1978. Informe sobre la flora actual en los alrededores del yacimiento arqueológico del paraje Sanate Abajo en el municipio de Higuey, provincia de la Altagracia. *Museo del Hombre Dominicano, Boletín* 7(10):131–132. Santo Domingo.

Thirty-two floral genera are identified in the environs of modern Sanate Abajo site.

854. Garcia Arévalo, Manuel A., and Julia Tavares. Presentación. *Museo del Hombre Dominicano, Boletín* 7(10):31–44. Santo Domingo.

Summary of results of the excavation of Sanate Abajo, a multicomponent site; earliest occupation (Ostionoid) is radiocarbon dated at ca. A.D. 1050.

855. Hall, Shirley M. 1978. Restos alimenticios. *Museo del Hombre Dominicano, Boletín* 7(10):95–124. Santo Domingo.

Summary reports on subsistence patterns and dietary reconstruction at the Ostionoid site of Sanate Abajo.

856. Morbán Laucer, Fernando, and Abelardo Jiménez Lambertus. 1978. Enterramientos humanos localizados en Sanate. *Museo del Hombre Dominicano, Boletín* 7(10):75–93. Santo Domingo.

Analysis of Ostionoid (ca. A.D. 820–1050) skeletal and associated lithic material from three excavated burials near Sanate, Altagracia province, Dominican Republic.

Azua Province

857. Guerrero, Jose G., and Fernando Luna Calderon. 1980. Informe de viaje a Padre Las Casas, provincia de Azua. *Museo del Hombre Dominicano, Boletín* 9(14):87–121. Santo Domingo.

Description of pottery, petroglyphs, and a possible plaza site at Loma Pie, Los Indios, and Monte Bonito.

Barreras

858.   Mañon Arredondo, Manuel de J. 1978. Aspectos prehistóricos no explicados de Barreras. *Museo del Hombre Dominicano, Boletín* 7(11):57–62. Santo Domingo.

Report on lithic material recovered from the Barreras area, Azua province, on the southwest coast of the Dominican Republic.

Barahona Province

859.   Vega, Bernardo. 1979. Arqueología de los Cimarrones del maniel del Bahoruco. *Museo del Hombre Dominicano, Boletín* 8(12):11–48. Santo Domingo.

Study of African American archaeology at Manifarto, Polo, Barahona, southwestern Dominican Republic, of *manieles* or refuge sites in the mountains where African American slaves sought refuge between 1522 and the end of the nineteenth century.

Las Salinas

860.   Veloz Maggiolo, Marcio, Plinio Pina Peña, and Bernardo Vega. 1971. Informe sobre un reconocimiento arqueológico en Las Salinas, República Dominicana. *Revista Dominicana de Arqueología y Antropología* 2(2–3):28–35. Santo Domingo.

Parque Nacional Jaragua

861.   López Rojas, Elba. 1990. Informe de un viaje de prospección al Parque Nacional Jaragua, 1987. *Museo del Hombre Dominicano, Boletín* 23:41–53. Santo Domingo.

Summary report on several prehistoric sites in the Parque Nacional Jaragua, Barahona province, including El Saladito, El Guanal, Cueva La Poza, Cueva Mongó, Río Pedernales, Cueva Roja, La Jinagosa, Las Mercedes, and La Ceiba.

Dajabon Province

Chacuey

862.   Boyrie Moya, Emile de. 1955. *Monumento megalítico y petroglifos de Chacuey, República Dominicana.* Universidad de Santo Domingo, Publicaciones, ser. 7, Antropología y Folklore, no. 1. Ciudad Trujillo: Editora del Caribe. 223 p.

Detailed report on the mapping and excavation of a ceremonial dance plaza as well as illustrations of petroglyphs; includes information on other sites in the Chacuey region.

863.   Castellanos, Reynaldo. 1981. La plaza de Chacuey: un instrumento astronómico megalítico. *Museo del Hombre Dominicano, Boletín* 10(16):31–40. Santo Domingo.

Author suggests many features of the plaza at Chacuey had astronomical significance.

864.   Marichal, Pragmacio. 1989. Destrucción del monumento indígena de Chacuey. *Museo del Hombre Dominicano, Boletín* 22:95–107. Santo Domingo.

Excellent summary of the destruction of the ceremonial plaza at Chacuey by road construction between 1980 and 1982.

Distrito Nacional

Cueva de Collantes

865.   Caba Fuentes, Angel, and Harold Olsen Bogaert. 1983. Descripción de tipos cerámicos de Cueva de Collantes, Distrito Nacional. *Museo del Hombre Dominicano, Boletín* 11(18):91–109. Santo Domingo.

Description of ceramic and non-ceramic artifacts from the historic period Collantes Cave site; author argues unfired clay balls were associated with geophagy.

866.   Veloz Maggiolo, Marcio, Renato O. Rimoli, and Fernando Luna Calderón. 1983. Investigaciones arqueológicas en Cueva Collantes, D.R.: informe preliminar. *Museo del Hombre Dominicano, Boletín* 11(18):73–96. Santo Domingo.

Authors conclude that a complex of caves in Santo Domingo were Taíno ceremonial sites occupied ca. A.D. 1000–1300.

El Caimito

867.   Veloz Maggiolo, Marcio, Elpidio Ortega, and Plinio Pina P. 1974. *El Caimito, un antiguo complejo ceramista de las Antillas Mayores.* Santo Domingo: Ediciones Fundación García-Arévalo. 25 p.

Important report on El Caimito, a Preceramic habitation site on the south coast of the Dominican Republic radiocarbon dated between 180 B.C. to A.D. 20.

Honduras del Oeste

868.   Rimoli, Renato O., and Joaquín Nadal. 1980. Cerámica temprana de Honduras del Oeste. *Museo del Hombre Dominicano, Boletín* 9(15):17–82. Santo Domingo.

Description of Honduras del Oeste, a site dated between 360 B.C.-A.D. 185 and southwest of Santo Domingo; lithic and ceramic artifacts are discussed.

Los Paredones

869.   Morban Laucer, Fernando A. 1968. *Los Paredones: un santuario prehistórico.* Universidad Autónoma de Santo Domingo, Instituto de Investigaciones Antropológicas, no. 2. Santo Domingo. 19 p.

Description of anthropomorphic and zoomorphic stone effigies found in the caves of Los Paredones manufactured by modifying riverine pebbles.

870.   Veloz Maggiolo, Marcio. 1968. Paredones: una nueva cultura antillana. *Mundo Hispánico* 21(248):42–46. Madrid.

Illustrated description of 28 anthropomorphic and zoomorphic figures found in the caves at Los Paredones; author argues carvings are made from stalactites and stalagmites.

Santo Domingo Viejo

871.   Jiménez Lambertus, A., and Hernán Olmos Cordones. 1979. Estudio de los restos biológicos de las excavaciones arqueológicas realizadas en el antiguo Colegio de Gorjón. *Museo del Hombre Dominicano, Boletín* 8(12):225–256. Santo Domingo.

872.   Monte Urraca, Manuel E. del. 1972. Capilla del Santísimo Sacramento de la Catedral de Santo Domingo de Guzmán: su historia y su restauración. *Museo del Hombre Dominicano, Boletín* 2:105–119. Santo Domingo.

873.   Olsen Bogaert, Harold. 1989. Investigaciones arqueológicas en la Capilla Nuestra Señora de la Antigua. *Museo del Hombre Dominicano, Boletín* 22:109–162. Santo Domingo.

Summary report on excavations in the colonial zone of Santo Domingo; includes a discussion of stratigraphy, faunal remains, and human burials.

874.   Olsen Bogaert, Harold, and Abelardo Jiménez Lambertus. 1990. La cerámica como relleno en construcciones coloniales; caso: techo sala de reflexiones del conjunto de Las Mercedes, Santo Domingo. *Museo del Hombre Dominicano, Boletín* 23:55–71. Santo Domingo.

875.   Ortega, Elpidio J. 1974. La mayólica hallada en las ruinas de San Francisco. *Museo del Hombre Dominicano, Boletín* 4:67–80. Santo Domingo.

876.   ———. 1980. *Introducción a la loza común o alfarería en el período colonial de Santo Domingo*. Santo Domingo: Fundación Ortega Alvarez. 166 p.

Ceramic analysis of materials from Plaza de los Curas, excavated in 1968; emphasis is on simple utilitarian ware, the most popular form used through the nineteenth century.

877.   ———. 1982. *Arqueología colonial de Santo Domingo*. Santo Domingo: Fundación Ortega Alvarez. 1982. 588 p.

878.   ———, and José M. Cruxent. 1977. Informe preliminar sobre las excavaciones en las ruinas del convento de San Francisco. *International Congress of Americanists (41 session, México, 1974), Proceedings* 3:674–689. México.

Summary report on excavation of the colonial Convent of San Francisco in Santo Domingo.

879.   ———, and Carmen Fondeur. 1978. *Arqueología de los monumentos históricos de Santo Domingo*. San Pedro de Macorís: Universidad Central del Este. 142 p.

Description of sixteen historical monuments excavated in the Dominican Republic; includes analysis of ceramic materials.

880.   ———, and Carmen Fondeur. 1979. *Arqueología de la Casa del Cordón*. Santo Domingo: Fundación Ortega Alvarez. 97 p.

Historical archaeological study of one of the oldest stone buildings in Santo Domingo, called the Rope House, because a monk's rope with tassels decorates its doorway.

881.   ———, and María Luisa Valdez. 1979. Informe de las excavaciones arqueológicas de la Casa de Gorjón. *Museo del Hombre Dominicano, Boletín* 8(12):161–223. Santo Domingo.

882.   Pina Peña, Plinio, Elpidio J. Ortega, and Marcio Veloz Maggiolo. 1972. Informe sobre reconocimiento arqueológico en la Casa no. 1 de la Calle Pellerano Alfau, Santo Domingo, República Dominicana. *Museo del Hombre Dominicano, Boletín* 2:73–103. Santo Domingo.

Higüey Province

Camino de los Indios de Macao

883.   Ortega, Elpidio J. 1984. Informe sobre las investigaciones arqueológicas en el Camino de los Indios de Macao, Provincia de Higüey. *Museo del Hombre Dominicano, Boletín* 19:13–23. Santo Domingo.

La Vega Province

884.   Olmos Cordones, Hernán, and Abelardo Jiménez Lambertus. 1980. Primer reporte de petroglífos de los sitios Palma Caña y El Palero, Provincia La Vega. *Museo del Hombre Dominicano, Boletín* 9(13):125–152. Santo Domingo.

Report on petroglyphs found at Palma Caña and El Palero sites in La Vega province.

La Concepción de La Vega

885.   Caceres Mendoza, Lourdes. 1980. Cerámica de las ruinas de La Vega Vieja. *Casas Reales* 5(11):101–113. Santo Domingo.

886.   Concepción, Mario. 1979. La evolución de la vivienda en La Vega Vieja. *Casas Reales* 3(8):79–101. Santo Domingo.

887.   Dalman, Virgilio. 1979. Informe de las investigaciones arqueológicas realizadas en el sitio histórico de La Vega. *Casas Reales* 3(8):103–117. Santo Domingo.

888.   González, José, and Fabio Pimentel. 1990. Rescate arqueológico y puesta en valor de La Vega Vieja. *Museo del Hombre Dominicano, Boletín* 23:97–1004. Santo Domingo.

Summary of conservation plans for Parque Nacional Historico de La Vega Vieja/Villa de la Concepción de La Vega, including descriptions of the monastery of San Francisco, and the fortress and cathedral.

889.   Jiménez Lambertus, Abelardo. 1979. Estudio antropológico físico del esqueleto humano descubrierto durante los trabajos arqueológicos de la Villa de la Concepción de La Vega. *Casas Reales* 3(8):119–133. Santo Domingo.

890.   ———. 1979. Estudio esqueleto 01 de las excavaciones de la Villa de la Concepción. *Museo del Hombre Dominicano, Boletín* 8(12):261–276. Santo Domingo.

891. Mendoza, Lourdes C. 1980. Cerámica de las ruinas de La Vega Vieja. *Casas Reales* 11:101–113. Santo Domingo.

Site on the trail between La Isabela and Santo Domingo where, in 1498, Bartholomew Columbus temporarily held off the rebel leader Roldán while Christopher Columbus was absent from Hispaniola.

892. Moya Pons, Frank. 1979. Historia de La Vega. *Casas Reales* 3(8):39–54. Santo Domingo.

893. Ortega, Elpidio J., and Carmen Fondeur. 1979. *Estudio de la cerámica del periodo indo-hispano de la antigua Concepción de La Vega.* Santo Domingo: Fundación Ortega Alvarez. 101 p.

Analysis of 896 ceramic fragments found on the site of La Concepción de la Vega, a city occupied between 1510 and 1526, when it was destroyed by an earthquake.

894. Palm, Erwin. 1952. La fortaleza de la Concepción de La Vega. *Congreso Histórico Municipal Interamericano (5 session, Ciudad Trujillo, 1952), Memorias* 2:115–118. Ciudad Trujillo.

Los Huesos

895. Valdez A., Maria Luisa. 1978. Nuevos petroglífos localizados en la Cordillera Central, República Dominicana. *Museo del Hombre Dominicano, Boletín* 7(10):227–238. Santo Domingo.

Description of petroglyphs found near Los Huesos, La Vega province in central Dominican Republic.

Yuboa

896. Morales Ruiz, Carlos. 1968. Petroglifos taínos de Yuboa. *Revista Ahora* 7(265):4–45. Santo Domingo.

See also: C. Morales Ruiz, Rincón de Yuboa, nuevo e importante descubrimiento (*Revista Ahora* 7(276):45–48, 1969. Santo Domingo); C. Morales Ruiz, Informe sobre tres grupos petroglíficos (*Revista Dominicana de Arqueología y Antropología* 1(1):57–80, 1971. Santo Domingo).

897. Ortega, Elpidio, and Marcio Veloz Maggiolo. 1973. Plaza de Yuboa. *Museo del Hombre Dominicano, Boletín* 3:227–229. Santo Domingo.

María Trinidad Sanchez Province

Río San Juan

898.   Pena Sosa, Santiago. 1978. Aspectos arqueológicos del Río San
       Juan. *Museo del Hombre Dominicano, Boletín* 7(11):131–140. Santo
       Domingo.

       Ostionoid and Meillacoid components are identified at an
       archaeological site in the municipality of Río San Juan.

Monte Cristi Province

899.   Cruxent, José M. 1967. Nota sobre el hallazgo de una vasija de
       gres en los restos de un naufragio: Montecristi (República
       Dominicana). *Instituto Venezolano de Investigaciones Científicas
       (IVIC), Departmento de Antropología, Boletín Informativo* 5:23–26.
       Caracas.

900.   Ortega, Elpidio J., Pierre Dennis, and Harold Olsen. 1990.
       Nuevos yacimientos arqueológicos en Arroyo Caña. *Museo del
       Hombre Dominicano, Boletín* 23:29–39. Santo Domingo.

       Description of a Meillacoid period (ca. A.D. 1200–1300)
       ceremonial plaza near the provincial limits of Monte Cristi and
       Valverde.

Buenhombre

901.   Rimoli, Renato O., Marcio Veloz Maggiolo, and P. Marichal.
       1974. Buenhombre: un poblamiento ceramista en la costa norte.
       Instituto Montecristeño de Arqueología, Boletín 1:14–33. Santo
       Domingo.

Hatillo Palma

902.   Ortega, Elpidio J., and Marcio Veloz Maggiolo. 1971.
       Excavación arqueológica en el vasto residuario indígena de
       Hatillo Palma. *Revista Dominicana de Arqueología y Antropología*
       2(2–3):5–27. Santo Domingo.

Pedernales Province

903.   Veloz Maggiolo, Marcio, Fernando Luna Calderón, and Renato
       Rímoli. 1979. *Investigaciones arqueológicas en la provincia de
       Pedernales, República Dominicana.* San Pedro de Macorís:
       Universidad del Este. 99 p.

Summary of archaeological, physical anthropological, and zooarchaeological research conducted at four archaeological sites near the Haitian-Dominican border, including Río Pedernales, Cueva Roja, Jinagosa, and Las Mercedes.

Puerto Plata Province

Escalera Abajo

904.   Rimoli, Renato. 1980. Restos de fauna en el sitio arqueológico de Escalera Abajo, provincia Puerto Plata. *Museo del Hombre Dominicano, Boletín* 9(13):171–192. Santo Domingo.

Discussion of zooarchaeological remains from two cave sites in Escalera Abajo; see also: F. Luna Calderón, Estudio antropológico del

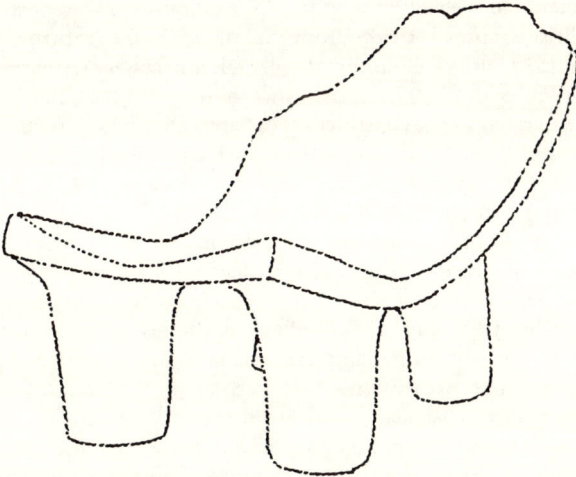

Figure 12. Stone seat or *duho*, Lomas de Cuzco, Pinar del Río, Cuba.
These ceremonial stools were usually low, four-footed,
with an upward-curving back, often carved in effigy form,
and were used by Taíno chieftains as a symbol of rank.

Source: M.R. Harrington, *Cuba Before Columbus*,
Museum of the American Indian, Heye Foundation, Indian Notes
and Monographs, no. 17. New York, 1921. Figure 22.

osario de Escalera Abajo (*Museo del Hombre Dominicano, Boletín* 9(13):193–211, 1980).

La Isabela

905.   Palm, Erwin W. 1945. Excavations of La Isabela, white man's first town in the Americas. *Acta Americana* 3:298–303. México.

Report on excavations at the La Isabela, which was the second Spanish settlement in Hispaniola, on the north coast of modern Dominican Republic; both indigenous and Spanish pottery was recovered. The unhealthy and unstrategic site was chosen after Columbus' fleet of the second voyage, having discovered the destruction of Navidad, was unable to make much headway eastward against the trade winds. The story of La Isabela's construction and history as the administrative seat of Columbus' government is one of disease, death, and disillusionment. Columbus, partly through others' cruel and aggressive treatment of the native peoples, lost their confidence as well as the support of the colonists. The reports of poor conditions spread throughout Spain with the return of many disgruntled settlers. Columbus finally felt it necessary to return himself in 1496 to defend his position. In his absence, Bartholomew Columbus began the construction of Santo Domingo, on the southern coast of Hispaniola at the mouth of the Ozama River, and moved the capital there. See also, J.A. Caro Alvarez, La Isabela (*Museo del Hombre Dominicano, Boletín* 3:48–52, 1973); C. Dobal, *Como pudo ser La Isabela* (Santiago: Pontifica Universidad Catolica Madre y Maestre, 1988. 165 p.) and J.A. Puig Ortiz, *Por la valorización histórica de las ruinas de La Isabela, primera ciudad del Nuevo Mundo* (Santo Domingo: Editora del Caribe, 1973. 111 p.) for reviews of the history of archaeological work and legislation pertaining to the site; B. Chiarelli and F. Luna Calderon, The excavation of La Isabela, the first city of the New World (*International Journal of Anthropology* 2:199–209, 1987) for a summary report on excavations at La Isabela by the Instituto di Antropología dell'Università in Firenze, Italy, and the Museo del Hombre Dominicano; see also, B. Chiarelli, La Isabela: the first seven years (1493–1500) of the European colonization of America (*International Journal of Anthropology* 2:195–197, 1987); B. Chiarelli, La Isabela: ascesa e declino della prima città europea del Nuovo Mundo (*L'Universo, Supplemento* 1:11–14, 1991); B. Chiarelli and R. Pieracciolo, La Isabela, prima città europea nel Nuovo Mondo (*L'Universo* 4:440–455, 1988); J.G. Guerrero and E. Ortega, La Isabela, primera ciudad del nuevo mundo aun no ha muerto (*Hoy* 117:6–9, 1983); F. Luna Calderon, Los esqueletos de La Isabela: testigos mudos de una gran hazana (*Hoy* 117:10–11, 1983); F. Luna Calderón and M. Masali, Lo scavo e lo studio preliminare del cimitero pericolombiano del Castillo de la Isabela a Santo Domingo (*L'Universo, Supplemento* 1:19–23, 1991); G.E. Pia, Recenti savi archeologici nel cimitero spagnolo della Isalbela (*L'Universo, Supplemento* 1:15–18, 1991).

La Unión

906. Veloz Maggiolo, Marcio, Elpidio J. Ortega, and Plinio Pina Peña. 1972. El cementerio de La Unión, Provincia de Puerto Plata. *Museo del Hombre Dominicano, Boletín* 2:130–146. Santo Domingo.

Samaná Province

907. Krieger, Herbert W. 1929. *Archaeological and Historical Investigations in Samaná, Dominican Republic.* Smithsonian Institution, Bulletin, no. 147. Washington, DC. 91 p.

908. Miller, Gerrit S., and Herbert W. Krieger. 1929. Expedition to Samaná Province, Dominican Republic. *Smithsonian Institution, Explorations and Fieldwork* 1928:43–54. Washington, DC.

909. Pinart, Louis A. 1945. Arqueología de Samaná, República Dominicana, 1881. In: *Samaná, pasado y porvenir*. E. Rodríguez Demorizi, ed. pp. 212–219. Santo Domingo: Editorial Montalvo.

Pinart was a Protestant missionary who visited the Dominican Republic in 1881 and explored caves near Bahía de San Lorenzo, south of the Bahía de Samaná.

910. Pagán Perdomo, Dato, and Abelardo Jiménez Lamberetus. 1983. Reconocimiento arqueológico y espeleológico de la región de Samaná: reporte de más de 45 nuevos sitios. *Museo del Hombre Dominicano, Boletín* 11(18):39–71. Santo Domingo.

Brief report on 45 archaeological sites, mostly cave sites, in eastern Dominican Republic.

San Cristóbal Province

Borbón

911. Pagán Perdomo, Dato. 1978. *Nuevas pictografías en la isla de Santo Domingo: las cuevas de Borbón.* Santo Domingo: Museo del Hombre Dominicano. 130 p.

Illustrated description of some 963 pictographs discovered in the Borbón caves in the province of San Crisóbal; pictographs show

Taíno deities and rituals; see also: D. Pagan Perdomo, Nuevas petrografías en la isla de Santo Domingo: las cuevas de Borbon (*Museo del Hombre Dominicano, Boletín* 9:31–53, 1978).

Yamasá

912.   García Arévalo, Manuel A., and Fernando Morbán Laucer. 1990. La plaza o batey aborigen de Yamasá. *Museo del Hombre Dominicano, Boletín* 23:79–96. Santo Domingo.

Report on a plaza site located at Sierra de Yamasá near Hato Viejo, San Cristobal province.

San Pedro de Macorís Province

913.   Mañon Arrendondo, Manuel de J., Fernando Morban L., and Aida Cartagena P. 1971. Nuevas investigaciones de areas indígenas al noreste de Guayacanes y Juan Dolio. *Revista Dominicana de Arqueología y Antropología* 1(1):81–133. Santo Domingo.

914.   Ortega, Elpidio. 1978. Informe sobre investigaciones arqueológicas realizadas en la región este del país, zona costera desde Macao a Punta Espada. *Museo del Hombre Dominicano, Boletín* 7(11):77–99. Santo Domingo.

Results of an archaeological survey from Macao al Cabo to Punta Espada, including Bávaro, Entrada a la Cuevita, Punta Cana, and Cabo San Rafael; identification of Ostionoid and Chicoid ceramics.

Ingenio Cristóbal Colón

915.   Booy, Theodoor H.N. de. 1919. Santo Domingo kitchen-midden and burial mound. *Museum of the American Indian, Heye Foundation, Indian Notes and Monographs* 1(2):107–137. New York.

Report on the excavation of a mound on Ingenio Cristobal Colón, San Pedro Macorís; includes description of marine and terrestrial shells, as well as mammal, bird, and fish remains.

Juan Dolio

916.   Boyrie Moya, Emile, and José M. Cruxent. 1956. Muestras arqueológicas de Juan Dolio, República Dominicana. *Museo de Ciencias Naturales, Boletín* 1(2):11–33. Caracas.

Report on the excavation of a Taíno habitation site east of Santo Domingo containing Boca Chica (Period IIIb–IV) pottery.

917. Jiménez Lambertus, Abelardo. 1980. Hallazgo de huesecillos del oido en craneos indígenas. *Museo del Hombre Dominicano, Boletín* 9(13):229–234. Santo Domingo.

Examination of human skeletal remains from Juan Dolio, San Pedro de Macorís.

918. Jimenez Lambertus, Abelardo. 1981. Variedades anatómicas el atlas en esqueletos precolombinos de Juan Dolio, San Pedro de Macorís. *Museo del Hombre Dominicano, Boletín* 10(16):63–72. Santo Domingo.

Juan Pedro
919. Veloz, Maggiolo, Marcio, and Elpidio J. Ortega. 1986. *Arqueología y patrón de vida en el poblado circular de Juan Pedro, República Dominicana.* Santo Domingo: Museo del Hombre Dominicano. 86 p.

La Caleta
920. Boyrie Moya, Emile de. 1952. Las piezas arqueológicas, de material travertínico, de las Cuevas de los Paredones (Caleta II), República Dominicana. *Congreso Histórico Municipal Interamericano (5 session, Ciudad Trujillo, 1952), Memorias* 1:181–186. Ciudad Trujillo.

Report on a stone carving near La Caleta consisting of human figures, cylindrical pendants, and beads.

921. Herrera Fritot, René, and Charles Leroy Youmans. 1946. *La Caleta: joya arqueológica antilliana; exploración y estudio de un rico yacimiento indígena dominicano y comparación de los ejemplares con los de Cuba y otros lugares.* La Habana: Imprenta El Siglo XX. 160 p.

Detailed description of the excavation and materials recovered from a large indigenous village site and cemetery east of Santo Domingo; five crania are described in considerable detail.

Maravillas
922. Morbán Laucer, Fernando. 1990. Las cuevas de las Maravillas: vestigios de una cultura precolombina en Santo Domingo, República Dominicana: enterramientos aborígenes. *Museo del Hombre Dominicano, Boletín* 23:15–27. Santo Domingo.

Report on investigations of caves with Sub-Taíno pottery and petroglyphs near San Pedro de Macorís and La Romana.

Punta de Garza
923.   Veloz Maggiolo, Marcio, Renato O. Rimoli, Fernando Luna
        Calderon, and Joaquin E. Nadal. 1977. *Arqueología de Punta de Garza.*
        San Pedro de Macorís: Universidad Central del Este. 237 p.

    Summary of excavations conducted at Punta de Garza in the
province of San Pedro de Macoris; evidence suggests the site was
occupied ca. 160 B.C. by marine collectors and was later reoccupied
by agriculturalists.

Talanquera
924.   Morbán Laucer, Fernando, Plinio Pina Peña, and Alejandro
        Peguero. 1989. Arqueología de la Talanquera, Republica
        Dominicana. *Museo del Hombre Dominicano, Boletín* 22:179–187.
        Santo Domingo.

    Summary report on the site of Los Corrales (ca. A.D. 640–670),
San Pedro de Macorís province.

925.   Lembert R., José E. 1989. Zooarqueología de Talanquera. *Museo
        del Hombre Dominicano, Boletín* 22:188–196. Santo Domingo.

Sánchez Ramírez Province
926.   Pagán Perdomo, Dato, and Manuel García Arévalo. 1980. Notas
        sobre pictografías y petroglifos de las Guácaras de Comedero
        Arriba y El Hoyo de Sanabe, República Dominicana. *Museo del
        Hombre Dominicano, Boletín* 9(14):13–56. Santo Domingo.

    Discussion of pictographs and petroglyphs from two cave sites
discovered in 1978; authors conclude that designs are similar to those
associated with Taíno mythology and ritual; description of examples
of rock art found at two cave sites in Sánchez Ramírez Province.

Las Guácaras
927.   Morales Ruiz, Carlos. 1968. Las Guácaras: origen, enigma y
        significado de sus petroglifos. *Revista Ahora* 7(259):44–48. Santo
        Domingo.

Santiago Province
Yabanal
928.   Ortega, Elpidio J., Marcio Veloz Maggiolo, and Plinio Pina Peña.
        1972. Los petroglifos de Yabanal, República Dominicana. *Museo
        del Hombre Dominicano, Boletín* 1:61–74. Santo Domingo.

HAITI

(Capital: Port-au-Prince)

Haiti, measuring 27,750 sq km in area, occupies the eastern third of the island of Hispaniola, which lies between Cuba and Puerto Rico. Mountains cover approximately two-thirds of the land area of Haiti and its principal population centers are near the coast. Some ranges rise sharply from a narrow coastal shelf, while others extend westward toward the Dominican Republic.

On his first voyage to the New World, on December 6, 1492, Columbus encountered an island that he named *Española*, or Hispaniola. The island first became the province of Spanish colonizers. Some 100,000 native Arawak Indians were wiped out by disease, maltreatment, and possibly culture shock, within 50 years.

General

929. Alexandrenkov, Eduard. 1979. La sociedad de los indios de Haití a fines del siglo XV. In: *Las Antiguas civilizaciones de América*. América Latina Estudios de Científicos Soviéticos, no. 4. Moscow: Ciencias Sociales Contemporáneas.

930. Aubourg, Michel. 1951. *Haiti préhistorique; mémoire sur les cultures précolombiennes, Ciboney et Taíno*. Bureau d'Ethnologie de la República d'Haiti, Publication no. 8. Port-au-Prince. 73 p.; Port-au-Prince: Editions Panorama, 1966. 64 p.

Summary of archaeological research in Haiti.

931. Corvington, Herman. 1942. *Histoire humaine des aborigènes d'Hayti*. Port-au-Prince: Librarie Samuel Devieux. 31 p.

932. Fisher, Kurt A. 1952. L'archéologie en Haiti. *Conjonction* 37:45–49. Port-au-Prince.

933. Herve, Georges. 1913. Inventaire des antiquites indigenes de Saint-Domingue (partie française), a la veille de la revolution. *Revue de l'Ecole d'Anthropologie* 23 (11):376–396. Paris.

934.   Krieger, Herbert W. 1932. Culture sequences in Haiti. *Smithsonian Institution, Explorations and Fieldwork* 1931:113–124. Washington, DC.

Summary of archaeological fieldwork conducted between January and May, 1931, at Arawak sites in Haiti to obtain pottery and other midden debris.

935.   Oriol, Jacques. 1969. *La vannerie Haitianne: generalities et particulares.* Port-au-Prince: Imprimerie Theodore. 35 p.

936.   Rouse, Irving. 1940. The use of classification in Haiti. *Southeastern Archaeological Conference, Newsletter* 2(4):10. Baton Rouge.

Bibliography

937.   Laguerre, Michel S. 1982. *The Complete Haitiana: A Bibliographic Guide to the Scholarly Literature, 1900–1980.* Millwood, New York: Kraus International. 2 v.

Includes books, articles, essays, dissertations and theses, and government publications; arranged in eleven major headings subdivided into 65 sections.

938.   Pratt, Frantz. 1991. *Haiti: Guide to the Periodical Literature in English, 1800–1990.* Bibliographies and Indexes in Latin American and Caribbean Studies, no. 1. New York: Greenwood Press. 310 p.

Museum Collections

939.   Viré, Armand. 1940. La préhistoire en Haïti. *Société Préhistorique Française, Bulletin* 37(4–5):108–137. Paris.

Description of artifacts in local collections; includes illustrations of petroglyphs.

Bureau d'Ethnologie d'Haiti

940.   Alexis, Stephen. 1941. *Catalogue du Musée National.* Port-au-Prince.

941.   Aubourg, Michel. 1953. La sección d'archéologie pré-colombienne. *Bureau d'Ethnologie de la República d'Haiti, Publication* 10:17–21. Port-au-Prince.

Illustrated guide to the archaeological exhibits in the Musée du Bureau d'Ethnologie d'Haiti; see also: K.A. Fisher, Rapport trimestriel du Bureau d'Ethnologie de la República d'Haiti (*Bureau d'Ethnologie de la República d'Haiti, Bulletin* 2–3:4–6, 1943).

942.   Fisher, Kurt A. 1943. Une amulette jumelée en os de la section d'archéologie du Bureau d'Ethnologie de la République d'Haiti. *Bureau d'Ethnologie de la República d'Haiti, Bulletin* 2–3:31–32. Port-au-Prince.

Brief description of a bone amulet from the archaeology section of the Bureau d'Ethnologie.

Colección Hodges
943.   Vega, Bernardo. 1982. Un objeto enigmático de la Colección Hodges. *Museo del Hombre Dominicano, Boletín* 10(17):21–28. Santo Domingo.

Report on a possible Meillac or Chicoid hollow tubular ceramic object from a private collection in Cape Haitian, Haiti; object was probably used for smoking tobacco rather than inhaling *cohoba*.

History of Archaeological Research

944.   Aubourg, Michel. 1947. Les recherches archéologiques de M. Herbert Krieger dans le nord d'Haiti. *Bureau d'Ethnologie de la República d'Haiti, Bulletin* 2(3):41–49. Port-au-Prince.

945.   Pressoir, Catts. 1952. *Haiti: Monuments Historiques et Arqueologiques*. Instituto Panamericano de Geografía e Historia, Publicación no. 143. Mexico. 32 p.

History of archaeological research in Haiti with bibliography and map of sites.

Environment

946.   Poole, A.J. 1929. Explorations in Haitian caves. *Smithsonian Institution, Explorations and Fieldwork* 1928:45–52. Washington, DC.

See also: A.J. Poole, Further explorations in Haitian caves (*Smithsonian Institution, Explorations and Fieldwork* 1929:63–76, 1930. Washington, DC).

Cultural Evolution and Society

Cultural Evolution and Development

947.   Coe, William R. 1957. A distinctive artifact common to Haiti and Central America. *American Antiquity* 22(3):280–282.

The Couri phase differs from other Caribbean or coastal South American traditions. Diagnostic artifacts include flint flake knives and daggers with distinctive unifacial retouching (969, 970). These are accompanied by groundstone dishes, double-bitted axes, peg-shaped pendants, shell pendants, and stone mortars and pestles. The less specialized hammerstones and other crude implements are common. A similar complex, the Cabaret, is reported near Port-au-Prince (255) and on the Dominican side of the island in the Marban phase. The Couri unifacially chipped knives and daggers are significant in that similar objects are known from the Maya lowlands and highlands of Central America at 2000 B.C. and Panama. Ripley P. Bullen suggests that they were introduced into the insular Caribbean directly from Central America.

948.   Fisher, Kurt A. 1947. La culture prehistorique d'Haiti (Ciboneys). *Bureau d'Ethnologie de la República d'Haiti, Bulletin* 2(2):22–26. Port-au-Prince.

Physical Anthropology

949.   Luna Calderon, Fernando. 1980. Estudio de un caso de amputación de Isla Gonave, Haiti. *Museo del Hombre Dominicano, Boletín* 9(13):213–227. Santo Domingo.

Description of skeletal remains from Cueva de En Café, La Genave, Haiti, at the Smithsonian Institution in Washington, DC.

Ethnography

950.   Bourguignon, Erika E. 1959. The persistence of folk belief: some notes on cannibalism and zombie in Haiti. *Journal of American Folklore* 72:36–46.

Ethnohistory

951.   Cheibaum, L.S. 1966. Indeytsy tainy ostrova gaiti do ispanskogo zavoevaniia. *Sovetsjaia Etnografia* 4:52–56. Moscow.

The Taíno Indians of Haiti prior to the Spanish conquest.

952. Corvington, Herman. 1942. *Caonabo, Seigneur de la Maguana.* Port-au-Prince: Librarie Samuel Devieux. 27 p.

953. ———. 1942. *Deux caciques du Xaragua: Bohéchio et Anacaona.* Port-au-Prince: Librarie Samuel Devieux. 40 p.

954. ———. 1942. *Guacanaharic.* Port-au-Prince: Librarie Samuel Devieux. 33 p.

955. Nau, Emile. 1855. *Histoire des Caciques d'Haïti.* Paris: T. Bouchereau; Paris: Guerin, 1894; Port-au-Prince: Editions Panorama, 1963. 365 p.

Important nineteenth-century work on the aboriginal inhabitants of Haiti.

Religious Organization

956. Safford, William E. 1916. Identity of cohoba, the narcotic snuff of ancient Haiti. *Washington Academy of Sciences, Journal* 6:547–562. Washington, DC.

Material Culture

Art

957. Barker, Paul, and Gerard Gayot. 1964. Le chien de pierre de chansolme, Opigielgourian, dieu des taínos. *Bureau d'Ethnologie de la República d'Haiti, Bulletin* 4(30):9–45. Port-au-Prince.

Description of a stone dog image found in northwest Haiti which authors claim represents the Taíno dog-god, Opigielgourian, and the first archaeological evidence of the domesticated dog in the prehispanic Caribbean.

958. Mangonès, Edmond, and Louis Maximilien. 1941. *L'Art Précolombien d'Haiti.* Port-au-Prince: Imprimerie de l'Etat. 29 p.

Petroglyphs and Pictographs

959. Hodges, William H. 1979. L'art rupestre précolombien en Haiti; étude descriptive des gravures de la Roche à l'Inde à Camp Coq dans la vallée du Limbé. *Conjonction* 143:5–34. Port-au-Prince.

Pottery

960.   Oriol, Jacques. 1974. La poterie Haîtienne: généralités et particularités. *Bureau d'Ethnologie de la República d'Haiti, Bulletin* 4(31):20–81. Port-au-Prince.

Lithics

961.   Roumain, Jacques. 1943. L'outillage lithique des Ciboney d'Haîti. *Bureau d'Ethnologie de la República d'Haiti, Bulletin* 2:22–27. Port-au-Prince.

Description of archaeological objects and a summary of Ciboney culture.

Regional and Site Reports

962.   Barker, Paul. 1961. Les cultures Cadet et Manigat: emplacements de villages précolombiens dans le nord-ouest d'Haiti. *Bureau d'Ethnologie de la República d'Haiti, Bulletin* 3(26):1–70. Port-au-Prince.

Report on the excavation of two sites in northeastern Haiti: Cadet, a village site near Port-de-Paix with Carrier-type pottery; and Manigat, a cave on Ile de la Tortugue with Meillac variant pottery. Two gold ear ornaments were found at Cadet, possibly the site of a village visited by Columbus.

963.   Rouse, Irving, and Clark Moore. 1984. Cultural sequence in southwestern Haiti. *Bureau d'Ethnologie de la República d'Haiti, Bulletin* 1:25–38. Port-au-Prince.

Reconsideration of archaic and ceramic sites in a little known southwestern peninsula of Haiti; results support Bartolomé de Las Casas' statement that farming settlements existed in the region and that inhabitants traveled across the Mona Passage to Puerto Rico.

Basseterre

964.   Pirate capital is explored: ruins of Basseterre. *Science Newsletter* 40:265, 1941.

See also: Pirate capital is explored: ruins of Basseterre (*Science Digest* 10:77, 1941).

Bois de Charrite

965. Ortega, Elpidio, and José Guerrero. 1982. El fecado del sitio
Mellacoide Bois de Charrite, Haiti. *Museo del Hombre Dominicano,
Boletín* 10(17):29–54. Santo Domingo.

Description of excavations at Mellacoid site Bois de Charrite,
Haiti near Cape Haitian; radiocarbon dates indicate occupation
between A.D. 1180–1440.

En Bas Saline

966. Cusick, James. 1989. Change in Pottery as a Reflection of Social
Change: A Study of Taíno Pottery Before and After Contact at
the Site of En Bas Saline, Haiti. M.A. thesis, Department of
Anthropology, University of Florida, Gainesville. 223 leaves.

967. Deagan, K.A. 1987. Searching for Columbus's lost colony.
National Geographic Magazine 176:672–675. Washington, DC.

For an account of the initial discovery of En Bas Saline, see also:
K. Deagan, The redoubtable Dr. Hodges (*Archaeology* 41:47, 1988).

Ft. Liberté Bay

968. Rainey, Froelich G. 1936. A new prehistoric culture in Haiti.
National Academy of Sciences of the United States, Proceedings 22(1):4–
8. Washington, DC.

Report on archaeological investigations conducted near Ft.
Liberté Bay, northern Haiti, in the spring of 1935; author establishes
the existence of a preceramic culture and a subsequent culture which
"correlates with the Shell Culture pattern (probably Arawak) that has
been found distributed over the Great Antilles and the Virgin Islands."

969. ———. 1941. *Excavations in the Ft. Liberté Region, Haiti.* Yale
University Publications in Anthropology, no. 23. New Haven.
48 p.

Description of the excavations in the Ft. Liberté Bay area and in
several other parts of Haiti in 1934 and 1935 leading to Rouse's
classification published as *Culture of the Ft. Liberté Region, Haiti.*

970. Rouse, Irving. 1941. *Culture of the Ft. Liberté Region, Haiti.* Yale
University Publications in Anthropology, no. 24. New Haven.
196 p.

Author constructs three broad sequences from sites in the Ft. Liberté region: Couri, Meillac, and Carrier; includes an extensive catalog of artifact plates and provides descriptions of subsistence strategies and some fundamental hypotheses concerning social life; includes appendices: 1. D. Horton and J. Berman, Preliminary report of the technological analysis of Meillac and Carrier sherds (pp. 169–172); 2. I. Rouse, Surface finds in Ft. Liberté region; 3. Animal remains in the Ft. Liberté sites; 4. Chronological summary of Meillac and Carrier pottery.

971.   ———. 1939. *Prehistory in Haiti: A Study in Method*. Yale University Publications in Anthropology, no. 21. New Haven; New Haven: HRAF Press, 1964. 202 p.

Technical study of some 12,000 specimens of material culture obtained by F.G. Rainey and Rouse from eleven archaeological sites near Ft. Liberté Bay in Haiti; a seminal work in constructing typologies in archaeology; publication of: I. Rouse, Contributions to the Prehistory of the Fort Liberté Region, Haiti. Ph.D. dissertation, Department of Anthropology, Yale University.

Savanne Carré no. 2

972.   Dávila y Dávila, Ovidio. 1978. Analysis of the lithic materials of the Savanne Carré no. 2 site, Fort Liberté region of Haiti. *Museo del Hombre Dominicano, Boletín* 7(10):202–226. Santo Domingo.

Preliminary typological study of a lithic assemblage from the Savanne Carré no. 2 site in the Ft. Liberté region of Haiti.

Ile à Cabrits

973.   Fisher, Kurt A. 1944. Une tête antropomorphique en pierre de l'Ile à Cabrits. *Bureau d'Ethnologie de la République d'Haiti, Bulletin* 3:39. Port-au-Prince.

Description of an anthropomorphic stone head from Ile à Cabrits.

Ile à Vache

974.   Rouse, Irving. 1947. Ciboney artifacts from Ile à Vache, Haiti. *Bureau d'Ethnologie de la République d'Haiti Bulletin* 2(2):16–21, 2(3):61–66. Port-au-Prince.

Report on excavations of flint and other lithic artifacts on Ile à Vache, off the south coast of Haiti.

La Navidad

975. Méhu, Raphael H. 1955. *Où fut érigé le fort de La Nativité?* Port-au-Prince: Les Presses Libres. 28 p.

976. Morison, Samuel E. 1940. The route of Columbus along the north coast of Haiti and the site of Navidad. *American Philosophical Society, Transactions* 31(4):239–285. Philadelphia.

Attempt to locate, through intensive study of relevant documents and personal reconnaissance, the location of the reef where the Santa Maria was wrecked and the site of Navidad, the first settlement attempted by Europeans in the New World; poses three problems: the site of the wreck of the Santa María, the site of Navidad, and the site of Guacanagari's village; Morison concludes that Navidad must be near the church at Limonade Bord-de-Mer; see also, K.A. Deagan, El impacto de la presencia europeo en La Navidad (La Española) *(Revista de Indias* 47(181):713–732, 1987); K.A. Deagan, Searching for Columbus' lost colony (*National Geographic* 172(5):672–675, 1987. Washington, DC); K.A. Deagan, The search for La Navidad, Columbus' 1492 settlement (In: *First Encounters: Spanish Explorations in the Caribbean and the United States, 1492–1570.* J.T. Milanich and S. Milbrath, eds. pp. 41–54. Gainesville: University of Florida Press, 1992).

Port-au-Prince

977. Bastien, Rémy. 1944. Archéologie de la Baie de Port-au-Prince: rapport préliminaire. *Bureau d'Ethnologie de la República d'Haiti, Bulletin* 3:33–38. Port-au-Prince.

Description of Preceramic material from the Port-au-Prince region.

Puerto Real

978. Ewen, Charles R. 1987. From Spaniard to Creole: The Archaeology of Hispanic American Cultural Formation at Puerto Real, Haiti. Ph.D. dissertation, Department of Anthropology, University of Florida, Gainesville. 275 p.

Author examines the effects of the colonization process on the Spaniards in the New World during the sixteenth century using the site of Puerto Real on the north coast of Haiti as a case study; results indicate that New World and African cultural elements were introduced into Spanish colonial culture almost at contact; author hypothesizes that the Spaniards practiced conservatism in those socially visible areas associated with male activities together with the incorporation of indigenous traits in the less visible, female-dominated areas; published as: C.R. Ewen, *From Spaniard to Creole: The Archaeology of Cultural Formation at Puerto Real, Haiti* (Tuscaloosa: University of Alabama Press, 1991. 155 p.); see also: C.R. Ewen and M.W. Williams, Puerto Real: archaeology of an early Spanish town (In: *First Encounters: Spanish Explorations in the Caribbean and the United States, 1492–1570.* J.T. Milanich and S. Milbrath, eds. pp. 66–76. Gainesville: University of Florida Press, 1992).

979.   Ewen, Charles R. 1988. The short, unhappy life of a maverick Caribbean colony: Puerto Real. *Archaeology* 41:41–47. New York.

980.   Fairbanks, Charles H., and Rochelle A. Merrinan. 1982. The Puerto Real Project: Haiti. *Journal of New World Archaeology* 5(2):67–72. Los Angeles.

981.   Hodges, William H. 1979. Puerto Real: excavation dans la Plaine de Limonade. *Conjonction* 147:37–48. Port-au-Prince.

Recovery of Meillac ceramics establishes an indigenous component at Puerto Real, Plains of Limonade, Haiti; further excavation revealed several colonial Spanish structures.

982.   McEwan, Bonnie G. 1983. Spanish Colonial Adaptation on Hispaniola: The Archaeology of Area 35 Puerto Real, Haiti. M.A. thesis, Department of Anthropology, University of Florida, Gainesville.

983.   ————. 1985. Backyard archaeology at Puerto Real, Haiti. *Bureau d'Ethnologie de la República d'Haiti, Bulletin* 1:65–69. Port-au-Prince.

Excavation of a probable high status area at Puerto Real indicates traditional Spanish food and European tableware were preferred over locally manufactured goods.

984.   ————. 1986. Domestic adaptation at Puerto Real, Haiti. *Historical Archaeology* 20(1):44–49. Bethlehem, Pennsylvania.

Economic and environmental factors had a significant impact upon adaptive strategies at Puerto Real.

985.   Reitz, Elizabeth J. 1986. Vertebrate fauna from Locus 39, Puerto Real, Haiti. *Journal of Field Archaeology* 13(3):317–328. Boston.

Zooarchaeological analysis of skeletal fragments from Locus 39 indicates a high frequency of cattle (*Bos taurus*) suggesting residential and cattle processing functions.

986.   Shapiro, Gary. 1984. A soil resistivity survey of sixteenth-century Puerto Real, Haiti. *Journal of Field Archaeology* 11(1):101–110. Boston.

Remote sensing techniques are used to identify and define subsurface location of the central building complex at Puerto Real.

987.   Smith, Greg C. 1986. Non-European Pottery at the Sixteenth-Century Spanish Site of Puerto Real, Haiti. M.A. thesis, Department of Anthropology, University of Florida, Gainesville.

988.   Williams, Maurice. 1986. Sub-surface patterning at Puerto Real: a sixteenth-century Spanish town on Haiti's north coast. *Journal of Field Archaeology* 13(3):283–296.

Systematic test excavations define town boundaries and variation in the distribution of material remains.

989.   Willis, Raymond. 1984. Empire and Architecture at Sixteenth-Century Puerto Real, Hispaniola: An Archaeological Perspective. Ph.D. dissertation, Department of Anthropology, University of Florida, Gainesville.

JAMAICA

(Capital: Kingston)

The third largest island in the Caribbean after Cuba and Hispaniola, Jamaica is located some 145 km south of eastern Cuba. The island is very mountainous and measures 230 km in length and 35 to 82 km in width, with a total area of some 11,525 sq km. The low coastal plains rise to a mountainous backbone along the center of the island. *Xamayca*, as the Arawak inhabitants named the island, means 'land of wood and water.' The name conveys some idea of the nature of Jamaica's scenery, its hills and mountains, some of them heavily wooded, and its numerous small streams and rivers.

General

990. Duerden, J.E. 1897. Aboriginal Indian remains in Jamaica. *Jamaica Journal* 2(4):309–364. Kingston.

Discussion of kitchen middens, burial caves, implements, pottery, ornaments, and petroglyphs; includes a "Note on the craniology of the aborigines of Jamaica" by A.C. Haddon.

991. Emmons, R.V. 1953. Jamaican site designation: a critique. *American Antiquity* 18:396. Washington, DC.

Discussion of system of archaeological site designation.

992. St. Clair, James. 1970. Problem oriented archaeology. *Jamaica Journal* 4(1):7–10. Kingston.

993. Sherlock, Philip M. 1939. *The Aborigines of Jamaica.* Kingston: Institute of Jamaica. 20 p.

Useful short account of the archaeology of the Arawaks of Jamaica.

994. Vanderwal, Ronald L. 1965. Jamaican prehistory. *Jamaica Historical Society, Bulletin* 4(4):64–70. Kingston.

Bibliography

995. Bryant, William J., and C.B. Lewis. 1975. Archaeology and ethnography: Jamaica bibliography. *Archaeology Jamaica* 75(4):1–5. Spur Tree, Jamaica.

996. Vanderwal, Ronald L., and J.W. Lee. 1975. Bibliography of archaeological literature of Jamaica and West Indies. *Archaeology Jamaica* 75(1):1–145. Spur Tree, Jamaica.

Museum Collections

997. King, K.C. 1992. Jamaica's enduring heritage. *Archaeology* 45(1):73–76. New York.

Popular description of the Arawak Museum, Seville, Port Royal, Spanish Town, Falmouth, and other sites of historic and archaeological interest; see also, W.B. Goodwin, *Spanish and English Ruins in Jamaica* (Boston: Meador, 1946. 239 p.).

History of Archaeological Research

998. Howard, Robert R. 1962. Aboriginal archaeology in Jamaica. *Scientific Research Council of Jamaica, Information Bulletin* 2(4):61–65. Nassau.

Review of the history of archaeological research on Jamaica; includes summary of excavations conducted by the author; see also, B. Reid, Arawak archaeology in Jamaica: new approaches, new perspectives (*Caribbean Quarterly* 38(2–3):15–20, 1992) in which the author argues that the interpretation of the archaeological record for Jamaica has been distorted by racism and cultural biases.

999. Robotham, D. 1980. Anthropology and archaeology in Jamaica. *América Indígena* 40(2):355–366. Mexico.

Survey of recent work in progress and of the institutional framework for research and teaching, including museums.

Environment

1000. Booy, Theodoor H.N. de. 1913. Certain kitchen middens in Jamaica. *American Anthropologist* 15(3):425–434. Washington, DC; Museum of the American Indian, Heye Foundation, Contributions 2, 1913. New York.

1001. Longley, G.C. 1914. Kitchen middens of Jamaica. *American Museum Journal* 14(8):295–303.

1002. Miller, Gerrit S. 1932. Collecting in the caves and kitchen middens of Jamaica. *Smithsonian Institution, Explorations and Field Work* 1931:65–72. Washington, DC.

Ethnohistory

1003. Cotter, C.S. 1946. The aborigines of Jamaica. *Jamaican Historical Review* 1(2):137–141. Kingston.

1004. Reidell, Heidi. 1990. The Maroon culture of endurance. *Americas* 42(1):46–49. Washington, DC.

   Conflict and compromise have shaped the identity of the Maroon population of Jamaica; includes discussion of the history of the Maroons, originally peaceful and indigenous Arawak who escaped slavery.

1005. Tyndale-Biscoe, J.S. 1962. The Jamaican Arawak: his origin, history, and culture. *American Historical Review* 3(3):1–9. Washington, DC.

   Account of the origin, evolution, and historical ethnography of indigenous groups on Jamaica; distinguishes four subcultures, each with different pottery.

Historical Archaeology

1006. Cornmar, Ivor. 1966. A unique clay pipe. *Jamaica Historical Society, Bulletin* 4(8):160–163. Kingston.

1007. Fremmer, Ray. 1973. Dishes in colonial graves: evidence from Jamaica. *Historical Archaeology* 7:58–62. Detroit.

1008. Mathewson, R. Duncan. 1971. Jamaican ceramics: an introduction to eighteenth-century folk pottery in West African tradition. *Jamaica Journal* 6(2):54–56. Kingston.

1009. Smith, Roger C. 1987. The search for the lost caravels. *American Archaeology* 6(2):109–113. Albuquerque.

   Results of a magnetometer survey of St. Ann's Bay, Jamaica.

Cultural Evolution and Society

Cultural Evolution and Development

1010. Howard, Robert R. 1950. The Archaeology of Jamaica and Its Position in Relation to Circum-Caribbean Culture. Ph.D. dissertation, Department of Anthropology, Yale University. 498 p.

1011. ———. 1956. The archaeology of Jamaica: a preliminary survey. *American Antiquity* 22(1):45–59. Washington, DC.

Summary of archaeological work on Jamaica; Sub-Taíno sequence extends from Period III to Period IV, as in central Cuba.

1012. ———. 1965. New perspectives on Jamaican archaeology. *American Antiquity* 31(2):250–255. Washington, DC.

Summary of Jamaican archaeology in which three pottery styles are described; initial population of the island is suggested ca. A.D. 700.

1013. Vanderwal, Ronald L. 1968. Problems of Jamaican prehistory. *Jamaica Journal* 2(3):10–13. Kingston.

Partition of indigenous Jamaican ceramics into a red-pottery period (A.D. 650) and a post-A.D. 900 period represented on the south by White Marl and on the north by Fairfield (subdivided into east and west aspects); see also: R.L. Vanderwal, The Prehistory of Jamaica: A Ceramic Study (M.A. thesis, University of Wisconsin, Madison).

Subsistence Patterns

1014. Beckwith, Martha W. 1927. N*otes on Jamaican Ethnobotany.* American Folklore Society, Memoirs, v. 21. New York. 47 p.

Includes discussion of medicinal and food plants; see also: M. Steggerda, Plants of Jamaica used by natives for medicinal purposes (*American Anthropologist* 31:431–434, 1929).

Material Culture

Art

1015. Lacaille, A.D. 1943. A mortar and a rock-carving in Jamaica. *Man* 43(66):87–88. London.

Summary description of objects.

Pottery

1016. Lee, James W. 1976. Jamaican redware. *Archaeology Jamaica* 76(2):1–5. Spur Tree, Jamaica.

1017. Lee, James W. 1980. Arawak burens. *Archaeology Jamaica* 80(2):1–15. Kingston.

Discussion of Arawak burens (griddles) from Jamaica.

Lithics

1018. Gann, Thomas W.F., and Theodore D. McCown. 1935. Two chert implements from the southeast coast of Jamaica. *Man* 35:1. London.

1019. Lovén, Sven. 1932. Stone dart points from the district of Old Habour (Jamaica) and qualified flint artifacts from the Antilles. *Universidad Nacional, Instituto de Etnología, Revista* 2:133–138. Tucuman.

Groundstone

1020. Lee, James W. 1962. Arawak stone artifacts. *Scientific Research Council, Bulletin* 2(4):70–72. Kingston, Jamaica.

Description of celts found in Jamaica.

Wood

1021. Handler, Jerome S. 1978. The Bird-Man: a Jamaican Arawak wooden idol. *Jamaica Journal* 11(3–4):25–29. Kingston.

Description of three Arawakan carved wooden figures from Jamaica; author suggests a Bird-Man figure was probably a *zemí* associated with plant protection and growth.

Regional and Site Reports

1022. De Wolf, Marian. 1953. Excavations in Jamaica. *American Antiquity* 18(2):230–238. Washington, DC.

Report on excavations at three sites in northern Jamaica (Periods IIIa-b and IV); C.S. Cotter, A comment on the Windsor site, Jamaica (*American Antiquity* 20(2):173–174, 1954. Washington, DC) argues earthworks mentioned by De Wolf are of sixteenth-century Spanish origin and not nineteenth-century English.

1023.　Higman, B.W. 1974. A report on excavations at Montpelier and Roehampton. *Jamaica Journal* 8(2–3):40–45. Kingston.

Cinnamon Hill

1024.　Osborne, Francis J. 1976. Preliminary report on the Cinnamon Hill site (J-10). *Archaeology Jamaica* 76(1):1–18. Spur Tree, Jamaica.

Includes a faunal analysis by Kathleen F. Johnson.

Drax Hall Plantation

1025.　Armstrong, Douglas V. 1990. *The Old Village and the Great House: An Archaeological and Historical Examination of Drax Hall Plantation, St. Ann's Bay, Jamaica.* Urbana: University of Illinois Press. 400 p.

Examination of the development of African-American cultural systems from slavery through the free-laborer settlements; seven house-area features were excavated and structural and material remains suggest a dual relationship of continuity of African elements and processes of change in response to European trends; extensive use is made of historical and botanical data; publication of: The Old Village at Drax Hall Plantation: An Archaeological Examination of an Afro-American Settlement (Ph.D. dissertation, Department of Anthropology, University of California, Los Angeles. 449 p.); see also: D.V. Armstrong, The Old Village at Drax Hall: an archaeological progress report (*Journal of New World Archaeology* 5(2):87, 1982); D.V. Armstrong, An Afro-American slave settlement: archaeological investigations at Drax Hall (In: *The Archaeology of Slavery and Plantation Life.* T.A. Singleton, ed. pp. 261–287. San Diego: Academic Press, 1985).

Hillshire Hills

1026.　Aarons, G.A. 1983. Archaeological sites in the Hillshire area. *Jamaica Journal* 16(1):76–87. Kingston.

Survey of prehistoric, historic, and marine sites in the Hillshire Hills and Bay region of Jamaica.

Nanny Town

1027.　Bonner, Tony. 1974. Blue Mountain expedition: exploratory excavations at Nanny Town. *Jamaica Journal* 8(2–3):46–50. Kingston.

Norbrook

1028.   Blake, Edith. 1890. The Norbrook kitchen midden. *Victoria Quarterly* 4(2):26–34. Kingston.

Port Royal

1029.   Hume, I. Noël. 1968. A collection of glass from Port Royal, Jamaica, with some observations on the site, its history, and archaeology. *Historical Archaeology* 2:5–34. Detroit.

1030.   Link, Marion C. 1960. Exploring the drowned city of Port Royal. *National Geographic Magazine* 117(2):151–183. Washington, DC.

Popular account of an expedition to explore the site of the sunken city of Port Royal.

1031.   Marx, Robert F. 1967. *Excavation of the Sunken City of Port Royal, December, 1965–December, 1966. A Preliminary Report.* Kingston, Jamaica: Institute of Jamaica. 73 p.

See also: R.F. Marx, Excavating the sunken city of Port Royal, 1966: the first year (*Jamaica Journal* 2(2):12–18, 1968); *Excavation of the Sunken City of Port Royal, January 1967–March 31, 1968. A Preliminary Report* (Kingston, Jamaica: National Trust Commission, 1968. 35 p.)

1032.   ———. 1967. Pirate Port: *The Story of the Sunken City of Port Royal.* Cleveland: World; London: Pelham. 190 p.

See also: R.F. Marx, Port Royal (*Oceans Magazine* 1(5):66–77, 1969); The submerged remains of Port Royal, Jamaica (*Museums and Monuments* 13:139–145, 1972); *Port Royal Rediscovered* (Garden City, NY: Doubleday, 1973. 304 p.), a personal account of a marine archaeologist employed by the Government of Jamaica to salvage artifacts from the sunken city of Port Royal; includes a frank discussion of dealings with officials and obstacles encountered during his fieldwork between 1966 and 1968.

1033.   ———. 1968. *Brass and Copper Items Recovered From the Sunken City of Port Royal: May 1, 1966–March 31, 1968.* Kingston, Jamaica: National Trust Commission. 103 p.

See also: R.F. Marx, *Wine Glasses Recovered From the Sunken City of Port Royal: May 1, 1966–March 31, 1968* (Kingston, Jamaica: National Trust Commission, 1968. 35 p.); *Silver and Pewter Items Recovered From the Sunken City of Port Royal: May 1, 1966–March 31,*

1968 (St. Thomas: Caribbean Research Institute, College of the
Virgin Islands, 1971).

1034.   ———. 1968. Discovery of two ships of Columbus. *Jamaica
Journal* 2(4):13–17. Kingston.

1035.   ———. 1968. Divers of Port Royal. *Jamaica Journal* 2(1):15–23.
Kingston.

1036.   Mayes, Philip. 1970. The Port Royal Project. *Caribbean
Conservation Association Environmental Newsletter* 1(1):37–38.

1037.   Mayes, Philip. 1972. *Port Royal, Jamaica: Excavations 1969–1970*.
Kingston: Jamaica National Trust Commission. 136 p.

Summary of the results of the first major land excavation of Port
Royal, which was destroyed by earthquake in 1692; a detailed and
technical account of the material culture and architecture uncovered;
included is an account of earlier excavations and a history of the site.

1038.   Priddy, Antony. 1975. The seventeenth and eighteenth-century
settlement pattern of Port Royal. *Jamaica Journal* 9(2–3):8–10.
Kingston.

1039.   Williamson, D.E., R.T. Cochran, and F.A.B. Ward. 1970. Notes
on a seventeenth-century watch found at Port Royal:
correspondence. *Jamaica Historical Society, Bulletin* 5(5):71–75.
Kingston.

Sevilla Nueva

1040.   Cotter, C.S. 1948. The discovery of the Spanish carvings at
Seville. *Jamaican Historical Review* 1(3):227–233. Kingston.

1041.   Cotter, C.S. 1970. Sevilla Nueva: the story of an excavation.
Jamaica Journal 4(2):15–22. Kingston.

1042.   López y Sebastián, Lorenzo E. 1982. Arqueología de Jamaica:
Sevilla la Nueva. *Revista de Indias* 42(167–168):223–242. Madrid.

Report on Arawak, Spanish, and English occupations of Sevilla
la Nueva. The most ambitious attempt of the Spaniards to found a
major city on Jamaica was made early in the sixteenth century on the
north shore at St. Ann's Bay. The settlement was named Sevilla la
Nueva and seems to have been founded about 1510; it lasted only a
few years, with the population gradually drifting to the south coast,
leaving the city deserted by 1534; see also, B.G. McEwan, Faunal

remains from Sevilla Nueva (*Jamaica Archaeology* 84(3):21–29, 1984). P. Bryan, Spanish Jamaica (*Caribbean Quarterly* 38(2–3):21–31, 1992) argues that racism and cultural bias were part of the apparatus of Spanish conquest and control of Jamaica; author surveys the Spanish occupation of Jamaica from the time of Columbus in 1492 to the ceding of the island to England by the Treaty of Madrid in 1655.

Spanish Church

1043.   Osborne, Francis J. 1974. Spanish Church, St. Ann's Bay. *Jamaica Journal* 8(2–3):33–35. Kingston.

Spanish Town

1044.   Mathewson, R. Duncan. 1972. History from the earth: archaeological excavations at Old King's House. *Jamaica Journal* 6(1):3–11. Kingston.

Account of an investigation of Old King's House site in Spanish Town, undertaken in July 1971 by the Institute of Jamaica; the site represents some 400 years of occupation, including Arawak, Spanish, and English settlement; for a more specialized account see R.D. Mathewson, Archaeological analysis of material culture as a reflection of sub-cultural differentiation in eighteenth-century Jamaica (*Jamaica Journal* 7(1–2):25–29, 1972. Kingston).

White Marl

1045.   Howard, Robert R. 1962. Arawak remains at White Marl. *Jamaica Historical Society, Bulletin* 3(4–5):1–10. Kingston.

Preliminary report on excavations at the White Marl site on the south coast of Jamaica.

PUERTO RICO

(Capital: San Juan)

The easternmost island of the Greater Antilles, Puerto Rico is situated on one of the main approaches to the Caribbean Sea and the Isthmus of Panama. Roughly rectangular in shape, the island extends about 160 km from east to west and about 55 km from north to south, and is separated from the island of Hispaniola to the west by the 120 km wide Mona Passage. With its principal adjacent islands of Vieques (Crab Island), Culebra, and Mona, it has a total area of 8,900 sq km. The island consists of a complex of mountains surrounded by broken coastal plain, and is mountainous throughout most of its area.

Columbus made a landfall on Puerto Rico during his second voyage to the New World on November 19, 1493. The indigenous inhabitants called the island *Boriquén* or *Borinquén*, but Columbus named it San Juan Bautista. In the first years of the colony the island was known as San Juan, and its capital city as Puerto Rico. After 1521, when the capital had been refounded on its present site and was given the name San Juan, the island came to be called Puerto Rico.

Before the arrival of the Spaniards some 30,000 Taíno Indians inhabited Puerto Rico. Ponce de León, with about 50 followers, quickly subdued them and within 75 years the indigenous population practically disappeared from the coastal plains, but a considerable number of them survived in the mountains, where they intermarried with Europeans and were eventually acculturated.

General

1046. Coll y Toste, Cayetano. 1907. *Prehistoria de Puerto Rico*. San Juan: Tipográfia Boletín Merrcantil. 298 p.; 2d ed. San Juan, 1975. 261 p.

A thorough discussion of Puerto Rican Taíno culture.

1047. Fewkes, Jesse W. 1902. Prehistoric Porto Rico. *American Association for the Advancement of Science, Proceedings* 51:487–512. Washington, DC; *Science* 16:94–109, 1902. New York.

Overview of the prehistory of Puerto Rico, intended to draw attention of United States anthropologists to the new possession acquired from Spain; see also: J.W. Fewkes, Further notes on the archaeology of Porto Rico (*American Anthropologist* 10(4):134–147, 1908).

1048.   Gómez Acevedo, Labor, and Manuel Ballesteros Gaibrois. 1980. *Vida y cultura precolombinas de Puerto Rico.* Río Piedras, Puerto Rico: Editorial Cultural. 132 p.

Interesting synthesis of indigenous life and culture in Puerto Rico.

1049.   Haeberlin, Herman K. 1917. Some archaeological work in Porto Rico. *American Anthropologist* 19:214–238. Washington, DC.

1050.   Krug, L. 1876. Indianische Alterthümer in Porto Rico. *Zeitschrift für Ethnologie* 8:428–436. Berlin.

1051.   Mason, Otis T. 1876. The antiquities of Porto Rico. *American Association for the Advancement of Science, Proceedings* 25:294–299. Salem, Massachusetts.

1052.   Rouse, Irving. 1937. New evidence pertaining to Puerto Rican prehistory. *National Academy of Sciences, Proceedings* 23:182–187. Washington, DC.

Museum Collections

1053.   Alegría, Ricardo E. 1974. La primera exposición de piezas arqueológicas y el establecimiento del primer museo en Puerto Rico. *Instituto de Cultura Puertorriqueña, Revista* 17(64):37–42. San Juan.

Description of exhibits and the establishment of the first museum in 1854 in Puerto Rico.

1054.   *Catalogue Commemorating the Exhibition: The Art Heritage of Puerto Rico, Precolumbian to the Present.* New York: Metropolitan Museum of Art; El Museo del Barrio, 1974. 120 p.

1055.   Hostos, Adolfo de. 1955. *Una colección arqueológica antillana.* San Juan: First Federal Savings and Loan Association of Puerto Rico. 106 p.

Account of how an archaeological collection assembled by Hostos was prevented by a local women's club from being sold to Yale University; it was eventually donated to the University of Puerto Rico.

Bailey Collection

1056. Rouse, Irving. 1961. The Bailey Collection of stone artifacts from Puerto Rico. In: *Essays in Pre-Columbian Art and Archaeology.* S.K. Lothrop, ed. pp. 342–355. Cambridge: Harvard University Press.

Description of a collection of of miscellaneous stone objects, including stone rings, three-pointed stones, and pendants, deposited in the John and Mabel Ringling Museum of Art in Sarasota, Florida; the collection is significant because it includes carved objects dissimilar from Taíno examples from Puerto Rico.

Latimer Collection

1057. Mason, Otis T. 1877. The Latimer Collection of antiquities from Porto Rico in the National Museum at Washington, DC. *Smithsonian Institution, Annual Report,* 1876:372–393. Washington, DC.

Detailed description of the pottery and lithic artifacts bequeathed to the Smithsonian Institution by George Latimer, the son of a Philadelphia merchant, who lived for many years in Puerto Rico.

Stahl Collection

1058. Stahl, Agustín. 1889. *Los indios borinqueños: estudios etnograficos.* San Juan: Imprenta y Librería de Acosta. 206 p.

Description of fifteenth-century Puerto Rico and some 740 archaeological objects in the author's collection.

History of Archaeological Research

1059. Alegría, Ricardo E. 1960. *El Instituto de Cultura Puertorriqueña: los primeros 5 años.* San Juan: Instituto de Cultura Puertorriqueña. 103 p.

Summary of activities of the Instituto de Cultura Puertorriqueña, including establishment of archaeological monuments at the indigenous site of Capá in Utuado and the first Spanish settlement of Caparra near San Juan.

1060. Blanco, Nell N. 1973. Primer Simposio Puertorriqueño de Arqueologia del Caribe. *Fundación Arqueológica, Antropológica e Histórica de Puerto Rico, Boletín Informativo* 4(1):4–6. San Juan.

1061. Hostos, Adolfo de. 1938. *Investigaciones históricas.* San Juan.

1062.   López de Molina, Diana. 1978. La arqueología como ciencia social. *Museo del Hombre Dominicano, Boletín* 7(11):27–44. Santo Domingo.

Critical analysis of the archaeology of Puerto Rico; see also: M. Veloz Maggiolo, Comentarios a la ponencia: La arqueología como ciencia social (*Museo del Hombre Dominicano, Boletín* 7(11):45–56, 1978).

1063.   Miller, G.S. 1933. Fieldwork in Puerto Rico. *Smithsonian Institution, Explorations and Fieldwork* 1932:25–28. Washington, DC.

Environment

1064.   Barrett, O.W. 1933. The origins of the food plants of Puerto Rico. *Scientific Monthly* 37:241–256. Lancaster, Pennsylvania.

1065.   Vega, Jesús E. 1981. Excavation of a Submerged Sub-Taíno Site in Puerto Rico. M.A. thesis, Department of Anthropology, Florida Atlantic University. 114 p.

Underwater excavations at Isla Verde, east of San Juan, revealed a coastal settlement inhabited ca. A.D. 800 by Arawak Neo-Indians and characterized by coastal and maritime adaptations such as shellfish collecting and the hunting of manatees and turtles; root crop cultivation was also part of the subsistence diet; the site preceded the Taíno chiefdoms encountered by European explorers at the end of the fifteenth century; the site was submerged as a result of erosion produced by wave patterns diffracted by offshore reef patches.

1066.   Vega, Jesús E. 1990. The Archaeology of Coastal Change, Puerto Rico. Ph.D. dissertation, Department of Anthropology, University of Florida, Gainesville. 174 p.

Archaeological investigation of tectonic and eustatic land/sea level changes indicates a dynamic Holocene environmental history for the Caribbean region; by 15,000 B.C. sea level may have been 100–130 m below the present level thereby facilitating the movement of maritime hunter-gatherers; 29 prehistoric and nine historic littoral sites were examined on Puerto Rico.

Linguistics

1067.   Green-Douglass, Lisa C. 1990. Puerto Rico as a Microcosm for Toponymic Study. Ph.D. dissertation, Department of Linguistics, University of Iowa. 446 p.

Examination of place names of Puerto Rico; semantic, phonological, and morphological analyses provide information about the historical stages of Taíno and Spanish, and clarify meanings found in legends and folklore; see also, E. Zacarias de Justiniano, *Mini-bibliografía selectiva sobre la influencia de nuestros indios en diferentes aspectos de la vida puertorriqueña.* (Mayaguez: Universidad de Puerto Rico, Recinto Universitario de Mayaguez, Biblioteca General, 1987).

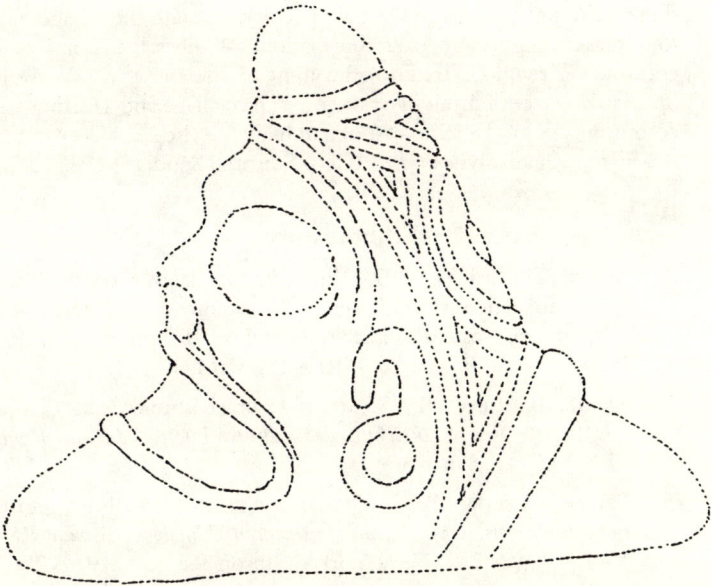

Figure 13. Anthropomorphic *zemi*, Dominican Republic.
Zemí refers to a deity or the objectification of a deity and is usually applied to a characteristic three-cornered deity form.

Source: M.A. García Arévalo, *Los signos en el arte Taíno* (Santo Domingo: Fundación García-Arévalo, 1989. Figure 1.

1068. Malaret, Augusto. 1963. Puerto Rico indígena. *Perú Indígena* 5(12):128–142. Lima.

Ethnography

1069. Davila, Ovidio. 1978. The Igneri Indians of Puerto Rico. *Caribe* 2(3):17–20. Santo Domingo.

Descriptive summary of the Igneri Indians of Puerto Rico; includes information on origins, organization and structure of the society, religion, subsistence patterns, and material culture.

1070. Zaragoza, Edward C. 1990. Portraits of a 'Santo': The Masks of Loiza Aldea, Puerto Rico. Ph.D. dissertation, Drew University. 212 p.

Anaysis of a three-day fiesta of religious processions during which three statues of the patron saint are paraded through the village while four masked figures reenact the exploits of the saint. Loiza Aldea continues a religious tradition brought to the New World by the Spaniards; the community was once a Taíno village and a former slave community some 15 miles east of San Juan; see also, A. Diaz Marrero, *Las jicoteas* (Levittown, Puerto Rico: Editorial Sendero, 1985. 24 p.).

Ethnohistory

1071. Alegría, Ricardo E. 1977. Episodios de la historia de Puerto Rico: el ataque y destrucción de la ciudad de Puerto Rico (Caparra) por los indios caribes en el año 1513. *Instituto de Cultura Puertorriqueña, Revista* 20(74):15–18. San Juan.

1072. Alegría, Ricardo E. 1979. Apuntes para el estudio de los caciques de Puerto Rico. *Instituto de Cultura Puertorriqueña, Revista* 22(85):25–41. San Juan.

1073. Fewkes, Jesse W. 1907. The aborigines of Porto Rico and the neighboring islands. *Bureau of American Ethnology, Annual Report* 1903–1904:3–220. New York: Johnson Reprint, 1970. 296 p.

Includes sections on population, race and kinship, physical characteristics, political divisions, houses, secular customs, religion, archaeological sites, and material culture; concludes that the population of Puerto Rico originated from South America. This report was intended to shed light on the inhabitants of the island that had come into the possession of the United States.

1074.   Hostos, Adolfo de. 1948. The ethnography of Puerto Rico. In: *The Circum-Caribbean Tribes.* J.H. Steward, ed. pp. 540–542. Handbook of South American Indians, v. 4. Bureau of American Ethnology, Bulletin 143. Washington, DC.

Summary of the historical ethnography of Cuba, including a reconstruction of Arawak *cacicazgos* (chiefdoms) and a discussion of primary historical sources.

1075.   Morales Cabrera, Pablo. 1932. *Puerto Rico indígena: prehistoria y protohistoria de Puerto Rico; descripcion de los usos, costumbres, lenguaje, religion, gobierno, agricultura, industrias del pueblo taíno de Boriquen, según los cronistas de Indias en la epoca del descubrimiento de America.* San Juan: Imprenta Venezuela. 381 p.

Summary of the history and prehistory of Puerto Rico; includes a glossary of indigenous terminology.

1076.   Pantel, A. Gus. 1973. Poblamiento Cibonez. *Fundación Arqueológica, Antropológica e Histórica de Puerto Rico, Boletín Informativo* 6(1):4–5. San Juan.

1077.   Sued-Badillo, Jalil. 1979. *La mujer indígena y su sociedad.* Río Piedras: Editorial Antillana. 81 p.

Contribution to the ethnohistory of Puerto Rican women based on accounts by early chroniclers; examines role of women as mothers, in politics, in the economy, social activities, family, and as *caciques*; see also, J. Sued Badillo, *La mujer indígena y su sociedad* (Hato Rey: Editorial Cultural, 1989. 81 p.).

1078.   Watlington, Francisco. 1972. Taínos versus Caribes: una nueva perspectiva. *Fundación Arqueológica, Antropológica e Histórica de Puerto Rico, Boletín Informativo* 3(1):5–6. San Juan.

Cultural Evolution and Society

Cultural Evolution and Development

1079.   Alegría, Ricardo E. 1965. On Puerto Rican archaeology. *American Antiquity* 31(2):246–249. Washington, DC.

Summary of Puerto Rican prehistory presented at the 1964 Caribbean symposium; author notes that radiocarbon dates favor a Central American origin for Preceramic populations although early ceramic traits are traced to Venezuela, ca. A.D. 120; the late ball game and associated features (stone yokes and ball courts) are linked with Mesoamerica.

1080. Moscoso, Francisco. 1980. Chiefdom and encomienda in Puerto Rico: the development of tribal society and the Spanish colonization to 1530. In: *The Puerto Ricans*. A. López, ed. Cambridge, Massachusetts: Schenkman.

1081. Rainey, Froelich G. 1935. Puerto Rican Archaeology. Ph.D. dissertation, Department of Anthropology, Yale University. 379 p.

1082. Rainey, Froelich G. 1935. A new prehistoric culture in Puerto Rico. *National Academy of Sciences, Proceedings* 21(1):12–16. Washington, DC.

Subsistence Patterns

1083. Fernández Méndez, Eugenio. 1960. Los corrales de pesca indígenas de Puerto Rico. *Instituto de Cultura Puertorriqueña, Revista* 9:9–13. San Juan; *Museo del Hombre Dominicano, Boletín* 7:171–179, 1976.

Religious Systems

Cohoba

1084. Oliver, Andrés L. 1973. Más sobre la cohoba. *Fundación Arqueológica, Antropológica e Histórica de Puerto Rico, Boletín Informativo* 5(1):7. San Juan.

Ball Game

1085. Alegría, Ricardo E. 1951. The ball game played by the aborigines of the Antilles. *American Antiquity* 16(4):348–352. Washington, DC.

Preliminary report on excavations at the ball court site of Capá by the Center of Archaeological Research at the University of Puerto Rico; author argues for a connection between ball courts and stone collars of Puerto Rico; Spanish translation: El juego de pelota entre los aborígenes antillanos (*Revista Mexicana de Estudios Antropológicos* 12:95–102, 1951. México); see also, R. Diaz y Paz, *Los Taínos, Puerto Rico: sus centros ceremonias y ritual de la pelota (batey) y sus conexiones con la cultura olmeca-maya-toltec de México* (New York: Toth; Pan American Institute, 1990. 83 p), for an attempt to establish a relationship between the Taíno and the indigenous peoples of Central America and Mexico before the Europeans.

1086.   ———. 1983. *Ball Courts and Ceremonial Plazas in the West Indies.* Yale University Publications in Anthropology, no. 79. New Haven. 185 p.

    Publication of: Ball Courts and Ceremonial Plazas in the West Indies (Ph.D. dissertation, Department of Anthropology, Harvard University, 1977).

Burial Patterns

1087.   Aitken, Robert T. 1917. Porto Rican burial caves. *International Congress of Americanists (19 session, Washington, DC, 1915), Proceedings* 1:224–228. Washington, DC.

    See also: R.T. Aitken, A Porto Rican burial cave (*American Anthropologist* 20:296–309, 1918).

Settlement Patterns

1088.   Haag, W.G. 1963. Puerto Rico and the Virgin Islands. In: *Early Indian Farmers and Villages and Communities.* W.G. Haag, ed. pp. 326–345. Washington, DC.

Material Culture

Petroglyphs and Pictographs

1089.   Davila, Ovidio. 1976. Apuntes sobre el arte rupestre prehispánico de Puerto Rico. *Cuadernos Prehispánicas* 4:61–68. Valladolid.

1090.   Fewkes, Jesse W. 1903. Prehistoric Porto Rican pictographs. *American Anthropologist* 5:441–467. Washington, DC.

1091.   Frassetto, Monica F. 1960. Preliminary report on petroglyphs in Puerto Rico. *American Antiquity* 25(3):381–391. Washington, DC.

    Classification of Puerto Rican petroglyphs into two types paralleling the development of Taíno culture in Periods III and IV.

1092.   Lothrop, Rachel W., and Samuel K. Lothrop. 1927. The use of plaster on Porto Rican stone carvings. *American Anthropologist* 29:728–730. Washington, DC.

1093.   Mason, J. Alden. 1940. Painted cave petroglyphs in Puerto Rico. *International Congress of Americanists (27 session, Lima, 1939), Proceedings* 1:305–310. Lima.

1094. Sued-Badillo, Jalil. 1972. Los grabados rupestres en Puerto Rico. *Fundación Arqueológica, Antropológica e Histórica de Puerto Rico, Boletín Informativo* 1(1):5–7. San Juan.

Pottery

1095. Lothrop, Samuel K. 1927. Two specimens from Porto Rico. *Museum of the American Indian, Heye Foundation, Indian Notes* 4:323–332. New York.

1096. Warrek, George. 1972. The cross-hatch design of the Hacienda Grande style. *Fundación Arqueológica, Antropológica e Histórica de Puerto Rico, Boletín Informativo* 1(2):3–5. San Juan.

Lithics

1097. Beauvois, E. 1886. Les colliers de pierre trouves a Puerto Rico et en Eoosse. *Materiaux pour l'Histoire Primitive et Naturelle de l'Homme* 3:388–392. Paris.

1098. Pantel, A. Gus. 1973. Working tool. *Fundación Arqueológica, Antropológica e Histórica de Puerto Rico, Boletín Informativo* 4(1):3; 5(1):4. San Juan.

1099. Pike, Dorothy W. 1974. Primer sitio de elaboración del pedernal encontrado en Puerto Rico. *Museo del Hombre Dominicano, Boletín* 4:97–107. Santo Domingo.

Groundstone

1100. Ekholm, Gordon F. 1961. Puerto Rican stone collars as ballgame belts. In: *Essays in Pre-Columbian Art and Archaeology.* S.K. Lothrop, ed. pp. 342–355. Cambridge, Massachusetts: Harvard University Press.

Offers evidence that stone yokes found in Puerto Rico were used as belts.

1101. Fagg, Bernard. 1957. Rock gong and rock slides. *Man* 57(32):30–32. London.

Argues that stone collars and elbow stones of Puerto Rico may have been used as gongs.

1102. Fewkes, Jesse W. 1905. Porto Rican stone collars and tripointed idols. *Smithsonian Institution, Smithsonian Miscellaneous Collections* 47(2):163–186. Washington, DC.

Description of precolumbian tripointed stones and collars found in Puerto Rico and presents various interpretations for their use and significance.

1103.   Fewkes, Jesse W. 1913. Porto Rican elbow-stones in the Heye Museum, with discussion of similar objects elsewhere. *American Anthropologist* 15(3):435–459. Washington, DC; Museum of the American Indian, Heye Foundation, Contributions 4, 1913. New York.

Analysis of twelve elbow stones and explanation that these were used for ceremonial purposes.

1104.   Fewkes, Jesse W. 1914. A prehistoric stone collar from Porto Rico. *American Anthropologist* 16:319–330. Washington, DC.

1105.   Hostos, Adolfo de. 1952. Gods of the garden. *Américas* 4(1):16–18. Washington, DC.

Three-pointed stones of Puerto Rico thought to be fertility idols.

1106.   Lothrop, Rachel W., and Samuel K. Lothrop. 1927. Porto Rican collars and elbow stones. *Man* 27:185–186. London.

1107.   Lothrop, Samuel K. 1928. A Porto Rican three-pointed stone. *Museum of the American Indian, Heye Foundation, Indian Notes* 5:154–157. New York.

1108.   Saville, Marshall H. 1926. The stone collars of Porto Rico. *Museum of the American Indian, Heye Foundation, Indian Notes* 3:177–188. New York.

Jade
1109.   Smith, Raymond J. 1973. Artefactos taínos de jade en Puerto Rico. *Instituto de Cultura Puertorriqueña, Revista* 16(60):25–28. San Juan.

Discussion of jade use among the Taíno of Puerto Rico; author suggests a source may be in the vicinity of the serpentine deposits near Mayaguez.

Shell

1110.   Montalvo Guenard, J.L. 1949. A shell collar from Puerto Rico. *American Antiquity* 15(2):160–161. Menasha, Wisconsin.

Description of a shell object similar to the stone collars of Puerto Rico.

Regional and Site Reports

1111.   Mason, J. Alden, 1917. Excavation of a new archaeological site in Porto Rico. *International Congress of Americanists (19 session, Washington, DC, 1915), Proceedings* 1:220–223. Washington, DC.

1112.   New York Academy of Sciences. 1940–1952. *Scientific Survey of Porto Rico and the Virgin Islands: vol. 18, pts. 1–4: Porto Rican Archaeology.* New York: New York Academy of Sciences. 577 p.

Important report on excavations conducted in Puerto Rico during 1934–1935 by the Peabody Museum, American Museum of Natural History, and the University of Puerto Rico; contents include: 1. F.G. Rainey, Porto Rican archaeology (1940, 208 p.); 2. J.A. Mason, A large archaeological site at Capá, Ultando, with notes on other Puerto Rican sites visited in 1914–1915; Appendix: I. Rouse, An analysis of the artifacts of the 1914–1915 Porto Rican survey (1941); 3. I. Rouse, Porto Rican prehistory: introduction, excavations in the west and north (pp. 307–460, 1952); 4. I. Rouse, Porto Rican prehistory: excavations in the interior, south and east; chronological implications (pp. 463–578, 1952).

The most famous Chicoid village with stone-bordered plazas is Capá in west central Puerto Rico. It was exacavated by Mason in 1915 and the pottery collection from these excavations was later studied by Rouse and identified as belonging to the Capá variant of the Chicoid stylistic series. It is the largest indigenous site on the island. Stone lined plazas or ball courts are usually found as single structures in villages although Capá has at least nine structures. The site is on the end of a small spur of land surrounded on three sides by fairly deep ravines. On the remaining side the spur probably had been fortified at a narrow point, thus isolating a large area. This surface was artificially leveled in preparation of it as a major center. The most imposing Capá structure (Structure A) is a rectangular enclosure measuring some 37 m by 50 m, and oriented along a north-south axis. Capá was the focal center of a very important paramount *cacique* (chieftain) and it was probably taken and destroyed by the Spaniards in the early sixteenth century. It provides possibly the best archaeological information on the size, configuration, and construction of a protohistoric Taíno center.

1113.   Pantel, A. Gus. 1973. North Coast Survey. *Fundación Arqueológica, Antropológica e Histórica de Puerto Rico, Boletín Informativo* 6(1):7–8. San Juan.

Caguanas

1114. Oliver, José R. 1980. A Cultural Interpretation of the Iconographic Art Style of Caguanas Ceremonial Center, Puerto Rico. M.A. thesis, Department of Anthropology, University of Illinois, Urbana.

Cayo Cofresi

1115. Guarch Delmonte, José M., and E. Questell Rodríguez. 1975. *Cayo Cofresi: un sitio precerámico de Puerto Rico*. Santo Domingo: Ediciones de Taller. 90 p.

Illustrated excavation report on a Preceramic site (Cayo Cofresi); material culture is generally similar to that found in Santo Domingo.

1116. Veloz Maggiolo, Marcio, Juan González Colón, and Edgar J. Maiz. 1977. El Precerámico de Puerto Rico a la luz de los hallazgos de Cayo Cofresi. *International Congress of Americanists (41 session, Mexico, 1974), Proceedings* 3:786–801. Mexico.

Evidence from Cayo Cofresi indicates a semisedentary sea-oriented population ca. 600 B.C.

1117. Veloz Maggiolo, Marcio, Juan González Colón, and E. Questell Rodríguez. 1975. *Cayo Cofresi: un sitio precerámico de Puerto Rico*. Santo Domingo: Ediciones de Taller. 90 p.

Report on Cayo Cofresi, a Preceramic site radiocarbon dated at 325 B.C. and 295 B.C.; authors argue inhabitants exploited sea and land animals.

Cerrillo

1118. Pantel, A. Gus. 1977. Cerrillo Complex: an Aceramic site, southwestern coast of Puerto Rico: progress report. *International Congress of Americanists (41 session, Mexico, 1974), Proceedings* 3:691–692. Mexico.

Report on a Preceramic complex in southwest Puerto Rico; lithic similar to Mordan-Barrera Complex of the Dominican Republic.

Convento de Santo Domingo

1119. Pons Alegría, Carmen A. 1973. The Igneri Ceramics From the Site of the Convent of Santo Domingo: A Study of Style and

Form. M.A. thesis, Department of American Studies, State University of New York at Buffalo.

Guayanilla

1120.   Chanlatte Baík, Luis A. 1976. *Cultura igneri: investigaciones arqueológicas en Guayanilla, Puerto Rico: pt. 1, Tecla II.* Santo Domingo: Museo del Hombre Dominicana. 168 p.

Description of the Tecla II Igneri (Ostionoid) site located in Guayanilla; includes description of ceramics, lithics, shell, and bone.

1121.   Chanlatte Baík, Luis A. 1977. *Primer adorno corporal de oro (Nariguera) en la arqueologia indioantillana: investigaciones arqueológicas en Guayanilla, Puerto Rico, Tecla I.* Santo Domingo: Museo del Hombre Dominicano; Fundación García-Arévalo. 66 p.

1122.   Chanlatte Baík, Luis A. 1985. *Arqueología de Guayanilla y Vieques.* Río Piedras: Centro de Investigaciones Arqueológicas, Universidad de Puerto Rico.

Hacienda Grande

1123.   Bullen, Ripley P., and Adelaide K. Bullen. 1974. Tests at Hacienda Grande, Puerto Rico. *Fundación Arqueológica, Antropológica e Histórica de Puerto Rico, Boletín Informativo* 1:1–14. San Juan.

Presents the results of two tests at multicomponent Hacienda Grande.

1124.   Oliver, Andrés L. 1972. Vasija inhalatoria Saladoide del Bajo Igneri, Hacienda Grande. *Fundación Arqueológica, Antropológica e Histórica de Puerto Rico, Boletín Informativo* 3(1):2–4. San Juan.

Isla de Vieques

1125.   Chanlatte Baík, Luis A. 1976. *La Hueca y Sorcé (Vieques, Puerto Rico): Nuevo esquema para los procesos culturales de la arqueología antillana.* Santo Domingo: Fundación García Arévalo.

1126.   ———. 1979. Excavaciones arqueológicas en Vieques. *Museo de Antropología, Historia y Arte de la Universidad de Puerto Rico, Revista* 1(1):55–59. Río Piedras.

1127.   ———. 1981. La Hueca y Sorcé *(Vieques, Puerto Rico): primeras migraciones agroalfareras Antillanas: nuevo esquema para los procesos culturales de la arqueología Antillana.* Santo Domingo.

1128. ———. 1983. *Catálogo arqueología de Vieques: Exposición del 13 del marzo al 22 de abril de 1983.* Río Piedras: Museo de Antropología, Historia y Arte, Universidad de Puerto Rico.

1129. ———. 1984. Nuevos descubrimientos arqueológicos en la isla de Vieques. *Instituto de Cultura Puertorriqueña, Revista* 86:29–36. San Juan.

Archaeological research on the island of Vieques reveals four occupations, Agro I through IV (2000 B.C.–A.D. 1492); includes description of ceramics, lithics, and shell artifacts.

1130. ———, and Yvonne M. Narganes Stordes. 1983. *Vieques, Puerto Rico: asiento de una nueva cultura aborigen antillana.* Santo Domingo: Centro de Investigaciones Arqueológicas de la Universidad de Puerto Rico.

1131. ———, and Yvonne M. Narganes Stordes. 1989. La nueva arqueología de Puerto Rico: su proyección en los Antillas. *Museo del Hombre Dominicano, Boletín* 22:9–49. Santo Domingo.

Review of the archaeological sequence for Puerto Rico and a revision of Irving Rouse's scheme of unilineal evolution based on results from excavations at La Hueca, Vieques, Puerto Rico.

1132. Figueredo, Alfredo E. 1975. The Vieques Archaeological Project. *Virgin Islands Archaeological Society, Journal* 2:20–24. St. Thomas.

1133. Narganes Sordes, Yvonne M. 1982. Vertebrate Faunal Remains From Sorcé, Vieques, Puerto Rico. M.A. thesis, Department of Anthropology, University of Georgia, Athens.

La Cueva El Convento

1134. Oliver, José R. 1973. La Cueva El Convento: informe preliminar. *Fundación Arqueológica, Antropológica e Histórica de Puerto Rico, Boletín Informativo* 5(1):7. San Juan.

La Mina

1135. Oliver, José R. 1973. Petroglífos en La Mina. *Fundación Arqueológica, Antropológica e Histórica de Puerto Rico, Boletín Informativo* 6(1):12. San Juan.

Loíza

1136.   Alegría, Ricardo, H.B. Nicholson, and Gordon R. Willey. 1955. The Archaic tradition in Puerto Rico. *American Antiquity* 21(2):113–121. Washington, DC.

Essay considers the existence of a Preceramic occupation of Puerto Rico prior to the Arawaks; includes descriptions of finds from the Loíza Cave excavations.

1137.   Geigel, Alma S. de. 1972. Renombrado arqueólogo realiza excavación de salvamento en Loíza aldea. *Fundación Arqueológica, Antropológica e Histórica de Puerto Rico, Boletín Informativo* 3(1):8–9. San Juan.

1138.   Rouse, Irving, and Ricardo E. Alegria. 1990. *Excavations at Maria de la Cruz Cave and Hacienda Grande Village Site, Loíza, Puerto Rico.* Yale University Publications in Anthropology, no. 80. New Haven. 133 p.

Includes an appendix: E.C. Wing, Animal remains from the Hacienda Grande site (pp. 103–110). The Preceramic complex known as the María de la Cruz has hammerstones and used flakes similar to those from Krum Bay on St. Thomas, although it lacks certain large blade and celt forms. Instead, the characteristic artifacts are the pebble edge-grinders and edge choppers like those of central coastal Venezuela.

Los Chorros

1139.   Veloz Maggiolo, Marcio, and Mao Ramos Ramírez. 1980. Informe sobre una nueva maraca monoxillas indígena hallada en Puerto Rico. *Museo del Hombre Dominicano, Boletín* 9(15):11–16. Santo Domingo.

Recovery of wooden maraca fragment from the Los Chorros site suggests widespread Taíno influence; possible dual function as a maraca and spatula used in *cohoba* ritual.

Magueyes Island

1140.   Coomans, H.E. 1965. Shells and shell objects from an Indian site on Magueyes Island, Puerto Rico. *Caribbean Journal of Science* 5:15–23. Mayaguez.

Description of shells from an indigenous midden.

Maisabel

1141. France, Susan de. 1988. Zooarchaeological Perspective on Saladoid and Ostionoid Subsistence Adaptations at the Maisabel Site, Puerto Rico. M.A. thesis, Department of Anthropology, University of Florida, Gainesville.

Mora Island

1142. Pantel, A. Gus. 1973. Mora Island. *Fundación Arqueológica, Antropológica e Histórica de Puerto Rico, Boletín Informativo* 6(1):5. San Juan.

San Juan

1143. Smith, Hale G. 1962. *Archaeological Excavation at El Morro, San Juan, Puerto Rico.* Florida State University, Department of Anthropology, Notes in Anthropology, v. 6. Tallahassee. 97 p.

Report on a National Park Service excavation intended to make available information for the restoration and interpretation of El Morro fort.

1144. Vila Vilar, Enriqueta. 1977. Algunas consideraciones en torno a las fortificaciones de Puerto Rico. *International Congress of Americanists (50 session, Roma-Genova, 1972), Proceedings* 3:271–275. Roma-Genova.

Discussion of problems associated with the construction of fortifications in the Caribbean, especially El Morro in Puerto Rico.

Tibes

1145. Alvarado Zayas, Pedro A. 1981. La cerámica del centro ceremonial de Tibes: estudio descriptivo. M.A. thesis, Centro de Estudios Avanzados de Puerto Rico y El Caribe, San Juan.

1146. González Colón, Juan. 1984. Tibes: un centro ceremonial indígena. M.A. thesis, Centro de Estudios Avanzados de Puerto Rico y El Caribe, San Juan.

Villa Taína de Boquerón

1147. Goodwin, R. Christopher, and Jeffrey B. Walker. 1975. *Villa Taína de Boqueron: The Excavation of an Early Taíno Site in Puerto Rico.* San Juan: Inter-American University Press. 112 p.

Excellent site report on the artifact and skeletal remains excavated from the Villa Taína de Boquereón site on the west coast of Puerto Rico; radiocarbon dates and ceramics suggest Taíno occupation ca. A.D. 1000 (Period III).

LESSER ANTILLES

General

1148. Allaire, Louis. 1973. *Vers une préhistoire des Petites Antilles.* Fond St.-Jacques, Ste-Marie, Martinique: Université de Montréal, Centre de Recherches Caraibes. 53 p.

1149. McNamare, Rosalina. 1960. Recent archaeological developments. *The Caribbean* 14(4):90–91. Port-of-Spain.

Summary of archaeological research in Antigua, Surinam, and the Netherlands Antilles.

1150. Petitjean-Roget, Jacques, and Edgar Clerc. 1970. L'archéologie précolombienne aux Antilles françaises. *Parallèles* 36–347:1–106. Fort-de-France.

Bibliography

1151. Myers, Robert A. 1981. *Amerindians of the Lesser Antilles: A Bibliography.* New Haven: Human Relations Area Files. 158 leaves.

Classified bibliography of some 1,300 references to archaeological, historical, and linguistic research on the Ciboney, Arawak, and Carib populations of the eastern Caribbean; includes geographical and author indexes.

Museum Collections

1152. Moreau, Jean-Pierre. 1988. *Guide des trésors archéologiques sous-marins des Petites Antilles d'après les archives anglaises, espagnoles et françaises des XVIe, XVIIe et XVIIIe siècles.* Paris: Editions J.-P. Moreau. 276 p.

Inventory of sixteenth- and seventeenth-century shipwrecks in the Lesser Antilles.

History of Archaeological Research

1153.   Olsen, Fred. 1974. *On the Trail of the Arawaks.* Norman: University of Oklahoma Press. 408 p.

Personal account of the author's efforts to trace the origin of the Arawak who inhabited the Antilles at the time of first European contact; useful for background information on the peoples of the Caribbean; contains first report on Yale University-Antigua Archaeological Society excavations at large Indian Creek site on Antigua, Lesser Antilles.

Environment

1154.   Fewkes, Jesse W. 1914. Relations of aboriginal culture and environment in the Lesser Antilles. *American Geographical Society, Bulletin* 46(9):662–678. New York; *Museum of the American Indian, Heye Foundation, Contributions* 1(8):662–678, 1914. New York.

1155.   Harris, David R. 1965. *Plants, Animals and Man in the Outer Leeward Islands, West Indies: An Ecological Study of Antigua, Barbuda, and Anguilla.* Berkeley: University of California Press. 164 p.

Linguistics

1156.   Girard, Victor J. 1972. Proto-Carib Phonology. Ph.D. dissertation, Department of Linguistics, University of California, Berkeley.

1157.   Wesche, Marjorie B. 1973. Place names as a reflection of cultural change: an example from the Lesser Antilles. *Caribbean Studies* 12(2):74–98. Mona, Jamaica.

Study of the process by which place-names are given, maintained intact, modified, or replaced on Tobago, Grenada, St. Vincent, and Dominica, between 1763 and the 1960s.

Ethnohistory

1158.   Ratch, Christian, and Andrew R. Craston. 1983. Ultsheimer's remarks on the Caribs in the years 1599–1601. *Belizean Studies* 11(1):16–25. Belize City.

Discussion of manuscripts, dated 1616, by Andrew Ultshmeinmer, referring to the Caribs of St. Vincent and Dominica.

Cultural Evolution and Society

Cultural Evolution and Development

1159.   Allaire, Louis. 1980. On the historicity of Carib migrations in the Lesser Antilles. *American Antiquity* 45(2):238–245. Washington, DC.

Author questions the historicity of Carib migrations to the Lesser Antilles using documentary and archaeological evidence; proposes a very late migration of Arawakan peoples rapidly acculturated to mainland Carib culture; rejects Jalil Sued Badillo's thesis that there were no ethnic differences between the Island Carib and the Taíno and that these distinctions were a European fabrication to enslave indigneous populations.

1160.   Bullen, Ripley P. 1976. The Preceramic periods of Florida and the Lesser Antilles. *Puerto Rican Symposium on Archaeology (1 session, San Juan, 1973), Proceedings* 1:9–24. San Juan.

Author rejects possibility of prehispanic contact between Florida and the West Indies during the Preceramic and Ceramic periods; Gulf Stream is seen as a major natural barrier; article also considers the movement of people from South and Central America to the Greater Antilles via the Lesser Antilles.

1161.   Petitjean-Roget, Henry. 1975. Contribution à l'étude de la préhistoire des Petites Antilles. Ph.D. dissertation, Department of Anthropology, Ecole Pratique des Hautes Etudes, Paris. 360 p

1162.   Pinchon, Robert. 1952. Les peuples précolombiens dans les Petites Antilles et leurs migrations. In: *Congreso Histórico Municipal Interamericano (5 session, Ciudad Trujillo, 1952), Memorias* 1:155–168. Ciudad Trujillo.

Archaeological and historical summary of Igneri and Carib culture; author reconstructs the invasion of the Lesser Antilles by the Carib and an historical ethnography of Carib culture; see also: R. Pinchon, Les Caraibes d'àpès l'archéologie et l'histoire (*Annales des Antilles* 1–2:79–92, 1956. Martinique).

1163.   Sanoja, Marío, and Iraida Vargas. 1976. Las culturas alfareras tempranas del oriente de Venezuela y sus relaciones con las del area andina nuclear y las Antillas. *Puerto Rican Symposium on Archaeology (1 session, Santurce, 1976), Proceedings* 1:139–147. Santurce.

Material Culture

Art

1164.   Petitjean-Roget, Henry. 1978. *L'art des Arawak et des Caraibes des Petites Antilles; analyse de la décoration des céramiques.* Fort-de-France: Centre d'Etudes Regionales Antilles-Guyane/CERAG. 60, 105 p.

Analysis of selected design motifs on Carib and Arawak pottery from the Lesser Antilles.

Petroglyphs and Pictographs

1165.   Petroglyphs of the Windward Islands. *Bejan* 6(11):22–24, 1959. Bridgetown.

Description of petroglyphs on Dominica, St. Lucia, St. Vincent, and Grenada.

Pottery

1166.   Bilbaut, Théophile. 1893. *La céramique des colonies françaises: âge de terre-âge de pierre, poteries de la Guyane et des Antilles françaises.* Paris: Société d'Editions Scientifiques. 159 p.

1167.   Haag, William G. 1965. Pottery typology in certain Lesser Antilles. *American Antiquity* 31(2):242–245. Washington, DC.

1168.   McKusick, Marshall B. 1960. The Distribution of Ceramic Styles in the Lesser Antilles, W.I. Ph.D. dissertation, Department of Anthropology, Yale University. 203 p.

ANTIGUA

(Capital: St. John's)

At the southern end of the Leeward Islands, Antigua has an area of 280 sq km with a varied landscape including small, scrub-covered hills in the north, a fertile central plain, and in the southwest, eroded remains of volcanoes, with valleys that support tropical vegetation. The dependencies of Antigua are Barbuda (160 sq km) and Redonda (1.3 sq km).

General

1169. Dawud, Al Hajji Talib Ahmad. 1971. Archaeological and historical sites in Antigua. *Caribbean Conservation Association, Environmental Newsletter* 2(1):29–39. St. Michael, Barbados.

1170. Nicholson, Desmond V. 1976. Archaeology in Antigua: the living past. *Caribbean Conservation News* 1(5):10–12. Barbados.

1171. Nicholson, Desmond V. 1983. *The Story of the Arawaks in Antigua and Barbuda*. Antigua: Antigua Archaeological Society; London: Linden Press. 36 p.

Cultural Evolution and Society

Settlement Patterns

1172. Davis, Dave D. 1982. Archaic settlement and resource exploitation in the Lesser Antilles: preliminary information from Antigua. *Caribbean Journal of Science* 17:107–122. Mayaguez, Puerto Rico.

Material Culture

Pottery

1173. Handler, Jerome S. 1964. Notes on pottery making in Antigua. *Man* 64:150–151. London.

Regional and Site Reports

1174. Hoffman, Charles A. 1963. Archaeological Investigations on Antigua, W.I. M.A. thesis, University of Florida, Gainesville.

Indian Creek

1175. Jones, Alick R. 1980. A report on two types of modification to gastropod mollusc shells from Indian Creek, Antigua. *Virgin Islands Archaeological Society, Journal* 9:31–40. St. Thomas.

Discussion of whorl removal techniques on shells from Indian Creek.

1176. ———. 1985. Dietary change and human population at Indian Creek, Antigua. *American Antiquity* 50(3):518–536. Washington, DC.

Zooarchaeological study of the Indian Creek site in Antigua; includes a reconstruction of dietary change and available protein through time; see also: A.R. Jones, Dietary changes of the Arawaks at Indian Creek, Antigua. *Caribbean Conservation News* 1(12):13–15, 1978).

1177. Olsen, Fred. 1974. *Indian Creek, Arawak Site on Antigua, West Indies: 1973 Excavation by Yale University and the Antigua Archaeological Society.* Norman: University of Oklahoma Press. 58 p.

Description of excavations and material culture from Indian Creek; see also: F. Olsen, Preceramic findings in Antigua (*Puerto Rican Symposium on Archaeology (1 session, Santurce, 1976), Proceedings* 1:85–95, 1976).

1178. Rouse, Irving. 1977. Cultural development on Antigua, West Indies: a progress report. *International Congress of Americanists (41 session, México City, 1974), Proceedings* 3:701–709. México.

Author identified three ceramic complexes for the Indian Creek site extending from 1775 B.C. to A.D. 1470; Island Carib are seen to have developed from the Island Arawaks.

Mill Reef

1179. Hoffman, Charles A. 1979. The ceramic typology of the Mill Reef Site, Antigua, Leeward Islands. *Virgin Islands Archaeological Society, Journal* 7:35–51. St. Thomas.

1180. Wing, Elizabeth S., Charles A. Hoffman, and C.E. Ray. 1968. Vertebrate remains from Indian sites on Antigua, West Indies. *Caribbean Journal of Science* 8(3–4):123–139. Mayaguez, Puerto Rico.

Analysis of food remains excavated from Mill Reef (ca. A.D. 500–1150); conclude a decrease in the frequency of rice rat bones and increase in the exploitation of birds was related to hunting pressure; fish was the primary food source.

BARBADOS

(Capital: Bridgetown)

Located in the Windward Islands about 160 km east of St. Vincent, Barbados is the easternmost of the Caribbean islands and lies south of the path usually taken by hurricanes. Roughly triangular in shape, the island is 34 km long and about 22 km at its widest point, and is composed chiefly of coral, which accounts for the magnificent white sand beaches. Temperatures are pleasant because of the latitude, the ocean, and the trade winds that sweep unimpeded across the island from December to June. Although tamarinds, other fruit trees, ornamental palms, banyan trees, and other exotic plants are grown, almost half the total area of Barbados is devoted to the cultivation of sugar cane.

In ancient times Barbados was inhabited by Arawak and then by Carib Indians, but was uninhabited when the first European settlers arrived from England in 1627.

General

1181. Barton, G.T. 1953. *The Prehistory of Barbados*. Bridgetown: Advocate. 88 p.

A somewhat dated, although basic guide to the archaeology, geography, history, and ethnography of indigenous Barbados.

1182. Cooksey, C. 1912. The first Barbadians. *Timehri* 2:142–144. Georgetown.

An early account seeking to resolve the mystery of the first inhabitants of Barbados.

1183. Fewkes, Jesse W. 1915. Archaeology of Barbados. *National Academy of Sciences, Proceedings* 1:47–51. Washington, DC.

1184. Roach, C.N.C. 1936–1939. Old Barbados. *Barbados Museum and Historical Society, Journal* 3(3–4):137–148, 211–222, 1936; 4(1–4):12–21, 53–67, 109–122, 167–179, 1936–1937; 5(1–3):3–11, 85–100, 130–143, 1937–1938; 6(1–4):26–40, 74–86, 139–151, 191–197, 1938–1939). St. Ann's Garrison.

A series of articles considering the prehistory of Barbados; essays include a discussion of the shell implements and pottery uncovered at Golders Green and Indian Mount sites in the parish of St. Lucy, as well as conch shell implements, chipped and ground stone tools and implements, bone tools, etc.

Museum Collections

1185.   Drewett, Peter L., Mary Hill Harris, and Caroline R. Cartwright. 1987. Archaeological survey of Barbados: first interim report. *Barbados Museum and Historical Society, Journal* 38(1):44–80. St. Ann's Garrison.

Ceramic, shell, and lithic artifacts in museum and private collections from Barbados are described.

1186.   *Guide to the Barbados Museum.* 3 ed. Barbados Museum and Historical Society, Bulletin no. 14. St. Ann's Garrison, 1969. 44 p.

History of Archaeological Research

1187.   Boomert, Aad. 1987. Notes on Barbados prehistory. *Barbados Museum and Historical Society, Journal* 38(1):8–43. St. Ann's Garrison.

Summary of the history of archaeological research in Barbados.

Ethnography

1188.   Handler, Jerome S. 1964. Land Exploitative Activities and Economic Patterns in a Barbados Village. Ph.D. dissertation, Department of Anthropology, Brandeis University, Waltham, Massachusetts.

Ethnohistory

1189.   Handler, Jerome S. 1969. The Amerindian slave population of Barbados in the seventeenth and early eighteenth centuries. *Caribbean Studies* 8(4):38–64. Río Piedras, Puerto Rico.

1190.   ———. 1970. Aspects of Amerindian ethnography in seventeenth-century Barbados. *Caribbean Studies* 9(4):50–72. Río Piedras, Puerto Rico.

1191.   ———. 1982. Slave revolts and conspiracies in seventeenth-century Barbados. *Nieuwe West-Indische Gids* 56:5–43. Gravenhague.

1192.   ———., and Charlotte J. Frisbie 1970. Aspects of slave life in Barbados: music and its cultural context. *Caribbean Studies* 11(4):5–46. Río Piedras, Puerto Rico.

1193.   Sinckler, E. Goulbrun. 1918. The Indians of Barbados. *Timehri* 5(22):48–55. Georgetown.

Cultural Evolution and Society

Cultural Evolution and Development

1194.   Bullen, Ripley P. 1966. Barbados and the archaeology of the Caribbean. *Barbados Museum and Historical Society, Journal* 30(2):16–19. St. Ann's Garrison.

Author suggests that Barbados was first inhabited ca. A.D. 400 by a pre-Arawak population and that the island was abandoned until ca. A.D. 800 when it was occupied by the Arawaks, who were conquered by the Caribs about A.D. 1200.

Physical Anthropology

1195.   Corruccini, Robert S., and Jerome S. Handler. 1980. Temporomandibular joint size decrease in American Blacks: evidence from Barbados. *Journal of Dental Research* 59:1528. Baltimore.

1196.   Corruccini, Robert S., Jerome S. Handler, R. Mutaw, and Frederick W. Lange. 1982. The osteology of a slave burial population from Barbados, West Indies. *American Journal of Physical Anthropology* 59:443–459. New York.

See also: J.S. Handler and R.S. Corruccini, Plantation slave life in Barbados: a physical anthropological analysis (*Journal of Interdisciplinary History* 14(1):65–90, 1983).

1197.   Corruccini, Robert S., Jerome S. Handler, and Keith Jacobi. 1985. Chronological distribution of enamel hypoplasoias and weaning in a Caribbean slave population. *Human Biology* 57:699–711. Detroit.

See also: R.S. Corruccini, K. Jacobi, J.S. Handler, and A. Aufderheide, Implications of tooth root hypercementosis in a Barbados slave skeletal collection (*American Journal of Physical Anthropology* 74:179–184, 1987); J.S. Handler, R.S. Corruccini, and R. Mutaw, Tooth mutilation in the Caribbean: evidence from a slave population in Barbados (*Journal of Human Evolution* 11:297–313, 1982); and J.S. Handler and R.S. Corruccini, Weaning among West Indian slaves: historical and bioanthropological evidence from Barbados (*William and Mary Quarterly* 43:111–117, 1986).

Burial Patterns

1198. Handler, Jerome S., Michael D. Conner, and Keith P. Jacobi. 1989. *Searching for a Slave Cemetery in Barbados, West Indies: A Bioarchaeological and Ethnohistorical Investigation*. Center for Archaeological Investigations, Southern Illinois University at Carbondale, Research Paper no. 59. Carbondale, IL. 118 p.

Material Culture

Pottery

1199. Diksic, M., J.L. Galinier, and L. Yaffe. 1981. Barbados and the archaeology of the Caribbean. *Barbados Museum and Historical Society, Journal* 36(3):229–235. St. Ann's Garrison.

Reports the results of x-ray fluorescence analysis of elementary micro-constituents of Saladoid-Barrancoid pottery.

1200. Handler, Jerome S. 1963. Pottery making in rural Barbados. *Southwestern Journal of Anthropology* 19(3):314–334. Albuquerque.

1201. ———. 1963. A historical sketch of pottery manufacture in Barbados. *Barbados Museum and Historical Society, Journal* 30:129–153.

Groundstone

1202. Forte, Joseph. 1882. Note on Carib chisels. *Royal Anthropological Institute of Great Britain and Ireland, Journal* 11:2–3. London.

Extract of a letter from J. Forte to W.L. Distant from Bennetts, Barbados, pertaining to Carib chisels.

Regional and Site Reports

1203. Bullen, Adelaide K., and Ripley P. Bullen. 1966. Barbados, a Carib centre. *Bejan* 155:20–22. Bridgetown, Barbados.

Popular account of field work done in Barbados in 1966.

Mapps Cave

1204.   Lange, Frederick W., and Jerome S. Handler. 1980. The archaeology of Mapps Cave: a contribution to the prehistory of Barbados. *Virgin Islands Archaeological Society, Journal* 9:3–17. St. Thomas.

Summary of excavations at multicomponent Mapps Cave site; chronological assessment is based on the presence of Suazey (Carib) and the lack of Caliviny (Arawak) ceramics.

Newton Plantation

1205.   Handler, Jerome S., and Frederick W. Lange. 1978. *Plantation Slavery in Barbados: An Archaeological and Historical Investigation.* Cambridge, Massachusetts: Harvard University Press. 368 p.

Historical and archaeological investigation of fourteen plantations, with extensive excavations undertaken at the large Newton Plantation in Christ Church; includes detailed archaeological record of skeletons and associated material culture; see also: J.S. Handler and F.W. Lange, Plantation slavery on Barbados, West Indies (*Archaeology* 32(4):45–52, 1980); J.S. Handler, An archaeological investigation of the domestic life of plantation slaves in Barbados (*Barbados Museum and Historical Society, Journal* 34(2):64–72, 1972), a description of a research project on Barbados slaves and the archaeological component of the work.

1206.   Handler, Jerome S., Frederick W. Lange, and Charles Orser. 1979. Carnelian beads in necklaces from a slave cemetery in Barbados, West Indies. *Ornament* 4(2):15–20. Los Angeles.

Grave goods from a slave cemetery include glass beads and two carnelian beads, possibly from India; authors suggest carnelian beads were transported to Barbados from southeast Africa.

1207.   Handler, Jerome S., Alfred Aufderheide, and Robert S. Corruccini. 1986. Lead contact and poisoning in Barbados slaves: historical, chemical, and biological evidence. *Social Science History* 10(4):399–426. Beverly Hills.

Interesting ethnohistorical and physical anthropological study of lead toxicity among slaves at Newton Plantation; see also: R.S. Corruccini, A. Aufderheide, J.S. Handler, and L.E. Wittmers,

Patterning of skeletal lead content in Barbados slaves (*Archaeometry* 29:233–239, 1987. Oxford, England).

1208.   Lange, Frederick W. 1977. Slave mortuary practices, Barbados, West Indies. *International Congress of Americanists (41 session, México, 1974), Proceedings* 2:477–483. México.

Consideration of theoretical and methodological problems associated with archaeological research of slave communities.

BARBUDA

(Capital: Hamilton)

One of the Leeward Islands, Barbuda has an area of 160 sq km and is situated about 40 km north of Antigua. The island is well stocked with wild pigs and guinea fowl, and has Sea Island cotton as its principal crop.

Cultural Evolution and Society

Subsistence Patterns

1209. Watters, David R., Elizabeth Reitz, David Steedman, and Gregory Pregill. 1984. Vertebrates from archaeological sites on Barbuda, West Indies. *Carnegie Museum, Annals* 53:383–412. Pittsburgh.

   Identification of fish, reptile, bird, and mammal from Indiantown Trail, Sufferers, and Overview sites on Barbuda.

Settlement Patterns

1210. Watters, David R. 1980. Transect Surveying and Prehistoric Site Locations on Barbuda and Montserrat, Leeward Islands, West Indies. Ph.D. dissertation, Department of Anthropology, University of Pittsburgh. 430 p.

   Author examines the relationship between environment and site locations at two physiographically dissimilar locations in the Lesser Antilles, Barbuda and Montserrat; the Montserrat data support site location parameters similar to those on nearby islands; the data from Barbuda are different because of dissimilar physiography.

DOMINICA

(Capital: Roseau)

Dominica is situated in the Windwards between the islands of Martinique and Guadeloupe. Some 47 km long and up to 26 km wide, it has an area of about 780 sq km. Dominica is a fairly mountainous island of volcanic origin, with a rich soil that produces tropical fruit, cacao, vanilla beans, and spices. Columbus made his landfall there on November 3, 1493, during his second voyage. The name of the islands derives from the Latin *Dies Dominica* (day of the Lord), commemorating the fact that the day of discovery was a Sunday. In 1690 a Franco-British treaty assigned Dominica to the Carib Indian inhabitants, but French settlers moved in to establish plantations under a French governor. A community of several hundred Carib Indians remains in the interior of the island.

General

Linguistics

1211. Rat, Joseph N. 1897. The Carib language as now spoken in Dominica, West Indies, February, 1897. *Royal Anthropological Institute of Great Britain and Ireland, Journal* 27(2):293–315. London.

1212. Taylor, Douglas M. 1946. Loan words in Dominica Island Carib. *International Journal of American Linguistics* 12(4):213–216. Bloomington, Indiana.

1213. ———. 1954. Names on Dominica. *Names* 2(1):31–37. Potsdam, New York.

Discussion of the impact of Amerindian, French Creole, and English cultures on the names of places, flora, fauna, mountains, plantations, and people of Dominica; see also: D.M. Taylor, Names on Dominica (*West-Indische Gids* 36:121–124, 1954).

Ethnography

1214. Banks, Eugene P. 1954. An Inquiry into the Structure of Island Carib Culture. Ph.D. dissertation, Department of Anthropology, Harvard University, Cambridge, Massachusetts.

233

1215.   Bell, H. Hesketh. 1938. Last of the Caribs. *National Review* 110(6):227–234. Orange, Connecticut.

1216.   Birge, William S. 1900. *In Old Roseau: Reminiscences of Life as I Found It In The Island of Dominica and Among the Carib Indians.* New York: I.H. Blanchard. 105 p.

1217.   Frederick, Faustulus J., and Elizabeth Shepherd. 1971. *In Our Carib Village.* New York: Lothrop, Lee and Shepard. 96 p.

1218.   Hawtayne, G.H. 1887. Remarks on the Caribs. *Royal Anthropological Institute of Great Britain and Ireland, Journal* 16:196–198. London.

1219.   Napier, Elma. 1949. The Caribs of Dominica. *West Indian Review* 6(1):24–25, 27–31.

1220.   Peter, Imelda. 1934. The Caribs of Dominica, then and now. *Canada-West Indies Magazine* 23(8):247–248, 250.

1221.   Ross, Charlesworth. 1970. Caribs and Arawaks. *Caribbean Quarterly* 16(3):52–59. Mona, Jamaica.

Popular, personal account by the author who was once 'Officer in charge of the Caribs.'

1222.   Taylor, Douglas M. 1935. The Island Caribs of Dominica, B.W.I. *American Anthropologist* 37(2):265–272. Washington, DC.

Presentation of ethnographic information collected during several short visits to the Carib Reserve between 1930 and 1934; see also: D. Taylor, Additional notes on the Island Carib of Dominica, B.W.I. (*American Anthropologist* 38(1):462–468, 1936).

1223.   ———. 1938. The Caribs of Dominica. In: *Anthropological Papers*, no. 3. pp. 103–159. Bureau of American Ethnology, Bulletin 119. Washington, DC.

Extensive ethnography of the Island Caribs, including description of most aspects of everyday life and the life-cycle on the Carib Reserve, including childhood games, sexuality, shelter and houses, fishing, canoe-building, cultivation, and legends; see also: D.M. Taylor, Columbus saw them first (*Natural History* 48(1):40–49, 1941), for a popular and illustrated survey of Island Carib history, culture, and lifeways.

1224.   Thomas, Leon. 1953. La Dominique et les derniers Caraibes insulaires. *Les Cahiers d'Outre-Mer* 6(21):37–60. Bordeaux.

1225. Twiston-Davies, Suzanne. 1963. Carib Indians: a vanishing race. *Contemporary Review* 204(1172):203–204, 208. London.

1226. Weller, Anthony, and Alen MacWeeney. 1983. Conquerors of the Caribbean. *Geo* 5:68–76, 102, 105–106. New York.

Popular account of the current life and socio-economic problems of the Island Caribs.

Culture Change

1227. Baker, Patrick L. 1988. Ethnogenesis: the case of the Dominica Caribs. *América Indígena* 48(2):377–401. México.

1228. Delawarde, J.-B. 1938. Les derniers Caraïbes, leur vie dans une réserve de la Dominique. *Société des Américanistes de Paris, Journal* 30:167–204. Paris.

Account of Carib culture in 1936; provides historical and contemporary information on religion and traditions, farming and hunting activities, material culture, and legends.

1229. Layng, Anthony. 1985. The Caribs of Dominica: prospects for structural assimilation of a territorial minority. *Ethnic Groups* 6(2–3):209–221. New York.

Discussion of the Island Caribs as a distinct minority group characterized by differential access to material resources, prejudicial treatment and stereotypes, endogamy, assumed identifiability, and common fate identity; see also: A. Layng, Ethnic identity, population growth, and economic security on a West Indian reservation (*Revista/Review Interamericana* 9(4):577–584, 1979–1980).

1230. Myers, Robert A. 1976. I Love My Home Bad, But ...: The Historical and Contemporary Contexts of Migration on Dominica, West Indies. Ph.D. dissertation, Department of Anthropology, University of North Carolina at Chapel Hill. 518 p.

Ethnicity

1231. Layng, Anthony. 1979–1980. Ethnic identity, population growth, and economic security on a West Indies Reservation. *Revista/Review Intermericana* 9(4):577–584. Hato Rey, Puerto Rico.

1232. Owen, Nancy H. 1974. Land and Politics in a Carib Indian Community: A Study of Ethnicity. Ph.D. dissertation,

Department of Anthropology, University of Massachusetts, Amherst. 230 p.

See also: N.H. Owen, Land, politics, and ethnicity in a Carib Indian community (*Ethnology* 14(4):385–393, 1975), for an analysis of Carib ethnicity on Dominica; group membership is based on physical appearance, the chieftaincy, legends, and control of the Carib Reserve lands; N.H. Owen, Conflict and ethnic boundaries: a study of Carib-Black relations (*Social and Economic Studies* 29(2–3):264–274, 1980), for an examination of the relations between Island Caribs and Afro-Dominicans using the concept of ethnic boundaries.

1233.   Gregoire, Crispin, and Natalia Kanem. 1989. The Caribs of Dominica: land rights and ethnic consciousness. *Cultural Survival Quarterly* 13(3):52–55. Cambridge, Massachusetts.

Discussion of the Caribs on Dominica; authors argue that maintaining communal land tenure is a means of community survival and continues an ability to resist European colonialism.

Folklore

1234.   Banks, Eugene P. 1955. Island Carib folktales. *Caribbean Quarterly* 4(1):32–39. Mona, Jamaica.

Description of the work by Raymond Breton, Jacques Bouton, and Douglas Taylor on the Caribs.

1235.   Taylor, Douglas M. 1945. Carib folk-beliefs and customs from Dominica, B.W.I. *Southwestern Journal of Anthropology* 1(4):507–530. Albuquerque.

Description of Carib beliefs and customs, particularly regarding the supernatural world; includes beliefs about the origin of man, magicians, spiritual entities or zombies, ghosts, dreams, omens, sickness, charms, etc.; see also: D.M. Taylor, Tales and legends of the Dominica Caribs (*Journal of American Folklore* 65(257):267–279, 1952) for a commentary on eight folktales pertaining to celestial myths, local legends, and entertainment tales, collected between 1938 and 1941.

Religious Organization

1236.   Layng, Anthony. 1979. Religion among the Caribs. *Caribbean Review* 8(2):36–41. Miami.

Account of Roman Catholicism and folk beliefs among Dominica's Island Caribs, and the role of religion in maintaining social boundaries between the Caribs and Afro-Dominicans.

Social Organization

1237. Banks, Eugene P. 1956. A Carib village in Dominica. *Social and Economic Studies* 5(1):74–86. Mona, Jamaica.

Description of the village of Bataka, the largest Carib community in Dominica's Carib Reserve; author discusses the importance of kin relations, marriage patterns, the extended family, work patterns, and village structures among the 201 residents of 35 households.

1238. Taylor, Douglas M. 1946. Kinship and social structure of the Island Carib. *Southwestern Journal of Anthropology* 2(2):180–212. Albuquerque.

Using seventeenth-century French works in addition to his own extensive field observations, author describes the traditional and contemporary Island Carib social system, especially with respect to kinship relations; see, D.M. Taylor, A note on marriage and kinship among the Island Carib (*Man* 53(175):117–119, 1953) for a brief account of the marriage and kinship practices reported by French missionaries visiting Dominica in the seventeenth century.

Carib Reserve

1239. Bell, H. Hesketh. 1937. The Caribs of Dominica. *Barbados Museum and Historical Society, Journal* 5(1):18–31. St. Ann's Garrison.

Abridged version of a 1902 report proposing the establishment of a Carib Reserve.

1240. Fermor, Patrick L. 1950. The Caribs of Dominica. *Geographical Magazine* 23(6):256–264. New York.

Account of Island Carib life on the Reserve.

1241. Layng, Anthony. 1983. *The Carib Reserve: Identity and Security in the West Indies*. Washington, DC: University Press of America. 177 p.

Author argues Reserve maintains a distinct Carib identity; views continuation of reservation status as an adaptive strategy reducing

competition with non-Caribs for land; publication of: A. Layng, The
Carib Populations of Dominica (Ph.D. dissertation, Department of
Anthropology, Case Western Reserve University, 1976. 243 p.); see
also: A. Layng, The Carib Reserve of Dominica: issues pertaining to
its boundary and title (*Caribbean Monthly Bulletin* 9(8):18–20, 1975).

1242.   Luke, Harry. 1947. Remnants of a Caribbean conquering race:
        1. Last refuge of Island Caribs in Dominica. *Crown Colonist*
        17(193):639–643. London.

Ethnohistory

1243.   Dreyfus, Simone. 1983–1984. Historical and political
        anthropological interconnections: the multilinguistic indigenous
        polity of the Carib Islands and mainland coast from the sixteenth
        to the eighteenth century. *Antropológia* 59–62:39–55. Caracas.

Figure 14. Stone *zemí*, Mesa del Sordo, Cuba.
Zemí refers to a deity or the objectification of a deity and
is usually applied to a characteristic three-cornered deity form.

Source: M.R. Harrington, *Cuba Before Columbus*,
Museum of the American Indian, Heye Foundation, Indian Notes
and Monographs, no. 17. New York, 1921. Figure 35.

1244.   Myers, Robert A. 1972. A Social History of Dominica, West Indies. M.A. thesis, Department of Anthropology, University of North Carolina at Chapel Hill. 146 p.

1245.   ———. 1984. Island Carib cannibalism. *Nieuwe West-Indische Gids* 58(3–4):147–184. Gravenhague.

Review of the literature debating the existence of Island Carib cannibalism.

1246.   Neveu-Lemaire, M. 1921. Les caraïbes des Antilles: leur représentants actuels dans l'île de la Dominique. *La Géographie* 35(2):127–146. Paris.

An early twentieth-century summary account of the Dominican Island Caribs, including a comparison of the Carib vocabulary collected by Daniel Thaly in 1916 and 1918 with the seventeenth-century vocabulary from Raymond Breton's Carib-French dictionary.

1247.   Taylor, Douglas M. 1949. The interpretation of some documentary evidence on Carib culture. *Southwestern Journal of Anthropology* 5(4):379–392. Albuquerque.

Corrective commentaries using primary source materials from the seventeenth century.

Cultural Evolution and Society

Subsistence Patterns

1248.   Hodge, W.H. 1942. Plants used by the Dominica Caribs. *Journal of the New York Botanical Garden* 43(512):189–201. New York.

Account of the uses made of plants by the Carib Indians, including plants used for dugout canoes, baskets, fish poisons, household articles, and cultivation; see also: W.H. Hodge and D.M. Taylor, The ethnobotany of the Island Caribs of Dominica (*Webbia* 12(2):513–644, 1957. Firenze) for a presentation of historical notes, as well as indexes to scientific, French-based Creole, and Island Carib names of plants, and descriptions of uses.

1249.   Taylor, Douglas M. 1950. The meaning of dietary and occupational restrictions among the Island Caribs. *American Anthropologist* 52(3):343–349. Washington, DC.

Description of seventeenth-century accounts of dietary and occupational restrictions, and the remnants of such practices among the contemporary Island Carib and the Black Carib of British Honduras.

Physical Anthropology

1250. Harvey, R.G., Marilyn J. Godber, A.C. Kopec, A.E. Mourant, and D. Tills. 1969. Frequency of genetic traits in the Caribs of Dominica. *Human Biology* 41(3):342–364. Detroit.

Material Culture

Groundstone

1251. Soustelle, Jacques. 1934–1935. Un pierre à trois pointes de la Dominique. *Musée du Trocadéro, Bulletin* 8:12–14. Paris.

Basketry

1252. Taylor, Douglas M., and Harvey C. Moore. 1948. A note on Dominican basketry and its analogues. *Southwestern Journal of Anthropology* 4(3):328–343. Albuquerque.

Technical description of basketry among the Dominica Carib.

Intellectual Life

Astronomy

1253. Taylor, Douglas M. 1946. Notes on the star lore of the Caribees. *American Anthropologist* 48(2):215–222. Washington, DC.

Discussion of Carib beliefs concerning the sun, moon, stars, and planets.

GRENADA

(Capital: St. George's)

Grenada is the southernmost island in the Windwards, lying 135 km north of Trinidad. The island is 34 km long and up to 19 km wide, and has an area of 310 sq km. The terrain consists of narrow coastal plains and eroded volcanic mountains, with ridges that run north-south, enclosing steeply sloped valleys.

General

1254. Bullen, Ripley P. 1964. *The Archaeology of Grenada, West Indies.* University of Florida, Contributions of the Florida State Museum, Social Sciences, no. 11. Gainesville. 67 p.

Report on results of archaeological research on Grenada yielding material from ca. A.D. 1 and extending through the historic period; three major periods are defined, including pre-Arawak, Caliviny (Arawak), and Suazey (Carib); see also: R.P. Bullen, Archaeological research at Grenada, West Indies (*American Philosophical Society, Yearbook* 1963:511–514, 1964).

Ethnohistory

1255. Petitjean-Roget, Jacques, Bénigne Bresson, and Elisabeth Crosnier. 1975. *Histoire de l'Isle de Grenada en Amérique, 1649–1659.* Montreal: University of Montreal Press. 230 p.

1256. Robertson, Windom J. 1958. The Caribs of Grenada. *Canada-West Indies Magazine* 48(12):27–28.

Cultural Evolution and Society

Cultural Evolution and Development

1257. Bullen, Ripley P. 1965. Archaeological chronology of Grenada. *American Antiquity* 31(2):237–241. Washington, DC.

Author argues that pre-Arawak agriculturalists, the Arawaks, and the Caribs (and possibly the Preceramic Ciboney) all entered the

241

West Indies through Grenada; see also: R.P. Bullen, The archaeology of Grenada, West Indies, and the spread of ceramic people in the Antilles (*International Congress of Americanists (36 session, Seville, 1964), Proceedings* 1:435–439, 1966. Seville) for a discussion of the ceramic periods on Grenada, possible origins in South America, and extensions throughout the Greater Antilles; includes a correlation of Insular Carib and Arawak pottery complexes for the Lesser Antilles.

Economic Organization

1258.   Cody, Ann K. 1991. Prehistoric Patterns of Exchange in the Lesser Antilles: Materials, Models, and Preliminary Observations. M.A. thesis, Department of Anthropology, San Diego State University. 435 p. San Diego.

Artifacts from the Pearls site on Grenada provide evidence for the Saladoid importation of exotic rocks and minerals to the island; these data are used to reconstruct long-distance exchange networks in order to understand sustained island-mainland and inter-island interactions, and Grenada's role in the regulation of exchange between the Lesser Antilles and mainland South America; author proposes that the site of Pearls acted as a 'gateway community' in the regulation of commerce between the Lesser Antilles and South America.

Material Culture

Petroglyphs and Pictographs

1259.   Huckerby, Thomas. 1921. Petroglyphs of Grenada and a recently discovered petroglyph in St. Vincent. *Museum of the American Indian, Heye Foundation, Indian Notes and Monographs* 1:139–164. New York.

GUADELOUPE

(Capital: Basse-Terre)

Guadeloupe consists of two islands, Basse-Terre on the west, and Grand-Terre on the east, separated by a narrow channel in the Leewards. The area of Basse-Terre is 940 sq km and that of Grande-Terre is 566 sq km. To the east are the island dependencies of Désirade and the Iles de la Petite-Terre; to the south lie Marie-Galante and the Ile des Saintes. All of these are within 25 km of the main islands. Other dependencies of Guadeloupe, St. Barthelmey and the northern part of St. Martin, are 208 to 240 km to the northwest.

General

1260.   Breton, Raymond. 1978. *Relations de l'Ile de la Guadeloupe.* Bibliothèque d'Histoire Antillaise, 1. Basse Terre: Société d'Histoire de la Guadeloupe. 211 p.

1261.   Clerc, Edgar. 1965. *Exposition d'archéologie précolombienne.* Basse-Terre: Société d'Histoire de la Guadeloupe. 39 p.

1262.   Montbrun, Christian. 1984. *Les Petites Antilles avant Christophe Colomb: vie quotidienne des Indiens de la Guadeloupe.* Paris: Karthala. 172 p.

General summary of the prehispanic populations of Guadeloupe and Martinique; includes discussion of geographical aspects of settlement, religion, and family structure.

1263.   Nadaillac, Jean F.A. du P. 1886. La Guadeloupe prehistorique. *Materiaux pour l'Histoire Primitive de l'Homme* 3:373. 15 p.

Museum Collections

Guesde Collection

1264.   Hamy, Ernest T. 1884. La Collection Guesde à la Pointe-à-Pitre. *Revue d'Ethnographie* 3:266–268. Paris.

See also: E.T. Hamy, Les aquarelles archéologiques de M. Guesde de la Pointe-à-Pitre (*Decades Americanae* 1–2:156–160, 1884. Paris);

O.T. Mason, The Guesde Collection of antiquities in Pointe-à-Pitre, Guadeloupe, West Indies (*Smithsonian Institution, Annual Report* 1884:729–837, 1899).

Ethnohistory

1265. Farrugia, Laurrent. 1975. *Les Indiens de Guadeloupe et de Martinique.* Paris: A.P. Collet. 180 p.

1266. Rennard, Joseph. 1929. *Les Caraibes la Guadeloupe, 1635–1656: d'après les relations du R.P. Breton.* Histoire Coloniale, 1. Paris: G. Ficker. 182 p.

Cultural Evolution and Society

Cultural Evolution and Development

1267. Mountbrun, Christian. 1977. Les homme et le milieu naturel dans le région caribe: le cas de la Guadeloupe. Ph.D. dissertation, University of Paris.

Physical Anthropology

1268. Barbotin, F. Maurice. 1978. Découverte de cranes, fémurs et autres os. *Société d'Histoire de la Guadeloupe, Bulletin* 38:3–37. Basse Terre.

1269. Hamy, Ernest T. 1902. Roches graves de la Guadeloupe. *Société des Americanistes de Paris, Journal* 4(1):82–87. Paris; *Decades Americanae* 5–6:94–107, 1902.

Material Culture

Art

1270. Clerc, Edgar. 1971. Les trois-pointes des sites précolombiens de la côte nord-est de la Grand-Terre. *Société d'Histoire de la Guadeloupe, Bulletin* 15–16:41–52. Basse Terre.

Discussion of shell and three-pointed stones from Guadeloupe.

Groundstone

1271. Hamy, Ernest T. 1884. Un anthropolithe de la Guadeloupe. *Revue d'Ethnographie* 3:516–520. Paris; *Decades Americanae* 1–2:41–45.

Regional and Site Reports

1272. Clerc, Edgar. 1970. Recherches archéologiques en Guadeloupe. *Parallèles* 36–37:68–98. Fort de France.

Illustrated account of archaeological research by the author at Morel, Anse-à-l'Eau, and Damencourt sites on Guadeloupe; using radiocarbon dating defines four prehistoric periods dating from A.D. 220 to ca. A.D. 900.

Marie-Galante

1273. Barbotin, Maurice. 1969. Arawak et Caraibes à Marie Galante. *Société d'Histoire de la Guadeloupe, Bulletin* 11–12:77–119. Basse Terre.

Brief summary of archaeological and historical research on Marie-Galante by the author; describes subsistence patterns, dwellings, burial patterns, etc.; also published: Arawaks: à Marie-Galente premier occupants (*Parallèles* 36–37:99–102, 1970); see also: M. Barbotin, Archéologie caraibe et chroniqueurs (*Société d'Histoire de la Guadeloupe, Bulletin* 15–16:53–67; 21:41–68, 1971–1974) for an archaeological and ethnographic description of Caribs on Marie-Galante.

Morel

1274. Clerc, Edgar. 1964. Le peuplement précolombien des Antilles et ses vestiges en Guadeloupe. *Société d'Histoire de la Guadeloupe, Bulletin* 2:18–31. Basse Terre.

Chronological assessment and description of ceramics at the Morel site; occupation extends from A.D. 200 (Saladoid tradition Morel I) to A.D. 850 (Morel IV); the most recent, possibly Carib, deposits contained thick, large pottery vessels, legged griddles, pottery stamps, and a shell gouge.

Trois-Rivières

1275. Froidevaux, Henri. 1920. La station des Trois-Rivières (Guadeloupe) et ses pétroglyphes. *Société des Américanistes de Paris, Journal* 12:127–140. Paris.

MARTINIQUE

(Capital: Fort-de-France)

Martinique, an island in the Windwards, measures 65 km in length and 700 sq km in area, and is one of the largest of the Lesser Antilles. The island, located about 600 km southeast of Puerto Rico, is rugged and studded with volcanic peaks, notably the volcano Mont Pelée and the Pitons du Carbet. There are dense, little-exploited rain forests in the mountainous north, and many narrow, fertile valleys with streams which become torrents in the rainy season. The coastline is deeply indented by numerous coves and harbors, and there are many small islets off the east coast.

Columbus landed on Martinique during his fourth voyage in 1502, but the island was subsequently ignored by the Spaniards, partly because of the ferocity of the Carib inhabitants. By the end of the seventeenth century the Carib population had been nearly wiped out.

General

1276. Bataillon, Claude. 1966. Recherches précolombinnes à la Martinique. *Société des Americanistes de Paris, Journal* 55(2):679–684. Paris.

1277. Delawarde, Jacques-Baptiste. 1937. *Préhistoire Martiniquaise; les gisements du Precheur et du Marigot.* Fort-de-France: Imprimerie Officialle. 30 p.

1278. Goyhénèche, E., and M. Nicolas. 1956–1957. *Des Iles et des Hommes.* Fort-de-France: Editions des Horizons Caraíbes. 2 v.

Includes a summary of the archaeology and ethnography of the Arawak and Carib of Martinique.

1279. Petitjean-Roget, Jacques. 1970. Introduction to Martiniquan archaeology. *Parallèles* 36–37:48–51. Fort-de-France.

Illustrated historical summary of archaeological (stratigraphic) and ethnographic research in Martinique; French translation: J. Petitjean-Roget, L'archéologie Martiniquaise (*Parallèles* 36–37:4–7, 1970).

1280. ———. 1970. New research. *Parallèles* 36–37:57–67. Fort-de-France.

French translation: J. Petitjean-Roget, Nouvelles recherches (*Parallèles* 36–37:25–47, 1970).

1281. Pinchon, Robert. 1952. Introduction à l'archéologie Martiniquaise. *Société des Americanistes des Paris, Journal* 41(2):305–352. Paris.

Author differentiates two cultures, an earlier Arawak and a later Carib, and describes sites and objects based on seven years of research on Martinique; the earlier pottery corresponds to the white-on-red ware of the region while the later pottery appears to be a local development.

1282. Revert, Eugène. 1949. *La France d'Amérique: Martinique, Guadeloupe, Guayane, Saint-Pierre et Miquelon.* Paris: Société d'Editions Géographiques, Maritimes et Coloniales. 287 p.

Includes summaries of the archaeology of Martinique and Guadeloupe.

Museum Collections

Musée de l'Homme

1283. d'Harcourt, Raoul. 1952. Collections archéologiques Martiniquaises du Musée de l'Homme. *Société des Americanistes de Paris, Journal* 41(2):353–382. Paris.

Description of archaeological material from five sites excavated by Eugène Revert in the 1940s; author argues that Carib culture of Martinique developed from an Arawak base.

History of Archaeological Research

1284. Petitjean-Roget, Jacques. 1970. Histoire des recherches archéologiques. *Parallèles* 36–37:19–24. Fort-de-France.

Environment

1285. Barrau, Jacques. 1976. Biogéographie ou ethnobiogéographie? Une réflexion à propos de la Martinique et plus généralement, des Petites Antilles. *Société de Biogéographie, Comptes Rendus* 469:83–96.

1286. ———, and C. Montbrun. 1978. La mangrove et l'insertion humaine dans les écosystèmes insulaires des Petits Antilles: le cas de la Martinique et de la Guadeloupe. *Social Science Information* 17(6):897–919.

Ethnography

1287. Price, Richard, and Sally Price. 1966. A note on canoe names in Martinique. *Names* 14(3):157–160. Potsdam, New York.

Ethnohistory

1288. Petitjean-Roget, Jacques. 1969. Arawaks et Caraibes: thème d'études pré-Colombiennes à Fort-de-France du 3 au 9 juillet 1961. *Annales des Antilles* 9:1–9. Martinique.

Summary of the ethnohistory and archaeology of Martinique.

Cultural Evolution and Society

Cultural Evolution and Development

1289. Allaire, Louis. 1977. Later Prehistory in Martinique and the Island Caribs: Problems in Ethnic Identification. Ph.D. dissertation, Department of Anthropology, Yale University. 425 p.

1290. Mattioni, Mario. 1967. Deux horizons précolombiens à la Martinique. *Parallèles* 24:8–10. Fort-de-France.

1291. Mattioni, Mario. 1969. *Archéologie de la Martinique.* Centre d'Etudes Régionales Antilles-Guyane, Cahiers 20. Fort-de-France. 68 p.

Discussion of the peopling of the Lesser Antilles and summary of archaeological knowledge regarding Martinique.

1292. Mattioni, Mario. 1969. Etude des migrations Arawak et Caraïbe aux antilles sur la base de 4 ans de fouilles archéologiques. *International Congress of Americanists (38 session, Stuttgart-München, 1968), Proceedings* 1:309–316. Stuggart-München.

Summary of cultural chronology of the Lesser Antilles with emphasis on Martinique and use of ethnographic analogy in the analysis of certain ceramic types from Martinique.

1293. Petitjean-Roget, Jacques. 1976. Un preceramico de Martinica. *Museo del Hombre Dominicano, Boletin* 7:180–190. Santo Domingo.

Demography

1294. Fauquet, G. 1912. Note sur la population de la Martinique. *Société des Americanistes de Paris, Bulletin et Memoires* 3–4:154–161. Paris.

1295. Petitjean-Roget, Jacques. 1970. Pre-Columbian populations. *Parallèles* 36–37:52–54. Fort-de-France.

French translation: J. Petitjean-Roget, Connaissance des populations précolombiennes (*Parallèles* 36–37:10–18, 1970).

Material Culture

Art

1296. Mattioni, Mario, and Maurice Nicolas. 1972. *Art précolombien de la Martinique*. Fort-de-France: Musée Départemental de la Martinique; Paris: Horizons Caraibes. 89 p.

Illustrated description of pottery and other artifacts from Martinique.

Pottery

1297. Mattioni, Mario. 1967. Symbolisme dans la poterie Arawak. *Terra Ameriga* 3(9):5–8. Genova.

Artistic analysis of art motifs on white-on-red Saladoid restored vessels; see also: M. Mattioni, La culture Arawak aux Antilles (*Archeologia* 45:30–33, 1972) for a discussion of the Arawak-Carib problem and suggests ceremonial-symbolic aspects of Modified Saladoid ceramics.

1298. Petitjean-Roget, Jacques, and Henri Petitjean-Roget. 1976. Methodological guidelines for the study of the decoration of the pre-Columbian ceramics of Martinique. *Puerto Rican Symposium on Archaeology (1 session, Santurce, 1976), Proceedings* 1:95–103. Santurce.

Theoretical discussion of the analysis of ceramic form, decoration, and function.

Regional and Site Reports

Anse-Belleville

1299.   Reichlen, Henry, and Paule Barret. 1940. Contribution à l'archéologie de la Martinique; le gisement de l'Anse-Belleville. *Société des Americanistes de Paris, Journal* 32:227–274. Paris.

Appendix: M. Friant, R. Hoffstetter, and P. Chabana, Appendice sur la faune précolombienne de l'Anse-Belleville (pp. 259–274). Report on the first extensive excavation in the French Antilles made in 1939 by Revert for the Musée de l'Homme.

1300.   Revert, Eugène. 1949. *La Martinique.* Paris: Nouvelles Editions Latines. 560 p.

Includes a discussion of archaeology and author summarizes his work for the Musée de l'Homme at L'Anse Belleville and Sainte-Marie; concludes that original Igneri (Arawak) ceramic tradition survived the Carib as part of the captive women's culture.

Diamant

1301.   Mattioni, Mario. 1966. Fouilles archéologiques à la Martinique. *Terra Ameriga* 2(2):5–8. Genova.

Popular account of archaeological work at the Diamant site.

Macabou

1302.   Allaire, Louis. 1981. Macabou excavations: Martinique, 1972–1979. *Museo del Hombre Dominicano, Boletín* 10(16):41–48. Santo Domingo.

Report of archaeological excavation at Macabou site on the southeast coast of Martinique; excavation at seven areas revealed three Suazoid phases (ca. A.D. 1100–1400) and author concludes Island Caribs should not be associated with Suazoid prehistoric or historic components.

1303.   Fraser, Linda J. 1981. The analysis of the vertebrate fauna from the Macabou site, Area F, Martinique. *Museo del Hombre Dominicano, Boletín* 10(16):49–60. Santo Domingo.

Summary of vertebrate remains excavated by Allaire at the Macabou site; includes comparisons between different areas of the site and with comparable material from Barbados, Grenada, and St. Lucia.

Paquemar

1304.   Reichlen, Henri, and Paule Barret. 1941. Contribution à l'archéologie de la Martinique: le gisement de Paquemar. *Société des Americanistes de Paris, Journal* 33:91–117. Paris.

Description of a collection made in 1938; authors argue that single-bitted, eared axes and modeled-incised pottery of the Lesser Antilles were Arawak rather than Carib manufactures.

Sainte Marie

1305.   Revert, Eugène. 1952. Rapport de M.E. Revert sur ses fouilles à Sainte-Marie, Martinique en 1940. *Société des Americanistes de Paris, Journal* 41(2):373–382. Paris.

Vivé

1306.   Bullen, Ripley P., and M. Mattioni. 1972. Some ceramic variations at Vivé, Martinique. *International Congress of Americanists (40 session, Roma-Genova, 1972), Proceedings* 1:225–229. Genova.

Discusses variation in ceramics between two cultural deposits (Saladoid and Barrancoid) separated by volcanic ash; radiocarbon dates at the site of Vivé.

1307.   Mattioni, Mario. 1972. Découverte d'une sépulture Arawak du II siècle à la Martinique. *International Congress of Americanists (40 session, Roma-Genova, 1972), Proceedings* 1:231–237. Roma.

Brief discussion of the discovery and excavation of an intact Arawak burial in Martinique; see also: M. Mattioni, Discovery of three third-century pre-Columbian tombs in Martinique (*Puerto Rican Symposium on Archaeology (1 session, Santurce, 1976), Proceedings* 1:79–85, 1976. Santurce).

1308.   ———. 1977. Essai de réconstitution d'une parcelle de 100m2 d'un village arawak du 2ème siècle à la Martinique. *International Congress of Americanists (41 session, México, 1974), Proceedings* 1:579–595. México.

Report on excavations at Vivé site, an Arawak village on Martinique radiocarbon dated to A.D. 420 and A.D. 220.

MONTSERRAT

(Capital: Plymouth)

Montserrat, one of the Leeward Islands, is about 40 km southwest of Antigua. It is 18 km long and up to 11 km wide, with an area of 97 sq km. It has a mountainous terrain with many streams and waterfalls, and a dense tropical vegetation.

1309. Harrington, Mark R. 1924. A West Indian gem center. *Museum of the American Indian, Heye Foundation, Indian Notes* 1(4):184–189. New York.

Regional and Site Reports

Galways Plantation

1310. Goodwin, Conrad M. 1982. Archaeology on the Galways Plantation. *Florida Anthropologist* 34(4):251–257. Gainesville.

Report on excavation of a sugar-boiling house.

1311. Pulsipher, Lydia M. 1983. Galways Plantation project. *Caribbean Geography* 1(2):141–142.

General synthesis of archaeological, historical, and geographical research on Galways Plantation, an eighteenth-century sugar estate.

1312. Pulsipher, Lydia M., and Conrad M. Goodwin. 1982. A sugar-boiling house at Galways: an Irish sugar plantation in Montserrat, West Indies. *Post-Medieval Archaeology* 16:21–27.

Description of the construction, equipment, and arrangement of an eighteenth-century sugar-boiling house at Galways Plantation.

1313. Zachs, Sarah. 1985. An Eighteenth-Century Plantation Support Structure on the Caribbean Island of Montserrat. M.A. thesis, Department of Anthropology, Brown University, Providence, Rhode Island. 56 p.

Report on the excavation and a functional analysis of an eighteenth-century building on the Galways Plantation site; description of ceramic remains and pipestems.

Harney

1314.   Mann, Robert W., Lee Meadows, William M. Bass, and David R. Watters. 1987. Description of skeletal materials from a Black slave cemetery from Montserrat, West Indies. *Carnegie Museum, Annals* 56(19):319–336. Pittsburgh.

Results of excavation of the Harney site, an eighteenth-century cemetery on Montserrat; skeletal pathology (e.g., anemia, fractures, malnutrition, osteoarthritis, etc.) suggests harsh conditions during life.

1315.   Petersen, James B., and David R. Watters. 1988. Afro-Montserratian ceramics from the Harney site cemetery, Montserrat, West Indies. *Carnegie Museum, Annals* 57(8):167–187. Pittsburgh.

Analysis of historic artifacts from excavations at a slave cemetery on Montserrat.

1316.   Watters, David R. 1981. A Turlington Balsam phial from Montserrat, West Indies: genuine or counterfeit? *Historical Archaeology* 15(1):105–108. Washington, DC.

Discussion of the authenticity of an eighteenth-century pharmaceutical bottle.

1317.   Watters, David R. 1987. Excavations at the Harney slave cemetery, Montserrat, West Indies. *Carnegie Museum, Annals* 56(18):289–318. Pittsburgh.

Description of artifacts, features, and skeletal material associated with the Harney site; author concludes the cemetery was used during the late eighteenth century for black slaves; an important contribution to plantation archaeological literature.

Trant

1318.   Steedman, David, David R. Watters, Elizabeth Reitz, and Gregory Pregill. 1984. Vertebrates from archaeological sites on Montserrat, West Indies. *Carnegie Museum, Annals* 53:1–29. Pittsburgh.

Zooarchaeological study of fish, reptile, bird, and mammalian remains at the Trant and Radio Antilles sites on Montserrat; authors conclude that Saladoid exploited local marine and land vertebrates.

1319. Watters, David R. 1980. A problematic artifact from Trant's Montserrat. *Virgin Islands Archaeological Society, Journal* 9:18–21. St. Thomas.

Functional discussion of a slate or shale artifact from the Trant site in Montserrat.

NETHERLANDS ANTILLES

(Capital: Willemsted)

General

1320. *Beiträge zur Anthropologie, Ethnographie und Archaeologie Niederl. Westindiens; Bijdragen tot de Anthropologie, Ethnographie en Archaeologie van Niederl. Westindie.* Mittheilungen aus dem Niederl. Reichsmuseum für Völkerkunde, Veröffentlichung, 2(9). Haarlem: H. Kleinman, 1904. 22 p.

Contents include: J.D.E. Schmeltz, Uber Sammlungen aus Niederl. Westindien und Surinam (pp. 1–6); C. Leemans, Altertümer von Curaçao, Bonaire und Aruba (pp. 7–17); G.A. Koeze, Schädel von Curaçao und Aruba (pp. 18–22).

1321. Boerstra, Egbert H.J. 1972. *Archeologie in de Nederlandse Antillen.* Nederlandse Stichting voor Culturele Samenwerking met Suriname en de Nederlandse Antillen, nos. 36–40. La Haya, Netherlands.

1322. ———. 1982. *De precolumbiaanse bewoners van Aruba, Curaçao en Bonaire.* Zutphen: Walburg Pers. 79 p.

1323. Heekeren, H.R. van. 1963–1964. Studies on the archaeology of the Netherlands Antilles, III: Prehistorical research on the islands of Curaçao, Aruba and Bonaire. *Nieuwe West-Indische Gids* 43:1–24. Gravenhague.

Preliminary survey and excavation results on Aruba, Bonaire, and Curaçao.

1324. Heekeren, H.R. van. 1969. De pre-Columbiaanse bewoners van de Benedenwindse eilanden. In: *De onderste steen boven: Belevenissen van een globetrotter.* H.R. van Heekeren, ed. pp. 132–143. Assen: Van Gorcum.

1325. Institute of Archaeology and Anthropology of the Netherlands Antilles. 1987. *Collected Papers on Netherlands Antilles Archaeology,*

1985. Curacao: Institute of Archaeology and Anthropology of the Netherlands Antilles. 133 p.

1326.　Wagenaar Hummelinck, P. 1955–1956. Caribische beelden, I-V. *West-Indische Gids* 36:125–132. Gravenhague.

Contents include: I. Huisje met wrijfsteen op Aruba; II. De Martello Tower op Barbuda; III. Mourera fluviatilis een sieraad van de Surinaamse volken; IV. De Old Dutch Church van St. Croix; V. Mensenfiguurtjes als rotskening op Bonaire.

Bibliography

1327.　Coomans-Eustatia, Maritza, and Henry E. Coomans. 1987. *Bibliography of the Archaeology and Amerindians of the Netherlands Antilles and Aruba.* Institute of Archaeology and Anthropology of the Netherlands Antilles, Reports no. 6, Uitgave, 31. Curaçao: Univeridat Nashonal di Antia. 69 p.

Bibliography covering the Netherlands Antilles up to 1986.

History of Archaeological Research

1328.　Geijskes, D.C. 1962. Het eerste Internationale Congrès voor de Studie van de Prae-Columbiaanse Culturen in de Kleine Antillen. *Nieuwe West-Indische Gids* 41(3):272–284. Gravenhague.

Report on the first International Congress for the Study of Prehistory in the Lesser Antilles in 1961; concludes there is no distinction between Arawak and Carib pottery in the Lesser Antilles.

Cultural Evolution and Society

Demography

1329.　Josselin de Jong, J.P.B. de. 1918. The precolumbian and early postcolumbian aboriginal population of Aruba, Curaçao, and Bonaire. *Internationles Archiv für Ethnographie* 24:51–114, 25:1–26. Leiden.

Physical Anthropology

1330.　Wagenaar Hummelinck, P. 1959. Studies on the physical anthropology of the Netherlands Antilles I: Indiaanse skeletvondsten op Aruba en Curaçao. *Nieuwe West-Indische Gids* 39: 72–94. Gravenhague.

Material Culture

Art

1331.   Heekeren, H.R. van. 1960. Studies on the archaeology of the Netherlands Antilles, II: A survey of the nonceramic artifacts of Aruba, Curaçao and Bonaire. *Nieuwe West-Indische Gids* 40:103–120. Gravenhague.

Includes a history of archaeological research in the Netherlands Antilles, a summary of 1923 excavations by J.P.B. Josselin de Jong, and a description of nonceramic artifacts collected by Josselin de Jong.

1332.   Josselin de Jong, J.P.B. de. 1924. A natural prototype of certain three-pointed stones. *International Congress of Americanists (21 session, The Hague, 1924), Proceedings* 1:43–45. The Hague.

Petroglyphs and Pictographs

1333.   Wagenaar Hummelinck, P. 1953. Rotstekeningen van Curaçao, Aruba en Bonaire. *De West-Indische Gids* 34:173–207. Gravenhague.

Illustrated description of rock paintings and carvings on the Dutch Leeward Islands; continued by: P. Wagenaar Hummelinck, Rotstekeningen van Curaçao, Aruba en Bonaire (*De West-Indische Gids* 37:93–126, 1956); P. Wagenaar Hummelinck, P. 1961. Rotstekeningen van Curaçao, Aruba en Bonaire (*De West-Indische Gids* 41:83–126, 1961); P. Wagenaar Hummelinck, Rotstekeningen van Curaçao, Aruba en Bonaire (*Nieuwe West-Indische Gids* 49(1–2):1–66, 1972).

Pottery

1334.   Du Ry, C.J. 1960. Studies on the archaeology of the Netherlands Antilles, I: Notes on the pottery of Aruba, Curaçao and Bonaire. *Nieuwe West-Indische Gids* 40(2):81–102. Gravenhague.

Examination of pottery from Aruba, Bonaire, and Curaçao in the Rijksmuseum voor Volkenkunde, Leiden, excavated by J.P.B. de Josselin de Jong in 1923.

Regional and Site Reports

1335. Boerstra, E.H.J. 1971. Opgravingen op Santa Barbara: rapport over de archeologische werkzaamheden in de Nederlandse Antillen gedurende de maand februari, 1971. *STICUSA Journaal* 1(3):6.

1336. Josselin de Jong, J.P.B. de. 1919–1920. De Beteekonis van het archeologisch onderzoek op Aruba, Curaçao en Bonaire. *West-Indische Gids* 1(2):317–334. Gravenhague.

Discussion of the significance of archaeological research on Aruba, Curaçao, and Bonaire.

1337. Kuilenburg, J. van. 1973. De oorspronkelijke bewoners van Aruba en Curaçao. *Fibula* 14(2):16–21.

Aruba

An island of the Netherland Antilles 28 km north of the coast of Venezuela. Aruba is 31 km long and some 8 km wide with an area of 179 sq km. The western part is mostly flat and there are cliffs on the north coast, and a coral reef along part of the south coast. Aruba's dry climate restricts agriculture to some corn and beans grown in isolated parts, and a succulent desert plant, aloe, introduced in 1840, whose juice is used in medicines.

1338. Boerstra, E.H.J. 1973. Skeletten van oude Indianen op Aruba. *STICUSA Journaal* 3(1):8–10.

1339. Engels, Chris, and A.J. van Bork Feltkamp. 1970. *Opgravingen te Malmok op Aruba: de Westie Gigan.* Willemstad: Het Curaçaosch Museum. 44 p.

Archaeological finds in Malmok on Aruba: the case of Gigan.

1340. Gould, Stephen J. 1971. The paleontology and evolution of Cerion II: age and fauna of Indian shell middens on Curaçao and Aruba. *Breviora* 31:1–26. Cambridge, Massachusetts.

1341. Hartog, Johannes. 1953. *Aruba: zoals het was, zoals het werd; van de tijd der Indianen tot op heden.* Aruba: Gebroeders De Witt. 480 p.

Includes an illustrated summary of the archaeology, ethnography, and history of indigenous Aruba; see also: J. Hartog, *Aruba Past and Present, From the Time of the Indians Until Today.* J.A. Verleun, trans. (Aruba: D.J. De Wit, 1961. 451 p.).

1342.   Koolwijk, A.J. van. 1882. De Indianen-Caraiben van het Eiland Aruba (West Indie). *Koninklijk Nederlands Aardrijkskundig Genootschap, Tijdschrift* 6:222–229.

1343.   Stearns, Richard E. 1948. Indian artifacts on the island of Aruba. *Maryland: A Journal of Natural History* 15(2):34–39. Baltimore; Artefactos indígenas de la isla de Aruba. *Acta Venezolana* 3:63–67, 1951. Caracas.

   Discovery of a shell gouge, pottery fragments, and other objects at the entrance of an Aruban cave.

1344.   Tacoma, Jouke. 1959. Studies on the physical anthropology of the Netherlands Antilles, II: Indian skeletal remains from Aruba. *Nieuwe West-Indische Gids* 39:95–112. Gravenhague.

1345.   Tacoma, Jouke. 1963. Studies on the physical anthropology of the Netherlands Antilles, III: Kunstmatige schedeldeformatte in Aruba. *Nieuwe West-Indische Gids* 43:211–222. Gravenhague.

Henriquez I

1346.   Heidecker, Lorraine, and Michael I. Siegel. 1969. Preliminary excavation of the Henriquez I site, Tanki Flip, Aruba, Netherlands Antilles. *Florida Anthropologist* 33(1–4):12–16. Gainesville.

Bonaire

   Bonaire is 50 km east of Curaçao and has an area of 290 sq km. The sea-salt industry of the island was revived in the late 1960s, goats and sheep are raised, and aloe plants are grown for a juice used in cosmetics.

1347.   Beiter, Gary N. 1989. Pictographs at Two Sites on Bonaire, N.A.: Description, Analysis and a Regional Comparison. M.A. thesis, Department of Anthropology, Florida Atlantic University. 96 p. Boca Raton.

   Report on two previously unrecorded sites on Bonaire; pictographs were subjected to a formal analysis to determine relationships between representational and nonrepresentational elements; pictographs on Bonaire are primarily nonrepresentational; rock art from the Lesser Antilles and adjacent Venezuela is primarily representational; examples from western Cuba, Aruba, and Curaçao are nonrepresentational with recurring motifs; rock art from the Dominican Republic and eastern Cuba is representational.

1348.   Gaay Fortman B. de. 1942. *Geschiedkundige sprokkelingen: de Indianen op Bonaire*. West-Indische Gids 24:251–256. Gravenhague.

1349.   Hartog, Johannes. 1957. *Bonaire: Van Indianen tot Toeristen*. Aruba: Gebroeders De Wit. 456 p.

Includes a summary of the archaeology of Bonaire.

Curaçao

Curaçao is located 61 km north of Venezuela and has an area of 426 sq km. It has a rocky volcanic base, overlain in part by sandstone and in part by coral hardened into limestone. The natural vegetation consists of drought-resistant plants such as aloe, agave, and cactus.

1350.   Hartog, Johannes. 1961. *Curaçao van kolonie tot autonomie*. Aruba: D.J. De Wit. 2 v.

Includes a chapter summarizing the archaeology and ethnohistory of Curaçao.

1351.   Haviser, Jay B. 1987. *Amerindian Cultural Geography on Curaçao*. Leiden: Rijksuniversiteit te Leiden. 212 p.

Study of the local and regional aspects of Curaçao's past and a site catchment analysis of some 97 archaeological sites recorded on the island; publication of: J.B. Haviser, Amerinidian Cultural Geography on Curaçao (Ph.D. dissertation, Rijksuniversiteit te Leiden, 1987).

1352.   Koolwijk, A.J. van. 1881. *De Indianen-Caraiben oorspronkelijke bewoners van Curaçao*. Koninklijk Nederlands Aardrijkskundig Genootschap, Tijdschrift 5:57–68.

1353.   Meeteren, N. van. 1951. Wie waren de eerste bewoners van Curaçao? *Curaçao* 13(30–31):205, 208.

1354.   Traylor, Ellen T. 1977. *Design Aspects of Pre-Columbian Pottery of the Arawaks and Caribs of Curaçao*. n.p.: Carenage Press. 19 p.

1355.   Walle, J. van de. 1948. De industriele voorsprong van Curaçao. *West-Indische Gids* 29:1–6. Gravenhague.

Saba

1356.   Josselin de Jong, J.P.B. de. 1947. Archaeological material from Saba and St. Eustatius, Lesser Antilles. *Mededelingen van het Rijksmuseum voor Volkenkunde*, no. 1. 54 p. Leiden.

Report on archaeological investigations at sites on Saba and St. Eustatius in 1923.

St. Eustatius (Sint Eustatius)

An island in the Netherlands Antilles, situated about 280 km east of Puerto Rico. Geographically one of the Leeward Islands, St. Eustatius is a volcanic island with an area of 30 sq km.

1357. Dethlefsen, Edwin. 1982. The historical archaeology of St. Eustatius. *Journal of New World Archaeology* 5(2):73–86. Los Angeles.

1358. Versteeg, Aad. 1987. Archaeological research on St. Eustatius: Indian farmers in the Netherlands Antilles in the fifth-century A.D. *Netherlands Foundation for the Advancement of Tropical Research, Report* 1986:25–40.

St. Martin (Sint Maarten)

A hilly island in the Leeward Islands is situated 250 km east of Puerto Rico. The northern 50 sq km is French and is called Saint-Martin. The remaining 40 sq km, called Sint Maarten, is Dutch.

1359. Bullen, Ripley P., and Adelaide K. Bullen. 1966. Three Indian sites on St. Martin. *Nieuwe West-Indische Gids* 45(2–3):137–147. Gravenhague.

1360. Haviser, Jay B. 1987. *An Archaeological Survey of St. Martin/St. Maarten.* Institute of Archaeology and Anthropology of the Netherlands Antilles, Reports no. 7. Willemstad. 48 p.

Report on a settlement survey of St. Martin in which 39 prehistoric sites were located; includes a comparison of settlement patterns, artifact assemblages, and subsistence strategies.

ST. KITTS-
NEVIS-ANGUILLA

(Capital: Basseterre)

General

Environment

1361. Merrill, Gordon C. 1957. The Historical Geography of St. Kitts and Nevis, British West Indies. Ph.D. dissertation, Department of Geography, University of California, Berkeley.

Regional and Site Reports

Anguilla

A flat, rocky island measuring some 91 sq km in area.

1362. Cope, Edward D. 1885. On the contents of a bone cave in the island of Anguilla, West Indies. *Smithsonian Institution, Contributions to Knowledge*, no. 489. Washington, DC. 30 p.

Nevis

An island in the Leeward Islands, about 3 km southeast of St. Kitts. It is approximately 93 sq km in area, volcanic in origin, and has a conical shape.

1363. Wilson, Samuel M. 1989. The prehistoric settlement pattern of Nevis, West Indies. *Journal of Field Archaeology* 16(4):427–450. Boston.

St. Kitts (St. Christopher)

An island in the Leeward Islands, about 320 km east-southeast of Puerto Rico.

1364. Armstrong, Douglas V. 1978. Archaic Shellfish Gatherers of St. Kitts, Leeward Islands: A Case Study in Subsistence and

Settlement Patterns. M.A. thesis, Department of Anthropology, University of California, Los Angeles.

1365. Armstrong, Douglas V. 1979. Scrap or tools: a closer look at *Strombus gigas* columella artifacts. *Virgin Islands Archaeological Society, Journal* 7:27–34. St. Thomas.

1366. Branch, C.W. 1896. On kitchen middens of St. Kitts. *Nature* 53:580. London.

1367. ———. 1907. Aboriginal antiquities in Saint Kitts and Nevis. *American Anthropologist* 9(2):315–333. Washington, DC.

1368. Goodwin, R. Christopher. 1978. The Lesser Antillean Archaic: new data from St. Kitts. *Virgin Islands Archaeological Society, Journal* 5:6–16. St. Thomas.

Report on two Archaic shell middens on St. Kitts; radiocarbon dates of 2123 B.C. and 198 B.C. suggest two distinct Archaic traditions.

1369. ———. 1978. *The Prehistoric Cultural Ecology of St. Kitts, West Indies: A Case Study in Island Archaeology. Part I: The Research Design.* Behavioral Sciences Foundation, Occasional Paper in Archaeology, no. 1. Estridge Estate, St. Kitts.

See also: R.C. Goodwin, *The Prehistoric Cultural Ecology of St. Kitts, West Indies: A Case Study in Island Archaeology* (Ph.D. dissertation, Department of Anthropology, Arizona State University, Tempe, 1979. 539 p.).

1370. Hoffman, Charles A. 1973. Archaeological investigations on St. Kitts. *Caribbean Journal of Science* 13(3–4):237–250. Mayaguez, Puerto Rico.

1371. Matheson, D.L. 1976. Descubrimiento arqueológico en St. Kitts (San Cristobal). *Caribbean Conservation News* 1(7):14–15. St. Michael, Barbados.

Prince of Wales Bastion

1372. Matheson, D.L. 1971. C.C.A. demonstration project: restoration of the Prince of Wales Bastion, Brimstone Hill, St. Kitts. *Caribbean Conservation Association, Environmental Newsletter* 2(2):34–36. St. Michael, Barbados.

Sugar Factory Pier

1373. Goodwin, R. Christopher, and Cyd Heymann. 1977. St. Kitts salvage archaeology. *Explorers Journal* 55(1):20–23. New York.

Brief report on salvage excavations of the Sugar Factory Pier site on St. Kitts; occupation at the site extends from A.D. 120 to ca. A.D. 650; authors suggest dietary stress and protein deficiency as causal factors in demise of the local sequence.

ST. LUCIA

(Capital: Castries)

The second largest of the Windward Islands is situated some 320 km north of Trinidad and separated from St. Vincent, to the southeast, by the St. Vincent Passage, and from Martinique, to the north, by St. Lucia Channel. St. Lucia is 45 km long with a maximum width of 19 km, and an area of about 620 sq km. It is mountainous and many short rivers intersect the mountains, and some flow into broad, fertile valleys.

Information about the initial European exploration of St. Lucia is unknown although England tried unsuccessfully to settle the island in 1605. A second English attempt, begun in 1638, also failed, due to fierce attacks by the Caribs. French claims to the island were confirmed by a treaty with the Caribs in 1660. St. Lucia subsequently changed hands several times before being captured by the British in 1803 and ceded to them by the Treaty of Paris in 1814.

General

1374. Jesse, Charles A. 1960. The Amerindians in Iouanalao: an introductory essay on the archaeology of St. Lucia. *Barbados Museum and Historical Society, Journal* 27(2):49–65; St. Lucia: Archaeological and Historical Society, 1960. 18 p.

Summary of the archaeology, ethnohistory, and ethnography of the Arawak of St. Lucia; includes principal archaeological sites with locations and major artifact classes.

1375. Jesse, Charles A. 1968. *The Amerindians in St. Lucia.* 2 ed. Castries: St. Lucia Archaeological and Historical Society. 41 p.

Includes: R.P. Bullen and A.K. Bullen, Two stratigraphic tests at the Grand Anse site, St. Lucia (pp. 24–39), a summary of archaeological research at the ceremonial Lavourte site.

1376. Jesse, Charles, and Harold F.C. Simmons. 1956. St. Lucia in the Lesser Antilles: a field for exploration. *Archaeology* 9(2):122–125. New York.

Illustrated summary of the history and archaeology of St. Lucia.

Museum Collections

1377. Pinchon, Robert. 1961. L'outillage lithique de Sainte-Lucie. *Société d'Histoire de la Martinique, Bulletin* 9:11–29. Fort-de-France.

Description of more than 700 stone artifacts in local collections on St. Lucia.

Ethnography

1378. Vérin, Pierre M. 1958. Carib survivals at Pointe Caraibe, St. Lucia. *Caribbean Society and Culture Notes* 1(3):1–2.

1379. ———. 1959. Sainte-Lucie et ses derniers Caraibes. *Les Cahiers d'Outre-Mer* 12:349–361. Bordeaux.

1380. ———. 1961. Les Caraibes à Sainte-Lucie depuis les contacts coloniaux. *Nieuwe West-Indische Gids* 41(2):66–82. Gravenhague.

Summary of the ethnohistory of the Carib of St. Lucia; argues that the Arawak preceded the Carib based upon the work of Marshall McKusick.

Ethnohistory

1381. Bullen, Ripley P. 1966. The first English settlement on St. Lucia. *Caribbean Quarterly* 12(2):29–35. Mona, Jamaica.

Summary of archaeological, historical, and geographic evidence pertaining to the location of a temporary early seventeenth-century English settlement on St. Lucia.

1382. Jesse, Charles A. 1963. The Spanish cedula of December 23, 1511, on the subject of the Caribs. *Caribbean Quarterly* 9(3):22–32. Mona, Jamaica.

1383. Nicholl, John, and Charles A. Jesse. 1966. An houre glasse of Indian newes: a record of settlement on St. Lucia in 1605. *Caribbean Quarterly* 12(1):46–67. Mona, Jamaica.

Publication of an important account of Carib agriculture and material culture on St. Lucia in 1605.

1384. Vérin, Pierre M. 1966. L'ancienne culture caraibe à l'époque colonial. *Société d'Histoire de la Guadeloupe, Bulletin* 5–6:16–26. Basse Terre.

St. Lucia 271

Cultural Evolution and Society

Cultural Evolution and Development

1385. Vérin, Pierre M. 1975. Note sur une culture de Sainte-Lucie du type Suazey et quelques perspectives comparatives pour l'archéologie guadeloupéenne. *Société d'Histoire de la Guadeloupe, Bulletin* 23(1):57–67. Basse Terre.

Material Culture

Petroglyphs and Pictographs

1386. Dubelaar, C.N. 1988. Petroglyphs in St. Lucia: introduction. *Latin American Indian Literatures Journal* 4(1):72–83. Beaver Falls, Pennsylvania.

1387. Jesse, Charles A. 1952. Rock-cut basins on Saint Lucia. *American Antiquity* 18(2):166–168. Washington, DC.

Description of a petroglyph and basins at Dauphin, St. Lucia.

Regional and Site Reports

1388. Friesinger, Herwig, ed. 1986. *Grabungen und Forschungen auf St. Lucia, 1984.* Wien, Osterreichischen Akademie der Wissenschaften. 79 p.

Contents include: H. Friesinger, Archäologische Ausgrabungen und Untersuchungen 1984 auf der Karibikinsel St. Lucia, West Indies; E. Reuer and S. Reuer-Fabrizii, Erster Bericht über die Skelettfunde von Pointe de Caille, St. Lucia, West Indies; F.F. Steininger, Erste Ernährungsstrategien des Arawakan-Siedlungsplatzes Pointe de Caille, NNW Vieux Fort, St. Lucia, West Indies; and P. Faupl, Mikroskopische Untersuchungen an prähistorischer Keramik von St. Lucia, West Indies.

Bequia

1389. Jesse, Charles A. 1953. A note on Bequia. *Caribbean Quarterly* 3(1):55–56. Mona, Jamaica.

Discovery of rock-cut basins corresponding to those known from other parts of the Lesser Antilles; author suggests Bequia may have been uninhabited by the Arawak because of lack of refuse middens.

Point Caribe

1390. Vérin, Pierre M. 1963. La Pointe Caraibe, Sainte-Lucie. M.A. thesis, Department of Anthropology, Yale University.

1391. Vérin, Pierre M. 1967. Quelques aspects de la culture matérielle de la région de Choiseul (Ile de Sainte-Lucie, Antilles). *Société des Américanistes de Paris, Journal* 56(2):460–494. Paris.

Description of contemporary pottery manufacture near Point de Caraibe, St. Lucia; also includes discussion of basketry and carved wooden objects.

ST. VINCENT

(Capital: Kingstown)

St. Vincent, an island of the Windward Islands with an area of some 345 sq. km., is situated 300 km north of Trinidad. Of volcanic origin, St. Vincent is traversed from north to south by a rugged mountain chain that reaches maximum elevation of over 1,200 m in the volcano of Soufgriere. Said to have been discovered by Columbus in 1498, the island was not occupied by Europeans until the seventeenth century, when the British and French began a long contest for its possession. British rule was recognized in 1763, but the Caribs resisted and, in 1773, a special district was set aside for them. In 1795 they revolted with French support, and were defeated. Many were then deported to Roatán in the Bay Islands off the north coast of Honduras.

General

1392. Bullen, Ripley P., and Adelaide K. Bullen. 1972. *Archaeological Investigations on St. Vincent and the Grenadines, West Indies.* William L. Bryant Foundation, American Studies, Report no. 8. Orlando. 170 p.

Presentation of results of a site survey; including definition of ceramic types, listing of radiocarbon dates, and comparsion with Venezuela and Puerto Rico; authors conclude Lesser Antilles and Venezuela form an interacting sphere until ca. A.D. 1000 when Ostinoid influences from Puerto Rico predominated until ca. A.D. 1200.

Linguistics

1393. Taylor, Douglas M. 1958. Names on St. Vincent. *West-Indische Gids* 38:97–105. Gravenhague.

Ethnography

1394. Gullick, Charles J.M.R. 1969. The Changing Society of the Black Caribs. B. Litt. thesis, Oxford University.

1395. ———. 1974. Tradition and Change Amongst the Caribs of St. Vincent. D. Phil. thesis, Oxford University.

1396. ———. 1975. The Caribs of St. Vincent: an historical background and research bibliography. *National Studies* 3(3):22–27. Belize City.

1397. ———. 1976. The Black Caribs in St. Vincent. *International Congress of Americanists (42 session, Paris, 1974), Proceedings* 6:451–466. Paris.

1398. ———. 1976. *Exiled From St. Vincent: The Development of Black Carib Culture in Central America up to 1945.* Malta: Progress Press. 152 p.

1399. Taylor, Douglas M. 1951. *The Black Caribs of British Honduras.* Viking Fund Publications in Anthropology, no. 17. New York: Wenner-Gren Foundation for Anthropological Research. 176 p.

Important ethnography of the descendents of St. Vicentian Caribs deported to Roatan Island in 1797; includes material on language, subsistence, social organization, life cycle, supernatural beliefs, rites and practices, etc.; see also, R.B. Bateman, Africans and Indians: a comparative study of the Black Carib and Black Seminole (*Ethnohistory* 37:1–24, 1990); M.H. Crawford, The anthropological genetics of the Black Caribs (Garifuna) of Central America and the Caribbean (*American Journal of Physical Anthropology, Supplement* 4:161–192, 1983); J.M. Hunter and R. DeKleine, Geophagy in Central America (*Geographical Review* 74:157–169, 1984); C.L. Jenkins, Ritual and resource flow: the Garifuna dugu (*American Ethnologist* 10:429–442, 1983).

Ethnohistory

1400. Boomert, Aad. 1986. The Cayo Complex of St. Vincent: ethnohistorical and archaeological aspects of the Island-Carib problem. *Antropológica* 66:3–68. Caracas.

1401. Gonzalez, Nancie L.S. 1988. *Sojourners of the Caribbean: Ethnogenesis annd Ethnohistory of the Garifuna.* Urbana: University of Illinois Press. 253 p.

See also: N.L. Gonzalez, From cannibals to mercenaries: Carib militarism, 1600–1840 (*Journal of Anthropological Research* 46:25–39, 1990); N.L. Gonzalez, New evidence on the origin of the Black Carib (*Nieuwe West Indische Gids* 57:143–173, 1983); R.W. Porter,

History and Social Life of the Garifuna in the Lesser Antilles and Central America (Ph.D. dissertation, Department of Anthropology, Princeton University, 1984. 844 p.); N.L. Whitehead, *Lords of the Tiger Spirit: A History of the Caribs in Colonial Venezuela and Guyana, 1498–1820* (Dordrecht, Netherlands: Foris, 1988); N.L. Whitehead, The snake warriors, sons of the tiger's teeth: a descriptive analysis of Carib warfare, ca. 1500–1820 (In: *The Anthropology of Warfare.* J. Haas, ed. pp. 146–170. Cambridge, England: Cambridge University Press, 1990); N.L. Whitehead, Carib ethnic soldering in Venezuela, the Guianas, and the Antilles, 1492–1820 (*Ethnohistory* 37:357–385, 1990).

1402. Kirby, I.A.E. 1971. *Pre-Columbian Indians in St. Vincent, West Indies.* St. Vincent: St. Vincent Archaeological and Historical Society. 6 p.

1403. Marshall, Bernard. 1973. The Black Caribs: native resistance to British penetration into the windward side of St. Vincent, 1763–1773. *Caribbean Quarterly* 19(4):4–19. Mona, Jamaica.

See also: J.P. Thomas, The Caribs of St. Vincent: a study in imperial maladministration, 1763–1773 (*Journal of Caribbean History* 18(2):60–74, 1984).

1404. Pinchon, Robert. 1961. Description de l'isle de Saint-Vincent, mauscrit inédit. *Annales des Antilles* 9:35–81. Martinique.

Archaeological summary of St. Vincent introduces an unpublished eighteenth-century description of Carib culture deposited in the archives of Martinique.

1405. Young, William. 1795. *An Account of the Black Charaibes in the Island of St. Vincent's; with the Charaib Treaty of 1779 and Other Original Documents.* London: J. Sewell; London: F. Cass, 1971. 125 p.

Cultural Evolution and Society

Physical Anthropology

1406. Hutchinson, Janice F. 1984. A Biocultural Analysis of Blood Pressure Variation Among the Black Caribs and Creoles of St. Vincent, West Indies. Ph.D. dissertation, Department of Anthropology, University of Kansas. 295 p.

Examination of blood pressure variation among the Black Caribs and Creoles of St. Vincent with emphasis on cultural (marital status, family size, educational status, church attendance) and biological (body build, nutrition, contributory components); see also, J. Hutchinson, Association between stress and blood pressure variation in a Caribbean population *(American Journal of Physical Anthropology* 71:69–79, 1986); J. Hutchinson and P.J. Bayard, Family resemblances for anthropometric and blood pressure measurements in Black Caribs and Creoles from St. Vincent Island *(American Journal of Physical Anthropology* 73:33–39, 1987).

Material Culture

Petroglyphs and Pictographs

1407.   Brinton, Daniel G. 1889. On a petroglyph from the island of St. Vincent, W.I. *Academy of Natural Sciences of Philadelphia, Proceedings* 1:417–420. Philadelphia.

1408.   Huckerby, Thomas. 1914. Petroglyphs of Saint Vincent, British West Indies. *American Anthropologist* 16(2):238–244. Washington, DC; *Museum of the American Indian, Heye Foundation, Contributions* 1:238–244, 1914. New York.

1409.   Kirby, I.A.E. 1969. *Pre-Columbian Monuments in Stone*. St. Vincent: St. Vincent Archaeological and Historical Society. 24 p.

An illustrated list of petroglyphs, sharpening stones, and stationary mortars from St. Vincent.

1410.   Sapper, Karl T. 1903. St. Vincent. *Globus* 84:297–303, 377–383. Braunschweig.

Groundstone

1411.   Spitzly, J.H. 1890. Notes on three stone adzes from Surinam (Dutch Guyana) and on eight stone implements from the islands of St. Vincent and St. Lucia. *Internationales Archiv für Ethnographie* 3:231–233. Leiden.

TRINIDAD AND TOBAGO

(Capital: Port of Spain)

Trinidad and Tobago are the southernmost islands in the West Indies, at the delta of the Orinoco, separated from Venezuela by the Gulf of Paria and by channels Dragon's Mouth and Serpent's Mouth. Trinidad comprises 4,800 sq km in area and Tobago some 300 sq km. There are also several small islands, the largest of which are Chacachacare and Little Tobago. Geologically an extension of the South American mainland, Trinidad is marked by three mountain ranges extending east and west. The terrain of Tobago is also rugged, with many hills and ridges.

General

1412. Bullbrook, John A. 1941. *The Aboriginal Remains of Trinidad and the West Indies*. Port-of-Spain, Trinidad: A.L. Rhodes. 14 p.; *Caribbean Quarterly* 1(1):16–21, 1(2):10–15, 1949. Mona, Jamaica.

Summary of information known about the Arawak; includes discussion of lifeways and diet, material culture, dress and personal ornamentation, religious systems, and origins and contacts.

History of Archaeological Research

1413. Bullbrook, John A. 1960. *The Aborigines of Trinidad*. Royal Victoria Institute Museum, Occasional Papers, no. 2. Port-of-Spain. 60 p.

Summary of the history of the archaeology of Trinidad and discussion of aboriginal sites and material culture; see also: J.A. Bullbrook, The aborigines of Trinidad (*Shell Trinidad* 4(9):4–7, 1956), for a semi-popular account of the history of archaeological research in Trinidad.

1414. Glazier, Stephen D. 1978. Theoretical approaches to the study of Trinidad's prehistory. *Virgin Islands Archaeological Society, Journal* 5:32–35. St. Thomas.

Brief description of theoretical approaches taken in Trinidadian archaeology.

1415. Harris, Peter O'B. 1976. Resúmen sobre la arqueología de Trinidad, 1973. *Museo del Hombre Dominicano, Boletín* 4(8):35–45. Santo Domingo.

Linguistics

1416. Lawrence, K.M. 1967. Notes of Iere, the Amerinidian name for Trinidad. *Caribbean Quarterly* 13(3):45–51. Mona, Jamaica.

1417. Penard, Thomas E. 1927. Remarks on an old vocabulary from Trinidad. *De West-Indische Gids* 10:265–270. Gravenhague.

Ethnography

1418. Glazier, Stephen D. 1978. Trinidad's Indians in the Guianas. *Virgin Islands Archaeological Society, Journal* 6:54–58. St. Thomas.

Ethnohistory

1419. Boomert, Aad. 1984. The Arawak Indians of Trinidad and coastal Guiana, ca. 1500–1650. *Journal of Caribbean History* 19(2):123–188. St. Lawrence, Barbados.

1420. Glazier, Stephen D. 1980. Aboriginal Trinidad in the sixteenth century. *Florida Anthropologist* 33(3):152–159. Gainesville.

Using archaeological, historical, and linguistic evidence, author argues that Carib-speaking groups shared protohistoric Trinidad with the Arawak.

1421. Newson, Linda A. 1976. *Aboriginal and Spanish Colonial Trinidad: A Study in Culture Contact.* London; New York: Academic Press. 344 p.

Cultural Evolution and Society

Cultural Evolution and Development

1422. Bullbrook, John A. 1956. The Carib-Arawak controversy. *Shell Trinidad* 4(10):7–9

1423. Harris, Peter O'B. 1976. The Preceramic period in Trinidad. *Puerto Rican Symposium of Archaeology (1 session, Santurce, P.R., 1976), Proceedings* 1:33–65. Santurce.

Similar to sites in northwestern Guyana and on the east coast of Venezuela, Banwari-Trace, St. John, Ortoire, and Poonah Road sites on Trinidad feature a chipped stone component of crude tools with stone grinders and milling slabs. In addition, there are notched stone net sinkers, stone paint mortars, as well as bone points and bone barbs. The site of Ortoire is significant because it reveals the modification of the earlier rough chipped stone complexes in northern Venezuela by the addition of grinding stones and other implements; author suggests Archaic patterns emerge ca. 7000 B.C. on Trinidad.

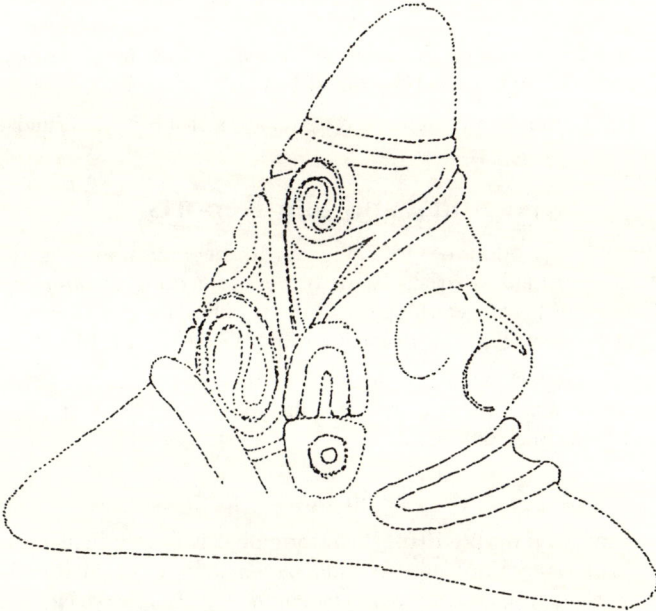

Figure 15. Anthropomorphic *zemí*, Dominican Republic.
Zemí refers to a deity or the objectification of a deity and is usually applied to a characteristic three-cornered deity form. These objects were originally made of shell but by A.D. 600 were replaced by three-pointed stone. After A.D. 1000 larger and more elaborate types were manufactured.

Source: M.A. García Arévalo, *Los signos en el arte Taíno*, Santo Domingo: Fundación García-Arévalo, 1989. Figure 7.

1424. Rouse, Irving. 1947. Prehistory of Trinidad in relation to adjacent areas. *Man* 47(103):93–98. London.

Subsistence Patterns

1425. Bullbrook, John A. 1963. *Notes Concerning Excavation of Shell Mounds or Kitchen Middens*. Royal Victoria Institute Museum, Occasional Papers, no. 3. Port-of-Spain. 27 p.

Material Culture

Pottery

1426. Sleight, Frederick W. 1946. Notes on a find from Trinidad. *American Antiquity* 11(4):260–261. Washington, DC.

Brief report on a prehistoric pottery vessel found in Trinidad.

Regional and Site Reports

1427. Booy, Theodoor de. 1917. Certain archaeological investigations in Trinidad, British West Indies. *American Anthropologist* 19(4):471–486. Washington, DC; *Museum of the American Indian, Heye Foundation, Contributions* 4(2):471–486, 1918. New York.

Brief report on excavations in shell-heaps on the St. Bernard estate near Cape Mayaro in 1915; includes descriptions of pottery vessels and other objects.

Erin Bay

1428. Fewkes, Jesse W. 1914. Prehistoric objects from a shell-heap at Erin Bay, Trinidad. *American Anthropologist* 16(2):200–220. Washington, DC; *Museum of the American Indian, Heye Foundation, Contributions* 7:200–220, 1914. New York.

Description of pottery, lithic, bone, and wood objects excavated in a shell-heap at Erin Bay in 1912–1913; compares objects from Trinidad with those found in other Caribbean islands. Pottery typically includes open bowls with thick rim flanges, incised designs on these flanges, and of effigy adornos, and elaborately produced stylized animal lug heads.

Palo Seco

1429. Bullbrook, John A. 1953. *On the Excavation of a Shell Mound at Palo Seco, Trinidad, B.W.I.* I. Rouse, ed. Yale University Publications in Anthropology, no. 50. New Haven: 114 p.

Important report on the excavation of the Palo Seco midden in 1919 by Bullbrook; a pioneer treatise in its detailed stratigraphic analysis, the first in the Antilles; author traces the history of archaeological research in Trinidad from 1898; includes desciption of pottery, lithics, bone artifacts, shell, animal, and human remains.

VIRGIN ISLANDS

(BRITISH)

(Capital: Road Town)

VIRGIN ISLANDS

(UNITED STATES)

(Capital: Charlotte Amalie)

The eastern Virgin Islands consist of 36 islands with a total area of 153 sq km. At the nearest point they are less than 1.5 km from the Virgin Islands of the United States. The British Virgin Islands are the easternmost extension of the Greater Antilles chain, and are separated from the Lesser Antilles by the Anegada Passage, one of the chief entrances into the Caribbean Sea. In climate, terrain, and natural resources, they are similar to the Virgin Islands of the United States, except that the British group has a main island which is low-lying and flat.

The United States Virgin Islands comprise 68 islands covering 340 sq km. Of the three main islands, St. Thomas is closest to Puerto Rico, which lies 65 km to the west. St. John is 5 km east of St. Thomas, and St. Croix is 65 km to the south. The land consists of a dramatic procession of craggy mountaintops rising from an underwater shelf.

General

1430.   Booy, Theodoor H.N. de. 1919. Archaeology of the Virgin Islands. *Museum of the American Indian, Heye Foundation, Indian Notes and Monographs* 1(1):1–100. New York.

General introduction to the archaeology of the Virgin Islands; includes a description of excavations at Magen's Bay village-site on St. Thomas, a midden at Salt River on St. Croix, and petroglyphs near Reef Bay on St. John and Congo Cay; illustrations of pottery, spindle-whorls, cassava griddles, and bone objects; for an analysis of faunal remains collected by Booy, see G.S. Miller, Mammals and reptiles collected by Theodoor de Booy in the Virgin Islands (*United States National Museum, Proceedings* 54: 507–511, 1918) and A. Wetmore, Bones of birds collected by Theodoor de Booy from kitchen-midden deposits in the islands of St. Thomas and St. Croix (*United States National Museum, Proceedings* 54:513–522, 1918).

1431.   Hatt, Gudmund. 1924. Archaeology of the Virgin Islands. *International Congress of Americanists (21 session, The Hague, 1924), Proceedings* 1:29–42. The Hague.

1432.   Krieger, Herbert W. 1938. Archaeology of the Virgin Islands. *Smithsonian Institution, Explorations and Fieldwork*, 1937:95–102. Washington, DC.

1433.   *Virgin Islands Prehistory.* St. Croix: Aye Aye Press, 1974. 22 p.

An examination of current archaeological research in the United States Virgin Islands, its expense, emphasis, and significance.

1434.   Yde, Jens. 1947. En vaerdfuld Gave fra Vestindien. *National Museets ts Arbejdsmark* 1947:29–37. Copenhagen.

Bibliography

1435.   Vescelius, Gary S. 1977. A bibliography of Virgin Islands archaeology. *Virgin Islands Archaeological Society, Journal* 4:1–16. St. Thomas.

Bibliography of published and manuscript materials dealing with the archaeology of the Virgin Islands.

Museum Collections

1436.   Bullen, Ripley P. 1965. Analysis of the Hatt Collection from the Virgin Islands and preserved at the Danish National Museum, Copanhagen. *American Philosophical Society, Yearbook* 1964:461–462. Philadelphia.

History of Archaeological Research

1437.   Figueredo, Alfredo E. 1974. History of Virgin Islands archaeology. *Virgin Islands Archaeological Society, Journal* 1:1–6. St. Thomas.

1438. Figueredo, Alfredo E. 1974. Current research in the Virgin Islands. *Liaison Bulletin of Archaeological Research (C.E.R.A.G.)* 2:1–5. Fort-de-France.

1439. Hatt, Gudmund. 1922. Den dansk-hollandske arkaeologiske ekspedition Vestindien. *Geografisk Tidsskrift* 26:236–237. Copenhagen.

1440. Morales Patino, O.I., and F. Royo Guardia. 1978. The Cuban Scientific Expedition to the Virgin Islands, 1951. *Virgin Islands Archaeological Society, Journal* 5:17–31. St. Thomas.

Historical Archaeology

1441. Antonsen, Inge M. 1972. En naivist i Vestindien, H.G. Beenfeldt. *National Museets ts Arbejdsmark* 1972:153–170. Copanhagen.

Cultural Evolution and Society

Cultural Evolution and Development

1442. Booy, Theodoor H.N. de. 1917. Archaeological investigations in the Virgin Islands to solve the riddle of the origin of their aborigines. *Scientific American* 84(2180):232–234. New York.

1443. Figueredo, Alfredo E. 1974. El hombre en las Islas Vírgenes. *Revista Dominicana de Antropología e Historia* 4(7–8):133–140. Santo Domingo.

Presents new evidence on the antiquity of human and Archaic cultural patterns of the Virgin Islands; see also: A.E. Figueredo, El hombre en las Islas Vírgenes: nuevas evidencias de su antigüedad y patrones de cultura arcaicos (*International Congress of Americanists (41 session, México City, 1974), Proceedings* 3:608–614, 1977. México) for a proposed taxonomic revision of the Krum Bay and Magens Bay temporal sequences.

Physical Anthropology

1444. Buxton, K.H. Dudley, J.C. Trevor, and Alvarez H. Julien. 1938. Skeletal remains from the Virgin Islands. *Man* 38(47):49–51. London.

Material Culture

Architecture

1445. Brown, Robert S. 1979. The vernacular architecture of Fredriksted. *Virgin Islands Archaeological Society, Journal* 8:3–43. St. Thomas.

Description of three types of domestic architecture and statement of need for preservation.

Pottery

1446. Bradstreet, Theodore E. 1975. Ceramic culture site location parameters for the Virgin Islands. *Virgin Islands Archaeological Society, Journal* 2:5–11. St. Thomas.

1447. Hatt, Gudmund. 1938. On pottery from the Virgin islands. *Man* 38(48):52–53. London.

1448. Willock, N.A. 1976. The potter's art. *Virgin Islands Archaeological Society, Journal* 3:5–6. St. Thomas.

Shell

1449. Armstrong, Douglas V. 1979. Scrap or tools: a closer look at *Strombus gigas* Columella artifacts. *Virgin Islands Archaeological Society, Journal* 7:27–34. St. Thomas.

Regional and Site Reports

1450. Figueredo, Alfredo E. 1972. The British Virgin Islands archaeological survey: first season. *Museum of the American Indian, Heye Foundation, Indian Notes* 8(4):131–135. New York.

Summary of the results of the first professional archaeological survey conducted in the British Virgin Islands; excavation and surface survey of the island of Virgin Gorda indicates an occupation extending from Saladoid times to Chicoid or Esperanza times.

1451. ———. 1978. The Virgin Islands as a buffer zone between the Taínos and the Caribs. *Revista/Review Interamericana* 8(3):393–399. Hato Rey, Puerto Rico.

Examination of the influences of Taíno and Carib cultures on the Virgin Islands; see also, A.E. Figueredo, *The Virgin Islands as a Historical Frontier Between the Taínos and the Caribs* (Frederiksted, St. Croix, 1979. 12 p.).

Anegeda Island

1452. Gross, Jeffrey M. 1975. The archaeology of Anegeda Island. *Virgin Islands Archaeological Society, Journal* 2:12–16. St. Thomas.

Arboretum

1453. Tilden, Bruce E. 1975. Excavations at the Arboretum site. *Virgin Islands Archaeological Society, Journal* 2:17–19. St. Thomas.

Gun Creek

1454. Figueredo, Alfredo E. 1980. Pottery from Gun Creek, Virgin Gorda. *Virgin Islands Archaeological Society, Journal* 9:27–30. St. Thomas.

Summary of midden excavations at Gun Creek site; ceramics suggest terminal insular Saladoid type dated at A.D. 500–600.

St. Croix

The largest of the Virgin Islands of the United States is about 65 km south of St. Thomas and about 145 km southeast of San Juan, Puerto Rico. It is 37 km long and 10 km across at its widest point. The terrain ranges from arid and rocky in the east, through rolling upland pastures, to lush tropics, in the west. Mountains rise abruptly from the northeastern shore of St. Croix.

1455. Gartley, Richard T. 1979. Afro-Cruzan pottery: a new style of colonial earthenware from St. Croix. *Virgin Islands Archaeological Society, Journal* 8:47–61. St. Thomas.

Description of unglazed pottery manufactured on St. Croix after 1750 and used until the nineteenth century; author argues it was originally made by African slaves.

1456. Skinner, Alanson. 1925. Archaeological specimens from St. Croix, Virgin Islands. *Museum of the American Indian, Heye Foundation, Indian Notes* 2(2):109–115. New York.

1457. Tilden, Bruce E. 1980. Cotton Garden red-on-brown ware: some preliminary observations. *Virgin Islands Archaeological Society, Journal* 9:22–26. St. Thomas.

Description of Cotton Garden red-on-brown ware, found at Fair Pain, Cramer Park, and Salt River Point sites on St. Croix; author argues this pottery represents a continuation of local earlier traditions within new Chicoid context in the Virgin Islands.

1458. Vescelius, Gary S. 1952. The Cultural Chronology of St. Croix. B.A. thesis, Department of Anthropology, Yale University, New Haven.

1459. Weiss, Malcolm, and William B. Gladfelter. 1978. A pre-Columbian conch midden, St. Croix, U.S. Virgin Islands. *Virgin Islands Archaeological Society, Journal* 6:23–31. St. Thomas.

1460. Morse, Birgit F. 1990. Precolumbian ball and dance court at Salt River, St. Croix. *Folk* 32:45–60. Copenhagen.

St. John

Third largest of the United States Virgin Islands, St. John is 5 km east of St. Thomas and some 130 km east of San Juan, Puerto Rico. The island is about 14 km long and 8 km wide. The terrain is rugged, with mountains of volcanic origin and an irregular coastline.

1461. Baum, Paul. 1976. Petroglyphs and other discoveries in St. John and St. Kitts. *Ohio Archaeologist* 26(2):29–22. Plain City, Ohio.

1462. Booy, Theodoor H.N. de. 1917. Archaeological notes on the Danish West Indies, the petroglyphs of the island of St. John and of Congo Cay. *Scientific American* 84(2189):376–377. New York.

1463. Sleight, Frederick W. 1962. *Archaeological Reconnaissance of the Island of St. John, U.S. Virgin Islands.* William L. Bryant Foundation, American Studies Report, no. 3. Orlando. 49 p.

St. Thomas

The second-largest of the United States, St. Thomas is some 60 km east of Puerto Rico. It is about 23 km long and 3 km wide. The island is of volcanic origin and has a rugged terrain and a deeply indented coastline.

1464. Bullen, Ripley P. 1962. *Ceramic Periods of St. Thomas and St. John Islands, Virgin Islands.* William L. Bryant Foundation, Central Florida Museum, American Studies Report, no. 4. Maitland, FL. 74 p.

Report on surface collections and stratigraphic testing on St. John and St. Thomas reveal two ceramic complexes: Coral (A.D. 100–700), similar to Saladoid, and Magens (A.D. 700–1500), similar to later Puerto Rican complexes.

1465.   Hannon, Tom, and Andrea Hannon. 1976. Bottles found in St. Thomas, Virgin Islands, waters. *Virgin Islands Archaeological Society, Journal* 3:29–45. St. Thomas.

1466.   Kay, Katheryne. 1976. Sculptured stone from St. Thomas, U.S. Virgin Islands. *Virgin Islands Archaeological Society, Journal* 3:15–18. St. Thomas.

Description of two carved stone artifacts from St. Thomas, a petaloid celt with a carved human face and an elbow stone, carved in low relief with a geometric design.

1467.   Lundberg, Emily R. 1985. Interpreting the cultural association of aceramic deposits in the Virgin Islands. *Journal of Field Archaeology* 12(2):201–212. Boston.

Investigation of several Preceramic sites, including the Arboretum site on St. Vincent, suggests aceramic deposits may be associated with ceramic deposits in the same coastal valley.

Hull Bay

1468.   Ubelaker, Douglas H., and J.L. Angel. 1976. Analysis of the Hull Bay skeletons, St. Thomas. *Virgin Islands Archaeological Society, Journal* 3:7–14. St. Thomas.

Krum Bay

1469.   Bullen, Ripley P. 1962. The Preceramic Krum Bay site, Virgin Islands, and its relationship to the peopling of the Caribbean. *International Congress of Americanists (34 session, Wien, 1960), Proceedings* 1:398–403. Vienna.

Preliminary report on excavations at Krum Bay sites; author suggests Panama-Antillean connections for Preceramic cultures.

1470.   ———., and Frederick W. Sleight. 1963. *The Krum Bay Site: A Preceramic Site on St. Thomas, United States Virgin Islands.* William L. Bryant Foundation, American Studies Report, no. 5. Orlando. 46 p.

A midden at Krum Bay is one of the most thoroughly explored Preceramic sites in the Caribbean region. The site has been known for many years from earlier excavations by Booy (1430, 1462) and Hatt (1431), and the authors carried out extensive work at the site. It is a shell midden on a protected bay on the south side of St. Thomas. Cultural refuse measures less than 50 cm in depth and contains shell, fish and turtle skeletal remains, burned rocks, and stone chips. It was presumably a residential and shellfish collecting location as well as a workshop for manufacturing stone tools. This volume is a report summarizing research at the site, including a detailed analysis of Preceramic sites in the Caribbean and Florida; authors conclude that Central America was the probable source for the West Indian Archaic.

1471.   Figueredo, Alfredo E. 1980. A chert point from Krum Bay, St. Thomas. *Virgin Islands Archaeological Society, Journal* 9:41–42. St. Thomas.

Comments on an Archaic period chert point from Krum Bay.

1472.   Lundberg, Emily R. 1989. Preceramic Procurement Patterns at Krum Bay, Virgin Islands. Ph.D. dissertation, Department of Anthropology, University of Illinois, Urbana. 376 p.

Krum Bay site is a small, Preceramic stratified shell midden composed predominantly of pearl oysters radiocarbon dated between 2900 and 1700 B.C.; vertebrate, macrobotanical remains, and microbotanical remains, as well as artifact assemblages, are used to formulate a model of successive site reoccupations by small communities using multiple settlements for specific activities in subsistence resource procurement.

PERSONAL NAME INDEX

(Numbers in index refer to entry numbers.)

PLACE NAME INDEX

(Numbers in index refer to entry numbers.)

Africa, 362, 365, 1206
Aguas Verdes, 684
Albisola (Italy), 221
Altagracia, 842–856
Ambergris Cay, 468
Ambrosio, cave, 655
Andros Island, 501, 502
Anegeda Island, 1452
Angelina, 708
Anguilla, 381, 1362
Anse-à-l'Eau, 1272
Anse Belleville, 1299, 1300
Anse Marguerite Dit Gros Cap, 374
Antigua, 372–374, 1149, 1153,
 1169–1180; *see also* Barbuda,
 Indian Creek, Indiantown
 Trail, Mill Reef, Overview,
 Sufferers
Apure River, 276
Arboretum, 374, 1453, 1467
Arroyo Caña, 900
Arroyo del Palo, 686
Aruba, 276, 373, 374, 379, 381,
 1320, 1322, 1323, 1326, 1327,
 1329–1331, 1333, 1334, 1338–
 1347; *see also* Ceru Noka,
 Henríquez, Malmok, Taki
 Leendert, Tanki Flip
Azua, 221, 374, 809, 838, 857, 858

Bahamas, 40, 227, 378, 458, 468–
 516; *see also* Ambergris Cay,
 Andros Island, Bimini Island,
 Cat Island, Clifton Pier
 Rockshelter, Crooked Island,
 Egg Island, Eleuthera Island,
 Fehling, Gordon Hill, Grand
 Caicos Island, Harbor Island,
 Hartford Cave, Highborn Cay,
 Long Bay, Mariguana Island,
 Minnes/Ward, Mores Island,
 New Providence Island, North
 Caicos Island, Pigeon Creek,
 Providenciales Island, Rum
 Cay Cave, San Salvador Island,
 Spring Point Cave, St.
 George's Cay, Turks and
 Caicos Islands, Watling Island
Bañador, 375
Banes, 687
Baní, 592
Banwari Trace, 372, 762, 775, 844,
 1423
Baracoa, 570
Barahona, 859–861
Barbados, 293, 370, 377, 1181–
 1208; *see also* Golders Green,
 Indian Mount, Mapps Cave,
 Newton Plantation
Barbuda, 376, 1209, 1210, 1326
Barquisimento Valley, 276
Barreras, 775, 858
Basseterre, 964
Batabanó, 662
Batey Negro, 760
Bávaro, 914
Bayahá, 220
Bayamo, 688, 689
Beane Field, 372
Belize, 47, 88, 1399, 1401
Bequia, 1390
Berna, cave, 737, 844

305

SUBJECT INDEX

(Numbers in index refer to entry numbers.)

Cotton, 326, 389, 726, 833–836; *see also* Cordage and textiles
Cotubanama, 843
Cranial deformation. *See* Physical deformation
Creole, 25, 50, 71, 72, 84, 1213, 1406; *see also* Linguistics, Transculturation
Cuban Scientific Expedition, 1440
Culin, S., 523
Cultural chronology, 14, 18, 233, 236–243, 371, 378, 381, 412, 414–416, 419, 515, 589, 775, 1254, 1292
Cultural ecology. *See* Environment
Cultural evolution and society, 223–285, 373, 375, 382, 412–422, 487–491, 517, 586–599, 755–757, 947, 948, 1010–1013, 1079–1082, 1159–116, 1194, 1257, 1267, 1289–1293, 1385, 1422–1424, 1442, 1443; *see also* Social complexity
Cultural patrimony, 335, 375, 864, 1445
Cultural resources management. *See* Salvage archaeology
Culture change, 976, 1227–1230
Culture contact. *See* Colonialism

Danajuroid tradition, 276
Dance plazas, 857, 862–864, 1460
Danish National Museum, 1436
Deities, 4, 372, 433, 451, 688, 689, 795, 869, 870, 957, 1021; *see also* Cosmology, Opigielgourian, Religious organization, Yucahu Bagua Maorocoti
Demography, 227, 293, 303–305, 376, 384, 424–426, 496, 600, 777, 1231, 1294, 1295, 1329; *see also* Epidemics, Ethnocide
Denevan, W.M., 304
Dental mutilation. *See* Physical deformation
Dentition, 781, 786, 787, 1197

Descent. *See* Kinship
Dictionaries, 56, 78, 82, 115, 116, 367, 376, 1417; *see also* Linguistis
Diet, 375, 699, 769, 771, 776, 855, 983, 1176, 1249, 1373, 1412; *see also* Subsistence patterns
Dobyns, H., 304
Dogs, 373, 957; *see also* Zooarchaeology
Dreams, 1235
Dress, 5, 12, 13, 384, 1412
Duhos, 4, 387, 388, 430, 500; *see also* Wood
Dwellings, 293, 766, 377, 384, 591, 598, 766, 886, 916, 1223, 1273

Ear plugs, 329
Earthworks, 1022
Ecology, 293, 370, 375, 1172, 1188, 1210, 1369; *see also* Environment
Economic organization, 285, 293, 397, 403, 492, 772, 1258; *see also* Commerce, Plantations
Effigy vessels, 378, 808, 822; *see also* Pottery
Encomienda, 403, 745
Endogamy. *See* Marriage
English, 159, 1025, 1042, 1044, 1381, 1403; *see also* Pirates
Enriquillo, 744
Environment, 41–44, 245, 293, 376, 477, 487, 488, 491, 517, 563–566, 736–738, 946, 1000–1002, 1064–1066, 1154, 1155, 1267, 1285, 1286, 1361; *see also* Ecology, Hydrology, Mangrove, Oceanography, Palynology, Topography
Epidemics, 306, 473; *see also* Demography
Ethnicity, 370, 395, 1229, 1231–1233, 1289; *see also* Social organization
Ethnobotany, 290, 423, 853, 766, 1014, 1248; *see also* Capsicum

annum, Capsicum frutescens,
Maize
Ethnocide, 406, 424, 425, 478, 577;
see also Demography
Ethnography, 12, 13, 129–133, 567,
577, 739–742, 950, 995, 1069,
1070, 1181,1188, 1214–1242,
1278, 1279, 1320, 1341, 1374,
1287, 1378–1380, 1394–1399,
1418; see also Life cycle, Racial
studies, Sexuality, Suicide
Ethnohistory, 12, 13, 129, 134–219,
227, 276, 375, 376, 392–410,
478–484, 578–582, 743–746,
929, 951–955, 1003–1005,
1071–1078, 1158, 1159, 1189–
1193, 1198, 1243–1247, 1255,
1256, 1265, 1266, 1288, 1350,
1374, 1380–1384, 1400–1405,
1419–1421
Ethnozoology. See Zooarchaeology
Exchange. See Commerce
Exposición Histórico-Americana de
Madrid, 723

Faunal extinctions, 563, 666; see also
Sloths
Faunal remains. See Zooarchaeology
Fertility symbols, 4
Fewkes, J.W., 39, 523, 729
Figurines, 377, 827
Fire, 792
Fishing, 293, 370, 493, 513, 773,
915, 1180, 1209, 1223, 1318;
see also Subsistence patterns
Fish traps, 493
Flint, 373, 947, 1019; see also
Lithics
Folklore, 790, 1070, 1228, 1234,
1235
Formative, 265, 271, 282, 382; see
also Preceramic
French, 136, 154
French Creole. See Creole

Games, 1223
García Feria, 546, 547

García y Grave de Peralta, F., 548
Garifuna, 47, 49, 60, 102, 128, 375,
1249, 1394, 1397–1399, 1401,
1403, 1405, 1406
Gateway communities, 1258
Genetics, 1250, 1399, 1406; see also
Physical anthropology
Geophagy, 316, 865, 1399
Ghosts, 1235
Glass, 1029, 1316, 1465; see also
Wine bottles, Wine glasses
Glottochronology, 117, 127, 242,
283; see also Linguistics
Gold, 378, 637, 687, 832; see also
Metals
Grammar, 94–101; see also
Linguistics
Greenstone, 358; see also Lithics
Griddles, 375, 627, 1017, 1430; see
also Pottery
Grinding implements, 261, 292,
636, 1015, 1409, see also
Groundstone
Groundstone, 352–358, 519, 633–
636, 830, 831, 1100–1108,
1202, 1251, 1271, 1411; see
also Axes and celts, Grinding
implements, Lithics
Guamá group, 556
Guanahatabeye. See Archaic
Guayabitoid tradition, 378
Guayabo Blanco, 524, 543, 553

Henige, D., 304
Herrera y Tordesillas, A. de, 197
Historical archaeology, 220, 411,
485, 486, 583–585, 664, 665,
677, 693, 747–754, 871–882,
885–894, 964, 967, 975, 976,
978–989, 997, 1006–1009,
1025, 1029–1044, 1169, 1310–
1317, 1357, 1372, 1381, 1441,
1455; see also Architecture,
Pewter
Historical linguistics, 58, 78–83;
see also Linguistics, Proto-
Arawakan, Proto-Carib

596, 656, 686, 691, 755, 765,
842, 854, 867, 965, 1079,
1117, 1147, 1272, 1306, 1308,
1368, 1392, 1472
Rainey, F., 507
Raleigh, W., 218
Real Biblioteca de Madrid, 82
Refuge sites, 859; see also African
Americans
Regional and site reports, 501–516,
521–523, 639–706, 838–928,
962–989, 1022–1045, 1111–
1147, 1175–1180, 1203–1208,
1272–1275, 1299–1308, 1310–
1319, 1335–1360, 1362–1373,
1388–1391, 1427–1429, 1450–
1472
Relationships with Mesoamerica
and Central America, 259–263,
586, 1470
Relationships with North America,
264–273, 625, 1160
Relationships with South America,
274–284, 1163, 1257, 1258
Religious organization, 5, 12, 13,
262, 382, 384, 389, 397, 403,
405, 429–432, 447, 612, 790,
956, 1228, 1236, 1262, 1412;
see also Cosmology, Deities,
Magic, Shamanism,
Supernatural, Vomit spatulas,
Zemi, Zombi
Remote sensing, 986, 1009
Repartimiento, 403
Residence patterns. See Social
organization
Resistance patterns. See
Insurrections
Revert, E., 1283, 1299
Revolts. See Insurrections
Rice rats, 1180; see also
Zooarchaeology
Rijksmuseum voor Volkenkunde,
Leiden, 1334
Rivero de la Calle, M., 570
Rochefort, C. de, 219

Rock basins, 1387, 1389
Rodríguez Ferrer, M., 523
Ronquoid tradition, 282, 374
Rouse, I., 591

Saladoid tradition, 293, 341, 374,
377, 1199, 1258, 1297, 1306,
1318, 1450, 1454, 1464
Salt, 491
Salvage archaeology, 373, 376, 378,
379, 754, 1373
Santa María, 976
Schomburgk, R., 740
Sculpture, 341–343, 371, 374, 378,
386, 806, 920, 973, 1466; see
also Art, Stone collars, Stone
elbows, Stone spheres
Sea level change. See
Environment
Seafaring. See Watercraft
Semantics, 105–114; see also
Linguistics
Seminole Indians, 1399
Settlement patterns, 12, 13, 293,
328, 370, 376, 488, 499, 508,
515, 798, 799, 1038, 1172,
1210, 1262, 1360, 1363, 1364,
1450; see also Site surveys
Sexuality, 1223; see also
Ethnography
Shamanism, 12, 13, 376, 446; see
also Religious organization
Shell, 288, 371, 375–377, 495, 505,
515, 638, 673, 674, 676, 684,
686, 690, 726, 833–836, 915,
1110, 1175, 1184, 1185, 1270,
1274, 1340, 1343, 1425, 1427–
1429, 1449, 1459, 1472; see
also Strombus gigas
Shellfish, 376, 491, 774, 1364; see
also Subsistence patterns
Shell middens. See Middens
Shell mounds. See Mound sites
Shipwrecks, 509, 521–523, 899;
Conde de Tolosa, 220, 754;
Nuestra Señora de la Concepción,
220, 754; Nuestra Señora de
Guadalupe, 220, 754